Cambridge Studies in Social and Emotional Development
General Editor: Martin L. Hoffman

The development of children's friendships

The development of children's friendships

Edited by

STEVEN R. ASHER *and* JOHN M. GOTTMAN

University of Illinois, Urbana-Champaign

CAMBRIDGE UNIVERSITY PRESS
Cambridge
London   New York   New Rochelle
Melbourne   Sydney

Published by the Press Syndicate of the University of Cambridge
The Pitt Building, Trumpington Street, Cambridge CB2 1RP
32 East 57th Street, New York, NY 10022, USA
296 Beaconsfield Parade, Middle Park, Melbourne 3206, Australia

First published 1981

Printed in the United States of America
Typeset by David E. Seham, Inc., Metuchen, New Jersey
Printed and bound by Vail-Ballou Press, Inc., Binghamton, New York

Library of Congress Cataloging in Publication Data
Main entry under title:
The development of children's friendships.
(Cambridge, studies in social and emotional development)
Includes index.
1. Childhood friendship. I. Asher, Steven R.
II. Gottman, John Mordechai. III. Series.
BF723.F68D48   155.4'18   80-25920
ISBN 0 521 23103 5 hard covers
ISBN 0 521 29806 7 paperback

To Ross Parke

Contents

vii

Contributors

Vernon L. Allen
Department of Psychology
University of Wisconsin
Madison

Steven R. Asher
Bureau of Educational Research
University of Illinois
Urbana

William A. Corsaro
Department of Sociology
Indiana University

Carol S. Dweck
Department of Psychology
University of Illinois
Urbana

Gary Alan Fine
Department of Sociology
University of Minnesota

Susan R. Goldman
Graduate School of Education
University of California
Santa Barbara

Jay Gottlieb
Department of Educational
Psychology
New York University

John M. Gottman
Department of Psychology
University of Illinois
Urbana

Maureen T. Hallinan
Department of Sociology
University of Wisconsin
Madison

Yona Leyser
Department of Learning and
Development
Division of Special Education
Northern Illinois University

Martha Putallaz
Department of Psychology
University of Illinois
Urbana

Peter D. Renshaw
School of Education
Riverina Advanced College of
Education
Wagga Wagga, N.S.W.
Australia

Janet Ward Schofield
Psychology Department
University of Pittsburgh

ix

Robert L. Selman
Laboratory of Human
Development
Harvard Graduate School of
Education

Nancy L. Stein
Department of Education
University of Chicago

Editorial preface

The topic of children's friendships is attracting scholars from diverse fields of inquiry. Psychologists, educators, sociologists, anthropologists, ethologists, and others have been drawn to the study of children's relationships with their peers. Yet present-day boundaries between the disciplines are strong, and researchers in one field are often uninformed about highly relevant work being pursued in a different field. In fact, most of the authors in this volume knew the work of only a few other contributors prior to the study group we organized that preceded and led to the preparation of this volume. Our hope, therefore, is that this book will stimulate interdisciplinary communication.

The volume is divided into two parts. Part I, "Group Processes," focuses on various aspects of the peer-group setting and structure that influence relationships between peer-group members. Part II, "Social-Cognitive Processes," emphasizes intrapsychic processes that relate to the formation and maintenance of friendships. Each section concludes with a commentary by a scholar whose own work is associated with the study of group influences (Vernon Allen) or the study of social cognition and behavior (Carol Dweck).

Both sections of the book highlight theoretical and practical questions about the study of friendship. Among the many intriguing theoretical questions are: What functions do friendships serve in children's lives? How does children's thinking about friendship change over age and how does their thinking influence their behavior? How do children form peer groups and what is the nature of these groups? What are the critical social skills that underlie a child's acceptance by the peer group? To what extent does the social-skill basis of peer relations change over age? Questions of considerable practical significance also abound: How many children are without friends and what possible consequences do peer-relationship problems have for later life adjustment? What educational strategies are effective in helping children who are isolated or rejected by their peer group? What conditions foster acceptance and friendship between children of different races or between children of markedly different intellectual ability?

As this volume demonstrates, theoretical and practical questions are often intertwined. For many of the contributors to this volume, applied problems offer useful contexts for studying theoretical questions. What is particularly noteworthy is the dual concern with facilitating constructive change and developing an adequate understanding of the psychological and social processes that account for children's peer relationships. Thus, the boundaries between basic and applied research that have characterized previous thinking are becoming more flexible.

The attraction of the study of children's friendships is by no means new. Renshaw's chapter on the history of peer relations demonstrates that the study of children's friendships was launched nearly fifty years ago when psychologists, sociologists, and educators undertook the scientific investigation of children's social relationships. Significant advances were made in the 1930s, particularly in the development of sociometric methodology, observation strategies, and the use of experimental research designs in field settings. We are very much aware of our historical roots, and this volume is a testimony to the vitality of the research traditions that began developing a half century ago.

Indeed, the vitality of these traditions is evident in the methodological advances discussed in this volume. The sociometric tradition is represented in research by Hallinan, Putallaz and Gottman, Gottlieb and Leyser, and Asher and Renshaw. These chapters reflect increased sensitivity to the distinct purposes of different sociometric measures. Peer status is a multidimensional phenomenon; various measures index different aspects of a child's integration into the peer group. Methodological advances are also evident in the way in which sociometric data are analyzed. Particularly promising are techniques discussed by Hallinan for studying clique structure and changes in relationships over time.

The observational tradition is represented in the volume by the participant-observation methods of Corsaro and Fine, the ethnographic methods used by Schofield, and the more quantitative methods of Putallaz and Gottman. In chapters by Corsaro, Fine, and Schofield, children's naturally occurring behavior and conversations are observed in such everyday contexts as the nursery school, the racially desegregated middle school, and the Little League. In the chapter by Putallaz and Gottman, an analogue or contrived situation is used to study behaviors (children's entry styles) that might occur relatively infrequently in the natural environment but that are nonetheless of considerable significance to children's success in peer relations. Also represented in this chapter are new sequential analysis techniques used to study the way in which particular social behaviors lead to particular outcomes. Overall, these chapters illustrate diversity in observational methods and demonstrate their value for both generating and testing hypotheses.

The use of field-experimental methodology is also represented. Gottlieb and Leyser review the accumulated evidence from major studies of social relationships of mainstreamed handicapped children. This research capitalizes on a natural experiment to study the social acceptance of mentally retarded children by handicapped and nonhandicapped peers. Asher and Renshaw, in their chapter, analyze research on social-skill training with children who lack friends. Here, the field experiment is initiated by the investigator in order to test certain hypotheses concerning the reasons why some children lack friends.

The study of children's friendships is being influenced by other research traditions as well. Selman takes a Piagetian approach to the study of children's philosophies and friendship. The impact of contemporary cognitive psychology can be seen in Stein and Goldman's analysis of the way in which children comprehend social events and in Asher and Renshaw's analysis of the dimensions of social skillfulness and of why social-skill training might be effective. Corsaro brings the perspectives of a sociolinguist to the study of children's conversations and their rules for denying access to play groups in the nursery school. Both Fine and Schofield use symbolic-interaction theory as an interpretive framework for their respective studies of Little League team players and middle-school students.

Historically, research on children's friendships has been characterized by relatively little emphasis on developmental issues. Studies have typically focused on one age group, and few attempts have been made to account for transformations in friendship relations over age. Several authors in this volume have begun to address developmental questions. Perhaps their chapters will stimulate further research to build on these promising and important beginnings.

This volume is thus a call for integrated thinking and research on many levels. We seek to remove barriers between disciplines, between applied and theoretical research, between the study of social action and social cognition, and between ourselves and our historical heritage.

This volume is the result of an interdisciplinary study group sponsored by the Society for Research in Child Development (SRCD), and financially supported by the Foundation for Child Development. The aim of SRCD-sponsored study groups is to bring together scholars from different disciplines who are working on a common frontier problem in child development, yet who are unaware of each other's work because of disciplinary boundaries. We are very grateful to the Society and the Foundation for their sponsorship and support. The royalties from this volume will go to the Society to support future interdisciplinary conferences.

Two individuals, in addition to the study group participants, contributed significantly to the work of the study group and to the resulting volume. We wish to thank Shelley Hymel and Angela Taylor for their considerable help with conference arrangements and manuscript preparation.

Our volume is dedicated to Ross D. Parke, Professor of Psychology at the University of Illinois, Urbana-Champaign. Ross's outstanding research, his sensitive guidance of others, and his enthusiastic support for systematic inquiry has done much to stimulate research on children's social development. We are delighted to have this opportunity to acknowledge the contributions of a good friend.

S. R. A.
J. M. G.

1   The roots of peer interaction research: a historical analysis of the 1930s

Peter D. Renshaw

Introduction

The period from the late 1920s to the start of World War II was a critical one for the study of children's peer relationships and friendships. The work of that era is uniquely relevant to our current research, much of which is based on methodologies that were developed during the 1930s. These approaches – observational methodology, sociometry, and experimental intervention – are alive and thriving, as the other chapters in this volume testify. It is hoped that the present chapter will enable readers to search out their roots and to appreciate the historical conditions that made the 1930s so productive.

The extent of the contribution of the 1930s to current research on peer interaction and friendship can be appreciated by noting the classic theoretical works published during that decade. Moreno launched the field of sociometry by publishing *Who Shall Survive* in 1934. Sherif initiated a lifetime investigation of groups with the publication of *The Psychology of Social Norms* in 1936. Lewin's writings on field theory (Lewin, 1931) and group climates (Lewin, Lippitt, & White, 1939) established the experimental method as an indispensable tool for studying group phenomena. Piaget (1926, 1932b) demonstrated the importance of studying the social-cognitive development of children, and Lois Murphy showed that even young children acted altruistically toward each other (Murphy, 1937).

These classic studies, however, are only part of the large body of peer research that was conducted and reported during the era. Studies by Parten (1932) on children's play, by Koch (1933) on popularity, and by Isaacs (1933) on children's social development are noteworthy examples of the efforts that were being made. And interest in peer interaction was not confined to school-age children. The social interaction of children below the age of 2 was systematically studied by Buhler (1930), Bridges (1933), Shirley (1933), and Maudry and Nekula (1939). In the 1930s, then, important theoretical writing was supplemented by extensive empirical re-

1

search on the peer interaction of children from infancy through adolescence.

Two important events at the end of the 1920s heralded the new era of research on peer interaction. The first, Thrasher's 1927 study of child and adolescent gangs in Chicago, was the finest empirical research on peer groups thereto published. In the early years of this century, children's gangs and clubs had been the focus of considerable interest (Bonser, 1902; Forbush, 1900, 1909), but there were no first-hand observational studies. Thrasher's study, in contrast, was based on extensive first-hand observation of gangs in their natural environment. Thrasher's theoretical roots were derived from sociology – from Cooley's theory of social organization and from the ecological sociology of Park. Cooley (1902) was one of the first social scientists to emphasize the importance of peers as socialization agents, and Park (1915, 1936) highlighted the pervasive influence of urban environments on behavior. Thrasher used Cooley's and Park's insights to study the formation, location, membership, and behavior of gangs in Chicago. Thrasher's contribution was to demonstrate how an observer could study the mobile and unpredictable behavior of groups in a natural setting. This required the invention of new observational methods, and Thrasher's technique stands as an early instance of participant observation (see Kluckhorn, 1940; Thrasher, 1928).

The second event that marked the beginning of the new era of research was the growth of child-welfare institutes in the late 1920s. At this time, the child-welfare institutes received an infusion of funds, with substantial long-term grants being made to the institutes at Iowa, Minnesota, Yale, Teachers College Columbia, and the University of California at Berkeley (Sears, 1975, p. 21). Almost immediately these institutes initiated programs of research on children's development in the social, cognitive, and physiological domains. In surveying the research being conducted, Thomas and Thomas (1928) noted researchers' interest in children's peer relationships. These early investigations of children's peer relationships had certain common features. They were observational studies of young children, conducted with considerable care, and their purpose was to establish a detailed and accurate description of the young child's social behavior. Beaver (1929), for example, partly in response to Thrasher's study of gangs, published a preliminary investigation of a "preschool gang." Beaver's goal was to collect a detailed description of the behavior of a preschool group so that future studies could be formulated. This investigation typifies the spirit of the times – it was future oriented, conceived as part of a cumulative series of studies, and concerned with careful observation. When Thomas and Thomas published their survey in 1928, few studies on children's peer interaction were completed. As the research came to fruition, a new and exciting era of research on children's peer relationships began.

Children's peer relationships as the focus of research

Three reasons for the upsurge of interest in children's peer groups in the 1930s are examined below: societal influences; theoretical debate concerning children's spontaneous social inclinations; and the spread of experimental nursery schools.

Societal influences

There was widespread concern in many Western countries during the 1930s that democratic social institutions were failing (Becker, Ulich, Piaget, Lindemann & van der Leeuw, 1932; Zorbough, 1938). Zorbough (1938), in an article entitled "Which Way America's Youth?," recounted the history of social unrest during the Depression. Zorbough's account revealed a deep anxiety about the unemployment of youth, their revolutionary ideals, and their potential for disillusionment with democratic social values and institutions. According to Thelen (1967), one response to this situation was to allow youth in high schools considerable freedom. Adults apparently were unsure of their social values and looked toward the young for new solutions to the enduring problems of the times.

Jean Piaget expressed a similar concern at this time. Piaget was prominent in the New Education Fellowship, an organization devoted to progressive educational reforms. In 1932, he wrote a paper for that organization, arguing for the encouragement of peer interaction in order to ensure truly cooperative and democratic social institutions. Piaget (1932a) wrote:

If we watch the child when he is not with adults . . . we will see him develop a social life with other children, and we will notice that while he is developing socially he is also intellectually acquiring the power of thought and criticism . . . But too often education ends by destroying instead of using and developing the desire to cooperate . . . All the new active methods of education . . . stress the relation of children to one another. Group work, common study, self-government, etc. imply cooperation in both the intellectual and the social sphere. That is where the solution lies. [p. 20]

Piaget hoped, therefore, that early exposure to peer groups would establish an appreciation of and capacity for democratic living.

It was during the 1930s also that Lewin and his colleagues studied group "climates," which were described in highly political terms as either

"democratic," "autocratic," or "laissez-faire." Indeed, Lewin and Lippitt (1938) asked the socially relevant question, "Are not democratic
groups more pleasant but autocratic groups more efficient?" (p. 292).
Given their democratic political outlook, these researchers must have
been pleased to show that democratic group climates facilitated both output and satisfaction. It can be seen, therefore, that a variety of researchers expressed general anxiety about the need to preserve democratic social institutions and that this concern was instrumental in
directing their attention to children's peer relationships.

Debate concerning children's spontaneous social inclinations

A second factor that led to the study of peer interaction and friendship
was an interest in the spontaneous social inclinations of children. One
view, expressed by Anna Freud (1935), was that young children were
inconsiderate, self-centered, and cruel. These antisocial traits were seen
as the inevitable outcome of the struggle between the child's spontaneous
and self-centered impulses, and the restrictions imposed by the environment (Freud, 1935, p. 46). The alternative view was formulated gradually
as systematic observations of children's peer interactions were conducted. Cocknell (1935) noted that children were overwhelmingly cooperative even when they were unobtrusively observed by adults. Isaacs
(1933) recorded many episodes of friendly and sympathetic interactions
between children. Parten (1932) found that cooperative-play behavior developed in quite young children, and Murphy (1937) noted many instances
of sympathetic behavior, especially when older children interacted with
younger playmates.

   These researchers were intrigued by the question of whether children
were naturally cooperative or were forced to be so by adult discipline.
They hoped that by observing the social interaction of very young children the true inclinations of human nature could be discovered. Parten
(1932) stated the fundamental issues:

By the time individuals have acquired their human nature, their overt group responses are determined by such a multiplicity of factors . . . that many scientists
have despaired of ever finding uniformities in their behavior. The genetic [devel-
opmental] approach to the study of social motivation and adjustment promises to
reveal group behavior which is only slightly affected by these complex social factors. The reactions of children are more or less spontaneous and therefore percep-
tible to investigators. [p. 243]

   This quotation from Parten shows the way in which the effort to discover children's spontaneous social inclinations led researchers to focus
on the peer interaction of very young children.

Murphy's 1937 investigation of the sympathetic behavior of pre-schoolers was a persuasive and sophisticated contribution to the debate. Murphy's study was conducted in a variety of preschool contexts, using both naturalistic observation and observation in contrived helping situations. In summarizing her research, Murphy noted that children reflected the influence of their surrounding culture in their strongly cooperative and aggressive tendencies. Murphy noted that the behaviors that were most prominent in children's play were the nurturant patterns of parenting (eating together, playing mother and baby, doctoring the babies) and the aggressive patterns of attack and defense (shooting and killing). The generality of these contrasting tendencies across all the groups of preschoolers Murphy studied caused her considerable consternation, because it seemed that children were imitating the destructive as well as the cooperative tendencies of their surrounding culture. Murphy's research on the origins of children's sympathetic behavior, therefore, led her to consider children in the context of the surrounding environment and the influence of that environment on their behavioral inclinations.

Experimental nursery schools

The third factor that directed researchers to the topic of children's peer relationships and friendships was the opportunity to observe very young children interact in peer groups. In North America, the expansion of the child welfare institutes and their attached nursery schools occurred at this time (see Sears, 1975). These nursery schools provided the opportunity to observe young children's daily social interaction. Nursery schools were available to very few children at this time. The White House Conference on Child Health and Protection found that 5 percent of the preschool population attended nursery schools, and only 30 percent of the 5-year-olds were in kindergarten (J. Anderson, 1936, p. 266). Virtually no children of lower socioeconomic status families attended nursery schools. Furthermore, even for the families at the highest income level, fewer than 25 percent of the preschoolers attended nursery schools (J. Anderson, 1936, p. 267). Groups of young children had simply not been readily available for observation on a regular basis. The experimental nursery schools, therefore, provided the most convenient context in which programmatic observations of young children could be made.

The fact that so few children were in nursery schools may suggest that children were deprived of opportunities for peer interaction. The data from the White House Conference (J. Anderson, 1936) suggests that they were not. Indeed, by age 2 all but 6 percent of the children surveyed had had the opportunity to play with other children (J. Anderson, 1936, p.

255). Moreover, parents reported the formation of special companionships even between toddlers. Thus 40 percent of the 2-year-olds were reported to have a favorite playmate, and by age 4 this had increased to 60 percent (J. Anderson, 1936, p. 260). Children were also given considerable freedom at a young age to play away from home. For example, although about half of the 1-year-olds played only at home, the play of less than 20 percent of 4-year-olds was restricted to their homes (J. Anderson, 1936, p. 255). These data indicate that peer interaction was a salient feature of children's lives whether or not they attended nursery schools. It was in the nursery schools, however, that almost all the research on young children's peer interaction was conducted.

The research climate of the 1930s

The creativity of the research at this time is quite striking, both in theory development (e.g., Lewin, 1931; Moreno, 1934; Piaget, 1932b; Sherif, 1936) and in the growth in methodological sophistication in such areas as observational methods, sociometry, and experimental approaches. Evidence suggests that the creativity of the researchers was facilitated by conditions unique to the period. In this section such factors are identified.

A fusion of paradigms

First, at this time, there was an openness to alternative paradigms and research methods that allowed researchers to draw on the strengths of other views, to consider a problem from a variety of perspectives, and to combine ideas from separate paradigms in order to create new insights. For example, Sherif (1936) cited both Lewin's and Piaget's contributions to his own ideas. Lewin's general field theory suggested to Sherif that the group itself should be the unit of analysis, and Piaget's research on the development of children's rules for regulating social behavior during games (Piaget, 1932b) suggested the importance of shared norms for understanding group behavior.

The merging of observational and experimental methods is a second example of the fusion of paradigms. Researchers moved easily between naturalistic observation and controlled experimental manipulation (Jack, 1934; Murphy, 1937; Page, 1936). In a study of children's personality traits, for example, Jack (1934) combined observations of children in natural settings with observations of children in a contrived setting that was analogous to the children's everyday experience. Having established a reliable means of measuring children's personality traits using an observational methodology, Jack devised an intervention procedure to change their behavior. In this way, Jack demonstrated how observational and experimental approaches could be combined in the study of children's personality traits.

Still another example of the fusion of paradigms can be seen in Isaacs's 1933 study of children's social development. Although her study was conducted within a psychoanalytic framework, Isaacs used an observational methodology that was subsequently adopted by Murphy (1937) in her study of children's sympathy and formalized by Barker and Wright (1955) in their ecological investigation of the day-to-day behavior of children and their families. Isaacs's commitment to an empirical approach to child study enabled her to provide a rounded picture of the child's behavior. Her observations were not biased toward children's anxieties and fears. Indeed, Isaacs (1933) was impressed by the cooperativeness and friendliness of children and framed her general discussion of children's social interaction by stating, "Only the more explicit and dramatic instances of friendliness and cooperation are quoted here as separate events. There were countless minor incidents of mutual helpfulness and common activity which could not be recorded and long stretches of quiet constructive work" (Isaacs, 1933, p. 93). Isaacs's psychoanalytic viewpoint did not prevent her from reporting data that contradicted the psychoanalytic view of young children as self-centered and self-serving.

Communication networks

The openness of researchers to alternative paradigms was facilitated by the establishment of formal and informal communication networks between researchers. Formal means of communication, such as journals and handbooks, proliferated during the late 1920s and 1930s. Following the publication of *The Child in America* (1928) by Thomas and Thomas, Murchison edited a *Handbook of Child Psychology* in 1931 and a revision in 1933. The journal *Child Development* began publication in 1930, and the various child welfare institutes began publishing their own research reports in monograph form. A distinctive feature of these publications was the mix of European and American authors. For example, in the first edition of the *Handbook of Child Psychology*, Isaacs, from Britain; Piaget, from Switzerland; Buhler, from Austria; and Lewin, from Germany contributed to the reviews of research. In addition to these formal networks, the researchers communicated with each other by personal contact. For example, information about Buhler's research on infants' social development was spread by her visits to the United States during the late 1920s. With the rise of the Nazis in Germany, Lewin, Buhler, and Moreno settled permanently in the United States. These European researchers helped maintain the creative research that had begun in the child welfare institutes.

An important instance of new ideas from European researchers building on established research at the child welfare institutes occurred at Iowa in the mid-1930s. Lewin's innovative research on group climates (Lewin, Lippitt, & White, 1939) was foreshadowed at Iowa in the research by Jack (1934), Page (1936), and H. Anderson (1937) on children's style of interaction. Anderson's distinction between integrative and dominative styles of peer interaction, in particular, parallels the distinction that Lewin and Lippitt (1938) made between democratic and autocratic group structures. Thus, while Lewin's contribution should be acknowledged as a new and creative one, it appears that his going to Iowa in 1936 and reading the research already completed there on styles of peer interaction was a significant influence on the development of his ideas.

The 1930s were characterized, therefore, by an unusual openness to new ideas that enabled researchers to combine insights from different paradigms in their study of peer interaction. The establishment of effective communication networks both formally and informally gave researchers access to new methodologies and theories. Finally, the security and continuity provided by the child welfare institutes helped researchers to conduct systematic and cumulative research on peer interaction. The following discussion will highlight specific advances in three areas: the growth of behavior observation techniques, the measurement of social relations using sociometric methods, and the use of experimental intervention approaches to study peer relationships.

Observational methodology

There was a sudden upsurge of observational studies in the 1930s, particularly from the child welfare institutes and from European researchers who had access to nursery-school facilities (e.g., Isaacs, 1933; Piaget, 1926). Observational studies were conducted on children's choice of companions (Challman, 1932; Hagman, 1933; Wellman, 1926), on quarreling between children (Dawe, 1934; Green, 1933), on the developmental stages of play (Bott, 1928, Parten, 1932), on children's assertiveness (H. Anderson, 1939; Jack, 1934; Page, 1936), on aggression (Fite, 1940; Jersild & Markey, 1935), and on sympathy (Murphy, 1937).

The widespread use of observational methodologies was spurred by a variety of factors. First, the observational method was advocated by significant researchers, particularly by Thomas (1929) and Blatz and Bott (1929). These child psychologists were convinced that a science of child psychology would emerge only after the accumulation of basic observable facts (Blatz & Bott, 1929). As a result, they adopted methodologies that avoided predetermined categories for coding behavior and attempted to provide unprejudiced reflections of the actual behavior of children. In their zeal for objectivity, some researchers described the most overt and perhaps least interesting aspects of social interaction. For example, Bott (1928) summarized the play behavior of the child simply in terms of the number of peers involved (alone, with one other child, with two children, with more than two children).

Other researchers sought answers to general problems in sociology or epistemology by observing young children's social interaction. Thus, Parten's (1932) study of children's play was reported within the framework of genetic sociology:

Genetic Sociology is as yet a little developed field of science. Investigators of social behavior have overlooked the period when adjustment to the group is first acquired and practiced. In so doing, they have ignored a source that ought to contribute not only to the explanation of child behavior but to the understanding of adult group habits which persist from childhood. [p. 243]

Even though Parten's study focused on young children it was conceived as part of a larger endeavor – the eventual explanation of adult social behavior. Likewise, Piaget's observational studies of children (1926, 1932b) were motivated by his determination to show that long-standing problems regarding the nature of knowledge could be answered by observing the development of knowledge systems in children. Piaget's approach was revolutionary in that he suggested that philosophical discussion alone could not solve epistemological problems – only by the observation and interviewing of children could solutions ultimately be forged.

Other researchers were disenchanted with the unscientific methods that had characterized much of child research up to this time. Munsterberg (1899) had berated the lack of rigor of child psychologists. A student of his, John Anderson (1933), was later to help set child psychology on a more rigorous course. During the late 1920s and early 1930s, Anderson guided many observational studies at the University of Minnesota Institute of Child Welfare that were marked by considerable methodological rigor. Under Anderson's influence and that of Goodenough (1928), new observational techniques were tested, including the use of an equal number of observational periods for each subject and the use of short time samples of behavior rather than continuous records. These innovations promoted the use of more sophisticated statistical techniques in analyzing observational data.

Three applications of the observational method that were used to study children's peer interaction are examined in more detail below.

Observational studies of children's companionship

Friendship bonds between children can be inferred by observing the frequency of contact between them. The use of this method of inferring friendships has been called "observational sociometry" (Moreno, 1978, p. 100) or "moving sociometrics" (Hartup, 1975). Wellman's 1926 study of the companionship choices of junior-high-school children initiated this way of determining peer companionships. The companions of each child were determined by observing children's associates when there was freedom to choose – for example, during trips to and from the lockers, free-play periods, and lunchroom and assembly time. Wellman was primarily interested in dyadic relationships and the similarity of the members of the dyad in such personality traits as introversion–extroversion, physical attributes (e.g., height and strength), and developmental markers (mental age and chronological age). Wellman's study illustrates the types of variables that were considered likely to influence companionships between children. The study showed that friends were quite similar on some indexes: for example, scholastic ability for girls and IQ for boys. The innovative aspect of the study, however, was the use of the observed frequency of association between children as a means of determining friendship relations. This observational method was subsequently adopted by Challman (1932) and Hagman (1933) in studying preschoolers' friendships and later by Florence Moreno (1942) in studying the process of rejection in a group of elementary-school children.

Hagman's 1933 investigation, in addition to correlating the degree of companionship between children with measures of personality, developmental age, and physical attributes, included a procedure to elicit verbal choices of each child's friends and compared the verbal choice with the observed frequency of companionship. Hagman also set up an experimental situation to observe both the quantity and quality of interaction between children who were either most- or least-frequent companions. In the experimental setting, both the quality and quantity of interaction were judged to be higher where the play partners were frequent companions. Hagman's interest in comparing alternative indexes of friendship, such as frequency of contact versus verbal choice, and her interest in the quality of interaction between friends and nonfriends are topics of current interest.

Observation of behavior in context

Thrasher (1927) found it useful to observe children in their everyday activities. So did the new generation of child psychologists. For example, Piaget's study of children's social interactions began when he followed two preschoolers around the Jean Jacques Rousseau Institute in Geneva and manually recorded their speech. Similarly, his study of children's moral judgment began by observing spontaneous street games (Piaget, 1932b). It was the research of Isaacs (1933), however, that was most influential in guiding other psychologists to observe children's behavior in context. Isaacs was well known in the 1930s, as demonstrated by her chapter in the *Handbook of Child Psychology* (Isaacs, 1931), and the credit other investigators gave her ideas (e.g., Murphy, 1937). Isaacs's approach to observing peer interaction was to record whole episodes of behavior by noting the actors involved, the context, the precipitating events, and the consequences. An example of one of Isaacs's observations is:

12-11-24   The children were all modelling very quietly and Dan made a boat and gave it to Benjie. Benjie told the others, "He has made a boat for me." Dan remarked, "Yes, I like you very much, and I'm going to kiss you." He kissed Benjie's hand. Benjie told the others, "He likes me." Dan then said to Harold, "I like *you,* and I'm going to kiss you," and kissed Harold's hand. Harold said, "He's a dear little thing," and all the others agreed. [1933, pp. 93–94]

Isaacs's approach is really an example of event sampling, as defined by Wright (1960). This approach was used by numerous other investigators of children's social interaction, most notably by Dawe (1934) and Murphy (1937). Dawe recorded over two-hundred quarrels between preschool children by noting the characteristics (age, sex, and name) of the contestants, the events that precipitated the quarrel, the context of the quarrel (indoor or outdoor), the resolution process, and the aftereffects. Murphy used a similar approach to study the sympathetic behavior of preschoolers. Both of these studies provide data on children's social behavior that is readily intelligible and of use in isolating factors that facilitate or inhibit particular types of social behavior.

Barker and Wright (1949, 1955) started with the ideas of these child psychologists and transformed the event-sampling technique by formalizing the observational procedures. They defined the types of contexts in which behavior occurred (behavior settings), established boundaries between sequences of action (episodes), and addressed the problems of reliability in order to standardize the method across observers. The pioneering work of Thrasher, Isaacs, Dawe, Murphy, and particularly Barker and Wright in preserving both the sequence of social interaction and its context is still useful today as ethnographers struggle with the task of relating changing patterns of peer interaction to contextual and setting variables (see Cook-Gumperz & Corsaro, 1977).

Observation using time-sampling procedures

The evolution of systematic observation using time-sampling procedures occurred in the late 1920s, and the University of Minnesota Institute of Child Welfare was particularly influential in demonstrating the usefulness of the procedure. Pioneering research by Goodenough (1928) and Olson (1929) paved the way for many subsequent studies of children's social interaction using time sampling. Studies by Green (1933) of children's friendships and quarrels, by Mallay (1935) of children's techniques for successful social interaction, by Caille (1933) of resistance and acquiescence in social transactions, and by Parten (1932) of children's play are only a few of the studies that employed a time-sampling procedure. Parten's study is a classic example of this approach. Specific categories of interaction – solitary play, onlooker play, parallel play, associative play, and cooperative play – were defined a priori as representing progressively more interdependent forms of peer interaction. It was hypothesized that as children aged they became capable of higher levels of interdependent play. By observing children at different ages and obtaining the same number of observations of each child, Parten could correlate age with the relative occurrence of the behavioral categories, thereby determining whether peer interaction became more interdependent with age. In conducting the study, the reliability of observers was assessed and every effort was made to control the time of day observations were made. The methodology of the study is widely employed today, but it should be remembered that in 1932 it was an elegant example of the methodological rigor advocated by Anderson and Goodenough.

The sociometric tradition

Sociometric methodology, which was invented during the 1930s, is a process of assessing and describing the interpersonal attraction among members of a group. Moreno, who was responsible for the widespread use of sociometric methods, began his research on groups in institutions such as prisons and reform schools. One of his early studies (Moreno, 1932) was conducted at the Sing Sing Prison in New York, while a second study was conducted at the New York State Training School for Girls. The fact that Moreno's initial research focused on the interpersonal relationships of institutionalized subjects is significant. Moreno argued that bureaucratic decision making, which took no account of the spontaneous interpersonal attractions of group members, resulted in group conflicts and individual maladjustment. When individuals' interpersonal choices were used in forming groups (for dormitories, for recreation, for work, and so on) Moreno argued that groups were cohesive and the social adjustment of group members was enhanced.

Moreno's theory and research were brought together in 1934 in the first edition of *Who Shall Survive*. It should be noted, however, that other researchers also contributed to the sociometric tradition. For example, Bott (1934, p. 79) represented the group structure of a preschool class using a diagrammatic scheme similar to Moreno's sociogram. Koch (1933) had published a thoughtful study of children's popularity using a paired-comparison sociometric measure. Koch's sociometric method allowed a ranking of the whole group in terms of comparative peer status to be computed. Koch's study of the popularity of children stemmed from her concern to show that social effectiveness with one's peers was related to other measures of social adjustment. Thus she correlated popularity with behavioral indexes of adjustment such as compliance with classroom routines and avoidance of behaviors such as ignoring others, playing alone, or aggression. Koch's interest, therefore, was directed to individual differences between children and helping children who were having peer relationship problems (Koch, 1935).

Whereas Koch was primarily interested in individual differences and in describing the characteristics of children who were popular or unpopular, Moreno was concerned with the types of group structures and the interpersonal relationships that resulted from different group structures. Thus, even though Moreno used the terms "star" and "isolate," his intention was to describe a group position, not a type of child. He believed that as the activity and the composition of the group changed, different children would come to occupy the star or isolate role.

Sociometric research continued to reflect the contrasting traditions represented by Koch's focus on individuals and Moreno's concern with whole-group processes. Koch's study of the correlates of popularity was followed by the research of Lippitt (1941), Bonney (1943a, 1943b), and, particularly, Northway (1943, 1944, 1946). Northway's purpose was to identify the behavioral characteristics of unpopular children and devise ways of helping these children gain in peer acceptance. Like Koch, therefore, Northway was interested primarily in individual differences and in intervention to aid particular types of children. Northway's approach (1944) is captured in the statement: "Because of the potential dangers

isolated individuals hold for a democratic society and because of the effects isolation has on personality development, we have been concerned
with studies of the children who are least acceptable to their age mates"
(p. 10). In studying these children, Northway was struck by the heteroge-
neity of the least acceptable children. She proposed a subclassification of
these children based on observation, teacher reports, and information in
the pupil records. She distinguished among *recessive children,* who were
listless, below average in intelligence, and lacking physical and mental
vitality; the *socially uninterested,* who were unmotivated to become socially involved; and the *socially ineffective,* who were noisy, rebellious
and arrogant. Using these subclassifications, Northway suggested the
type of help each child might need.

The contrasting tradition, that closely followed Moreno's prescriptions,
focused on group characteristics such as the number of cliques in a group
or the occurrence of chains, of stars, and of unreciprocated choices. Research in this tradition was done by Criswell (1939a, 1939b) on race and
sex cleavage in classrooms and by Jennings on leadership and isolation
(1937; 1952). Jennings had worked with Moreno from the beginning of the
1930s and was particularly influential in the initial dissemination of the
sociometric method. Her approach was identical to that of Moreno, and
although she studied leadership and isolation, her interest was not in
leaders and isolates as "types":

The why of leadership appears, however, not explainable by any personality quality or constellation of traits . . . The why of leadership appears to reside in the
interpersonal contribution of which the individual becomes capable in a specific
setting . . . Similarly, isolation appears as but the opposite extreme on this
continuum of interpersonal sensitivity between the membership and the individual
in the sociogroup. [Jennings, 1952, p. 317]

Jennings argued, therefore, that specific situations elevate individuals to
leadership or relegate them to isolation. Jennings believed that as children
move from context to context it is likely that they will occupy a variety of
group roles.

Jennings's suggestions to teachers on how to maintain a good group
climate contrasted with Northway's concern with individual children.
Jennings suggested that teachers reshape grouping practices in schools to
allow for more spontaneity (such as conversations in hallways) and establish homerooms on the basis of choice. In addition, Jennings suggested
that teachers monitor children's interactions to ensure that no child was
left out or stimatized. Where a child seemed to be excluded, Jennings
suggested manipulating the classroom roles to give the child some important group role. Jennings avoided the notion that the individual child may

be deficient in social skills or need assistance in learning how to interact with peers (Jennings, 1959).

Experimental intervention

The spread of experimental interventionist research is a third feature of the 1930s. There were notable attempts by Jack (1934), Page (1936), and Chittenden (1942), to change the interactional styles of children. There were attempts within the sociometric tradition to help unpopular or unsocial children gain in peer acceptance (Koch, 1935). There were also the studies by Lewin and his colleagues on group climates and peer interaction. The twofold purpose of the interventionist attempts was to assist children and to illuminate the psychological processes underlying change in peer relationships.

The field-experimental approach

Kurt Lewin argued persuasively during the 1930s for an experimental approach to the study of group phenomena. Lewin's viewpoint was that new groups should be established, so that the experimenter could know the history of the group and chart the conditions that influence group processes. At the same time, Lewin favored maintaining an environment that was as natural as possible so that the spontaneous and unpredictable dynamics of the group could be expressed. Lewin summarized his double-edged approach by stating that ''a relatively-free but well-defined set of conditions'' be established to study group phenomena (Lewin & Lippitt, 1938, p. 292). His approach is illustrated in the Lewin, Lippitt and White (1939) study of group climates. In this classic study, groups of boys were established with adult leaders who adopted either autocratic, democratic, or laissez-faire styles of interaction. The experiment was a realistic experience for the boys conducted in a natural setting over a lengthy time period.

Lewin reported the study in a preliminary fashion in the first volume of *Sociometry* (Lewin & Lippitt, 1938). The report suggested that the interaction pattern of groups of boys was quite different under democratic and autocratic styles of leadership. It was found that the expression of affect, the expression of discontent, and types of conversations varied according to leadership style. Group members in a democratic group climate were more friendly, group-minded, and work-minded than those in the other groups. It was found also that these tendencies were general across the personnel who acted the various leadership roles. All personnel adopted similar patterns of behavior when playing the particular leadership roles; it was thus clear that the group climate was not dependent on peculiar individual characteristics of the group leaders. Rather, the climate resulted from patterns of behavior that anyone could learn and adopt. This investigation highlighted the plasticity of human behavior and demonstrated the utility of the field-experimental approach for identifying the determinants of social interaction.

Lewin's influence on the subsequent history of peer-interaction research was pervasive. The field of group dynamics can be traced to Lewin's theory and research (Sears, 1975, p. 54). Likewise, the ecological psychology of Barker and Wright (1949, 1955) was inspired by Lewin's approach to the investigation of the effects of environments on social behavior. In addition, the classic study by Sherif on the interaction of children's groups at summer camps (Sherif, Harvey, White, Hood & Sherif, 1961) embodied Lewin's maxim that a relatively free but well-defined set of conditions should be established to study group processes. Finally, Lewin's ability to translate such complex social concepts as "autocracy" and "democracy" into experimental variables demonstrated the potential of social science to use an experimental paradigm to investigate the social conditions under which people work and live.

Intervention in children's style of interaction

The studies on children's interactional styles (H. Anderson, 1937, 1939; Chittenden, 1942; Jack, 1934; Page, 1936) were also influential in demonstrating the utility of an interventionist approach for furthering the understanding of peer interaction. Jack's 1934 study was instigated by Allport's research on adults' personality traits. Allport (1928) was interested in whether adults tended toward ascendant or submissive roles in interpersonal relationships. The ascendant personality tended to be socially gregarious, assertive, and at times a leader. In contrast, the submissive personality was quiet, nonassertive, and a follower. Jack wanted to know whether the personality traits Allport discovered in adults could be reliably measured in preschool children. An equally important goal was to demonstrate by experimental intervention that children who were observed to be submissive could be trained to be ascendant.

Jack's approach was to observe children in a paired-play situation and record categories of behavior that were either ascendant (defending one's right to toys, commanding, snatching back toys) or submissive (not defending one's right to toys, acquiescing). Having classified the children as either ascendant or submissive, Jack taught the submissive children how to play a game that was novel for the group of children. The submissive children, therefore, were given a specific skill: knowledge of how to play the new game. In a paired-play situation where the task was to play that game, the submissive children appeared more confident and exhibited significant increases in their ascendant behavior. The results Jack obtained were replicated by Page (1936).

The success of Jack's study had an immediate impact on the field. Murphy (1937) commented that the study's fundamental importance was that it suggested "that confidence could be built up in fairly limited periods of time through simple techniques of giving skills to the child which increase his resources" (p. 403). It is intriguing that Jack's study was interpreted as a skill-training study. The skill, however, was not a social skill such as how to initiate conversation, but the knowledge of a new game. The competence of the submissive children at the new game apparently enabled them to be more assertive in their style of peer interaction.

Although Jack's study was highly regarded, subsequent researchers challenged the value of training children to be ascendant. In particular, Harold Anderson, who had worked at the Iowa Child Welfare Research Station with Jack and Page, argued that more attention should be given to the social acceptability of the strategies children used in being assertive. In Anderson's view, it was harmful to promote ascendance in children without due regard to the strategies children employed.

Anderson defined the goal of interventionist attempts as that of helping children reduce dominative strategies and increase integrative strategies. Dominative strategies, in Anderson's definition, were those that take no account of the rights or needs of the other individual, whereas integrative strategies were responsive to the rights and needs of the other. Page (1936), in particular, had been aware of Anderson's viewpoint and reported that in her preschool sample submissive children who increased in ascendance as the result of training did use more of the integrative social strategies. Moreover, it was clear to Jack and Page that submissive children may be excluded from peer interaction opportunities. In support of this view, Jack showed that social responsiveness (playing with, smiling at, responding to, touching, and talking to other children) correlated + .62 with her measure of ascendance.

The debate that was generated by Jack's study illustrates the problems researchers confronted when they embarked on intervention studies of children's social relationships. A minimum requirement of such studies was that the change in children's behavior be seen as worthwhile. In Jack's study, the goal of helping children be more ascendant seemed desirable because greater ascendancy enabled them to defend their rights in the peer group and to participate in games more actively. However, Jack consciously decided not to evaluate the strategies children used in reaching those desirable goals. Anderson, in contrast, argued that the social strategies used by children in the peer group should reflect a respect for the rights of others. Anderson's viewpoint was influential in subsequent intervention research with children. Thus Chittenden (1942), in her classic intervention study with preschoolers, used Anderson's distinction between dominative and integrative (cooperative) social strategies. Chittenden reasoned that children who used a high percentage of dominative strategies did so because they were unable to think of cooperative alternative strategies for reaching their goals. In her training procedure, therefore, Chittenden showed these children how interpersonal conflicts over toys could be solved by means of cooperative strategies such as taking turns with the materials or sharing the toys.

Beginning with Jack's study (1934), therefore, a fruitful debate emerged in the 1930s concerning the goals of intervention with children. It appears that a consensus was established by the early 1940s that both the goals and the strategies taught to children should reflect an awareness of the rights of others. Chittenden's study, in particular, reflects a concern with enabling children to reach their social goals using cooperative strategies.

In summary, the 1930s was a uniquely creative period in the history of peer interaction research. The conditions that contributed to researchers' creativity included their openness to alternative paradigms and methodologies, the establishment of formal and informal communication networks, and the spread of the child welfare institutes with their attached experimental nursery schools. These conditions coincided with an unusual interest in children's peer relationships, some of which was generated by the availability of groups of young children in the experimental nursery schools. These schools provided a new opportunity for researchers to observe young children's social interactions in controlled situations over a period of time. Other researchers were interested in extending the genetic-developmental approach in order to study the genesis of social rules and social coordination. Others were motivated by a desire to identify the basic social inclinations of children as either cooperative or mutually antagonistic. Still others wanted to help children lacking in social skills.

The widespread interest in peer interaction motivated the evolution of the three dominant approaches to the study of peer interaction: observational methodology, sociometry, and experimental intervention. It should be noted also that Piaget's major contribution to the area of social-cognitive development was completed by the early 1930s (Piaget, 1926; 1932b).

The post-1930s era

Research on peer interaction did not cease at the end of the 1930s, but a significant change in the climate for research took place in the decades that followed. First, there was a dramatic reduction at the beginning of the 1940s in the number of personnel at the child welfare institutes. As Sears (1975) noted, World War II depleted the ranks of the child psychologists, because many of them were required to perform war-related tasks. Those researchers who remained at the institutes had to cover a number of duties, and intensive research endeavors on peer interaction were truncated.

After the war, research on children's peer relationships revived, but the intensive observational studies of young children that had characterized research at the child welfare institutes did not continue with the same vitality. Wright (1960) tabulated the number of observational studies in all areas of child psychology for each decade from 1890 through to 1960. The number of observational studies of children's behavior per decade was less than ten until the 1930s, when it increased to fifty-three; in the 1940s and 1950s combined, fewer than forty observational studies were reported, and few of these were concerned with peer interaction.

There are a variety of reasons for this. First, important theoretical shifts occurred in child and social psychology. In child psychology, renewed interest in Freudian theory led to a new emphasis on parent–child relationships to the exclusion of child–child relationships. This was especially true of the peer relationships of young children (2 years and younger), which remained a neglected research topic until it was revived in the 1970s (see Goldman & Ross, 1978). In social psychology, persuasive theoretical papers on social perception (Bruner & Postman, 1948; Dennis, 1948) influenced the research on peer interaction by focusing attention on the covert perceptual and cognitive processes that were hypothesized to mediate children's responses to each other. Peer research that reflected this influence included studies of the perception of sociometric status (e.g., Ausubel, Shiff, & Gasser, 1952), children's racial and ethnic attitudes toward each other (e.g., Radke, Trager, & Davis, 1949), and the development of children's concepts of race, religion, and ethnicity (e.g., Hartley, Rosenbaum, & Schwartz, 1948a, 1948b).

Second, the observational studies did not seem compatible with the emerging trend toward the laboratory. The laboratory was advocated by learning theorists in the postwar era as the best context in which to study children and establish the laws governing human behavior. Keller (1950), for example, addressed the membership of the Society for Research in Child Development in a paper entitled *Animals and Children*, in which he argued that it was time for the experimental method as developed with animals to be applied to the study of the child. Other influential voices were advocating an experimental approach for child psychology (Skinner, 1947), and even nonbehaviorists sought a new science of child psychology based on the exhaustive testing of principles and laws of behavior (Sears, 1947). The overall effect of these endeavors was to devalue the earlier naturalistic observational studies of children's social development and diminish the likelihood of further observational studies being conducted.

Thus in the post-1930s period there was reduced emphasis on peer interaction research and a change in the nature of the research conducted. The current scene is, however, reminiscent of the 1930s. First, there is a common concern for detailed observation of children's peer interaction. In the 1930s, the accurate description of children's ongoing peer interaction was facilitated by such innovative observational techniques as time sampling (e.g., Parten, 1932), event sampling (e.g., Dawe, 1934), and participant observation (e.g., Thrasher, 1927, 1928). The utility of these observational techniques continues to be demonstrated in current research, and there is an increasing use of audiovisual equipment to make complete records of children's interaction (e.g., Gottman & Parkhurst, 1980; Putallaz & Gottman, this volume). This method of recording interaction facilitates finely grained analysis of the unfolding sequence of interaction, and it holds the promise that cause–effect relationships in children's ongoing interactions may be discovered.

In the 1930s, sociometric methodology was used to study the effects of various institutional structures on children's friendships (e.g., Moreno, 1934), children's race relationships (Criswell, 1939a), and the characteristics of unpopular children (Koch, 1933). The adaptability of the sociometric technique is demonstrated both in these early studies and in current research, in which the effects of contrasting classroom structure on children's friendships (Hallinan. 1976. this volume). the race relationships of children in integrated school districts (Schofield. this volume; Singleton & Asher. 1977). and the cognitive and behavioral characteristics of unpopular children (Asher & Renshaw. this volume; Putallaz & Gottman. this volume) are being studied.

In contrast to the 1930s, sociometric measures are being used more often as outcome measures in social-skill training studies (e.g., Gottman, Gonso, & Schuler, 1976; Ladd, in press, Oden & Asher, 1977). In the 1930s, the impact of intervention programs was typically assessed by observing behavioral change in controlled experimental settings and in the child's everyday peer group (e.g., Chittenden, 1942; Jack, 1934; Page, 1936). Although behavioral measures are still utilized, sociometric measures are being included because of their importance as indicators of long-term social adjustment (e.g., Roff, Sells, & Golden, 1972; Ullmann, 1957).

Finally, in both the 1930s and the present era, peer interaction is studied by researchers from various disciplines and theoretical viewpoints. It was suggested above that researchers' ability in the 1930s to draw on ideas from alternative paradigms enhanced the creativity of their work. It remains to be seen whether the researchers of the 1980s in university, clinical, and educational settings will be able to combine forces in a similarly productive fashion.

References

Allport, G. A test for ascendance–submission. *Journal of Abnormal and Social Psychology,* 1928, *23,* 118–136.

Anderson, H. H. Domination and integration in the social behavior of young children in an experimental play situation. *Genetic Psychology Monographs,* 1937, *19,* 343–408.

Domination and social integration in the behavior of kindergarten children and teachers. *Genetic Psychology Monographs,* 1939, *21,* 287–385.

Anderson, J. E. The methods of child psychology. In C. Murchison (Ed.), *A handbook of child psychology* (Vol. 1). New York: Russell and Russell, 1933.

The young child in the home: A survey of three thousand American families. New York: Appleton-Century, 1936.

Ausubel, D. P., Schiff, H., & Gasser, E. A preliminary study of development trends in socioempathy: Accuracy of perception of own and other sociometric status. *Child Development,* 1952, *23,* 111–128.

Barker, R., & Wright, H. Psychological ecology and the problem of psychosocial development. *Child Development,* 1949, *20,* 131–144.

Midwest and its children. White Plains, N.Y.: Row Peterson and Co., 1955.

Beaver, A. P. A preliminary report on a study of a preschool "gang." In D. S. Thomas (Ed.), Some new techniques for studying social behavior. *Child Development Monographs: Teachers College Columbia University,* 1929, No. 1, 99–117.

Becker, C., Ulich, R., Piaget, J., Lindemann, E., & van der Leeuw, J. The changing social structure. *The New Era,* 1932, *13,* 283–289.

Blatz, W., & Bott, H. *Parents and the preschool child.* New York: William Morrow, 1929.

Bonney, M. Personality traits of socially successful and socially unsuccessful children. *Journal of Educational Psychology,* 1943, *34,* 449–472.(a)

The relative stability of social, intellectual, and academic status in grades III to IV, and the interrelationships between these various forms of growth. *Journal of Educational Psychology,* 1943, *34,* 88–102.(b)

Bonser, F. G. Chums: A study of youthful friendships. *Pedagogical Seminary,* 1902, *9,* 221–256.

Bott, H. Observations of play activities in a nursery school. *Genetic Psychology Monographs,* 1928, *4,* 44–88.

Personality development in young children. *University of Toronto Studies: Child Development Series I,* 1934, No. 2.

22   P. D. RENSHAW

Bridges, K. A study of social development in early infancy. *Child Development*, 1933, *4*, 36–49.

Bruner, J. S. & Postman, L. An approach to social perception. In W. Dennis (Ed.), *Current trends in social psychology*. Pittsburgh: University of Pittsburgh Press, 1948.

Buhler, C. *The first year of life*. New York: John Day, 1930.

Caille, R. Resistant behavior of preschool children. *Child Development Monographs: Teachers College Columbia University*, 1933, No. 11.

Challman, R. C. Factors influencing friendships among preschool children. *Child Development*, 1932, *3*, 146–158.

Chittenden, G. F. An experimental study in measuring and modifying assertive behavior in young children. *Monographs of the Society for Research in Child Development*, 1942, *7* (1, Serial No. 31).

Cocknell, D. L. A study of the play of children of preschool age by an unobserved observer. *Genetic Psychology Monographs*, 1935, *17*, 377–469.

Cook-Gumperz, J., & Corsaro, W. Social-ecological constraints on children's communicative strategies. *Sociology*, 1977, *11*, 411–433.

Cooley, C. H. *Human nature and the social order*. New York: Charles Scribners Sons, 1902.

Criswell, J. H. A sociometric study of race cleavage in the classroom. *Archives of Psychology*, 1939, No. 235.(a)

Social structure revealed in a sociometric test. *Sociometry*, 1939, *2*, 69–75. (b)

Dawe, H. C. Analysis of two hundred quarrels of preschool children. *Child Development*, 1934, *5*, 139–157.

Dennis, W. *Current trends in social psychology*. Pittsburgh: University of Pittsburgh Press, 1948.

Fite, M. Aggressive behavior in young children and children's attitudes toward aggression. *Genetic Psychology Monographs*, 1940, *22*, 151–319.

Forbush, W. B. The social pedagogy of boyhood. *Pedagogical Seminary*, 1900, *7*, 307–346. Boys' clubs. *Pedagogical Seminary*, 1909, *16*, 337–343.

Freud, A. *Psychoanalysis for teachers and parents*. New York: W. W. Norton, 1979. (Originally published, 1935)

Goldman, B. D. & Ross, H. S. Social skills in action: An analysis of early peer games. In J. Glick & K. A. Clarke-Stewart (Eds.), *The development of social understanding*. New York: Gardner Press, 1978.

Goodenough, F. Measuring behavior traits by means of repeated short samples. *Journal of Juvenile Research*, 1928, *12*, 230–235.

Gottman, J., Gonso, J., & Schuler, P. Teaching social skills to isolated children. *Journal of Abnormal Child Psychology*, 1976, *4*, 179–197.

Gottman, J., & Parkhurst, J. A developmental theory of friendship and acquaintanceship processes. In W. A. Collins (Ed.), *Minnesota symposia on child psychology* (Vol. 13). Hillsdale, N.J.: Lawrence Erlbaum, 1980.

Green, E. Friendships and quarrels among preschool children. *Child Development*, 1933, *4*, 237–252.

Hagman, E. P. The companionships of preschool children. *University of Iowa Studies in Child Welfare*, 1933, *7*, No. 4.

Hallinan, M. T. Friendship patterns in open and traditional classrooms. *Sociology of Education*. 1976, 49, 254–265.

Hartley, E., Rosenbaum, M., & Schwartz, S. Children's use of ethnic frames of reference: An exploratory study of children's conceptualizations of multiple ethnic group membership. *Journal of Psychology*, 1948, *26*, 367–386.(a)

Children's perceptions of ethnic group membership. *Journal of Psychology*, 1948, *26*, 387–398.(b)

Hartup, W. W. The origins of friendships. In M. Lewis & L. A. Rosenblum (Eds.), *Friendship and peer relations*. New York: Wiley, 1975.

Isaacs, S. The experimental construction of an environment optimal for mental growth. In C. Murchison (Ed.), *Handbook of child psychology*. Worcester, Mass.: Clark University Press, 1931.

Social development in young children: A study of beginnings. London: Routledge & Sons, 1933.

Jack, L. M. An experimental study of ascendant behavior in preschool children. *University of Iowa Studies in Child Welfare*, 1934, *9*(3), 9–65.

Jennings, H. Structure of leadership: Development and sphere of influence. *Sociometry*, 1937, *1*, 99–143.

Leadership and sociometric choice. In G. Swanson, T. Newcomb, & E. Hartley (Eds.), *Readings in social psychology*. New York: Holt, 1952.

Sociometry in group relations: A manual for teachers. Washington, D. C.: American Council on Education, 1959.

Jersild, A., & Markey, F. Conflicts between preschool children. *Child Development Monographs: Teachers College Columbia University*, 1935, No. 21.

Keller, F. Animals and children. *Child Development*, 1950, *21*, 7–12.

Kluckhorn, F. The participant-observer technique in small communities. *The American Journal of Sociology*, 1940, *46*, 331–343.

Koch, H. L. Popularity among preschool children: Some related factors and a technique for its measurement. *Child Development*, 1933, *4*, 164–175.

The modification of unsocialness in preschool children. *Psychology Bulletin*, 1935, *32*, 700–701.

The social distance between certain racial, nationality and skin-pigmentation groups in selected populations of American school children. *Journal of Genetic Psychology*, 1946, *68*, 63–95.

Ladd, G. Effectiveness of a social learning method for enhancing children's social interaction and peer acceptance. *Child Development*, in press.

Lewin, K. Environmental forces in child behavior and development. In C. Murchison (Ed.), *Handbook of child psychology*. Worcester, Mass.: Clark University Press, 1931.

Lewin, K., & Lippitt R. An experimental approach to the study of autocracy and democracy: A preliminary note. *Sociometry*, 1938, *1*, 292–300.

Lewin K., Lippitt, R., & White, R. K. Patterns of aggressive behavior in experimentally created social climates. *Journal of Social Psychology*, 1939, *10*, 271–299.

Lippitt, R. Popularity among preschool children. *Child Development*, 1941, *12*, 305–332.

Mallay, H. A study of some of the techniques underlying the establishment of successful social contacts at the preschool level. *Journal of Genetic Psychology*, 1935, *47*, 431–457.

Maudry, M., & Nekula, M. Social relations between children of the same age during the first two years of life. *Journal of Genetic Psychology*, 1939, *54*, 193–215.

Moreno, F. Sociometric status of children in a nursery school group. *Sociometry*, 1942, *5*, 395–411.

Moreno, J. L. *Application of the group method to classification*. New York: National Committee on Prisons and Prison Labor, 1932.

Who shall survive?: A new approach to the problem of human interrelations. Washington, D. C.: Nervous and Mental Disease Publishing Co., 1934.

Who shall survive: Foundations of sociometry, group psychotherapy and sociodrama. Beacon, N. Y.: Beacon House, 1978.

Munsterberg, J. *Psychology and life.* Boston: Houghton-Mifflin, 1899.

Murchison, C. *Handbook of child psychology.* Worcester, Mass.: Clark University Press, 1931.

Handbook of child psychology. New York: Russell & Russell, 1933.

Murphy, L. B. *Social behavior and child psychology: An exploratory study of some roots of sympathy.* New York: Columbia University Press, 1937.

Northway, M. L. Social relationships among preschool children: Abstracts and interpretations of three studies. *Sociometry,* 1943, *6,* 429–433.

Outsiders: A study of the personality patterns of children least acceptable to their age mates. *Sociometry,* 1944, *7,* 10–25.

Personality and sociometric status: A review of the Toronto studies. *Sociometry,* 1946, *9,* 233–241.

Oden, S., & Asher, S. R. Coaching children in social skills for friendship making. *Child Development,* 1977, *48,* 495–506.

Olson, W. *The measurement of nervous habits in normal children.* Minneapolis: University of Minnesota Press, 1929.

Page, M. L. The modification of ascendant behavior in preschool children. *University of Iowa Studies in Child Welfare,* 1936, *12,* 7–69.

Park, R. The city: Suggestions for the investigation of human behavior in the urban environment. *American Journal of Sociology,* 1915, *20,* 577–612.

Human ecology. *American Journal of Sociology,* 1936, *42,* 1–15.

Parten, M. B. Social participation among preschool children. *Journal of Abnormal and Social Psychology,* 1932, *27,* 243–269.

Piaget, J. *The language and thought of the child.* London: Kegan, Paul, 1926.

Social evolution and the new education. London: New Education Fellowship, 1932.(a)

The moral judgment of the child. New York: Harcourt, Brace, 1932. (b)

Radke, M., Trager, H., & Davis, H. Social perceptions and attitudes of children. *Genetic Psychology Monographs,* 1949, *40,* 327–447.

Roff, M., Sells, S. B., & Golden, M. M. *Social adjustment and personality development in children.* Minneapolis: University of Minnesota Press, 1972.

Sears, R. R. Child psychology. In W. Dennis (Ed.), *Current trends in psychology.* Pittsburgh: University of Pittsburgh Press, 1947.

Your ancients revisited. A history of child development. In E. M. Hetherington (Ed.), *Review of child development research* (Vol. 5). Chicago: University of Chicago Press, 1975.

Sherif, M. *The psychology of social norms.* New York: Harper, 1936.

Sherif, M., Harvey, O. J., White, B. J., Hood, W. R., & Sherif, C. W. *Intergroup conflict and cooperation: The robber's cave experiment.* Normal, Okla.: The University Book Exchange, 1961.

Shirley, M. *The first two years: A study of twenty-five babies* (Vol. 2). Minneapolis: University of Minnesota Press, 1933.

Singleton, L. C., & Asher, S. R. Peer preferences and social interaction among third-grade children in an integrated school district. *Journal of Educational Psychology,* 1977, *69,* 330–336.

Skinner, B. F. Experimental psychology. In W. Dennis (ed.), *Current trends in psychology.* Pittsburgh: University of Pittsburgh Press, 1947.

Thelen, H. A. *Classroom grouping for teachability.* New York: John Wiley, 1967.

Thomas, D. Introduction: The methodology of experimental sociology. *Child Development Monographs: Teachers College Columbia University,* 1929, No. 1, 1–21.

Thomas, W., & Thomas, D. *The child in America*. New York: Knopf, 1928.

Thrasher, F. M. *The gang: A study of 1,313 gangs in Chicago*. Chicago: University of Chicago Press, 1927.

   How to study the boys' gang in the open. *Journal of Educational Sociology*, 1928, *1*, 244–254.

Ullmann, C. Teachers, peers, and tests as predictors of adjustment. *Journal of Educational Psychology*, 1957, *48*, 256–267.

Wellman, B. The school child's choice of companions. *Journal of Educational Research*, 1926, *14*, 126–132.

Wright, H. Observational child study. In P. H. Mussen (Ed.), *Handbook of research methods in child development*. New York: John Wiley, 1960.

Zorbough, H. Which way America's youth?. *Journal of Educational Sociology*, 1938, *11*, 322–334.

Part I

Group processes

2   Friends, impression management, and preadolescent behavior

Gary Alan Fine

Introduction

Coexisting with adult society in contemporary America is a subsociety whose members are classified not by race, ethnicity, or religion, but by age. This is the social world of childhood – that stratum of social structure that Glassner (1976) termed "Kid Society." Children's society has a robust culture significantly different from that of parents and guardians. Increasingly, folklorists, anthropologists, and sociologists have become interested in exploring the social world of children. Their exploration seems to be an extension of research in youth culture and "adolescent society" (Coleman, 1961). The underlying contention is that children (and adolescents) maintain a social system relatively autonomous from adults. The goal of this chapter is to describe this social system, the abilities necessary to interact in it successfully, and the means by which members come to acquire these abilities; that is. how children become socialized to a "peer culture." In pursuit of this goal, we shall examine in some detail one particular social world – that of Little League baseball. Observations of Little League baseball players – both in the game and in their free time – suggest that boys by preadolescence have acquired skills in impression management and that their acquisition is, in part, a consequence of their friendships.

Research perspective: symbolic interactionism

My research perspective is symbolic interactionism, an approach to understanding social life developed by Charles Horton Cooley, George Herbert Mead, Herbert Blumer, and Erving Goffman, among others. Blumer

The author wishes to thank David Crist, Jeylan Mortimer, and Zick Rubin for helpful comments on a draft of this chapter.

(1969) argued that three premises are crucial to this perspective. First, human beings act toward things on the basis of the meanings that these objects have for them. Thus, actions or objects are said to have no a priori stimulus value. Second, the meanings of these stimuli emerge through social interaction. Third, and perhaps most important, these meanings are not static, but can be modified through an interpretive process. Meanings, therefore, are not reified, but are potentially subject to interpersonal negotiation. Through this assumption the symbolic interactionist perspective orients itself to change and development. A further assumption is that social meanings are shaped through communication and therefore that causes of action are not primarily biological and subconscious, but social and conscious.

The symbolic interactionist approach can be differentiated on two dimensions from the three major approaches to social development, psychoanalysis, learning theory, and cognitive stage theory. It differs from psychoanalysis and learning theory in rejecting the concept of the child as a relatively passive organism whose actions are largely predetermined by environment or biology (or in sophisticated analyses by their interaction); it construes the child as an active interpreter of situations (Faris, 1937/1971, p. 233). Further, it differs from psychoanalysis and cognitive stage theory in rejecting the existence of an invariable sequence of universal stages of development.

Socialization has been conceived of as a process by which the child becomes acculturated into adult standards; deviation from this ideal is thought to represent a failure of the acculturation process. This process is seen as deriving from the child's identification with the adult. For example, Parsons et al. (1951) claim that "there is approximate agreement that the development of identification with adult objects is an essential mechanism of the socialization process . . . The child becomes oriented to the wishes which embody for him the values of the adult, and his viscerogenic needs become culturally organized needs, which are shaped so that their gratification is sought in directions compatible with his integration into this system of interaction" (pp. 17–18).

Such a view is clearly "adultist." The concept of a single class of objects of identification is inadequate for the segmentation between adults and peers begins early, and the self is segmented according to situational needs. Frequently, several groups or individuals may be identified with (Fine & Kleinman, 1979). The conception of the child as having a single adult source of identification (role model or ego ideal) leads to children being seen as incomplete adults, lacking, but steadily learning, the norms that will incorporate them as full members of their society. Furthermore, identifications tend not to be total, but are situationally bounded, a function of the activation of latent cultures or systems of behaviors characteristic of sets of social relationships (Becker & Geer, 1960).

The distinctions between symbolic interactionism and other approaches should not be drawn too firmly. For example, the interactionist approach is congruent with Zigler and Child's (1969) definition of socialization as "the whole process by which an individual develops through transaction with other people, his specific patterns of socially relevant behavior and experiences" (p. 474). The interactionist perspective attempts to give the child (or any actor) more credit for his or her actions than deterministic theories allow, and this has led to criticism that symbolic interactionism is astructural and indeterminate (Zeitlin, 1973), although most interactionists admit there are biological and social constraints on behavior. No theory can reveal the whole truth of development, and symbolic interactionism is no exception; however, by exploring some of the implications of this approach for social development, childhood behavior can be better understood and traditional developmental approaches can be better informed about children's roles in shaping their own social worlds.

Issues underlying the symbolic-interactionist approach

Three important issues underlie the symbolic-interactionist approach to development, all of which represent processes that occur early in childhood and are well developed by preadolescence. These issues are: the development of the self through the perception of others, the importance of communication and the use of symbols, and the development of the ability to behave appropriately as a function of the expectations of others.

The relationship between self and other is seen by symbolic interactionists as crucial to the development of behavior (Wiley, 1980). The other is the mirror by which individuals learn of their selves (Mead, 1934, p. 158), and it is the other with whom the self must negotiate lines of collective action. Cooley (1902/1964) argues that the child's conception of the self is a product of interaction and that, when acquiring vocabulary, the child learns to know others before learning to be self-reflective (Cooley, 1908; Bain, 1936). Thus, the self-concept develops through social interaction and emerges from the child's ability to take the role of the other. This role taking is also seen as crucial by Piaget for the development of the concrete operations stage. However, contrary to the implications of cognitive approaches, symbolic interactionists argue that the child does not develop a conception of self (or "I") until after a conception of others has been acquired. Thus, the concept of an egocentric stage is not accurate according to the symbolic interactionist perspective. For the young child, the most important others typically are the child's parents or adult guardians, and these individuals are particularly significant in channeling the content of the child's self-concept. The shaping of the child's self by others is expanded with the onset of schooling, at which time the child must learn to deal with multiple others– what Mead (1925) termed the "game stage." This diverse social world shapes the child's self through exposure to a variety of behavioral options.

Simultaneous with the development of self (and a component of this development) is the growth of communication skills. Mastery of language and gestures is crucial for the preschool child in that it permits an understanding of and participation in interaction. The extent of symbolic universes of discourse varies depending on social factors; for example, the extent to which linguistic codes are elaborated or restricted (Bernstein, 1975). By the time the child is ready for formal schooling, this symbolizing process is well advanced (Denzin, 1977).

The third feature of development emphasized by interactionists is the acquisition of competence in behaving properly in a variety of social settings. The young child increasingly acquires the ability to interact with peers and near peers and spends more time in settings in which adults are not present to enforce their views of mannered interaction (Speier, 1973; MacKay, 1973). Situations in which dominance is not a direct result of age become common, and children must refine their techniques for constructing social meanings consensually; they mutually fit together lines of action, rather than have their situational definitions and courses of action constrained by adults (Elkin & Handel, 1978). Further, children learn, through the response of others, that their behaviors have consequences. While children may define situations as they feel proper and act according to these definitions in the presence of adults, if these definitions and actions are not congruent with adult prescriptions, children discover that their behaviors may have real (and painful) consequences. Among peers, contrary situational definitions may have negative outcomes as well, but in such situations there is no shared assumption that one party's definition is necessarily legitimate, although sociometric status influences the usage of social power.

Once the child recognizes that different sets of individuals have different expectations and that different situations may require different behaviors, the attempt to master a single, consistent set of core behavior patterns is no longer relevant. Symbolic interactionists emphasize the importance of the child's ability to see himself or herself as an object of appropriation (Mead, 1934). By this Mead means that the individual can place himself or herself in relation to an other or set of others (a process Blumer [1969] terms "self-indication") and can shape his or her behavior in light of others' expectations. Stone (1970, p. 399) conceived of identity as a "coincidence of placements and announcements" whereby the evaluation of one's self by others is similar to the desired evaluation of the self. By later childhood the key interactional task is to refine one's social identity and to acquire the skills necessary for the successful positioning of the self in multiple social worlds.

Preadolescent social development

Our focus in this chapter will be on the preadolescent period. During this period, the three features of development have become established. In particular, this chapter focuses on peer relations during preadolescence and examines, from the interactionist perspective, how they influence socialization.

Preadolescence (broadly, ages 7 to 12) represents a particularly significant period because in it children are expected to develop social lives that are not merely extensions of situations dominated by adults (parents and teachers). While this may occur somewhat earlier or later, in most locales preadolescents are not expected to be under the watchful eye of an adult chaperone and can thus develop their own private relationships. Researchers have noted the importance of friends – either the single chum or the gang – in preadolescent peer relations (see Fine, 1980a; Hartup, 1978 for a summary of this literature). These patterns of chumship and ganging are found in many areas of the globe, although not in every society, according to anthropological reports. It is believed that these relationships have considerable impact in shaping the child's social behavior and attitudes. For example, Sullivan (1953) writes: "In the company of one's chum, one finds oneself more and more able to talk about things which one had learned, during the juvenile era, not to talk about . . . about the last chance [troubled children] have of favorable change is based on their need for getting along with a chum in preadolescence" (pp. 227, 252). Whatever the validity of Sullivan's explicit connection between friendship and psychiatric therapy, friendships produce moments of shared fantasy that Cottle (1971) has argued allow children to escape the boundaries of their troubled existence. Groups also allow children to learn about themselves and society: "The school-age child spends as much of his time as possible in the company of his peers, from whom he learns at first hand about social structures, about in-groups and out-groups, about leadership and followership, about justice and injustice, about loyalties and heroes and ideals'' (Stone & Church, 1968, p. 364).

These groups are arenas for social action: They are social locations in which the preadolescent is able to explore available role options and to master methods of impression management in a supportive social environment. Having a set of close friends or a single chum is important to the child, because preadolescent interaction is generally not placid (Opie & Opie, 1959) but is filled with the possibilities of sudden denigration. As Stone and Church suggest, ''the feeling of inclusion seems to necessitate someone's exclusion'' (1957, p. 221). Thus, in this socially tempestuous time, having a friend with whom one can feel secure provides a solid base from which interpersonal confidence can be built, even given the notoriously fickle affections of children.

Preadolescent social relations and Little League baseball

This chapter is intended to be a theoretical analysis of the socializing effects of preadolescent friendship, not a description of a world of childhood activities. However, the theoretical assessment is grounded in a set of research experiences, some of which will be described in the following pages. The research consisted of a three-year participant-observation study of preadolescent males. During these three years, Little League baseball leagues in four American communities were examined by the author: (1) Beanville,[1] an upper-middle-class professional suburb of Boston, Massachusetts; (2) Hopewell, an exurban township outside of the Providence, Rhode Island metropolitan area consisting of a string of small towns, beachfront land, farms, and a campus of the state university; (3) Bolton Park, an upper-middle-class professional suburb of St. Paul, Minnesota, similar to Beanville except for geographical location; and (4) Sanford Heights, a middle- to lower-middle-class suburb of Minneapolis, Minnesota, comprised of a large number of modern mass-produced homes. A research assistant, Harold Pontiff, conducted a parallel investigation of a Little League baseball program in Maple Bluff, an urban, upper-middle-class area of St. Paul.

The Little League baseball organization was founded in Williamsport, Pennsylvania, in 1939 for the purpose of allowing boys (ages 9 to 12) to play organized baseball under adult supervision. (For an evaluation of this program see Fine and West, 1979.) The organization has grown enormously. It is now international and comprises over 600,000 players in about 5,000 leagues. The program was designed for boys and for a long time excluded girls. As a result of court suits, Little League now admits both boys and girls, although only ten girls played in the five leagues in the period under examination. Because of the small number of girls observed, I will limit my discussion to preadolescent boys. There is evidence that males and females differ in their play patterns (Lever, 1976) and relationships (Waldrop & Halverson, 1975), and thus we must be cautious in generalizing our analysis to girls without confirming evidence.

The primary methodology employed to collect data about Little Leaguers and their friends was participant observation (see Bogdan & Taylor, 1975). In order to focus the observations, two teams in each league were chosen for intensive study. Detailed records were kept of the players on ten teams (twelve to fifteen players per team), less detailed records were kept on thirty-two other teams, and information was collected on scores of preadolescents who were not involved in the league. At first the intention was to examine the Little League teams, but it soon became apparent that the only way in which preadolescent social behavior could be understood was through observing the larger context of their spring and summer leisure-time patterns. Thus, considerable time was spent with the players and their friends outside of the baseball context. (For a detailed treatment of this research see Fine and Glassner, 1979; Fine, 1980b). While it would be misleading to claim that the research settings are representative of the environments of American children, they do cover a substantial range. Like the Little League organization itself, the primarily middle-class sample has fewer rural children, urban children, and poor children than would be expected by chance. While I will speak in generalities, one should remember the sample from which this analysis derives.

Children and presentation of self

Central to the process of growing up is learning ways of displaying one's social self in public. Adults fear that children will say the wrong thing in public. For example, they may tell Aunt Millie about what they really think of her homemade apple pie, or they may tell rich Uncle Joe the private conversations their parents have had about him. Such images provide an endless source of jokes and indicate the anxiety that adults feel about the potential so-called indiscretions of their offspring. Somewhat facetiously, we might suggest that the danger is that the child has not mastered the art of being hypocritical. Less facetiously, one can note that the issue is one of learning situational proprieties – behavior that is deemed proper in one situation is considered grossly improper in another. While etiquette books for children emphasize rules for behavior appropriate in all situations (Cavan, 1970), these rules must be negotiated in their social contexts. Preadolescents do not behave toward their peers in the same way they behave toward their parents, a point that most parents recognize. While parents may not get upset if their children curse or tell dirty jokes with their friends, this does not mean that the children are given license to behave this way in front of their parents. Conversely, the fact that a child may be willing to admit affection to relatives does not imply that the same child will admit this to peers. Stone and Church comment that "no ten-year-old boy would be caught dead saying that he 'loved' anything" (1957, p. 220). This evaluation is confirmed by my observation that children who too readily admit to affection become the objects of teasing or scorn.

By preadolescence a boy normally finds himself in several distinct social worlds, and he discovers that appropriate behavior is dependent upon his interpretation of the nature of these worlds. The popular and socially integrated preadolescent is the one who has mastered techniques of impression management in order to present himself through flexible role performances (see Elkins, 1958) and to altercast others (Weinstein & Deutschberger, 1963; Weinstein, 1969) into roles that support his role position. In other words, through his actions the child is able to control the behavioral roles of his interaction partners in ways that complement his social position.

In his discussion of presentation of self, Goffman (1959) does not consider the development of impression-management skills, because his interest is primarily in knowledgeable adults. Goffman's model of a human being is of a schemer or actor who must manipulate a world of complex and deceptive meanings (see Goffman, 1974). The acquisition of this competence seems not to be confined to the preadolescent period but develops from birth. However, my research indicates that by puberty the child has acquired the basic techniques of impression management, although interactional subtlety is still to be mastered.

Cooley (1964; orig. 1902) notes the importance of the early development of the social self and suggests that very young children attempt to manipulate the impressions that others have of them: "The young performer soon learns to be different things to different people, showing that he begins to apprehend personality and to foresee its operation. If the mother or nurse is more tender than just she will almost certainly be 'worked' by systematic weeping" (p. 197). However, it is unlikely that prior to schooling children attempt to present different identities or even to shape the impressions that others have of them. More likely, children manipulate others to achieve some end, and their impressions are shaped indirectly. Cooley notes that "a child obviously and simply, at first, does things for effect. Later there is an endeavor to suppress the appearance of doing so; affection, indifference, contempt, etc., *are simulated* to hide the real wish to affect the self-image. It is perceived that an obvious seeking after good opinion is weak and disagreeable" (p. 199; emphasis added). This later concern involves constructing one's behavior so as to manipulate and constrain others. Corsaro's research with nursery-school children (this volume) indicates that some rather young children have considerable ability and finesse in structuring situations to their own advantage, particularly in terms of controlling the access of peers to ongoing play groups. However, it is during preadolescence, with its concern with peer status, that this ability and desire to position oneself in situations consciously to affect one's presentation of self becomes critical to long-term popularity. In order to manage the impressions of others, the preadolescent must expand his or her facility at taking the role of the other (Mead, 1934), and through this must role play to create the desired impression.[2] By preadolescence the child must deal with a wide range of others who may expect the child to behave according to several distinct standards of behavior. A 4-year-old can use a single behavioral repertoire, but the preteen must learn that several repertoires need to be mastered for different settings. The development of presentation-of-self ability is exemplified in the child's increasing sophistication in getting along with others and in developing moral and philosophical systems (Selman's stages 3 and 4) in which flexibility of interaction as a function of the needs of one's friend becomes recognized as a part of friendship (Selman, this volume).

Rules and negotiation

The growth of social competency can be observed in the child's increasing sophistication in the practice of game rules. Piaget suggests in his analysis of marble playing (1932/1962) that until the age of 3 the child has rules only in that there are ritual repetitions that he or she performs with play objects. At this stage rules are not grounded in social interaction, and what regularities exist appear to be idiosyncratic. Piaget suggests that until games are played collectively, rules in a meaningful sense do not exist.

The second stage is termed the stage of egocentrism and lasts until approximately the age of 6, although Piaget admits that these ages are not invariant in all cultures and social classes (p. 46). Marble playing at this age becomes social, but according to Piaget, children's rules are egocentric: "When they play together they do not watch each other and do not unify their respective rules even for the duration of one game" (p. 40). Piaget's data on two marble players suggest that although different sets of rules seem to be operating, the children construct a social interaction sequence that is satisfying to both parties and is dependent on the presence of each other (as indicated by the existence of different rules when the child plays alone). While these interactants are not playing a "game" (an adult-defined category of activity), they are interacting in a fashion that is meaningful for them.

The two later stages of the development of the practice of rules represent the growth of the preadolescent's ability to deal with peers. During early preadolescence (ages 7 through 10) the child recognizes the importance of rules as a regulator of others' behavior. Rules are claimed to ensure reciprocity in the game world. However, this notion of rules as a model for play does not imply that rules are not used to strategic advantage. For example, Piaget points out that in this stage knowledge of rule content may vary widely. Thus children construct their game reality (the rule structure) in the course of play: "It is only when they [the marble players] are at play that these same children succeed in understanding each other, either by copying the boy who seems to know most about it or, more frequently, by omitting any usage that might be disputed" (p. 42).

Although children claim that rules are absolute, in practice they are negotiated. Further, the rules may be used by the knowledgeable player to limit the options of the less familiar (or deliberately naive) player. In this case, Piaget says of himself, "When I play carelessly, and let the shooter drop out of my hand, Ben exclaims *'Fan-coup'* to prevent me from saying *'coup-passe'* and having another shot" (p. 44). Rules are conditional, and their use becomes something of a game. A player may get another shot if he says *'coup-passe,' unless* the opponent first says *"fan-coup."* This requires the ability to place oneself in the opponent's position in order to recognize the appropriate moment for such a challenge. This decision may be based upon the importance of the game and the relationship between player and challenger. While challenges are legitimate, they may create hard feelings and indicate that the game is "serious" and not "merely" play (Riezler, 1941). Rule-governed games carry with them the potential to be played according to several perspectives. These perspectives imply different social meanings, and when game meanings are disputed, inferences about the character of the disputants may be drawn by their fellow players.

By late preadolescence the negotiation of game rules provides almost as much interest as the game itself (Knapp & Knapp, 1976). Boys acquire techniques for "getting along" – they learn when to use threats of force, when to trade favors, when to use reason, when to back off gracefully, and when to leave the field angrily. Piaget notes that this is a period of "juridical discussions" (p. 43) in which "the dominating interest seems to be interest in the rules themselves." This observation of late preadolescence as a period in which a quasi-legal system operates has been confirmed by Glassner (1976), who notes that children are able to settle interpersonal disputes with a minimum of violence through informal processes of childhood jurisprudence. This process is evident when preadolescents must determine ordering. On one occasion I brought several empty beer cans from Colorado for preadolescent beer-can collectors in Minnesota. Because the cans had different values, it was necessary for the children to determine an order for choosing. After discussion, players were able to order themselves in such a way that no player felt publicly humiliated. For example, the high-status boy who chose first claimed that the next time I brought beer cans he would pick sixth. Opie and Opie (1959) speak of children as having a "Code of Oral Legislation" that binds them to allow social relations to take particular forms (e.g., possession typically being 100 percent of the law) if ritual declarations, such as those asserting ownership ("finders keepers, losers weepers"), are followed.

The rules as a code of conduct are not crucial during late preadolescence. More important is the social experience that derives from learning to manipulate the social order (the use of rules) – the issue is rights and privileges. Despite the supposed inflexibility of the rules (as explained to an interested adult), they are not enforced uniformly; some children are allowed leeway, and others are not. Both the legitimacy of rules and the legitimacy of preferential treatment are being acquired in this process. Knapp and Knapp (1976) note: "As they [children] argue about rules, add new ones, agree to exceptions, and censure a playmate who is cheating, they are exploring how necessary rules are, how they are made, and what degree of consensus is needed to make them effective. They are also learning something about the relationship of personality to power, and of fairness to order" (p. 17). Rules provide guidelines for interaction but do not control the interaction itself; they are topics for negotiation. The sometimes bewildering complex of rules exists not because preadolescents wish every contingency to be considered so that fights are impossible, but because a set of rules provides a store of information that boys can use in their arguments with each other in defining ambiguous situations in the game. It is the process of negotiation that is central to interaction, rather than the formal rules themselves.

An example of this negotiation process is depicted by Dennison (1969) in a description of a fight among five troubled boys with severe learning and behavior problems. These preadolescents are supposedly "out of control" and unable to cope with social interaction; they attend a school for delinquent children. In the course of the school year a hostile rivalry developed between three Puerto Rican friends (Jose, Julio, and Vicente) and two non-Hispanic buddies (Stanley, white, and Willard, black). These preadolescents engaged in a series of violent altercations, and finally the boys decided to fight it out, with Dennison, their teacher, only insisting that they not use weapons. I will quote from his account at some length, because it indicates the subtlety of preadolescent impression management and the development of standards for behavior as a result of interaction:

A great shout went up, a roar, and all five piled into each other . . . and stopped abruptly to let Jose take off his shirt. Stanley and Willard took their shirts off, too. They were about to clash again when Stanley paused and took off his shoes, and so Willard and Jose took their shoes off, too. The roar went up again and they tangled, Stanley and Willard against Jose, Julio, and Vicente . . . There was much cursing, many shouts of pain – strange shouts, really for each one had in it a tinge of protest and flattery. It was in these overtones that one could sense the fine changes in their relations. They were saying things for which they had no words, and the refinement of this communication was extraordinary and beautiful. It was apparent immediately that the boys had set some kind of limit to their violence, though they had not spoken of limits. Rules, codes, acknowledgements popped up spontaneously and changed swiftly. When anyone got hurt, he stepped off the mats . . . and the rule was accepted by all, without having been announced that no one could be attacked when he stepped off the mat . . . Occasionally as the boys rolled and squirmed, they also punched each other in the ribs. These blows, however, were almost formal and were very subtly adjusted. The loser must prove that he is really struggling, and so in order to ensure himself against the contempt of the victor, he punches him in the ribs. Delivered with just the right force, these punches remain compliments . . . They are tributes, too, to the reality of the fight. Delivered a bit harder, they are "unfair." Delivered still harder, they precipitate a bloodletting. And so they are very nicely attuned . . .
    Willard is grinning and trying different holds, but in between the grins he exerts himself to the utmost and still can't pin Jose. And so he shouts again and again, "Give up?" and Jose cries, "You have to kill me!" The decision is in Willard's hands. Soon he lets Jose up, but punches him on the arm so Jose won't think he has been let up. Willard shows great tact in his awareness of victory. He smiles openly at Jose, not a triumphant smile, but a friendly one. [Dennison, 1969, pp. 133–137]

These "maladjusted" preadolescents are highly sophisticated in techniques of impression management and in the staging of social encounters. Even an emotional fight is not a random sequencing of aggressive actions but is socially ordered, and this structuring occurs not before the event but during it. While there are certain characteristics that these boys could report about "fighting norms" or rules, the application of these procedures occurs during the fight and is responsive to immediate considerations. This structuring of interaction is equally relevant to games that have rules as part of the oral tradition, but these rules may not be followed or may be altered in the course of the game.

Individuals in these social situations have the power to altercast their fellow interactants. Thus, Willard had the opportunity to defeat his enemy Jose, with a presumable explicit loss of status to Jose; however, he refrained from doing this, possibly as an attempt to drain the encounter of emotional intensity. This process of constructing social meanings is characteristic of social interaction, even among children.

Friendship and socialization

By preadolescence, peer relationships have become central to the child's social world. Their centrality reveals itself in children's self-consciousness about the impressions that others have of them and in the importance they give to their friendships. By incorporating the needs for impression management and friendship. I argue that the friendship bond creates a setting in which impression-management skills are mastered and in which inadequate displays will typically be ignored or corrected without severe loss of face. Outside of friendship bonds, preadolescents have a critical eye for children's behaviors that are managed inadequately.

Typically, preadolescents name many children as friends. For example, in Sanford Heights, forty-eight of the fifty 12-year-olds in the Little League were asked to evaluate their relationships to the other 12-year-olds in the league. In our sample, 18 percent of all possible relationships are said to be close friends, 31 percent are friends, 2 percent are disliked, and 49 percent are neither friends nor disliked. It is the boys' rather large network of "friends" that comprises the bulk of the society in which they spend their social leisure time.

Friendship has generally been conceptualized as an affective bond, a relationship charged with positive feeling, in some cases approaching "love." Other features should be emphasized as well. Friendship is also a staging area for interaction, a cultural institution for the transmission of knowledge and performance techniques, and a crucible for the shaping of selves. Each of these aspects of the friendship relationship has implications for interaction within and outside of the friendship bond.

Friendship as a staging area

Friendship is a social relationship, a bond between two individuals. As such it is not a physical entity but a spiritual or ideational one. However, friendships are not continuously salient, and when they are not, their effects on social interaction are slight. One's position as a friend can be conceived of as akin to a partial identity that is activated when relevant, with the understanding that multiple friendship identities can be activated simultaneously. Obviously, a friendship identity is likely to be activated when the friend is physically present. Thus, the analysis can be expanded from an emphasis on the ideational aspect of the relationship to include an emphasis on the friendship context. A friendship bond, therefore, can be described as a staging area for action.

The presence of friends produces a social context that allows for the performance of actions that would otherwise be improper. For example, in an earlier paper (Fine, 1980a) I described the social ecology of preadolescent pranks among 12-year-olds in Sanford Heights. Of the seventy prank partners named for four different types of pranks, 89 percent were close friends of the namer, 9 percent more were friends and the remaining 2 percent were former friends. Close friendships thus can provide a staging area for pranks, which some scholars (Dresser, 1973; Knapp & Knapp, 1976) claim socialize children by allowing them to explore the boundaries of allowable behavior and to gain social poise in stressful situations.

The friendship bond, in allowing for a wide latitude of behavior, creates a setting in which the child is able to explore modes of expressing sexual attitudes, aggression, and attitudes toward school and work. Even if negatively sanctioned behavior occurs, the sanctioning typically does not imply a derogation of the actor, and the disapproved action is not seen as part of the actor's identity. Friends typically have sufficient "idiosyncracy credits" (Hollander, 1958) to allow for a wide range of technically inappropriate actions. The actions of a friend are much less likely to be defined as inappropriate than are the identical behaviors of others.

The friendship group seems of particular importance as a context for action in terms of the developing relationship between boys and girls. Broderick (1966) notes that at ages 12 and 13, 56 percent of the boys and 76 percent of the girls in his sample prefer double- or group-dating to single-dating. One group of 12-year-old boys in Hopewell even formalized this to the extent that they formed a club whose major function was the support of members in their dealings with girls. This form of social activity is also evident in private parties of preadolescents (Martinson, 1973). These parties, in which the boys are supported by their male friends and the girls are in the company of their friends, are staging areas for quasi-sexual and quasi-aggressive behavior. Boys in Sanford Heights informed me that "making out" occurred at these events, and this "making out" apparently consisted of kissing and above-the-waist petting ("getting to second base"). However, roughhousing may also occur, because boys are ignorant of adolescent social norms of chivalrous behavior to girls or ashamed of showing tenderness to girls. One young adult male recalled the way in which male peers are used for social support in situations where social norms are ambiguous and self-presentation becomes a considerable challenge: "As I remember there weren't many fellows who were on the dance floor. They were all in a group in the corner, and that is where I ended up too. We told jokes, tested our strength on the bars that stood along the walls, and teased any fellow who dared to ask a girl to dance" (Martinson, 1973, pp. 84–85).

On one occasion I went with three preadolescent friends from Sanford Heights to a large amusement park in the Minneapolis-St. Paul area:

The boys seem very interested in the girls that they see, and there is considerable whispering and teasing about them. Tom had received a small coin bank as a prize which he decides that he no longer wishes to keep. At this time we are standing in line for a roller coaster directly behind three girls – apparently a year or two older than these twelve-year-olds – one of whom is wearing a hooded jacket. Frank tells Tom to take the bank and "stuff it in her hood," which Tom does to the annoyance of his victim. When she turns around, Tom and Hardy tell her that Frank did it, and of course Frank denies this, blaming Tom. The girls tell the boys to shut up and leave them alone. As things work out, Hardy has to sit with one of these girls on the ride and he clearly appears embarrassed, while Tom and Frank are vastly amused. After the ride Tom and Frank claim that they saw Hardy holding her. Frank said that he saw them holding hands, and Tom said: "He was trying to go up her shirt." Hardy vehemently denies these claims. A short while later we meet these girls again, and Frank turns to Hardy, saying "Here's your honey." The girl retorts as she walks away, "Oh, stifle it." [Field notes]

The male friendship group provides a supportive staging area for these boys to practice their impression-management skills on each other and on their female contacts as they develop sexualized selves. It is attention rather than tenderness that orients the staging of boy–girl encounters in this period:

A group of boys come across a preadolescent girls' softball team from a different area of town, sitting around a park picnic table. The boys begin teasing them with sexual taunts: "Hey, suck me where the sun never shines," "Pluck my hairs," or "You're innocent like my butthole." The girls are not visibly outraged at this and actually seem to enjoy the attention that the boys are giving them – at one point singing to attract their attention. After whispering discussion about what they should do to their victims, the boys steal the girls' thermos and pour out the water in it – at which the girls squeal but don't get seriously upset. Later the boys return to the picnic table and throw beer cans at the girls, who giggle and scream. [Field notes]

The presence of one's friends seems to provide a legitimation for this type of activity, which has important consequences for the sexual social-

ization of preadolescents. It provides them with a range of experience in
dealing with the opposite sex and a testing of their social poise (Stone,
1965). Players are socialized to respond to the demands of a variety of
social situations, and their friendships serve to provide access to these
situations.

Friendship as a cultural institution

Suttles (1970) has described friendship as a social institution, and this
description certainly applies to the didactic function of friendship. Information transmitted through friendship ties varies in the extent of its diffu-
sion. Some information is highly localized, perhaps shared only by members of a dyad, while other information is widely known among
preadolescents or Americans in general. These dyads and groups not only
create a private culture (Suttles, 1970; Fine, 1980a), but also transmit cultural information relevant to the problems of growing up. This is of particular significance to socialization, in that it provides the child with a stock
of knowledge and repertoire of behavior useful for encounters with other
peers. Children acquire information from many sources – the media,
schools, religious organizations, and their families – all adult-dominated
institutions. In contemporary American society, adults typically share an
ideology that prescribes what children should and should not know. There
are several topic areas in which children are interested but that they cannot learn about from adults: the practice of sex, informal rules of institutions (how *really* to succeed in school), the art of making negative evaluations (insults), and how to have excitement and adventure (pranks,
mischief, and illegal behavior).

For example, one 12-year-old boy explained to his friends in clinical
detail how to "french" a girl. The first part of the account outlines the
basic behaviors in "frenching," but of perhaps greater importance is the
latter section of the transcript, which transmits signals about the structure
of sexual relations in contemporary America:

> Tom: First of all, you gotta make sure you don't get no more "Ahhhk!" burps in
> your mouth (Hardy and Frank both laugh). It would be very crude to burp.
> I mean you make sure you don't have a cold, cause greenies [mucus] going
> through there (Tom laughs), going through her mouth would taste awful
> horseshit (all laugh).
> Frank: And one thing, don't spit while frenching.
> Tom: And make sure . . . make sure you don't breathe out of your mouth (all
> laugh) unless you're doing mouth-to-mouth resuscitation. After all that
> frenching, you just gotta do mouth-to-mouth to keep your air up. OK, now
> you take a squirt of your favorite after-shave. You rub it on your hair, and
> you rub it all around you. And you (Tom giggles "hysterically") and you

rub it all around. It sure feels good (more giggling). Frank's choking under pressure. Listen (more "hysterical" laughter), he's got a boner (more laughter). He's got a boner. He's got a boner and he'd like to suck it off.

Hardy: Listen, listen, his lips are on it.

Tom: He's sucking (all laugh).

Frank: Nuhhh. Nuhhh. Nuhhh (joking, making almost mooing sounds, apparently designed to simulate a sexually excited woman) . . .

Tom: Hardy, do you like to put anything in my act?

Hardy: No.

Tom: Only that he's got a, Ahhh!, stiff boner (Hardy giggles). Frank. Frank ain't got stiff, uh-uh. Since we're talking about Hardy's girl friend, he's sorta, you know what I mean, doncha?

Hardy: No! (Frank laughs).

Tom: He sorta hit the jack, uh, hit the jack. Hit the jack-off, you know.

Hardy: No, I don't know.

Tom: I do (Tom and Hardy both laugh). Well, anyway, I get to my second lesson. First you walk in, you see a sexy girl in the telephone booth. You don't know who she is, just see the back of her. Gotta make sure she doesn't have a big butt, you know . . . You just walk into the telephone booth, put your arm around her and say "Hi." And she goes "Uhhh! Ohhh, hi" (tone sounds surprised at first, then "feminine" and "willing"). With her tongue around, wrapped around, wrapped around the microphone, her teeth, her teeth are chattering from so much shock. You just take your pants . . . no . . . well.

Hardy: You take her pants.

Tom: Well, you just stick out your tongue, and you say (Tom sings in a mocking romantic fashion): "Want to, oh baby, you mean it, you let me under your skin." [Taped transcript]

This is a fragment of a longer conversation that is one of numerous conversations among one set of close friends. This conversation is not much different from those of other precocious preadolescents. Taken together, these conversations allow for an examination of the dynamics of the acquisition of the male sex role. Through the content of these conversations boys learn what is expected of them by their peers. The importance of this talk does not derive from the acquisition of sophisticated techniques of french kissing (although specific content learning does occur); rather, boys learn how to present themselves to male peers as "males." This conversation suggests that males are expected by each other to be sexually aggressive and that females wait for their attempts with undisguised arousal. This short dialogue offers a world view that is consistent with male dominance and female submission. By this talk, preadolescents are learning skills that will allow them to handle themselves within the context of similar lines of talk and prepare them to act as "males."

The same process is evident in other areas as well. Preadolescents, in discussing how to evade schoolwork or cut classes (for example, claim that you have a church confirmation, since teachers never check), acquire rhetoric about schooling. Again, it is less important to learn specific facts and procedures than to learn ways to talk. These tools for interactional negotiation allow the child to deal competently with peers.

Through the support of friends, the child also learns techniques of evaluation, when to use insults and when to avoid them, and the social implications of this process of evaluation. The case of one 10-year-old boy in Sanford Heights who was criticized by several older boys is instructive. The 10-year-old, Tommy, is the son of a Little League manager. In one postseason practice in preparation for a state-wide tournament, Tommy and Harmon, a 12-year-old teammate, angrily traded insults. Harmon's temper had caused problems all season, and this episode was the final straw. Tommy's father announced that he was quitting as manager of the team. After the anger subsided he returned, but Harmon's father felt that it was in everyone's best interest if Harmon left the team. The following week some of Harmon's friends met Tommy on a school bus:

Hardy sees Tommy get on the bus and announces loudly, "Tommy sucks." Rod adds: "Tommy's a wuss." In unison Jerry and Rod tell Tommy as he approaches, "You suck." Rod particularly is angry at Tommy, "Harmon can't play because of you. What a fag!" Tommy doesn't respond to the abuse from his older tormentors, but looks dejected and perhaps near tears (which is what Rod and Hardy later tell Harmon). The insults build in stridency and anger as Hardy calls Tommy a "woman," Jerry knocks off his hat, and Rod says, "Give him the faggot award." Finally Jerry takes the baseball cap of Tommy's friend and seatmate and tosses it out the window of the moving bus. [Field notes]

It is a frequent observation that preadolescents can be distressingly cruel to each other, but the social context of this cruelty is not sufficiently emphasized. The cruelty is almost always expressed in the presence of friends. Insults seem to be expressed as much for reasons of self-presentation to one's peers as to attack the target. This point has also been made about sounding or playing the dozens by black adolescents (e.g., Kochman, 1972; Abrahams, 1970). The case cited above is representative in that there was an attempt by the insulters to test the boundaries of proper insults and the insult crescendo continued until the target either became upset and withdrew, or until one of the perpetrators did something that was outside the range of legitimate behavior in that situation. Thus, in this case, tossing the baseball cap out of the bus window ended the insults. Jerry's action was outside the realm of legitimate behavior, and he sullied his social self. Although he was not sanctioned by his friends, he apologized to the victim, claiming that he didn't really intend to get rid of the hat.

To summarize, socialization does not consist of rote learning of behaviors or of an encyclopedia of practical knowledge. Socialization can best be considered instruction in dealing with situations, or, as Denzin (1977) suggests, learning to fit together lines of action. The child needs to learn the process by which social meanings are constructed, ways of knowing the expectations of others, and methods of determining their likely actions (Mead's notion of the Generalized Other). The friendship group, by placing the child in such situations in a supportive environment, provides the opportunity to acquire and refine skills that are necessary for interaction with others.

Friendship as a shaper of the social self

The third way in which friendship contributes to the socialization of the preadolescent is through its effects on self-image. Friendship is a crucial factor in the development of the social self, both for popular boys and for boys with few close friends.

The literature on the correlates of popularity reveals a wide array of explanations of children's interpersonal success. The factors associated with interpersonal success include acceptance of school ideology (Gold, 1962), attractiveness of the first name (McDavid & Harari, 1966), role-playing skills (Mouton, Bell, & Blake, 1956), intelligence (Barbe, 1954; Gallagher, 1958), adjustment to parents and teachers (Feinberg, 1953), physical attractiveness (Dion & Berscheid, 1974), and attitude to school (Davis, 1957). I shall not review this extensively researched problem, but shall only agree with Hartup (1970) that acceptance or rejection is clearly a multidimensional phenomenon. One might be tempted to suggest that this area has been overstudied, because these correlations do not successfully convey the dynamics of making and breaking friends as they occur in children's societies.

There is some quantitative evidence that suggests that social interpretations are related to friendship choices. Davitz (1955), examining friendship patterns of male and female summer campers, found that those who are chosen as best friends are perceived as more similar to the chooser in activity preferences than are children who are not liked. Individuals perceive their best friends as more similar to themselves than they actually are; in this study these best friends were not more similar to the chooser than were children who were not liked. Elkins (1958) found in interviews with a sample of early adolescents that children who were the most chosen were more flexible in role performances and had the ability to meet the needs of others.

The friendship relation provides the nexus in which this development of self and role flexibility can occur. The child who has best acquired the ability to take the role of the other will be most flexible in role performance. Consequently, as Elkins's research suggests, this individual will be popular, perhaps because he or she is socially rewarding. Such individuals, through their flexibility of role performances, will likely be perceived as more similar to each of those with whom they interact than their self-ratings or average ratings might suggest. Thus, peer leaders are those who are most skilled at impression-management techniques.

Gottman and his colleagues (Gottman, Gonso, & Rasmussen, 1975; Putallaz & Gottman, this volume) have argued that popular children have more knowledge and ability of how to make friends than do their unpopular companions. Style of interaction seems central to friendship (Asher & Renshaw, this volume). Research indicates that social training may help isolated children learn techniques of making friends and thus improve their social standing (Asher & Renshaw, this volume; Gottman, Gonso & Schuler, 1976; Oden & Asher, 1977; Walker & Hops, 1973), lending support to the theory of the existence of presentational aspects of popularity. This process operates in both directions, for the support of friends provides a mechanism for the development of self-presentational ability.

From the symbolic interactionist perspective, individuals can be conceived of as having multiple selves, which are functions of setting and audience. From this standpoint, the developmental issue is not the traditional psychiatric one of the unitary development of the self, but the interactional issue of acquiring behavioral flexibility to cope with situations and of seeing the behaviors involved in this coping as part of one's repertoire of behavior.

In friendship there is less likelihood that any action will produce a negative evaluation and a dramatic change in the status of the relationship, because friendships tend to be relatively stable over time, even during preadolescence. Each action has a small incremental effect upon the person's image because of the larger base of previous experiences with that person. It follows that the actor will be freer of self-conscious constraints placed on his behavior in the presence of friends than of nonfriends. Further, friends tend to perceive themselves as relatively similar to each other in their preferred activities and thus believe that they share patterns of behavior. One of the frequent responses received when I inquired why a boy was friends with another dealt with common interests and activities: "He likes to do the things I like to do."

In childhood friendships, the child's self (the perceived unitary composite of his multiple selves) develops in situations in which serious threats to the self are not likely to be present. This argument returns us to the social psychiatric model of friendship proposed by Sullivan (1953). The affective ties between preadolescent chums consist of an interest in and acceptance of the other, and accompanying this interest is a close attention to role taking and assuming the perspective of the other. Sullivan (1953) argues that "your child [at preadolescence when he finds a chum] begins to develop a real sensitivity to what matters to another person. And this is not in the sense of 'what should I do to get what I want.' but instead, 'what should I do to contribute to the happiness or to support the prestige and feeling of worthwhileness of my chum' " (p. 245).

Because the chum has the same orientation, Sullivan suggests that this is the last. best chance for dramatic changes in the child's "self-system". It is a time for the individual's self (the "I" in Mead's terms) to be validated through social interaction. Whether Sullivan is correct about the relative importance of this period is not of concern; more important is the existence of this validation of the self through friendship.

Conclusion

In this chapter I have argued that children's friendships should be analyzed in terms of their contribution to the development of the child's interactional competence. As in all interaction, participants are able to generate social meanings through peer relations, and these meanings affect behavior and self-indication. I have argued that preadolescents develop considerable competence at mastering self-presentational skills and that regular interaction partners are of particular importance in this social learning. These social skills differ from many that the child is acquiring in that they do not consist of a core of knowledge, behavior patterns, or social norms; rather, they consist of techniques for negotiating social reality. This negotiation is a process that requires an understanding of the social dynamics of peer interaction.

In particular, preadolescent friendships serve three functions that contribute to the development of interactional skills – functions that are generally not considered in developmental literature on friendship. First, friendships provide a staging area for behavior. Friendships are situated in social environments that have implications for the acquisition of interactional competencies. Second, friendships are cultural institutions, and as such they provide didactic training. Third, friendships provide, a context for the growth of the child's social self. a context within which he or she can learn the appropriate self-image to project in social situations. While these functions of friendship are not limited to preadolescence, they seem characteristic of this period because at this age the child is simultaneously particularly influenced by peers and is striving to acquire information and behavior necessary for social competence in adult society.

Notes

1 All personal and place names used in conjunction with the discussion of the Little League baseball research are pseudonyms.
2 For the distinction between role taking and role playing, see Coutu, 1951.

References

Abrahams, R. *Deep down in the jungle* (Rev. ed.). Chicago: Aldine, 1970.
Bain, R. The self-and-other words of a child. *American Journal of Sociology,* 1936, *41,* 767–775.
Barbe, W. B. Peer relationships of children of different intelligence levels. *School and Society,* 1954, *80,* 60–62.
Becker, H. S., & Geer, B. Latent culture: A note on the theory of latent social roles. *Administrative Science Quarterly,* 1960, *5,* 304–313.
Bernstein, B. *Class, codes and control.* New York: Schocken, 1975.
Blumer, H. *Symbolic interactionism: Perspective and method.* Englewood Cliffs, N.J.: Prentice-Hall, 1969.
Bogden, R., & Taylor, S. J. *Introduction to qualitative research methods.* New York: Wiley-Interscience, 1975.
Broderick, C. B. Socio-sexual development in a suburban community. *Journal of Sex Research,* 1966, *2,* 1–24.
Cavan, S. The etiquette of youth. In G. P. Stone & H. A. Farberman (Eds.), *Social psychology through symbolic interaction.* Waltham, Mass.: Xerox, 1970.
Coleman, J. *The adolescent society.* New York: Free Press, 1961.
Cooley, C. H. A study of the early use of self-words by a child. *Psychological Review,* 1908, *15,* 339–357.
    Human nature and the social order. New York: Schocken, 1964. (Originally published, 1902.)
Cottle, T. J. Prospect Street moon. In T. J. Cottle, *Time's children.* Boston: Little, Brown, 1971.
Coutu, W. Role playing versus role taking: An appeal for clarification. *American Sociological Review,* 1951, *16,* 180–187.
Davis, J. A. Correlates of sociometric status among peers. *Journal of Educational Research,* 1957, *50,* 561–569.
Davitz, J.R. Social perception and sociometric choice of children. *Journal of Abnormal and Social Psychology,* 1955, *50,* 173–176.
Dennison, G. *The lives of children.* New York: Vintage, 1969.
Denzin, N. K. *Childhood socialization.* San Francisco: Jossey-Bass, 1977.
Dion, K., & Berscheid, E. Physical attractiveness and peer acceptance. *Sociometry,* 1974, *37,* 1–12.
Dresser, N. Telephone pranks. *New York Folklore Quarterly,* 1973, *29,* 121–130.
Elkin, F., & Handel, G. *The child and society: The process of socialization* (3rd ed). New York: Random House, 1978.

Elkins, D. Some factors related to the choice status of ninety eighth-grade children in a social setting. *Genetic Psychology Monographs*, 1958, *58*, 207–272.

Faris, E. *The nature of human nature*. New York: McGraw-Hill, 1971. (Originally published, 1937.)

Feinberg, M. R. Relation of background experiences to social acceptance. *Journal of Social Psychology*, 1953, *48*, 206–214.

Fine, G. A. The natural history of preadolescent male friendship groups. In H. Foot, A. H. Chapman, & J. Smith (Eds.), *Childhood and friendship relations*. Chichester: Wiley, 1980. (a)

Cracking diamonds: The relationship between observer role and observed content in Little League baseball settings. In W. Shaffir, A. Turowetz, & R. Stebbins (Eds.), *The social experience of fieldwork*. New York: St. Martin's Press, 1980. (b)

Fine, G. A., & Glassner, B. The promise and problems of participant observation with children. *Urban Life*, 1979, *8*, 153–174.

Fine, G. A., & Kleinman, S. Rethinking subculture: An interactionist analysis. *American Journal of Sociology*, 1979, *85*, 1–20.

Fine, G. A., & West, C. S. Do Little Leagues work: Player satisfaction with organized preadolescent baseball programs. *Minnesota Journal of Health, Physical Education and Recreation*, 1979, *7*, 4–6.

Gallagher, J.J. Social status of children related to intelligence, propinquity, and social perception. *Elementary School Journal*, 1958, *58*, 225–231.

Glassner, B. Kid society. *Urban Education*, 1976, *11*, 5–22.

Goffman, E. *Presentation of self in everyday life*. Garden City, New York: Anchor, 1959. *Frame analysis*. Cambridge, Mass.: Harvard University Press, 1974.

Gold, H. A. The importance of ideology in sociometric evaluation of leadership. *Group Psychotherapy*, 1962, *15*, 224–230.

Gottman, J., Gonso, J., & Rasmussen, B. Social interaction, social competence and friendship in children. *Child Development*, 1975, *46*, 709–718.

Gottman, J., Gonso, J., & Schuler, P. Teaching social skills to isolated children. *Journal of Abnormal Child Psychology*, 1976, *4*, 179–197.

Hartup, W. W. Peer interaction and social organization. In P. Mussen (Ed.), *Carmichael's manual of child psychology* (Vol. 2). New York: Wiley, 1970.

Children and their friends. In H. McGurk (Ed.), *Issues in childhood social development*. London: Methuen, 1978.

Hollander, E. P. Conformity, status, and idiosyncrasy credit. *Psychological Review*, 1958, *65*, 117–127.

Knapp, M., & Knapp, H. *One potato, two potato . . . : The secret education of American children*. New York: Norton, 1976.

Kochman, T. Toward an ethnography of black American speech behavior. In T. Kochman (Ed.), *Rappin' and stylin' out: Communication in urban black America*. Urbana: University of Illinois Press, 1972.

Lever, J. Sex differences in the games children play. *Social Problems*, 1976, *23*, 478–487.

MacKay, R. Conceptions of children and models of socialization. In H. P. Dreitzel (Ed.), *Childhood and socialization*. New York: Macmillan, 1973.

Martinson, F. M. *Infant and child sexuality: A sociological perspective*. St. Peter, Minn.: Book Mart, 1973.

McDavid, J. W., & Harari, H. Stereotyping of names and popularity in grade school. *Child Development*, 1966, *37*, 453–459.

Mead, G. H. The genesis of the self and social control. *International Journal of Ethics*, 1925, *35*, 251–277.

Mind, self and society. Chicago, Ill.: University of Chicago Press, 1934.

Mouton, J. S., Bell, R. L. Jr., & Blake, R. R. Role playing skill and sociometric peer status. *Group Psychotherapy*, 1956, *9*, 7–17.

Oden, S., & Asher, S. R. Coaching children in social skills for friendship making. *Child Development*, 1977, *48*, 495–506.

Opie, I., & Opie, P. *The lore and language of school children*. Oxford: Oxford University Press, 1959.

Parsons, T., Shils, E. A., Allport, G. W., Kluckhohn, C., Murray, H. A., Sears, R. R., Sheldon, R. C., Stoffer, S. A., & Tolman, E. C. Some fundamental categories of the theory of action: A general statement. In T. Parsons & E. A. Shils (Eds.), *Toward a general theory of action*. Cambridge, Mass.: Harvard University Press, 1951.

Piaget, J. *The moral judgment of the child*. New York: Collier, 1962. Originally published, 1932.)

Riezler, K. Play and seriousness. *Journal of Philosophy*, 1941, *38*, 505–517.

Speier, M. *How to observe face-to-face communication*. Pacific Palisades, Cal.: Goodyear, 1973.

Stone, G. P. The play of little children. *Quest*, 1965, *4*, 23–31.

Appearance and the self. In G. P. Stone & H. A. Farberman (Eds.), *Social psychology through symbolic interaction*. Waltham, Mass.: Ginn-Blaisdell, 1970.

Stone, L. J., & Church, J. *Childhood and adolescence*. New York: Random House, 1957. *Childhood and adolescence* (2nd ed.). New York: Random House, 1968.

Sullivan, H. S. *The interpersonal theory of psychiatry*. New York: Norton, 1953.

Suttles, G. D. Friendship as a social institution. In G. J. McCall, M. McCall, N. K. Denzin, G. D. Suttles, & S. B. Kurth (Eds.), *Social relationships*. Chicago: Aldine, 1970.

Waldrop, M. F., & Halverson, C. F. Jr. Intensive and extensive peer behavior: Longitudinal and cross-sectional analysis. *Child Development*, 1975, *46*, 19–26.

Walker, H. M., & Hops, H. The use of group and individual reinforcement contingencies in the modification of social withdrawal. In L. A. Hamerlynck, L. C. Handy, & E. J. Mash (Eds.), *Behavior change: Methodology, concepts, and practice*. Champaign, Ill.: Research Press, 1973.

Weinstein, E. A. The development of interpersonal competence. In D. A. Goslin (Ed.), *Handbook of socialization theory and research*. Chicago: Rand McNally, 1969.

Weinstein, E. A., & Deutschberger, P. Some dimensions of altercasting, *Sociometry*, 1963, *4*, 454–466.

Wiley, N. The genesis of self:From me to we to I. In N. K. Denzin (Ed.) *Studies in symbolic interaction* (Vol. 2). Greenwich, Conn.: JAI Press, 1980.

Zeitlin, I. *Rethinking sociology*. Englewood Cliffs, N.J.: Prentice-Hall, 1973.

Zigler, E., & Child, I. L. Socialization. In G. Lindzey & E. Aronson (Eds.). *The handbook of social psychology* (2nd ed., Vol. 3). Reading, Mass.: Addison-Wesley, 1969.

3 Complementary and conflicting identities: images and interaction in an interracial school

Janet Ward Schofield

Introduction

The social life of American preadolescents is deeply influenced by divisions along racial and gender lines. Isolation between the sexes reaches a peak during the late elementary and early junior high school years (Hartup, 1970). Cleavage between blacks and whites, which is often minimal in the early school years, also becomes extremely pronounced by preadolescence (St. John, 1975).

One need not be a social scientist to recognize that during the preadolescent years friendship and other lesser forms of association most frequently occur between children who have both gender and racial group membership in common. However, research has documented the extraordinarily pervasive nature of these divisions. For example, Hallinan's 1977 study of eleven classrooms in the fourth through sixth grades found that friendship cliques were completely segregated by sex, with not a single clique containing both boys and girls. A large number of other studies have found the same striking preference for association with members of their own sex in both young children and preadolescents (Hartup, 1970).

Early studies by Moreno (1934) and Criswell (1937) documented striking racial cleavage among preadolescents. More recent research using both sociometric questionnaires and direct observation of behavior continues to suggest that bringing black and white children together in desegregated schools by no means automatically leads to the development of strong interracial friendships (Cohen, 1975; McConahay, 1978; Schofield,

The research on which this paper is based was funded by the author's contract #400-76-0011 with the National Institute of Education. Other expenses related to preparation of the chapter were covered by a grant #1R01 MH31 602-01 from the National Institute of Mental Health. However, all opinions expressed herein are solely those of the author and no endorsement of the ideas by NIE or NIMH is implied or intended. The author wishes to express her deep appreciation to the students and staff of Wexler School for their generous cooperation and to H. Andrew Sagar and Elaine McGivern for their energetic and insightful assistance in the data gathering.

1978; St. John, 1975; Stephan, 1978). For example, Gerard and Miller's (1975) longitudinal sociometric study of desegregated elementary school children found clear evidence of marked and continuing racial cleavage. Silverman and Shaw (1973) observed with whom students walked as they exited from a junior high school. Only 5 percent of the students participated in this minimal sort of interracial interaction even though the student body was roughly half black.

Virtually every study that compares the impact of gender and race on interaction and friendship patterns in children of junior high school age or younger concludes that sex is a considerably stronger grouping criterion than race. Krenkel (1972) found that, when playing and eating, fourth, fifth, and sixth graders in a desegregated school were much more likely to form sexually segregated than racially segregated groups. St. John and Lewis (1975) concluded that sex has a much stronger influence than race on sociometric measures of friendship choice among sixth graders. Singleton and Asher (1977; 1979) assessed both sociometric choices and actual peer interactions in third-grade children. The tendency for ingroup choice to occur along gender lines was dramatically stronger than that for ingroup choice along racial lines. In the sociometric data, sex accounted for roughly twenty times as much variance as did race.

Previous research tells us that race and sex are strong barriers to friendship and that sex is generally a stronger barrier than race, at least for children and preadolescents. However, such research generally does not address questions such as why this is so, how children interact with outgroup members when situational constraints require that they do so, and whether such interaction lays a basis for the development of friendship at some future date. Exploring such questions seems to be the next logical step, given how clear and consistent the patterns of cleavage are.

Research on how children react to and deal with others who are members of racial or gender outgroups could reasonably be conducted in a wide variety of ways. One strategy is to combine extensive observation of peer relations over a relatively long period of time with repeated interviews with the children themselves. This strategy is an excellent way to become aware of the children's assumptions, of subtle nuances in relationships, and of differences between stated ideals and actual behavior (Rist, 1978). Such awareness is especially important when one is studying a topic as sensitive as relations between blacks and whites. Furthermore, longitudinal work provides a good opportunity to begin to discover why some relationships deepen while others remain static or are terminated.

The need for research of this sort to illuminate the development of relations between blacks and whites has been frequently noted in recent years (National Institute of Education, 1975; St. John, 1975). In the past few years, a number of studies exploring peer relations in desegregated schools through observational and interviewing techniques have begun to appear (Clement, Eisenhart, & Harding, 1979; Collins, 1979; Metz, 1978; Noblit. 1979; Rist. 1978; Scherer & Slawski. 1979; Schofield & Sagar, 1979; Sullivan, 1979). This research strongly confirms the finding of earlier very different studies that children tend to choose their friends from within their own racial group and to segregate themselves even for less intense forms of social contact. Some of these recent studies also provide rich detail on the strategies that black and white children use in dealing with each other. However. they rarely if ever devote much attention to relations between the sexes. so they provide little direct assistance in comparing the way that sex and race operate to influence peer relations.

The study on which much of this chapter is based was similar to the studies discussed immediately above in that the major data-gathering strategies were long-term observation of peer interaction in a desegregated school and repeated intensive interviewing of students. The study is different from the others in that it has focused attention on relations between boys and girls as well as on relations between blacks and whites.

In the remainder of this chapter, the reader is first introduced briefly to Wexler School,[1] the research site, and to the methodology employed in the study. Next some conceptual distinctions relating to the development of friendship are introduced to lay the groundwork for discussion of peer relations at Wexler. Then, relations between boys and girls are discussed and compared to those between blacks and whites. The study confirms the conclusion drawn by earlier researchers that cross-sex and cross-race friendships are quite rare for preadolescent children. It also supports the previous work suggesting that gender is a stronger grouping criterion than race. However, it goes beyond most previous work to analyze the very different meanings and implications of these two cleavages. It suggests that although there is less contact between boys and girls than between blacks and whites, the split between blacks and whites is more fundamental and less likely to narrow as the children mature.

The research site: Wexler Middle School

In choosing a site for the research, I adopted a strategy that Cook and Campbell (1976) have called "generalizing to target instances." The aim was not to study what happens in a "typical" desegregated school. Rather, it was to explore peer relations under conditions that theory suggests should be relatively conducive to positive relations between blacks and whites.

The vast majority of studies of peer relations in interracial settings have been conducted in schools that fail to approach the conditions that Allport (1954) and others, including Pettigrew (1967; 1975), have suggested are vital to fostering positive intergroup attitudes. Not surprisingly, their results often suggest that desegregation has little positive impact on inter-group relations and may even have a negative impact (Cohen, 1975; Scho-field, 1978; St. John, 1975; Stephan, 1978). Hence, I decided that it would be particularly illuminating to study a school that meets or comes close to meeting the conditions specified by Allport as conducive to development of improved intergroup attitudes and behavior.

Allport (1954) argues that intergroup contact may reinforce previously held stereotypes and increase intergroup hostility unless the contact situation is structured in a way that provides equal status for minority and majority group members and provides strong institutional support for positive relations. Hence, he argues, equality of status in formal roles is an important precondition to change. More recent work suggests that equal status may be neither an absolutely necessary prerequisite nor a sufficient condition for change; however, it does appear to be very helpful (Amir, 1969, 1976; Cohen, 1975; Cohen, Lockheed, & Lohman, 1976; Cook, 1978). Allport also held that an additional ingredient necessary to improved intergroup relations was cooperation toward shared, strongly desired goals. A rapidly growing body of research suggests that cooperation toward mutually desired goals is indeed generally conducive to improved intergroup relations (Aronson, Blaney, Stephan, Sikes, & Snapp, 1978; Ashmore, 1970; Cook, 1978; Sherif, 1979; Slavin, 1980; Worchel, 1979).

Wexler Middle School, which serves 1,400 children in the sixth through eighth grades, was chosen for study because the decisions made in planning for it suggested that it would come reasonably close to meeting the conditions that Allport specified. The school's strong efforts to provide a positive environment for interracial education can be illustrated by examination of its staffing policy. The administration, faculty, and staff of the school are biracial, with about 25 percent of the faculty being black. The top four administrative positions are filled by two blacks and two whites. Three of these four administrators are male. The school's commitment to maintaining an equal status staffing pattern is clear in the following excerpt from field notes from a meeting with a black vice-principal during Wexler's second year:

Vice-principal Cooper said, "You know . . . they were really careful about the staffing (of this school). You had to get it divided white/black, male/female and that sort of thing . . . Both of the counselors that worked with me last year were really good and both of them are interested in coming back; but I can't hire them because the person we have now is a white female, so I have to get a black male."

The extent to which Wexler met the conditions specified by Allport as conducive to the development of improved intergroup relations has been discussed at length elsewhere (Schofield, in press; Schofield & Sagar, 1979). Here I shall merely report the conclusion drawn in those discussions – that Wexler, especially during its first year, came considerably closer to meeting Allport's criteria than most desegregated public schools. Yet the school fell seriously short of meeting the conditions in a number of important ways, many of which were quite direct results of societal conditions over which Wexler had little or no control. For example, in spite of Wexler's commitment to a staffing pattern that would provide equal formal status for blacks and whites, the proportion of black teachers on its staff was considerably lower than the proportion of black students, because nowhere near 50 percent of the teachers in Waterford, the city in which Wexler is located, were black and the school system did not want to put too high a proportion of its black teachers in one school. In addition, and again reflecting the pool of available applicants, the black faculty members were disproportionately teachers of nonacademic subjects. In sum, Wexler made stronger than usual efforts to foster positive relations between blacks and whites, but fell markedly short of being a theoretically ideal milieu for the accomplishment of this goal.

As suggested by Vice-principal Cooper's discussion of staffing policy, Wexler made some effort to create an environment conducive to equal status, cooperative relations between males and females as well as between blacks and whites. All in all, however, relatively little attention was focused on this goal.

Wexler is located in a large industrial northeastern city. Just over 20 percent of the city's population is black. Wexler opened in the fall of 1975 with a student body that was almost precisely 50 percent black and 50 percent white. A large majority of Wexler's white students came from middle- or upper-middle-class homes. Although some of the black children were middle class, the majority came from either poor or working-class families.

During its first year, Wexler obtained its students through an open enrollment plan. Students were selected on a first-come, first-served basis within quotas set to obtain a racially and sexually balanced student body. In the school's second year, the open enrollment plan was dropped and students from about a dozen elementary schools were required to enroll in Wexler when they entered sixth grade. By the time the students who entered Wexler as sixth graders in 1975 graduated from the eighth grade, the proportion of whites in the student body had dropped substantially, and many individuals, both black and white, questioned whether the school was even coming close to fulfilling its early promise (Schofield, 1978).[2]

Students at Wexler are organized into groups of about 150, which are known as teams and which share five academic teachers. Each team is divided into five classes, which rotate from teacher to teacher during each day. Students generally stay with the same classmates for their academic subjects and take nonacademic subjects such as gym or art with teammates. Because the students at Wexler come from a very wide variety of elementary schools, it is quite usual for children to find that their classes contain few if any former acquaintances.

Data gathering

The analysis that follows is based on an intensive study of peer relations in the sixth and seventh grades at Wexler from its opening in 1975 to 1978.[3] The basic data-gathering strategy was intensive and extensive observation in Wexler's classrooms, hallways, playgrounds, and cafeteria. Observers used the full field note method for recording the events they witnessed (Olsen, 1976). A large number of events were observed, because they were representative of events that filled most of the school day at Wexler. However, an important subgroup of events was oversampled in relation to their frequency of occurrence because of their direct relevance to the study's focus. This strategy, which Glaser and Strauss (1967) call theoretical sampling, led to oversampling certain activities, such as affective education classes designed to help students get to know each other, meetings of Wexler's interracial student advisory group set up to handle the special problems students may face in a desegregated school, and health classes dealing with sex education. Over the course of the three-year study, more than 500 hours were devoted to observation of students and staff at Wexler.

A wide variety of other data-gathering strategies ranging from sociometric questionnaires to experimental work were also used. Interviews were employed extensively. For example, randomly selected panels of students participated in open-ended interviews twice a year. Teachers and administrators were also interviewed repeatedly. In addition, graffiti in the bathrooms and on the school walls were routinely recorded, school bulletins were collected, and careful note was taken of such phenomena and events as wall decorations and public address system announcements. Space does not allow full discussion of the many varied techniques that were employed in collecting and analyzing the data on which this paper is based. However, two general principles guided the research. First, both data-gathering and analysis were as rigorous and systematic as possible. For example, sampling techniques were employed where appropriate; trained coders, who were unaware of the race and sex of particular respondents, coded the open-ended interviews using reliable systems developed for this research; and field notes were carefully indexed so that all notes relevant to a given topic could be examined. Second, since it is often impossible to achieve extremely high levels of precision and control in field research, strong efforts were made to triangulate the data (Webb, Campbell, Schwartz, & Sechrest, 1966). Great care was taken to gather many different types of information bearing on the same issue, to minimize the potential problems with each data source, and to be sensitive in analyzing and interpreting the data to biases that could not be completely eliminated. The approach used in the analysis of the qualitative data was heavily influenced by Bogdan and Taylor (1975), Becker and Geer (1960), Campbell (1975), Glaser and Strauss (1967), Schatzman and Strauss (1973) and others. Fuller details on data-gathering and analysis are presented elsewhere, as is information on the strategies used to minimize observer reactivity and bias (Schofield, 1977; in press).[4]

The development of friendship

In order to provide a foundation for the presentation of the study's results, I will briefly discuss some conceptual issues relating to the development of friendship. Although friendship has been defined in a wide variety of ways, most of these definitions stress closeness, mutuality, and attention to the specific personal characteristics of the individuals involved. For example, Kurth (1970) defines friendship as an intimate personal relationship involving each individual as a total person. The emphasis on closeness and on awareness of the other as a unique individual as defining characteristics of friendship makes it clear that friendship must develop out of earlier less intimate relations.

Levinger and Snoek (1972) have argued that one can characterize relations between people as being on one of three basic levels: unilateral awareness, surface contact, and mutuality. At the first level, that of unilateral awareness, an individual is aware of another but has not yet interacted with him or her. At the second level, surface contact, individuals interact in a rather superficial way. Their lives touch, but no deep relationship exists and behavior is heavily determined by the roles the individuals have in the contact situation. Finally, mutuality may emerge when individuals increasingly disclose themselves to each other and build up a store of shared experience. These levels of relatedness may not constitute invariant stages in the development of a mutual relationship such as friendship. One can reasonably argue, however, that mutuality must be preceded by surface contact and that surface contact is often preceded by unilateral or bilateral awareness.

Levinger and Snoek (1972) point out that different characteristics of individuals are differentially important at the three levels of relatedness. At the level of unilateral awareness, the external characteristics of the person being perceived, such as physical characteristics, are likely to have a major impact on the perceiver's reaction and on his or her decision about whether to try to build an acquaintance with the other person. External characteristics undoubtedly remain important during interactions at the surface contact level. At this level, however, new factors, such as information about the occupational or other social roles of the individual, also play a large part in determining how a relationship will evolve. Finally, in mutual relationships partners share more and more information about themselves as unique individuals, and their reactions to these aspects of each other influence whether the relationship will progress (Levinger, 1974).

Social identity

External characteristics are especially important at the early stages of relatedness, because such characteristics may be virtually the only information one has about the other person. The mere fact that a characteristic is visible, however, does not mean that it necessarily has a strong impact on the early stages of a relationship. For example, although it is possible to distinguish hair color from a distance, most people do not react differently to black-haired strangers than to brown-haired strangers. I would argue that this is the case because the categories "black-haired" and "brown-haired" do not have any important associated social identity.

The term "social identity" is used here to refer to a widely shared image about the likely behavior and personal characteristics of individuals who are members of a given social category, such as black or white, or male or female. A social category is "a rule or set of specifications that a perceiver uses to classify people as similar" (Ashmore & Del Boca, 1979, p. 280). The categories "black" and "white" do not have the same clear and relatively unambiguous biological basis as the categories "male" and "female" (Harris, 1975); yet both pairs are social categories related to obvious physical characteristics. Research by Taylor, Fiske, Etcoff, and Ruderman (1978) shows quite clearly that individuals classify others whom they are observing by their race and sex.

The concept of social identity as employed in this paper is similar in meaning to what Ashmore and Del Boca (1979) have called a cultural stereotype and others have termed a social stereotype (Karlins, Coffman, & Walters, 1969; Secord & Backman, 1964). All of these terms refer to a shared pattern of beliefs about the personal attributes of the members of a given social category. However, for the purposes of this chapter, I prefer to use the term "social identity." There are advantages to avoiding the word "stereotype" in the present context. As Brigham (1971) points out in his review of the literature on ethnic stereotypes, stereotypes have historically been conceptualized as incorrect generalizations that are products of a faulty thought process. Further, stereotypes have traditionally been seen as rigid and not easily changed by new information. More recent work on stereotypes by Brigham (1971), Ashmore and Del Boca (in press), and others has seriously questioned the usefulness of definitions stressing such factors. However, "stereotype" still seems to conjure up associations based on earlier definitions. In this chapter, I do not directly address the veridicality of the social identities that emerged at Wexler other than to indicate that there was at least a kernel of truth in them. Furthermore, I emphasize the ways in which these images emerged quite naturally from certain types of exposure to and interaction with members of the other group, rather than arguing that special faulty thought processes were involved, and I make no claim that the images that developed were unusually rigid or impervious to new information.

The term "social identity" also has some important advantages over the term "stereotype". The word "social" calls attention to the close tie between the images that develop and social interaction. Indeed, the argument in this chapter is that such images both emerge out of interaction and direct the course of interaction. The term "identity" makes salient the important relation, stressed long ago by such theorists as Cooley and Mead, between others' images of an individual and that individual's own emerging sense of self. The social identities discussed in this paper are important not only because they influence the way individuals approach and think about each other but also because they may influence the way in which individuals come to view themselves.

Having introduced Levinger and Snoek's ideas on the development of relatedness, as well as the concept of social identity, this chapter will now turn to an analysis of peer relations at Wexler. First. I demonstrate that, as preadolescents, students do not often progress beyond mere awareness or surface contact to deeper, more mutual relations with classmates who do not share both their race and sex. Then, an analysis of the social identities that are linked to the categories of "boy" and "girl" and "black" and "white" is presented, because these social identities appear to be important factors inhibiting the development of positive mutual relationships. These social identities obviously do not develop overnight at Wexler, and they are undoubtedly influenced by the social identities that the children associated with these categories before entering Wexler. Nonetheless, it is instructive to look at the content of the social identities that exist at

Wexler and to explore the way in which these identities are related to the children's observation of and interaction with each other.

Self-segregation by race and sex at Wexler: an overview

With a few exceptions, classes in Wexler's sixth and seventh grades tend to have roughly equal numbers of blacks and whites and equal numbers of boys and girls. Such balance within the classrooms does not, however, guarantee that students will move beyond the most superficial level of surface contact with others who are different from themselves. The students at Wexler often resegregate themselves along racial and gender lines to a remarkable extent, avoiding even surface contact when possible. This pattern persists even when teachers attempt to reduce such cleavage. As one of the observers noted near the beginning of the study:

Today, Mr. Little has assigned the children to specific tables. He has not, however, assigned seats. At all but one table, there is a remarkably clear arrangement of students by both sex and race. For example, if you start with a white male at any given table and look to one side, skipping the other white males who might be at the table, you invariably come next to the black males. Next you find the black females. The black females abut against white females, which completes the circle.

Students not only sit near those who share their gender and race but also exert noticeable pressure on mavericks who through carelessness or preference try to break out of the segregated pattern.

The chairs in Mr. Socker's room are arranged in the shape of a wide shallow U. As the first few kids come into the room, Harry (white) says to John (white), who is starting to sit down in an empty section of the room along one side of the U, "Don't sit there, that's where all the girls sit." Harry and John sit elsewhere . . .

The pervasiveness and extent of the voluntary segregation by both race and sex is illustrated by examination of seating patterns in the school cafeteria. These patterns were mapped roughly once a week for two years. On a typical day, there were about 200 students in the cafeteria during any particular lunch period with fewer than ten cross-race adjacencies and significantly fewer cross-sex adjacencies (Schofield, 1979; Schofield & Sagar, 1977).

Observations in Wexler's classrooms, like those in the cafeteria, suggested that sex is generally a more potent grouping factor than race. The overriding importance of gender was made clear when children had to choose between interacting with someone of their own race or someone of their own sex. Virtually without fail, children in such situations interacted with a child from the other racial group. The resistance against joining a group of students of the opposite sex was so strong that students occasionally accepted a punishment rather than joining such a group.

Mr. Little instructs the students to form groups of *three* for a science experiment. None of the groups formed are sexually integrated . . . Mr. Little notices a group of four boys and instructs one of its members, Juan (black), "Go over and work with Diane." (Diane's group has two black girls in it). Shaking his head, Juan says, "No, I don't want to!" Mr. Little says quietly but with an obvious edge in his voice, "Then take off your lab apron and go back to the regular class." Juan stands absolutely still and doesn't reply. After a long heavy silence, Mr. Little says, "Okay, I'll do it for you." He unties Juan's apron and sends him out of the room.

As the foregoing suggests, students at Wexler act much like previous research would lead one to expect. Gender and race are both extremely important grouping criteria, with gender being even more important than race. Cross-group interaction is often actively avoided, and deep friendships between children of different race or sex are quite unusual.

Race and gender are similar, then, in that shared membership in racial or sexual categories is generally a precondition for the development of close friendship or even for voluntary mutual involvement in somewhat less intense social relationships. In spite of this fact, study of social relationships at Wexler strongly suggests that there are important qualitative differences between the types of interactions that do occur between boys and girls and blacks and whites. Furthermore, the social identities associated with gender categories are very different in content from those associated with racial categories. The content of specific social identities is important, because it strongly influences the ways in which children perceive and respond to each other. For example, if a white child believes that blacks are aggressive, he or she may interpret a black child's playful push as an attack rather than a friendly overture. Once this interpretation is placed on the behavior, the white child may respond in a hostile way, creating anger in the black child, who then repeats the push, this time actually expressing anger and hostility. Such behavior, of course, would confirm the originally inaccurate image.

The remainder of this chapter explores the social identities that are associated with racial and sexual group membership. In addition, it looks at the way in which these social identities influence preadolescents' behavior. The analysis suggests that the staff and students react in fundamentally different ways to race and gender. Although the separation of the sexes is virtually complete in many situations, much of the interaction occurring within the all-male or all-female groups involves preparation for future, more mature aspects of male and female sex roles that entail a great deal of cross-sex interaction. Furthermore, the cross-sex interaction that does occur often foreshadows the future romantic and sexual involvement between males and females. The situation with respect to racial cleavage is quite different.

Sex, social identity and peer interaction

Both students and teachers at Wexler acknowledge gender as an important identity element. Gender categories are readily and openly used in addressing individuals and in organizing the social world.

Mr. Count (white) says to a group of black girls who are talking, "Let's have your attention girls. We're trying to conduct a meeting here."

Laura, Brenda and Sally (all white girls) break out in loud giggles. Harvey (white) turns and says, "Would you ladies kindly shut up?"

Teachers feel free both to instruct students in behaviors that they feel are suitable to the child's sex and to lay down special rules that regulate relations between boys and girls.

Mr. Little begins passing out folders. He hands Sonya (black) hers then calls Don's name. Don (black), who is seated near Sonya, says,"Tell Sonya to get my folder." Mr. Little admonishes him, "You're the one that should be getting the folders. You're the gentleman!"

As is apparent above, sex roles are usually defined in a very traditional way at Wexler. Consistent with traditional sex roles is a strong emphasis on the boys' physical prowess and athletic skill.

John (white) says, "Did you see Iron Man? Man, he can do anything! He's so strong!" Harry (white) replies, "Aw, he's nothing. Spider Man's the one . . ." A discussion of the relative strength of Iron Man, Spider Man, and Tarzan continues as the boys try to decide which one to draw as the emblem on their notebooks.

A great deal of the interaction within male peer groups seems directed toward proving and displaying athletic skill and physical strength. Informal arm wrestling tournaments are legion, as are a variety of behaviors such as playful shoving, tussling, mock boxing matches, wrestling, and fun fights. Occasionally, boys will reenact particularly dramatic fights with great gusto. This behavior was never observed among girls.

The frequent occurrence of playful aggressive behavior is indicated by the following excerpts from notes taken during the first thirty minutes of a science class:

Richard (black) says to me (a male observer), "I just won a fight . . . I didn't even know him." I ask, "What were you fighting about?" He replies, "Oh, we just started wrestling around . . . I had him (Andy, who is white) in a full nelson and it was a choice of snapping his neck or running when the teacher came. So I ran."

Bobby (black) and Mark (black), who are wrestling by the light switch, fall on the floor and roll out into the hall . . . Joe (black) and Stan (black) have a "fun" fight at the drinking fountain while Jerry (white) and Steve (white) wrestle on the other side of the room. Stan heads over and joins this fracas.

These notes were taken in an unusually rowdy class, yet they are typical in four important ways. First, the girls neither joined in the boys' physical play nor exhibited such behavior in interaction with other girls. This is, of course, quite consistent with traditional sex roles and with previous studies of children's social behavior (Maccoby & Jacklin, 1974). Second, the black boys, who were approximately equal in number to the white boys in this class, accounted for a disproportionate amount of the playful physical behavior. Third, although the majority of the physical play was within racial groups, there was some involving both white and black boys. Finally, if we can believe Richard's report, in this case as in the majority of interracial physical contests, the black child emerged victorious.

Although girls rarely get involved in the boys' roughhousing, they do occasionally attempt to join the boys in athletics on an equal basis. These efforts are generally discouraged by both the teachers and the boys:

Rita (black) says, "It's been suggested that we have competition between the teams . . . spelling bees, and sports like softball." Judy (white) says, "Mixed games or just girls and just boys?" The girls chorus, "We want mixed games." The boys speak up in favor of separate teams . . . Ms. Johnson (black) says, "Please keep in mind, females, that we are not physically equal to men . . . Some of the boys are pretty strong and can hit that ball pretty hard. So it might be a good idea to have a girls' softball team and a boys' softball team. We really don't want anyone to get hurt."

Athletics and other forms of physical interaction are more than just play. Boys often use such interactions to compete with each other for highly valued places at the top of the male dominance hierarchy, which they rather systematically set about constructing. A sixth-grade guidance counselor tells of an incident that occurred in the time-out room, where children are sent if they become unruly in class:

John (white) and Greg (black) started talking . . . about who could "take" whom in a fight. They went through a whole list of names saying, "Well, Joe (black) can take Henry (black)" . . . "Henry can take Jack (white)" . . . "Bill (black) can take Martin (white)" until they came to two kids who could beat a lot of others, but who hadn't yet tested each other. One of these kids, Wilber (black) was in the time-out room. So, John, Greg, and Wilber tried to leave the room to find the other kid for a showdown.

Girls were rarely observed engaged in such efforts to establish a dominance hierarchy based on physical prowess.

Interviewer: You're saying that girls and white kids get suspended less than
    boys and black kids. Why do girls get suspended less than boys?
Ellen (white): They (girls) are not as much interested in all the power and every-
    thing. Boys are always interested in who's the strongest . . . Around here,
    girls don't care if they're the strongest one in the whole school and they can
    beat everybody up . . .

Omark, Omark and Edelman's (1975) cross-cultural research with somewhat younger children suggests that this difference between boys and girls
is not unique to Wexler nor to American children.

A great deal of the social interaction in girls' peer groups revolves
around grooming oneself and each other. The girls' interest in attractiveness is evident in the grooming behavior that occurs quite frequently even
in academic classes.

Sonya (black) goes over to a table of six white girls and starts combing the hair of
one of them. I've frequently seen black girls combing each others' hair. This is the
first time in two months that I've seen one of them comb a white girl's hair.

Discussion of hair, clothes, and other aspects of physical appearance is
frequent among girls who are friends, and girls who flaunt the dress norms
at Wexler are often teased and taunted.

Much of the girls' concern over appearance and dress appears to stem
from a desire to be attractive to boys. Indeed, relations with the opposite
sex are so important to girls that they are one of the major causes of girls'
fights.

Interviewer: What do (girls) fight about?
Vice-principal Barnes (black): Oh, the girls fight about boyfriends . . .
Interviewer: And what about the boys?
Vice-principal Barnes: The fellows fight as a result of horseplay that gets out of
    hand, bumping and wrestling, and so forth.

Relations with boys are so important for girls that popularity with other
girls is seriously influenced by their popularity with boys.

Interviewer: Are there certain students who are more popular than others with
    the girls?
Ellen (white): Yes, for example, Lois (white).
Interviewer: Why is she so popular?
Ellen: The boys always bother her . . . They push her and just a couple of days
    ago one kissed her in the hall.

In contrast, boys interviewed in the sixth and seventh grades never indicated that their places in their peer group depended on relations with girls.

The students' aspirations for adult life generally coincide with traditional sex roles. The large majority of students seem to prefer the types
of occupations that our society has traditionally assigned to those of
their gender.

The children are conducting a clinic in health class today. Ms. Crocker writes on the blackboard ten different jobs . . . Two white girls volunteer to be medical secretaries . . . Two boys, one white and one black, volunteer to be doctors.

Furthermore, the students, especially the boys, are extremely reluctant to assume roles that have traditionally been assumed by members of the opposite sex.

Mr. Little says, "Now each group appoint one person to be secretary for the science experiment." The boys in one group are arguing because no one wants to be the secretary. They maintain that being a secretary is women's work. Mr. Little says, "A boy can be a secretary . . . But let's call it a recorder. There is something about the word secretary that sounds feminine."

Given all the recent controversy over women's social and economic position in our society, one might think that girls would feel threatened or angered by the traditional occupational expectations that boys hold for them. Yet for a wide variety of reasons, there is very little friction over such matters at this age. A great many of the girls themselves hold traditional career expectations, planning to become nurses, teachers, or secretaries. The most frequent exception to this rule appeared to be girls from homes of high socioeconomic status. However, even such girls rarely seemed deeply concerned about or seriously threatened by the more traditional expectations of their peers. Perhaps this is because sixth and seventh graders are young enough so that occupational plans are not a particularly salient topic.

Male and female: compatible and complementary social identities

The social identities attached to the social categories "boy" and "girl" are quite clearly defined and widely shared at Wexler. Most students and staff have fairly clear and similar ideas about what it means to be male or female, both in the present and in the future. Boys are more interested than girls in physical prowess and athletic ability. Girls spend more time and energy than boys on grooming themselves and on openly planning how to attract the opposite sex. In many ways the boys and girls at Wexler are remarkably similar to the high-school students of a quarter of a century ago described in James Coleman's classic book, *The Adolescent Society*.

Wexler's students and staff not only have a fairly coherent shared picture of what boys and girls are and should be like, they also tend to see these male and female social identities as compatible or complementary. Take for instance the boys' emphasis on physical prowess and the girls' emphasis on attractiveness. Children in each group can work toward max-

imizing the extent to which they attain the characteristics associated with
their gender without interference or competition from the other group.
One might argue that the boys' emphasis on physical strength could lead
to domination or intimidation of the girls, thus creating a situation conducive to hostility and friction. Yet a variety of factors makes such behavior
quite infrequent. Perhaps the most important of these factors is the salience of the general societal norm that holds that it is unmanly for a male to
use his physical prowess to intimidate a female:

> Dr. Wells, a clinical psychologist working as a consultant at Wexler, told me that
> he's noticed that teachers often say to boys, "You should never punch a girl."
> However, they rarely, if ever, counsel girls to avoid punching boys.

In addition, girls at this age are often as big or bigger than boys. Hence,
unless a boy chooses his target carefully, he runs the risk of being igno-
miniously vanquished by the "weaker sex." Finally, the usual voluntary
or enforced separation into same-sex peer groups for nonacademic activities means that boys and girls have relatively little contact with each other
in school in those less supervised settings, such as the lunchroom, which
are most conducive to fights and physical intimidation.

Although the traditional male and female social identities that prevail at
Wexler do not threaten each other seriously or lead to a great deal of
friction, they do impede the development of friendship between boys and
girls. The children appear to feel that the gulf between male and female is
so basic that it is fruitless to try to form cross-sex friendships. A considerable amount of both research and theory suggests that common interests,
attitudes, and experiences are conducive to the development of friendship
(Berscheid & Walster, 1978; Byrne, 1971; Duck, 1973). Boys and girls see
themselves as quite dissimilar and see this dissimilarity as a reason for
staying within their single-sex peer groups.

> Interviewer: In your class, do the boys mix more with the boys or the girls?
> Harry (white): The boys!
> Interviewer: Why?
> Harry: Well, there's boy talk and girl talk.

> Interviewer: I've noticed in the lunchroom that very often boys sit together and
>   girls sit together. Why do you think that is?
> Bob (white): So they can talk. The boys talk about football and sports and the
>   girls talk about whatever they talk about.

Note that Bob knows what boys talk about. He apparently does not know
what girls discuss, but he assumes it is different.

Although Wexler's students generally maintain that boys and girls do
not become friends, they are very aware of members of the opposite sex
as potential partners in a romantic or sexual relationship. Indeed, the as-

sumption is that almost any personal relation between a boy and girl will be romantic or sexual in nature. Questions about children getting to know members of the opposite sex at Wexler were virtually always interpreted as questions about romantic or sexual relations by both teachers and students alike.

> Interviewer: How do boys and girls get to know each other?
> Jennifer (black): The boy just says he likes you, and he starts calling you, an after that you go steady.

> Interviewer: What kinds of interactions are there between boys and girls at Wexler?
> Ms. Ellis (white teacher): Mostly it's caveman stuff . . . There's probably only about six to eight sexually active girls in my classes . . . There is also the goofy stage, quietly breathing at each other.

The assumption that virtually all boy–girl relations are romantic is not unique to Wexler. Clement, Eisenhart, Harding, and Livesay (1977) report that the fifth and sixth graders in a southern school, like the students at Wexler, assume that boys and girls who spend time together or show interest in each other are romantically involved. This assumption often leads children to avoid the types of interactions that might lead to friendship. For example, Fine argues in this volume that preadolescent friends spend a great deal of time in activities designed to socialize them into adolescent or adult roles. One such activity is working together on class projects. Yet boys and girls at Wexler tend to avoid contact with each other during this sort of task, at least partly because of the possibility that working together might suggest romantic involvement.

> Interviewer: Do boys and girls mix much in your class while they are working?
> Stacey (black): No, because people like to work with their friends . . . When you're working on a project . . . your friend has to call and come over to your house. If it's a boy, it can be complicated.

Indeed, some children avoid even casual conversation with those of the opposite sex out of concern that it will be interpreted as a sign of romantic interest.

> Sandra (white): If you talk with boys they (other girls) say that you're almost going with him.
> Interviewer: What does the boy think?
> Sandra: I don't know. I can't tell what a boy thinks. It's hard.
> Interviewer: You mentioned you have deep conversations with your girlfriends. Do you ever have conversations like that with boys?
> Sandra: Never, I mean, it never crossed my mind.

It is ironic that the development of friendship between boys and girls is impeded at least partly because the children are aware that they are approaching the age when they may begin to become deeply involved with each other in a romantic or sexual way.

Much of the interaction within same-sex peer groups seems to be preparation for future relations with the opposite sex. For example, Fine (this volume) argues that male preadolescent play groups are an important arena for learning about sexuality. The observations at Wexler suggest that this is true in school settings as well. Boys often quite openly discuss sexuality.

Bob (black) is reading a *National Geographic*. Sam (white) says, "Hey Bob, are there any naked ladies in that book?" Bob laughs and says, "Yeah, here is a naked pygmy," as he shows the magazine to Sam.

Although the boys emphasize avoidance of girls in many situations, they clearly see heterosexuality as the only appropriate sexual orientation. Indeed, one of the most frequent terms of abuse used between boys is the epithet "faggot," which one boy announced "means a guy who loves other guys."

Girls were rarely if ever observed discussing sexuality in the relatively open manner that boys were. Further, they appear much less likely than boys to use epithets that question another's sexual prowess or orientation. Nonetheless, girls are far from unaware of their burgeoning sexuality:

Joan (black), who is remarkably mature physically for a sixth grader, is wearing a very tight fitting sweater and skirt today. While the other students work, she dances down the middle aisle showing off her body very effectively, throwing her arms around . . . rotating her hips and thrusting out her breasts . . .

The girls, even more than the boys, indicate an active romantic interest in peers of the opposite sex, and report that much of their conversation with friends revolves around romantic intrigues, covering subjects such as who they like and how this other person has behaved toward them. Both boys and girls show a strong awareness of the future intertwining of the male and female roles.

Looking up from his book, Vincent (black), says to Stan (black), "I want an education. Then, I'll get married and have a family."

Thus, although the children believe that they have few interests to share as friends with members of the opposite sex, they have definite romantic interests in the present and expect to form lasting mutual attachments with each other in the future. The complementary nature of the male and female roles in this sphere is obvious. The boys and girls will find proof of their masculinity or femininity in being able to attract a partner. They cannot fulfill goals such as being married or having children without each other. It is interesting to note that the children do not seem concerned about the potential contradiction between their conviction that boys and girls are not sufficiently similar to be friends and their intention to form deep and lasting cross-sex romantic and sexual relationships in the future.

The lively romantic interest that boys and girls have in each other is clearly seen in the ritualized patterns of behavior that are a part of a rather rudimentary courtship process. One common pattern includes the use of a same-sex peer as a messenger who conveys the initial indication of romantic interest. A more subtle but equally effective technique involves teasing about romantic interest within a single-sex peer group in a context that virtually ensures that such teasing will be overheard by the person who is the object of the group member's interest. In both cases, the person whose romantic interests are being discussed typically denies the allegations heatedly. Thus, the message of interest is transmitted rather subtly, allowing the person who feels the interest to gauge the other's reaction without the risk of admitting his or her own interest.

Another technique, used primarily by boys, involves overacting attraction or romantic interest in such a pronounced or playful way that the indication of interest can be written off as teasing or fooling around. Such behavior often occurs in the company of peers, who provide support and validation of the playful intent:

Daniel, a black boy, comes running up to Sara (white) . . . He grabs her, putting his arm around her shoulders. She tries to get away, but before she can completely extricate herself, Joe (black) who has run up behind Daniel with a camera snaps a picture. The two boys run away laughing gleefully. Joe says, "We've got the evidence!" Eric (white) jokes with a wide grin, "He tried to rape her."

This playful teasing and attention-seeking behavior occurs very frequently in less dramatic form. Typical of this type of behavior is the "bothering" and "pushing" which Ellen mentions in the interview about popular girls previously quoted. Such behavior often allows students to begin to explore what physical contact with the opposite sex is like:

Jeff (black), who teases Marion (white) a lot, leans over and touches her neck with his hand. The touch is in between a caress and a poke as he walks his fingers across her neck . . . Marion first smiles at Jeff. Then she frowns slightly, but she doesn't look angry. Jeff looks at her, giggles and quickly dashes off.

Analysis of the common patterns of courting behavior suggests that these patterns are not conducive to the development of friendship for a variety of reasons. Virtually none of these behavior patterns involves any significant amount of relaxed or extended contact. Typically, contact and communication during these episodes is highly constricted and contains virtually no content except for the indication of romantic or sexual interest. Levinger and Snoek's (1972) perspective suggests that if a significant amount of information on a variety of topics is not exchanged during surface contact between individuals, a deep mutual relation such as friendship is unlikely to develop.

Another important factor that seems to prevent courtship behaviors from laying the groundwork for friendship is that a child who is trying to attract a boyfriend or girlfriend is almost by definition concerned about appearing in a favorable light. Fine (this volume) argues that preadolescent friendship is, among other things, an arena for learning social skills in a relaxed relationship that permits some latitude for experimentation, ineptness, and awkwardness. The emphasis on presenting oneself in the most favorable light in order to attract the other adds an element of strain and threat to cross-sex interaction which is not as salient with same-sex peers. This strain is likely to be especially great in preadolescent cross-sex interactions, because preadolescents have had little experience in romantic relationships and hence are likely to handle them awkwardly.

The children's concern with rejection and failure in cross-sex relationships is highlighted by the fact that virtually all of the widely used courting techniques are structured in a way that lets the students deny the reality of their romantic interest or through other means protects them from embarassment should their overtures be met with indifference. For example, as discussed above, touching and "bothering" are recognized as an indication of romantic interest. They can, however, be treated as something quite different, such as an attempt to annoy, because no direct declaration of romantic interest is required. Thus, the child initiating the interaction is protected from rejection. If the response to his or her overture yields no indication that the other child reciprocates the romantic interest, the reality of its romantic motivation can easily be denied.

In summary then, male and female identities at Wexler are generally seen as compatible or complementary. This does not mean, however, that friendly relations develop between boys and girls. Rather, boys' and girls' awareness of each other as possible romantic and sexual partners, concern about rejection in such relationships, and strong sex-typing of interests and activities result in a great deal of informal segregation of the sexes and rather ritualized and constricted types of behavior when cross-sex interaction does occur.

Race, social identity, and peer interaction at Wexler

Although race is a very salient social category to the students, the staff at Wexler generally maintain that, unlike gender, race should not be considered a meaningful identity element. One way to capture this difference in the teachers' reactions to race and gender is to make a conceptual distinction between legitimate and illegitimate elements of an individual's identity. A legitimate element is one that is perceived as relevant to the interaction at hand. Thus, awareness of it or reference to it is seen as appropriate. An illegitimate element is one that is seen as irrelevant or otherwise not appropriate for consideration in a particular interaction. If the various parties to an interaction have different views about the legitimacy of an identity element, then the legitimacy of that element can be said to be contested. Of course, invocation of a particular identity element may be perceived as legitimate in some interactions but not in others. For example, a child asked as a classroom exercise to describe her parents might mention that her mother is a member of the School Board. Such a comment would most probably be perceived as legitimate. However, mention of this fact during a dispute with a teacher over a grade would most probably be perceived as an illegitimate use of the same identity element.

Both teachers and students see gender as an aspect of a student's identity that has real meaning that is legitimately considered in a wide variety of situations. In sharp contrast, the prevailing view among the staff at Wexler is that in virtually all circumstances, race is an illegitimate identity element – that is, racial group membership is seen as having little or no meaning and as not being relevant to what children are like or the way they should be treated. This perspective is clearly expressed in the following excerpt from an interview with a black vice-principal at Wexler:

I don't address myself to group differences when I am dealing with youngsters . . . I try to treat youngsters . . . as youngsters and not as black, white, green or yellow . . . Children are children . . .

The white staff at Wexler generally takes a similar view. Hence, most teachers do little or nothing to cultivate positive views of black and white identity in their students or to guide students as they begin to try to discover how to interact with outgroup members.

Interviewer: Do you think it is best to . . . deal openly with the fact that black and white kids may not be used to each other . . . or is it best to just treat them like . . . there is nothing special about the school?
Ms. Wire: I don't know. I guess I sort of prefer the second approach. I don't know how I would handle the first approach . . . is probably what I am saying . . . I would get too bogged down in it.

Indeed, virtually the only times that the staff members mention race to students are the very rare occasions when they urge students to ignore race. Teachers at Wexler often go to rather extreme lengths to avoid the mention of race (Schofield. 1977. in press; Schofield & Sagar. 1979). This tendency is especially pronounced in their interaction with students. Recent research suggests that this phenomenon is not unique to Wexler but occurs, although less pervasively, in other desegregated schools (Clement et al., 1979; Willie, 1973). On the other hand, it is clear that this tendency is not found in all such schools (Sullivan, 1979).

In spite of the teachers' insistence that race should be ignored, it is a vitally important identity element in peer interactions. The students tend to segregate themselves by race in a wide variety of settings. Furthermore, they often think of each other as black or white, as the following excerpts from interviews with students indicate:

> Interviewer: Would you tell me the names of some of your friends?
> Harry (black): Joe, Daryl, Stan, and Richard – and Andy even though he's white.

> Interviewer: How friendly are the kids at Wexler?
> Susan (white): The black kids or the white kids?

Most children entered Wexler with at least tentative ideas about what outgroup members would be like.

> Sara (white): All of the white mothers were kind of scared to send their kids here because of the blacks. Parents were afraid because they (blacks) are tougher . . . They (blacks) don't take anything (from anybody).

However, with little or no prior direct experience with outgroup members and little guidance from the teachers to help them understand each other, students initially seemed very anxious to learn about each other through first-hand observation. Unsure of what the other students would be like, children watched each other warily to pick up signals that would tell them how to act towards outgroup members and to get an idea of what types of behaviors to expect.

One fact that was soon obvious to both black and white students was that the white students at Wexler perform much better academically on the average than their black classmates:

> Mr. James (white) said to me (a white observer), "I have a large number of kids getting A's, very few getting C's and a lot getting D's and E's . . . Kids from Fairmount (white) and Belleview (white) are getting the A's and B's and those from areas like Knox (black) and Trenton (black) get the D's and E's. This disturbs me. I keep wondering, 'Is it me? Or is it what these kids have?' "

Both white and black students at Wexler have come to see academic effort and achievement as characteristically white:

> Sylvia (black): Blacks are badder than whites . . . I ain't never seen a white person in the seventh grade cut class. When you look around you see the

black kids walking the halls . . . I guess they (blacks) don't care about learning. The white kids, when it's time to get their education, they can't wait.

Ann (white): The black kids don't really care what (grades) they get . . . I don't know any black kids that are really smart . . . Some black girls in my class (are) pretty nice. They'll be happy if they get a B or a C . . . They smile and say, "I never expected to get this."

The strong association in students' minds between racial group membership and academic performance is not unique to Wexler. A number of other studies of children in desegregated schools suggest that such children often perceive whites as more intelligent or more academically motivated than blacks. It should come with little surprise to learn that this perception is sometimes found among the whites in a school but is not shared by their black peers (Brigham, 1974). Yet other schools resemble Wexler more closely, with blacks sharing the view that whites are brighter, more hardworking, or both (Collins & Noblit, 1977; Ogbu, 1974; Patchen, Hoffman, & Davidson, 1976). A few fairly sophisticated students seem conscious of the role that social class plays in the superior academic performance of white students. The large majority, however, tend to think in terms of racial group membership, which is, after all, more visible than social class background.

Whereas whites are associated with academic success by both groups at Wexler, blacks are associated with physical toughness and the inclination to use this toughness to defend themselves and to dominate others, both black and white. This finding at Wexler is also mirrored in numerous studies of other desegregated situations. For example, Patchen et al.'s 1976 study of nearly 4,000 black and white students in desegregated high schools found that both groups of students rated blacks as tougher than whites. Also, Brigham's (1974) study of white fourth- and fifth-grade students found a parallel tendency for white students to see blacks as hostile and easily angered.

The strength of the association at Wexler between being black and being tough is well illustrated by the responses of eighty sixth-grade boys, forty black and forty white, to a sentence-completion task. Embedded in a wide variety of other sentence fragments about life at Wexler were phrases like "Most of the black kids in the school . . ." and "A lot of people think that white kids . . ." Over one-half of both the black and white boys completed these questions in a way that emphasized the physical toughness and aggressiveness of blacks (Sagar, 1979).[5] Typical responses were:

> Tom (white): A lot of people think that black kids *fight too much*. A lot of people think that white kids *aren't strong enough*.
>
> Daryl (black): A lot of people think that black kids are *nasty, no good, mean*. A lot of people think that white kids are *smart*.

The association between toughness and blacks is strong among the girls as well:

> Donna (black): The white girls are scared of the black girls.
> Interviewer: Why do you think that is?
> Donna: They (black girls) just like to bully.
> Interviewer: Do they bully other black girls?
> Donna: Those who let them . . . Most of the time white girls . . . can't defend themselves as well as a black girl can.

Although black and white students agree that blacks are tougher and more aggressive than whites, they perceive and evaluate this identity element quite differently. Whites tend to see toughness as a characteristic of all or most blacks. In addition, whites are almost uniformly negative about the behavior that earns blacks this image. Blacks, on the other hand, are much more likely than whites to differentiate between "regular" blacks and "bad" blacks. Children who do this feel that toughness or aggressiveness is not characteristic of all, or virtually all, blacks, even though it is more likely to be found in blacks than in whites.

> Bobbi (black): Some blacks is friendly . . . The friendly blacks get along with whites. But the black people that think they're bad, they just don't like people that much . . . They pick fights with whites and then with blacks. They fight with everybody.

A large majority of the black children share the white children's strong negative reactions to aggressiveness in peer relations. A significant number, however, see no problem with it. For these children, the problem lies in the white children's lack of willingness or ability to stand up for themselves.

> Interviewer: Do you think white children have any trouble learning how to act toward black kids?
> Donna (black): Yes . . . They just can't take it. They don't know how to fight.
> Interviewer: Do you think black children have any trouble knowing how to act towards whites?
> Donna: No.

The image of blacks as physically strong and dominating is closely tied to the image of blacks as rule breakers. Recall Sylvia's assertion that black kids, not white kids, are the ones who cut classes. The sentence completions of a white boy, Martin, also illustrate the image of blacks as rule breakers:

A lot of people think that black kids are *mean or vandalize.*
A lot of people think that white kids are *hard workers.*

Whites, in contrast to blacks, are seen as being "good," sometimes even too good for other children's tastes:

> Harry (white): A lot of people think that white kids are *goody goody two-shoes.*

Both black and white children, when pressed for reasons that might explain the association of blackness with "toughness" and "badness," will sometimes make reference to social class. But this does not change the fact that they spontaneously organize their thought in terms of racial group membership rather than the less easily perceived social class membership.

Given the social class differences between blacks and whites at Wexler and the historical fact of past and continued prejudice and discrimination against blacks in our society, it should not be surprising to learn that blacks see prejudice and conceit as widespread among the white students at Wexler:

> Jerry (black): A whole lot of black kids think that everybody that's white hates them. So, they'll hate white people back.

Black girls are especially likely to complain of social isolation and to attribute it to white conceit.

> Terri (black): Some white kids act conceited. They don't want to talk to you . . . You be talking to them and they'll talk to you for about a minute or so, and then they'll go over to their other friends and act like they don't know you.

Many white students at Wexler are anxious to believe that they are not prejudiced. Research by both Dutton (1976) and Gaertner (1976) suggests that such feelings are not unusual. These students recognize that they often avoid blacks and feel superior to them. But these feelings of dislike and superiority are, in their minds, based on evidence and are not prejudice:

> Laura (white): I sound prejudiced, but I don't mean to . . . I have a friend who is colored. Don't get me wrong. How can I explain this? White people, er, OK, take Jewish first . . . (Laura is Jewish.) Jewish parents always want their children to go to college. That's a real big thing . . . I think it's the same with most white people . . . But, some black parents just don't care . . .

Thus, although there is agreement on a number of aspects of black and white identity at Wexler, there is no agreement on the issue of whether whites are prejudiced. Most whites argue that they are not conceited or prejudiced, but most blacks feel that they can discern evidence of prejudice and conceit in the behavior of many whites. This finding parallels Patchen et al.'s 1976 finding that black students see whites as much more likely than blacks to be stuck-up or to expect special privileges. Like the white children at Wexler, the whites in the Patchen study did not share this view. Indeed, they saw blacks as somewhat more stuck-up and likely to expect special privileges than whites.

Black and white: conflicting identities

Unlike gender identities, racial identities at Wexler are not complementary. The white domination of academic affairs raises serious problems, because the role of student is so salient for both white and black children. Although high achievers and teachers often argue that children who do poorly do not care about achieving, there is considerable evidence to the contrary. Discussions of academic achievement are common even among students whose grades are generally low. Such students seem pleased when they do well, showing their papers to other students and talking about them in loud tones. For black students, however, succeeding academically often means leaving their friends behind and joining predominantly white groups within their classes.

Mr. Cousins compliments Harry on his work and says that he will think about moving Harry from Group C (the "slow," predominantly black, math group) to group B. Ken (black), who is also in Group C, looks up and says, "We want to keep Harry. Please don't move him. We like having him sit here." Harry smiles broadly.

Children at all levels of the academic performance spectrum are sensitive to the fact that doing well means doing better than others. Thus, the whites' high level of academic performance can become a source of friction between blacks and whites. Lacking disconfirming information, black students often perceive white students' performance as an arrogant display. Sometimes such a display seems intended. More frequently, calling attention to one's prowess seems meant to gratify oneself or to please the teacher rather than to hurt less able peers. Yet such displays can put a child who cannot get the answers, or who cannot get them quickly, in an awkward or even humiliating position:

The teacher says, "Who knows the answer to question four?" and calls on Lilly (black) who starts to answer incorrectly. While she talks, children all around her wave their hands in the air, straining in the teacher's direction. Some call out, "I know," or "Call on me! Call on me!" The teacher calls on Cecilia (white) who gives the correct answer.

The white domination of academic life inhibits the development of friendship between blacks and whites in a variety of ways. Whites may come to feel superior or to have previous beliefs about superiority reinforced. Black jealousy of whites' performance is another factor contributing to friction in black–white relations.

> Interviewer: Are some kids more likely to be picked on than others?
> Sue (white): Yeah . . . People who are real smart or who they just don't like.

Since academic grouping within classes is fairly frequent, teachers, both black and white, often set up and enforce racially segregated seating patterns as a by-product of their desire for academically homogeneous subgroups in their classes.

Whites who try to assist lower-achieving blacks are sometimes unpleasantly surprised by the other student's reaction:

> Interviewer: Are there any things the white kids do that annoy the black kids?
> Vice-principal Cooper (black): Some of the better white students . . . want to be teachers . . . They offer advice and help where it is not wanted. Not necessarily not needed, but not wanted. That stimulated a lot of problems. The first year I was here . . . the majority of the problems that came to me [were of that type].

Black students often see such offers of help as yet another indication of white feelings of superiority and conceit. White students who do not perceive themselves as conceited feel mystified and angry when what seem to them to be friendly and helpful overtures are rejected.

In sum, at Wexler whiteness has become associated with success in what is the most fundamental role of children in the school situation– that of student. White children readily accept being part of a group that performs well in the student role. But the more whites work at achieving academically and obeying school rules, the more they tend to appropriate to themselves success in the role of student and to leave blacks the choice of accepting the role but admitting failure in it or rejecting the role and condemning themselves to conflict with the demands of the school.

The very obvious white domination of academic life at Wexler fosters in many black students a sense of alienation from the school, from academic work, and from whites that is evident in the following excerpt from the field notes:

Today the class is supposed to watch a rerun of the "Middle School Quiz" program which is modeled on the old television show, "The College Bowl." Wexler's team, which consists entirely of white children, is competing against another all white team . . . Marian (black) has been rather unruly all during class today. When the teacher tells her to sit down and watch the TV, Marian mutters in an undertone, "That's not Wexler School . . . might as well call it White School."

Both teachers and parents told researchers that black children who consistently perform very well are sometimes pressured by their black peers not to work so hard. A somewhat similar phenomenon is reported by Collins and Noblit (1977), who found that black students at the high school they studied often discouraged their peers from enrolling in the more advanced courses that were predominantly white by saying things like, "There ain't nothing but white faces in there" (p. 126).

In discussing gender identity at Wexler, I argued that strength or toughness as an element of the boys' masculine identity is compatible with the girls' general lack of desire to achieve toughness. The boys can be strong without threat to the girls, because the girls have no particular desire to compete with the boys in this way, and because clear norms specify that boys should not use their physical prowess to hurt or dominate girls. Furthermore, when boys do harass girls, it is often possible for the girls to interpret that behavior as a sign of attraction rather than as a challenge that demands a reply.

The situation with respect to toughness as an element of racial identity is quite different, because there are no widely accepted norms that inhibit blacks from using their physical prowess to dominate whites.

> Interviewer: Who do boys intimidate mainly?
> Bill (black): Other boys.
> Interviewer: OK, who do black kids intimidate mainly?
> Bill: Whites, but blacks too.
> Interviewer: Who are whites likely to intimidate?
> Bill: Other whites.

Research in other desegregated schools suggests a similar pattern. For example, when Scherer and Slawski (1978) compared the patterns of peer interaction found in five ethnographic studies of desegregated schools, they found that "hassling" of white students by blacks was common. These authors define "hassle" as "to purposely annoy or provoke the other" (p. 24) and illustrate the concept of hassling by means of an incident in which several students purposely walked between a boy and a girl who were talking as they walked down a hallway. Even though most instances of hassling seem trivial, it is clear that students do not perceive them as such. The pervasiveness and symbolic importance of such encounters leads many white students to feel both annoyed and afraid:

> Annie (white): Most of the black kids are really bad . . . There are little things I can't even remember, like a lot of times they just come in and pick on you. You can't really go tell the counselor because it's too small, but if you're here all year and those little things keep happening it seems a lot bigger.

A variety of factors make whites attractive targets for hassling, although blacks frequently hassle other blacks as well. Aware of past oppression, concerned about establishing and maintaining equality with whites, and at an academic disadvantage, black children sometimes seem to assert themselves to redress past grievances or to gain a sense of power:

> Interviewer: What do you like least about Wexler?
> Mary (white): There's lots of black kids . . . Yesterday a bunch of girls were going around saying, "Remember *Roots*," and pushing us . . . It happens a lot of times. They come and hit me for nothing.

Black children as well as white are aware of this phenomenon.

> Jim (black): Lots of times they (black students) . . . try to act like they're real tough towards white kids, so they'll be scared of them.

The fact that whites are widely believed to be conceited and to feel superior makes many black children quick to take offense and to act aggressively even though offense may not have been intended:

> Sue (white) hurt her neck a little tumbling in gym class. Andrea (white) and Gail (black) go over to help her up from the floor. They get her up, but then she says her neck still hurts and stretches out face down on the floor again. After a few minutes, she begins to kick her legs up and down and accidentally kicks Gail's foot. (I say accidentally because Sue was facing so that she couldn't see Gail and had been in that position for some time.) Gail says heatedly, "Do that again and I'll kick you back hard."

Also, some white children behave in a way that virtually invites harrassment. Many of them are so afraid of blacks that they do not stand up for themselves, even in very unthreatening encounters. This lack of willingness to assert themselves and to protect their own rights when interacting with blacks makes whites attractive targets, because their behavior reinforces others' attempts to dominate them:

> Interviewer: Are there certain kids who are more likely to get picked on than others?
> Barb(white): I think the kids that are scared to stand up to people get picked on. My friend [is an example]. She's scared of people just walking past her that look strange to her . . . She's scared of mostly everything I could name.

Scherer and Slawski (1979) indicate that blacks are often aware that many white students will tolerate behavior from them that they would not tolerate from a white peer. Interviews at Wexler gave evidence of a similar belief. Indeed, black children often seem to test whites to see how far they can be pushed. Once dominance has been clearly established, the interaction terminates:

> Prince (black) asks John (white) to lend him an eraser. After hesitating briefly, John hands his eraser to Prince who uses it industriously. Then, instead of returning the eraser to John who is looking at him expectantly, Prince puts it in the open palm of his own hand which is within reach of John but which is not very close to

the part of the table at which John is working. John eyes the eraser for about five seconds. Then he bends his head over his work. After about thirty seconds, he looks up again at the eraser which is cupped in Prince's motionless hand. John again bends over his work. After another short interval John looks up yet again. This time he looks at Prince's face for about fifteen seconds. Then just as John reaches over towards the eraser, Prince closes his hand into a fist around it . . . John quickly withdraws his hand and looks down at his paper. Immediately thereafter Prince returns the eraser.

The perception of blacks as "tough" and "bad" adds a strong element of threat to their image. Thus, mild hassling behavior appears more threatening than it might otherwise. Indeed, experimental work done at Wexler showed clearly that both black and white children interpret ambiguously aggressive behavior, such as light poking with a pencil, as more mean and threatening when performed by a black than when performed by a white (Sagar & Schofield, 1979). White children frequently interpret behavior that blacks intend as friendly as aggressive or threatening:

> Lynn (black): Most of them (the white girls) are scared of me.
> Interviewer: How do you know that?
> Lynn: 'Cause they act like it. When we're just playing around they get scared and run to the dean. I say, "I was just . . . kidding." They say "Oh, I thought you was for real."

This tendency is so strong that even innocuous acts, like a black girl lightly touching a white girl's hair, can result in tears and a situation that ends in the vice-principal's office.

White children frequently avoid blacks in an effort to keep from having to deal with children of whom they are at least a little afraid. This strategy obviously inhibits the development of positive relations between the two groups. A more serious result, however, is that it often fuels the blacks' perception that whites think they are too good to play or work with blacks.

Blacks' perception of whites as likely to be prejudiced or conceited is clearly incompatible with whites' fear of seeming prejudiced, thus creating a conflict over the "true" social identity of whites. The perception on the part of black children that whites are likely to be prejudiced and conceited leads to an intensification of pressures that exist in both gender and racial ingroups to avoid friendly contact with the outgroup. In fact, black children, especially black girls, often put considerable pressure on their peers not to make friends with whites, because such an alliance suggests to them a rejection of blacks. Both blacks and whites agree that there is less pressure among whites to avoid interracial friendships than vice versa.

Lydia (black): They [other black girls] get mad 'cause you've made a white
  friend . . . They say that blacks are supposed to have black friends and
  whites are supposed to have white friends.
Interviewer: Do all the students here feel like that?
Lydia: No, but quite a few.
Interviewer: Do white students feel that way, too?
Lydia: No. Some might; most of them don't.
Bonnie (white): White kids, a lot of them, know and like black kids. Their
  friends don't say, "Oh, you've got a black friend . . ." But the black kids
  really have a thing against white friends . . . Last year, the black girls in my
  art class . . . always picked on the white kids. This one black girl didn't, so
  the black kids didn't tell her all their secrets . . . Black kids just don't like
  their friends having white friends. That's the main reason why black kids
  don't make friends with white kids . . . They think any contact with whites
  and you're a traitor.

Summary and conclusions

Children at Wexler rarely move from awareness of or surface contact with
children of a different sex or race to the deep level of mutual relatedness
that is implied by the word "friendship." Reasonably smooth and comfortable surface contact does generally occur when the school requires
such contact. For example, children get along well with each other when
assigned to work together in class on a group project, but they rarely take
advantage of the forced surface contact to begin to build real friendships
with children who are not of the same race or sex. Strong peer pressures
inhibit the development of both cross-race and cross-sex friendships.

In ironic contrast to the pressures to avoid cross-sex friendship, much
of the social interaction in both same-sex peer groups and cross-sex situations is fundamentally influenced by the students' awareness of the mutuality that will develop in their relations with the outgroup in the near future. Cross-group interaction often consists of awkward attempts to
initiate romantic relations. The possibility of romance is so salient that the
development of friendship is stymied.

Boys and girls agree that males and females are and should be different.
Thus, both boys and girls are able to maximize the attainment of their
sex-related social identities without threat to each other. However, these
differences in the social identities of males and females are very important
in explaining why friendships generally do not develop between boys and
girls. Boys do not expect girls to want to join in the activities or talk they
engage in with their friends and vice versa. This may also be one of the
reasons that romantic relationships in preadolescence or early adoles-

cence are often so awkward. The children either do not or believe they do not share many interests. Hence conversation lags.

Black and white children, like boys and girls, tend in general to have little more than surface contact at Wexler. There are, however, a number of very important differences between the surface contact that evolves between boys and girls and blacks and whites. Even progressing to the level of surface contact with the racial outgroup is a big change for many of Wexler's students, who have had little prior contact with racial outgroup members in their families, their neighborhoods, or their previous schools. Because contact is so new and race is treated as an illegitimate identity element by most of Wexler's staff, the students must discover for themselves the meaning of the black and white identities of which they are so aware and formulate rules that lead to tolerably smooth interactions. This is not an easy task.

McCall and Simmons (1966) point out that interaction is likely to be smooth when the individuals involved have had a prior chance to observe the identity elements that the other interactants claim as salient to the situation. They also argue that prior contact between the individuals in an interaction is generally conducive to smooth interaction. The racial isolation of most children prior to their Wexler experience is hardly conducive to either of these interaction-facilitating conditions.

The children struggle to deal with the problem of constructing social identities for the categories "black" and "white" and to discover how they should act toward members of the outgroup. One major factor that affects the outcome of this struggle is the strong association between race and social class. In Wexler, as in the large majority of desegregated schools, whites on the average come from families of considerably higher socioeconomic status than blacks. Given the relation between academic achievement and socioeconomic status, it is hardly surprising that whites do better academically at Wexler than blacks. Many of the other differences between black and white social identities at Wexler also appear to be strongly related to social class differences. For example, Miller (1968) has argued that "toughness" and "excitement" are two core values that help to explain the gang behavior of working-class white boys. It seems reasonable to argue then that the class background of the black children at least partially accounts for the association of blackness with toughness and rule breaking at Wexler.

A crucial fact for the development of black and white social identities at Wexler is that race is very visible whereas social class background is not. In addition, the history and present state of race relations in our country create special tensions that may tend to magnify class-based differences between blacks and whites. For example, any tendency black children may have to value toughness, stemming from their social class background, seems likely to be exacerbated in their dealing with white children, because of a sensitivity to the historical subordination and exploitation of blacks in American society. Whatever the reasons for the rather different behavior patterns that came to be associated with being black or white at Wexler, children tend to categorize each other by their racial group membership and to attribute the differences they perceive to race rather than to class. Hence, differences in academic achievement and personal style between black and white children come to be perceived as racial differences.

The social identities that are attached to the categories "black" and "white" are not conducive to the development of friendship between black and white children. Because children are generally graded relative to the others in their classes, white achievement often means black failure. This fact can reinforce the image and reality of whites as conceited and prejudiced. The black image of toughness is frequently, although by no means entirely, gained at the expense of whites, who come to be viewed as weak and scared. Such an identity is unpleasant for whites and is especially threatening to white males. Further, children's reality-based images of racial outgroups come to be exaggerated through misunderstanding and awkward attempts to reach out to outgroup members. Whites who offer to assist blacks academically out of a desire to be helpful sometimes reinforce the blacks' image of whites as arrogant. Blacks who play with whites in a rougher manner than the whites expect may be seen as aggressors.

Whereas relations with gender outgroups are profoundly influenced by the expectation of future positive ties, relations between blacks and whites are shaped by the history and present existence of racial separation, hostility, and discrimination in our society. Under these conditions, relations between blacks and whites inside the school cannot be expected to be particularly comfortable or smooth, and it is perhaps unrealistic to expect that blacks and whites inside the school will form close and deep mutual relations easily or quickly. The tumultuous social upheavals of the 1960s made it painfully apparent that racial isolation is not a workable long-term solution for the racial tensions that beset our society. This chapter makes it clear that in spite of its efforts, Wexler was not able to heal deep racial divisions overnight or to create a small utopia. Yet, to be seen in its proper perspective, life at Wexler needs to be compared not only to some ideal standard but also to the realities of the larger society in which it is embedded:

Interviewer: Some people say that black and white kids in schools like Wexler get to know each other quickly and easily and others say that this isn't so. What do you think?

Mary (white): It's not really so easy 'cause you don't know how the kids are going to act toward you . . . But, you know, it's much easier to get along with black people (now) than it was at first.

Pat (black): My locker partner is white . . . We got to know each other by the third day in school . . . We're friends . . . Black kids are a lot more used to white kids now [in June, compared to September] . . . After a while you get to know what they're going to do usually . . . You learn . . . different things about being with them.

Notes

1 To protect confidentiality, pseudonyms are used throughout this paper for the school studied as well as for all students and staff.

2 Conditions have changed rapidly at Wexler during the years since it first opened. The school is described here as it was during its first two years, because most of the data on which this paper is based were gathered during that period.

3 Data from the eighth grade are not incorporated in this paper, because the structural arrangements in that grade were quite different from those in the sixth and seventh. Specifically, in the two lower grades, children were mixed in academically and racially heterogenous classes. In the eighth grade, on the other hand, children were tracked into different classes depending on their academic performance. This resulted in heavily white accelerated classes and heavily black regular classes.

4 To illustrate the variety of data gathered relevant to the conclusions drawn, I will briefly mention some of the types of data that underlie the point made later in this paper that, at Wexler, blacks are seen as tougher and as more likely to break rules than whites by both black and white children and that this perception is not without some basis in fact. First, there are the data mentioned in the text drawn from systematic coding of the sentence completions of eighty randomly selected black and white male sixth-graders. In addition, other evidence comes from interviews with forty other students who were randomly selected within quotas set to obtain equal numbers of children from each sex, race, and grade level (sixth and seventh). Open-ended responses to questions such as "What kinds of kids are most likely to fight?" were coded and analyzed. Appropriate statistical analyses were performed on relevant quantitative data obtained directly from students in these interviews, such as students' estimates of the number of black and white children who were suspended each year from school. Because suspensions are a reflection of the school's disciplinary procedures as well as students' behavior, these interviews also explored whether students felt the disproportionate suspension of black students, of which they were well aware, stemmed from black students' behavioral tendencies or from unfair school practices. Actual suspension rates, teachers' perception of these rates, and their thoughts about why rates were higher for blacks than whites were also investigated.

Finally, all the field notes were systemically examined for incidents such as serious rule breaking and rough physical play and for discussion of such topics by children, including threats made by students to either peers or teachers. Of course, in interpreting the meaning of the results of this coding, one must always be aware that observers are undoubtedly somewhat selective in recording field notes, as they did in this study, because more happens in any given moment than can be recorded. Space does not allow a full discussion of all the procedures undertaken to ensure a high level of objectivity in gathering, analyzing, and interpreting the field notes. However, one illustration may be useful. Care was taken to compare the patterns of results obtained by black and white observers whenever this was possible. When it was not, patterns obtained by different white observers were systemically compared. Similarly, all observers were instructed in techniques that minimized the probability of their focusing exclusively on one child or group of children. Results from both black and white observers suggested very noticeable differences between blacks and whites in a large majority of the categories analyzed. Blacks were roughly three to ten times as likely as whites to have been recorded as engaging in such behaviors. Although it would be unwise to consider these figures as firm estimates of the magnitude of group differences, the size of the differences found and their consistency across categories and observers does suggest a real phenomenon rather than one induced by observer bias.

It should be obvious from the foregoing why I have not chosen to discuss every piece of data that bears on all of the points made in this chapter. A rather complex and multifaceted argument is developed. Such an argument would be impossible within reasonable space limitations if the very varied evidence for each part of the argument were presented in full. It must, of course, be emphasized in this context that the excerpts from interviews and field notes used extensively in the text are examples or illustrations of the evidence that are used to give the reader a direct sense of the way children at Wexler think about things. They do not by themselves constitute the entire evidence.

5 The sentence completions were coded by two researchers who were not aware of the race of the respondents. The intercoder agreement was 97.5 percent. Cohen's kappa, which takes into account the chance level of agreement in arriving at its reliability estimate, was .95, indicating excellent reliability in coding these data.

References

Allport, G. W. *The nature of prejudice*. Cambridge, Mass.: Addison-Wesley, 1954.

Amir, Y. Contact hypothesis in ethnic relations. *Psychological Bulletin,* 1969, *71,* 319–342.
  The role of intergroup contact in change of prejudice and ethnic relations. In P. A. Katz (Ed.), *Towards the elimination of racism*. New York: Pergamon Press, 1976.

Aronson, E., Blaney, N., Stephan, C., Sikes, J., & Snapp, M. *The jigsaw classroom*. Beverly Hills, Cal.: Sage Publishers, 1978.

Ashmore, R. D. Solving the problem of prejudice. In B. E. Collins, *Social psychology: Social influence, attitude change, group processes, and prejudice*. Reading, Mass.: Addison-Wesley, 1970.

Ashmore, R.D., & Del Boca, F. K. Conceptual approaches to stereotypes and stereotyping. In D. L. Hamilton (Ed.), *Cognitive processes in stereotyping and intergroup behavior*. Hillsdale, N.J.: Lawrence Erlbaum Associates, in press.
  Sex stereotypes and implicit personality theory: Toward a cognitive-social psychological conceptualization. *Sex Roles,* 1979, *5,* 219–248.

Becker, H. S., & Geer, B. Participant observation: Analysis of qualitative data. In R. N. Adams & J. I. Preiss (Eds.), *Human organization research*. Homewood, Ill.: Dorsey Press, 1960.

Berscheid, E., & Walster, E. *Interpersonal attraction* (2nd ed.). Reading, Mass.: Addison-Wesley, 1978.

Bogdan, R., & Taylor, S. J. *Introduction to qualitative research methods: A phenomenological approach to social science*. New York: Wiley, 1975.

Brigham, J. C. Ethnic stereotypes. *Psychological Bulletin*, 1971, *76*, 15–38.
   Views of black and white children concerning the distribution of personality characteristics. *Journal of Personality*, 1974, *42*, 144–158.
Byrne, D. *The attraction paradigm*. New York: Academic Press, 1971.
Campbell, D. T. Degrees of freedom and the case study. *Comparative Political Studies*, 1978, *8*, 178–193.
Clement, D., Eisenhart, M., & Harding, D. The veneer of harmony: Social–race relations in a southern desegregated school. In R. C. Rist (Ed.), *Desegregated schools: Appraisals of an American experiment*. New York: Academic Press, 1979.
Clement, D., Eisenhart, M., Harding, J., & Livesay, J. *The emerging order: An ethnography of a southern desegregated school*. Unpublished manuscript, University of North Carolina, Chapel Hill, 1977.
Cohen, E. The effects of desegregation on race relations. *Law and Contemporary Problems*, 1975, *39*(2), 271–299.
Cohen, E., Lockheed, M., & Lohman, M. The center for interracial cooperation: A field experiment. *Sociology of Education*, 1976, *49*, 47–58.
Coleman, J. *The adolescent society*. New York: The Free Press, 1961.
Collins, T. W. From courtrooms to classrooms: Managing school desegregation in a deep south high school. In R. C. Rist (Ed.), *Desegregated schools: Appraisals of an American experiment*. New York: Academic Press, 1979.
Collins, T. W., & Noblit, G. *Crossover High*. Unpublished manuscript, Memphis State University, 1977.
Cook, S. W. Interpersonal and attitudinal outcomes in cooperating interracial groups. *Journal of Research and Development in Education*, 1978, *12*, 97–113.
Cook, T., & Campbell, D. The design and conduct of quasi-experiments and true experiments in field settings. In M. Dunnette (Ed.), *Handbook of industrial and organizational psychology*. Chicago, Ill.: Rand-McNally, 1976.
Criswell, J. H. Racial cleavage in Negro–white groups. *Sociometry*, 1937, *1*, 81–89.
Duck, S. W. *Personal relationships and personal constructs*. New York: Wiley, 1973.
Dutton, D. G. Tokenism, reverse discrimination, and egalitarianism in interracial behavior. *Journal of Social Issues*, 1976, *32*(2), 93–107.
Gaertner, S. L. Nonreactive measures in racial attitudes research: A focus on "liberals." In P. A. Katz (Ed.), *Towards the elimination of racism*. New York: Pergamon Press, 1976.
Gerard, H., & Miller, N. *School desegregation*. New York: Plenum Press, 1975.
Glaser, B. G., & Strauss, A. L. *The discovery of grounded theory: Strategies for qualitative research*. Chicago, Ill.: Aldine Publishing, 1967.
Hallinan, M. T. *The development of childrens' friendship cliques*. Paper presented at the American Sociological Association Convention, Chicago, Illinois, 1977.
Harris, M. *Culture, people, nature: An introduction to general anthropology* (2nd ed.). New York: Thomas Y. Crowell, 1975.
Hartup, W. W. Peer interaction and social organization. In P. H. Mussen (Ed.), *Carmichael's manual of child psychology* (Vol. 2). New York: Wiley, 1970.
Karlins, M., Coffman, T. L., & Walters, G. On the fading of social stereotypes: Studies in three generations of college students. *Journal of Personality and Social Psychology*, 1969, *13*, 1–16.
Krenkel, N. *Self-concept and interaction patterns of children in a desegregated school*. Master's thesis, California State University, San Francisco, 1972.
Kurth, S. B. Friendship and friendly relations. In G. J. McCall, M. M. McCall, N. K. Denzin, G. D. Suttles, & S. B. Kurth (Eds.), *Social relationships*. Chicago, Ill.: Aldine Publishing, 1970.

Levinger, G. A three-level approach to attraction: Toward an understanding of pair related-ness. In T. L. Huston (Ed.), *Foundations of interpersonal attraction*. New York: Academic Press, 1974.

Levinger, G., & Snoek, J. D. *Attraction in relationship: A new look at interpersonal attraction*. Morristown, N.J.: General Learning Press, 1972.

Maccoby, E. E., & Jacklin, C. N. *The psychology of sex differences*. Stanford, Cal: Stanford University Press, 1974.

McCall, G. J., & Simmons, J. L. *Identities and interactions*. New York: Free Press, 1966.

McConahay, J. The effects of school desegregation upon students' racial attitudes and behavior: A critical review of the literature and a prolegomenon to future research. *Law and Contemporary Problems*, 1978, *42*,(3), 77–107.

Metz, M. H. *Classrooms and corridors. The crisis of authority in desegregated schools*. Los Angeles: University of California Press, 1978.

Miller, W. B. Focal concerns of lower-class culture. In L. A. Ferman, J. L. Kornbluh, & A. Haber (Eds.), *Poverty in America*. Ann Arbor: University of Michigan Press, 1968.

Moreno, J. *Who shall survive? A new approach to the problems of human interrelations*. Washington, D. C.: Mental Disease Publishing Co., 1934.

National Institute of Education. *Resegregation: A second generation school desegregation issue*. Unpublished manuscript, Desegregation Studies Unit, Washington, D.C., 1975.

Noblit, G. Patience and prudence in a southern high school: Managing the political economy of desegregated education. In R. C. Rist (Ed.), *Desegregated schools: Appraisals of an American experiment*. New York: Academic Press, 1979.

Ogbu, J. U. *The next generation: An ethnography of education in an urban neighborhood*. New York: Academic Press, 1974.

Olsen, S. *Ideas and data: Process and practice of social research*. Homewood, Ill.: The Dorsey Press, 1976.

Omark, D. R., Omark, M., & Edelman, M. Formation of dominance hierarchies in young children. In T. R. Williams (Ed.), *Psychological anthropology*. Paris, France: Mouton, 1975.

Patchen, M., Hoffman, G., & Davidson, J. Interracial perceptions among high school students. *Sociometry*, 1976, *39*, 341–354.

Pettigrew, T. Social evaluation theory: Convergences and applications. In D. Levine (Ed.), *Nebraska Symposium on Motivation* (Vol. 15). Lincoln: University of Nebraska Press, 1967.

Racial discrimination in the United States. New York: Harper & Row, 1975.

Rist, R. *The invisible children*. Cambridge, Mass.: Harvard University Press, 1978.

Sagar, H. A. *Stereotypes and attribution: The influence of racial and behavioral cues upon social perception*. Unpublished doctoral dissertation, University of Pittsburgh, 1979.

Sagar, H. A., & Schofield, J. W. Racial and behavioral cues in black and white children's perceptions of ambiguously aggressive acts. *Journal of Personality and Social Psychology*, in press.

Schatzman, L., & Strauss, A. *Field research: Strategies for a natural sociology*. Englewood Cliffs, N.J.: Prentice-Hall, 1973.

Scherer, J., & Slawski, E. L. *Coping with desegregation: Individual strategies and organizational compliance*. Unpublished manuscript Sociology Department, Oakland University, Rochester, Michigan, 1978.

Color, class and social control in an urban desegregated school. In R. C. Rist (Ed.), *Desegregated schools: Appraisals of an American experiment*. New York: Academic Press, 1979.

Schofield, J. W. *Social process and peer relations in a "nearly integrated" middle school.* (Contract No. 400-76-0011, 1977.) Final project report for the National Institute of Education, 1977.

School desegregation and intergroup relations. In D. Bar-Tal and L. Saxe (Eds.), *Social psychology of education: Theory and research.* Washington, D. C.: Hemisphere Press, 1978.

Behind closed doors: Race relations in an American school. New York: Praeger Publishers, in press.

The impact of positively structured contact on intergroup behavior: Does it last under adverse conditions? *Social Psychology Quarterly,* 1979, *42,* 280–284.

Schofield, J. W., & Sagar, H. A. Peer interaction patterns in an integrated middle school. *Sociometry,* 1977, *40,* 130–138.

The social context of learning in an interracial school. In R. C. Rist (Ed.), *Desegregated schools: Appraisals of an American experiment.* New York: Academic Press, 1979.

Secord, P. F., & Backman, C. W. *Social psychology.* New York: McGraw-Hill, 1964.

Sherif, M. Superordinate goals in the reduction of intergroup conflict: An experimental evaluation. In W. G. Austin & S. Worchel (Eds.), *The social psychology of intergroup relations.* Monterey, Cal.: Brooks/Cole, 1979.

Silverman, I., & Shaw, M. E. Effects of sudden mass school desegregation on interracial interaction and attitudes in one southern city. *Journal of Social Issues,* 1973, *29*(4), 133–142.

Singleton, L., & Asher, S. Peer preferences and social interaction among third-grade children in an integrated school district. *Journal of Educational Psychology,* 1977, *69,* 330–336.

Racial integration and children's peer preferences: An investigation of developmental and cohort differences. *Child Development,* 1979, *50,* 936–941.

Slavin, R. E. Cooperative learning. *Review of Educational Research,* 1980, *50,* 315–342.

St. John, N. *School desegregation: Outcomes for children.* New York: Wiley, 1975.

St. John, N., & Lewis, R. Race and the social structure of the elementary classroom. *Sociology of Education,* 1975, *48,* 346–368.

Stephan, W. G. School desegregation: An evaluation of predictions made in *Brown* vs. *Board of Education. Psychological Bulletin,* 1978, *85,* 217–238.

Sullivan, M. L. Contacts among cultures: School desegregation in a polyethnic New York City high school. In R.C. Rist (Ed.), *Desegregated schools: Appraisals of an American experiment.* New York: Academic Press, 1979.

Taylor, S., Fiske, S., Etcoff, N., & Ruderman, A. Categorical and contextual bases of person memory and stereotyping. *Journal of Personality and Social Psychology,* 1978, *36,* 778–793.

Webb, E. J., Campbell, D. T., Schwartz, R. D., & Sechrest, L. *Unobtrusive measures: Nonreactive research in the social sciences.* Chicago, Ill.: Rand McNally, 1966.

Willie, C. *Race mixing in the public schools.* New York: Praeger Publishers, 1973.

Worchel, S. Cooperation and the reduction of intergroup conflict: Some determining factors. In W. G. Austin & S. Worchel (Eds.), *The social psychology of intergroup relations.* Monterey, Cal.: Brooks/Cole, 1979.

4   Recent advances in sociometry

Maureen T. Hallinan

Introduction

Sociometry is one of the oldest traditions within which social scientists have examined friendship bonds. Beginning with the ideas of Moreno (1953) and their application in the empirical studies of Moreno (1953) and Jennings (1950), sociometry has become a popular way of studying social relationships.

Strictly speaking, the term "sociometry" refers to a research method. Sociometry is defined as the measurement of social relations; it is a technique for collecting data about interpersonal choices, especially friendship choices of group members. A sociometric questionnaire is an instrument that asks respondents to name or identify those group members who satisfy a preference criterion, such as liking or esteem. Frequently asked sociometric questions are "Who are your best friends," "Who would you prefer to sit next to," and "Who do you like to play with?"

The term "sociometry" also has a more general meaning: It is often used to describe the study of social relations. Research studies in which data from a sociometric questionnaire are analyzed are often called sociometric studies. According to this usage, sociometry is more than a data collection technique; it is a body of research resulting from the analysis of data on preference choices.

Early sociometric studies were concerned with distribution of popularity or the number of friendship choices received by group members. Moreno (1953) used the terms "sociometric star," "neglectee," and "social isolate" to describe persons receiving many, few, or no choices, respectively, in a group. Most sociometric studies tried to relate ascribed and achieved characteristics of individuals to the positions they occupied in the friendship structure of a group. Rarely was the distribution of

Much of the research reported here was supported by grants from the National Institute of Mental Health and the Spencer Foundation.

friendliness examined or the number of choices given. These early studies were conducted primarily in the classroom, because of an overriding interest in children's popularity, a concern for helping children gain acceptance in a group, and the accessibility of the data. In general, these studies failed to reveal causal processes or to describe the dynamics of friendship formation, maintenance, and dissolution.

Over the past ten years, social scientists have renewed their interest in sociometry as a tool for understanding friendship. A new set of sociometric questions have been formulated and researchers have tried to link respondents' answers to these questions to theories of interpersonal attraction and friendship. More appropriate research designs and more powerful statistical techniques have been developed to aid in collecting and analyzing sociometric data.

The present chapter describes some of these recent advances in sociometry. It is written from a sociological perspective and is limited to the sociological tradition. The chapter is divided into three parts. The first section describes some of the research questions sociometricians currently ask about friendship. It includes a discussion of individual, situational, and structural determinants of friendship choice. The second section outlines recent developments in sociometric methodology, with particular attention to new statistical techniques for analyzing sociometric data. The last section presents the findings of selected sociometric studies that employ recent advances in sociometric methodology to study substantive questions that have been neglected in the past.

Current research interests in sociometry

Initially sociometricians were interested primarily in correlates of popularity and unpopularity. Not unlike research on the "great man theory" of leadership (see Gibb, 1954), early sociometric studies aimed at identifying constellations of personality and social traits that characterized individuals occupying different positions in the social system. Research on the social structure of the classroom showed that popular students generally possessed valued resources such as physical attractiveness, a high level of intelligence, academic achievement, athletic ability, and high social class. Unpopular students were found to have fewer talents and social skills and less social awareness than their peers. In describing the characteristics of social isolates, sociometry had a therapeutic intent. It aimed at helping teachers devise methods to integrate unpopular children into the social structure of a group. A review of this early literature is found in Glidewell et al. (1966).

Most of the early sociometric studies were atheoretical: They simply presented descriptions of friendship patterns or identified correlates of friendship choices. Some studies referred vaguely to a conceptual framework but failed to link the research questions and hypotheses to that framework. Only rarely did sociometry rely on theories of interpersonal attraction for explanations and predictions of findings.

Beginning in the late 1960s, attention shifted within sociology from an interest in the position of an individual in the friendship structure of a group to a concern with the determinants of friendship choice: that is, friendliness (number of friendship choices made) and popularity (number of friendship choices received). This change in perspective was partly due to a failure of previous studies to explain the development of social structure or to generate new research questions. It also may have reflected disillusionment with the idea that sociometry could suggest methods of changing social relations in the classroom.

The shift in focus to determinants of friendship choice created a new interest in sociometry and stimulated a number of research studies. In particular, researchers began to investigate the effects of individual, situational, and structural variables on the selection of friends. Study of the determinants of friendship choice was facilitated by the development of powerful mathematical and statistical techniques for analyzing sociometric data. The use of multivariate models made possible an examination of the differential impact of individual and group-level variables on friendship choice as well as a comparison of the determinants of friendliness and popularity. In this section of the chapter, theoretical developments in research on individual, situational, and structural effects on friendliness and popularity will be discussed.

Individual-level determinants of friendship choice

Several individual-level variables have been related to friendship choice. Among these are sex, race, academic achievement, age, and socioeconomic status. Although early sociometric studies correlated these variables with popularity or looked at the incidence of cross-sex or cross-race friendships, they generally failed to examine causal relationships among the variables.

Some of the recent research on individual-level effects of friendship relies on theories of interpersonal attraction to govern the selection of independent variables and to explain observed results. The most popular theoretical explanations of interpersonal attraction are balance theory (Heider, 1958), with its subsequent reconceptualizations (Festinger, 1957;

Newcomb, 1961), and social exchange theory (Blau, 1974; Homans, 1974; Thibaut & Kelley, 1959). These theories propose several bases of attraction: proximity, similarity, complementarity, status, and reciprocity. Recent studies have attempted to examine the effects on friendship choice of individual-level characteristics that are related to these bases of attraction.

Questions about similarity and status effects on friendship underlie some of the recent work in sociometry. Children are likely to select as friends those peers who are similar to themselves in relevant characteristics such as sex, race, or achievement. They may also use these characteristics to identify classmates who have higher rank or status than themselves. Similarity is expected to affect friendship by providing a basis for each person to validate his social identity (Schachter, 1959), by reducing potential conflicts (Sherif et al., 1961), and by increasing each person's approval of the other (Newcomb, 1961). Status effects on friendship are expected because high-status individuals tend to win the esteem and affection of their peers by conforming more closely to group norms (Homans, 1950). Moreover, friendship with a higher-status person is likely to be rewarding, because that person's prestige extends to his or her friends.

One question currently being asked (Tuma & Hallinan, 1979) is whether similarity or status is more salient to students as a basis for the selection of friends. It is possible that both factors influence friendship choice but that status plays a greater role in the formation of a friendship whereas similarity exerts a greater influence on the stability of a relationship. Because status characteristics are highly visible, they may be most influential during the initial contacts with a person. Children's similarities may be more important in the continuation of a friendship.

A status characteristic that is receiving particular attention is race. It is widely reported that children's friendships divide along racial lines, although less sharply than on the basis of sex (St. John & Lewis, 1975; Singleton & Asher, 1977). At the same time, academic achievement and race tend to be significantly related in the classroom (Coleman et al., 1966), and some previous evidence (e.g., Hargreaves, 1972) indicates that children's achievement influences friendship choices. Hence racial cleavage in friendship may be partly the result of differences in academic achievement. A critical task of researchers is to separate the effects of academic achievement from the tendency to make same-race friendships. This would make possible a more accurate assessment of the impact of school desegregation programs on cross-race friendliness.

Most previous sociometric studies ignored age as a factor in the formation of friendships except by occasionally comparing friendship patterns across grades. The effects of age on friendships within the classroom were largely ignored, because the age variation within a classroom was small. However, with the growing prevalence of ungraded classrooms in elementary schools, it is now possible to determine whether age acts as a status characteristic for children in the selection of their friends. If children primarily select same-age friends, then ungraded classrooms may be less effective than previously believed in fostering children's social development. Research on cross-age interactions shows that the content of children's interactions changes with the magnitude of the age difference between the children (Shatz & Gelman, 1973) and that social learning and modeling occur more effectively across age groups (Peifer, 1971; Thelen & Kirkland, 1976). How age differences affect friendship remains to be studied.

Sex is widely regarded as a status characteristic in the larger society. However, little is known about the effects of sex on friendship choice in the classroom except for a frequently documented "sex cleavage": that is, the restriction of children's friendship choices to classmates of the same gender. If sex does have status value for children, one may question whether being male is assigned a higher value than being female, as has typically been the case among adults. It may be that children assign a greater status value to being female because it is associated with higher academic achievement or greater maturity (Maccoby & Jacklin, 1974). A close examination of determinants of cross-sex friendship choices would shed some light on this issue. On the other hand, a sex cleavage may simply demonstrate a preference for similarity with one's friends, at least among elementary-school children. If sex is a status characteristic for children, its value may change with age. This could be a partial explanation of the increased number of cross-sex friendships among older children and in some elementary classrooms. Current research on the basis for sex cleavage should provide a better understanding of the role of sex in friendship choice.

Situational determinants of friendship choice

Most early sociometric studies were conducted in traditional classrooms. In these settings, student interaction was generally limited. Structural characteristics of traditional classrooms imposed constraints on students' behavior and largely determined the content, frequency, and duration of their interactions. Recently, researchers have questioned the appropriateness of generalizing the results of these studies to other types of classrooms (Epstein & McPartland, 1975; Hallinan, 1974). Attention has begun to focus on the effects on friendship of situational variables that alter the amount of student interaction in the classroom. Among these variables are the organization of the classroom and the assignment of students to groups for instructional purposes.

Traditionally organized classrooms constrain student interaction more than other kinds of classroom structures (Adams & Biddle, 1970; Brophy & Good, 1970). Students are generally assigned to particular stationary desks where they remain for much of the school day. Seating patterns necessitate that students interact with the few students who sit near them when they are permitted to talk. In traditional classrooms, children are grouped homogeneously by ability and are often segregated by age and sometimes by sex. On the other hand, open classrooms are characterized by frequent student interaction. For the purpose of this discussion, open classrooms are defined as those without rigid homogeneous grouping practices and that encourage joint student activity. Children in open classrooms are typically free to move about the room and interact with whomever they please. The nature of task assignments often encourages prolonged student interaction about work activities. Students periodically go to a resource center in the classroom for informal discussion.

The assignment of students to instructional groups within the classroom also affects their interaction patterns (Hallinan & Tuma, 1978). In traditional classrooms, students rarely work in subgroups; they remain together as a whole class for instruction. In open classrooms, children are generally assigned to one or more task groups based on criteria decided upon by the teacher or by the children themselves. Small-group instruction imposes proximity on some students and increases the likelihood that they will interact. Instruction in groups is also associated with a general tendency for the interaction level of the whole class to increase. The degree of task homogeneity within small groups also affects interaction. Being assigned the same task and the same instructional materials provides group members with reasons for talking and working together and creates common experiences.

Given the effect of classroom organization and grouping practices on student interaction, the question that arises is: To what extent do opportunities for interaction in the classroom affect children's friendship choices? One would anticipate that, in traditional classrooms with limited student interaction, a rigid status hierarchy based on student performance would emerge. Children who perform well are likely to receive many friendship choices, and those who perform poorly may receive few. On the other hand, in open classrooms the frequent interaction among students and the diversity of their activities probably alter the components of status and stimulate the development of different status systems. The wide variety of activities is likely to increase every child's chance of succeeding in at least one activity. At the same time, the chance of a child's excelling in all activities is small. To the extent that status accruing from success in classroom activities is associated with friendship choice, one would expect a more even distribution of popularity in open classrooms. Some evidence supporting these conjectures is found in Hallinan (1974) and Felmlee and Hallinan (1979).

Besides affecting the status system in a classroom, grouping practices and classroom organization are also expected to influence the extent to which similarity is a basis for friendship choice. The criterion employed to assign students to instructional groups draws attention to, or even exaggerates, existing similarities. An example is grouping by ability. Grouping practices can also create new similarities among children by involving them in the same tasks. This suggests that children assigned to the same groups or working together on classroom activities are more likely to become friends than students who do not have these opportunities. A study by Hallinan and Tuma (1978) supports these predictions.

Another important organizational variable believed to influence friendship choice is class size. Large class size increases the number of students in a class who have similar ascribed and achieved characteristics. In large classes students are more likely to meet peers who resemble themselves in relevant traits. To the extent that similarity is a basis of interpersonal attraction, children in large classes are expected to have more friends than those in small classes. At the same time, fewer cross-sex friendships are expected in large classes since students have more same-sex peers with whom to establish friendships. The number of social isolates may also decrease as class size increases, presumably because the chance of meeting compatible peers increases. On the other hand, some impressive evidence has been found that social isolation increases with class size (Barker & Gump, 1964).

A related question is how the racial composition of a class affects the friendship choices of black and white students. If friendship is based on similarity, one would expect that increasing the number of students of one race in a class would increase the friendliness of those students within their racial group. Moreover, increasing the number of black students should increase the probability that white students will find black peers whom they would like to have as friends. Similarly, the larger the number of white students in a classroom, the greater the likelihood that black children will make cross-race friendships. All of these questions are currently being researched; initial results demonstrate a powerful effect of situational variables on friendship patterns. Some of this evidence will be discussed in the section of this chapter on illustrative empirical studies.

Structural determinants of friendship choice

Most of the previous empirical work on friendship focused on individual- and organizational-level determinants of friendship choice. Rarely was a study concerned with the effects on friendship of structural or network properties; that is, patterns of interpersonal relationships among group members. Concern with network effects on friendship is a recent interest of sociometricians that emerges as part of a growing body of literature on properties of social networks and the dynamics of change in network structure over time.

A question that arises about network effects on friendship choice is how the structure of the set of relationships in which an individual's choice is embedded affects that individual's selection of friends. For example, a reciprocity effect (a tendency to reciprocate a friendship choice) could influence friendship choice if the other member of the dyad had already chosen the individual as a friend. Similarly, a transitivity effect (a tendency to restore balance) in a triad could lead a person to make a friendship choice in order to restore psychological or cognitive balance in the triad. Reciprocity and transitivity effects are among the structural properties most frequently studied by sociometricians (e.g., Hallinan, 1974, 1979a; Holland & Leinhardt, 1970).

A related question concerns whether characteristics of individuals or situations influence or modify structural effects on friendship choice. For example, is academic achievement related to a tendency to restore balance in a triad? This question has received attention only recently in network studies. Several individual-level characteristics are likely to interact with network properties to affect the selection of friends. It has been shown, for example, that sex interacts with a reciprocity effect to determine the likelihood that a friendship is reciprocated (Eder & Hallinan, 1978). Girls were found to be more reluctant to make choices that would expand their social network than boys for reasons that may have to do with socialization and the nature of their play activities.

Theories of cognitive consistency (Abelson et al., 1968), balance (Heider, 1958), and exchange (Homans, 1974; Thibaut & Kelley, 1959) suggest that the amount of interaction in a classroom affects the incidence of certain kinds of dyadic and triadic relationships. The psychological discomfort believed to result from unreciprocated friendship choices and from involvement in unbalanced triadic relationships is greatest when members are interacting face to face. The frequent intermingling and sharing of tasks in an open classroom should serve to deter these sociometric connections, because students are likely to avoid forming uncomfortable relationships or to resolve them more quickly when there are more opportunities to interact and where maintaining uncomfortable relationships could be a lasting source of stress.

Finally, questions arise about larger configurations of relationships within a social network. How cliques form and how their members are characterized is a particular interest of social psychologists. Cliques are viewed as one of the most powerful agents of the peer influences process. Recently, researchers (e.g., Cohen, 1977; Hallinan, 1979b) have examined the size and stability of cliques in various situations, the relationship of less popular class members to clique members, sex and race cleavage in cliques across age groups, and the relationship of newcomers to a group to members of existing cliques.

Developments in methodology

This section of this chapter outlines a number of recent developments in methods of collecting and analyzing sociometric data. It focuses on the construction of a sociometric questionnaire and on mathematical and statistical techniques for data analysis.

The sociometric questionnaire

Respondents to a sociometric questionnaire are asked to designate which members of a group they prefer based on a selected criterion. The responses are usually treated as binary data and coded as unity if a choice is made and zero if a choice is absent. A typical sociometric variable is a person's choice or nonchoice of another group member as a friend.

Measurement error can be introduced into sociometric data in a number of ways. One possible source of error is the choice criterion. The sociometric question may be based on a unidimensional or a multidimensional concept. Friendship, which is a multidimensional concept, is often measured by the questions "Who do you prefer to sit next to?" or "Who do you prefer to play with?" These questions may elicit different responses from subjects, because they measure different aspects of friendship. If a sociometric question taps only one dimension of a multidimensional concept, a respondent's choice list is likely to be incomplete. A preferred strategy is to ask multiple questions directed at the several dimensions of a concept. An alternative is to ask a more general question, such as "Who is your friend?"

Another concern in constructing a sociometric questionnaire is the validity of the instrument. A question such as "Who do you prefer to work with?'' has often been used to measure friendship. This question may actually be measuring esteem or admiration. Care must be taken to ensure that a sociometric questionnaire has construct and content (face and sampling) validity. One approach would be to validate sociometric data on friendship by observational methods.

Recently researchers have pooled sociograms based on different choice criteria to obtain large samples for tests of structural models. An example of a structural model is the transitivity model whose structure contains no intransitive triads (e.g., Davis, 1970; Holland & Leinhardt, 1970). Pooling has drawn attention to problems of measurement error in sociometric data and to questions about the validity of a sociometric instrument. The pooling of sociograms is likely to introduce considerable error when the sociograms are based on different questionnaires measuring different concepts or when some of the sociograms are based on multidimensional concepts measured by single questions. The errors are compounded as the number of sociograms pooled increases. The recent development of blockmodeling (to be discussed later) will further sensitize sociometricans to possible error in their data, because use of blockmodeling on sociometric data illustrates that different structures emerge when different choice criteria are used.

Another potential source of error in sociometric data is the format of the questionnaire. The three most familiar types of sociometric questionnaires are fixed choice, free choice, and ranking technique. In a fixed-choice questionnaire, respondents are asked to name a set number of group members who satisfy some preference criterion. Most typically three names are requested: for example, name your three best friends. In a free-choice questionnaire, the subjects are asked to list as many group members as satisfy the preference criterion: for example, name all your best friends. A ranking technique requires the respondents to rank some or all of the group members in order of preference on the designated criterion.

The type of technique employed to collect sociometric data can be the source of response error. (Little evidence is available about the reliability or validity of these techniques.) Holland and Leinhardt (1973) and Hallinan (1974) discussed various ways that a fixed-choice questionnaire might produce error. Constraining the number of responses might lead some subjects to select group members who did not satisfy the choice criterion in order to provide the required number of responses. The choice limitation may lead other respondents to exclude some names that satisfy the criterion. Both conditions are types of response error.

A ranking technique may be the source of a different kind of response error. A partial or complete ranking procedure assumes that it is possible for subjects to rank order group members on the choice criterion. While this may be true for some subjects, others may find ranking a difficult or meaningless task. The responses of these subjects are likely to contain error. Response error in a ranking technique may be reduced when respondents are allowed to make ties.

A free-choice sociometric questionnaire is less vulnerable to response error than a fixed-choice questionnaire or ranking procedure. Nevertheless, error may be introduced in the administration of the questionnaire. If the verbal instructions of the test administrator or the form of the questionnaire suggest that a certain number of responses are expected, error similar to that found with fixed-choice data is likely to appear. Moreover, if it is not clear to the respondents that they may name all or none of the group members if they prefer, then they may answer incorrectly in order to adhere to a norm of having a few friends among one's classmates.

While response error has always been a concern of sociometricians, it is a more serious problem in current analyses that employ a network structure, such as a dyad or triad, as the unit of analysis. For example, in a group of size n containing $n (n - 1) (n - 2) /3!$ triads, if a child makes one incorrect choice (compared to the child's true sentiments), that error appears in $(n - 1) (n - 2) /3!$ triads. Thus if a group contains 20 members, a single error affects 57 observations.

A recently devised sociometric technique (Hallinan, 1974) currently employed in some studies tends to reduce measurement and response error. Subjects are given a list of the names of group members. After each name are the words Best Friend, Friend, Don't Know. The respondent is asked to circle the correct response for each name on the list. This technique is similar to a ranking procedure with ties, but it allows the respondent to decide how many classmates to put in each category. Names may be ranked within the Best Friend and Friend categories, allowing for ties, if desired. This procedure is appropriate for collecting data on best friends or friends. Furthermore, the categories can be modified for other criteria. It will be noted that the technique does not allow for negative sentiment. Most social scientists have considerable difficulty obtaining data on negative affect because authorities – especially school personnel – are reluctant to have questions asked that might elicit unfriendly or hostile feelings. This is a loss, because positive and negative scores are often not highly correlated.

Methods of analysis

Until recently, analyses of sociometric data were limited to tabular or graphic descriptions of choice data. The most frequently used technique for presentation of data was the sociogram, in which points represented persons and directed arrows represented choices. The visual analysis of sociograms was unsatisfactory for several reasons. The arrangement of points in a graph was subjective, making comparisons across sociograms difficult. Moreover, if a group was large and had many choices, a graph representation was extremely cumbersome.

Another typical way of presenting sociometric data was in a sociomatrix. The rows of a sociomatrix contain choices from one individual to other members of a group and the columns contain choices to the individual in the group. Sociomatrixes are more easily analyzed than sociograms. They have the advantage of being manipulable by laws of matrix algebra. Techniques were developed to identify clique members, liaison persons, and isolates through algebraic operations on the sociomatrixes (Harary & Ross, 1957). However, most of these techniques require reciprocal choice data, and because sociometric data seldom contain only mutual choices, their applicability is limited.

Early work by sociometricians also included attempts to identify structural properties of a graph by comparing the incidence of dyad types to their frequency in a random graph. Katz, Taguiri, and Wilson (1958) used this approach to study a tendency toward mutuality in sociometric data. Sociometricians did little else with random graphs until the late 1960s and 1970s. Interest was renewed when Holland and Leinhardt (1970) developed a procedure for comparing the observed number of intransitive triads in a sociogram to the number expected by chance. Subsequent empirical studies used this approach (Felmlee & Hallinan, 1979; Hallinan, 1974). Although this method has the advantage of eliminating chance as an explanation for observed structural properties, it is not without methodological problems. An unresolved issue is the question of selecting appropriate controls for a random graph. In Holland and Leinhardt's random model, group size and the number of mutual, asymmetric, and null choices in a sociogram were controlled. However, these controls are not adequate. Because asymmetry, mutuality, and transitivity are interdependent structural properties, any random model that controls for two of these configurations necessarily underestimates the strength of a tendency toward the third property, as demonstrated by Hallinan and Sørensen (1973). Considerably more work must be done on random models before they can be used with confidence to identify components of group structure. When structural properties are to be compared across groups, a random model is inadequate. A more appropriate technique is a deterministic model that yields a ratio between the incidence of the observed property and the maximum or minimum number of similar configurations possible in a group of that size.

Factor analysis attained some popularity in the 1960s as a device for analyzing sociometric data, particularly for identifying friendship cliques. This method is based on the notion that persons belonging to the same clique are likely to give and receive choices among themselves and to ignore other group members. Factors are constructed to account for the variance in choices across group members. Members load on the different factors in proportion to the amount they vary with the factors. Overlapping cliques and social isolates can be detected. A critique of this method is found in Hubbell (1965). Factor analysis is used infrequently today because more sophisticated scaling techniques have become available.

More recently, multidimensional scaling and cluster analysis have been used to analyze sociometric data, especially ranked data or weighted choices (e.g., Elliott & Hallinan, 1975). In multidimensional scaling, a metric is defined to establish the distance between any two individuals. A straightforward metric may be obtained for ranked sociometric data by assuming that as the value or rank increases, the degree of closeness or friendliness of the two individuals decreases. Members of a group are located in a dimensional space, and those who are within a given radius are defined as belonging to the same clique.

One of the most recent techniques developed for the analysis of cross-sectional sociometric data is blockmodeling (White et al., 1976). The aim of blockmodeling is to abstract the structure of a group based on several different social ties or relationships. Members of a group are partitioned into subsets in such a way that members of a subset are approximately equivalent in their relationships to each other and the subsets themselves occupy a similar place in the group structure across the various group ties. While one of the advantages of blockmodeling is that it permits considerable data reduction, one can question the meaning of the structure obtained from pooling several diverse ties. A strong theoretical framework is essential before blockmodeling is used for structural analysis other than the simplest application of the technique to the detection of cliques based on a unidimensional relationship.

Over the last few years, multivariate techniques have been introduced to examine determinants of friendship choice and to study factors affecting the incidence of structural properties in a graph. A linear regression model can be used to regress a person's choice of another group member on characteristics of the chooser, the person chosen, and situational variables. The dependent variable in this kind of analysis is a dichotomous variable representing a person's choice or nonchoice of another. Using a dummy dependent variable in a regression analysis can present a number of methodological problems. These include heteroskedasticity, which causes ordinary least squares estimates to be inefficient, and the possibility of predicting probabilities to be greater than unity or less than zero. These problems are less serious when the sample size is large and when the mean of the dependent variable is close to one half. Under these conditions, use of a linear regression model with a dichotomous dependent variable is acceptable when the aim of the research is to identify variables that influence the process of friendship selection. More sophisticated models are needed to obtain precise estimates of the effects of the exogenous variables on friendship choice.

A linear regression model can also be used to study individual and situational effects on network structure. The incidence of particular network configurations, such as mutuality in dyads or intransitivity in triads, can be regressed on individual and situational independent variables. In one study using this approach, the dependent variable was deviation from randomness: that is, the difference between the number of intransitive triads observed in a group and the number expected by chance (Leinhardt, 1972). However, when a statistical index based on a random model is used as the dependent variable rather than the actual frequency of a structural property, the results merely show whether a relationship exists between the independent variables and the probability of obtaining the observed property by chance. It is preferable to employ the observed frequency of a configuration as the dependent variable in order to establish an association between the property and its hypothesized predictors.

All of the techniques described above, with the exception of a regresssion model with lagged variables, are static models designed for the analysis of cross-sectional data. Currently, more powerful dynamic models are being employed for the analysis of longitudinal sociometric data. In an early study, Katz and Proctor (1959) employed a discrete time Markov model to analyze change in dyadic relationships. Significant advances in the study of stochastic processes have been made since that time, particularly in the development and application of continuous time stochastic models (e.g., Singer & Spilerman, 1976). One advantage of these models is that they permit change in friendship choice to occur at any time rather than only at discrete time intervals. Stochastic models are currently being used to examine change in structural properties over time. Sørensen and Hallinan (1976) estimated the parameters of a continuous time stationary Markov model to study change in triads over time. Hallinan (1979a) used a similar model to observe dyadic change. Wasserman (1979) formulated two models that permit the estimation of reciprocity and popularity effects on change in dyadic relationships. These latter two studies demonstrated a tendency for persons to reciprocate friendship offers.

The last section of this chapter will present selected sociometric studies that ask theoretical questions about friendship, demonstrate new methodologies, and report important findings about children's friendships in the classroom. These studies will be divided into three categories: studies examining the effects of individual characteristics on friendship choices, studies investigating the effects of situational variables on friendship choices, and network studies.

Illustrative empirical studies

Effects of individual characteristics on friendship choice

In a recent longitudinal study, Tuma and Hallinan (1979) examined the effects of sex, race, age, and academic achievement on the formation, stability, and dissolution of schoolchildren's friendships. These independent variables were selected to demonstrate how status and similarity influence friendship choice. Sociometric data were obtained from fourth-grade, fifth-grade and sixth-grade children in eighteen classrooms in two public elementary schools. The classes were similar in size (approximately twenty-five students), sex composition (about half female) and socioeconomic status (lower- to lower-middle class). Ten classes were about 80 percent black and 20 percent white, and the remaining eight classes were almost entirely black. The data were collected five times during the 1975–76 school year, at six-week intervals. The modified ranking technique with individual cutoff points described earlier was employed to obtain the data. Responses were classified as best friend, friend, and nonfriend.

A linear regression model was employed to analyze the data. The dichotomous dependent variable represented P's choice of O at a point in time. This was coded as unity if P chose O as a best friend and zero otherwise. P's choice of O at the preceding data collection was a critical variable that was expected to interact with the effects of the children's individual characteristics. Consequently, separate analyses were performed for each of P's possible choices of O at the previous time point. In other words, the data were divided into three samples, each of which contained those dyads in which P chose O as best friend, friend, or nonfriend at the previous time point. Classroom characteristics and an effect of O's choice of P at the previous time point (reciprocity effect) were controlled for.

The study showed that similarity of sex had a significant positive effect on increased friendliness. In other words, when P and O were of the same sex, their choices were more likely to change from nonfriend to friend or from friend to best friend. Moreover, similarity of sex had a statistically significant effect on the stability of friend and best-friend choices. Cross-sex friendship choices were markedly less stable than same-sex choices. Status effects of sex were found to be different than in the larger society. Change to a closer friendship choice was less likely when O was male. This result may be interpreted as a status effect if female is viewed as higher status than male. This is possible in an elementary classroom, where girls tend to conform more closely to teachers' expectations for appropriate attitudes and behaviors and often attain higher levels of academic achievement than boys. On the other hand, it may simply be that boys value intimacy less than girls do.

Racial similarity had no significant effect on any type of change in friendship choice. However, racial effects were observed. Black children were more likely to change to friendlier relations than whites: that is, to change from "know" to "friend" or from "friend" to "best friend." Moreover, P's choice of O as best friend was more stable when O was black. This finding suggests that if race is viewed by the students as a status characteristic, then black is more highly valued than white in these classrooms. This is not surprising in majority-black schools. This result needs to be examined in classrooms with greater racial balance.

Academic achievement had both similarity and status effects on the stability of best friendships. The greater the difference in achievement levels of two students, the less stable was a best-friend choice between them, indicating an effect of similarity. A status effect was seen in that the higher the achievement of O the greater the stability of best friend choices directed to O. This finding suggests that children value the academic achievement of their peers and that achievement serves to foster friendly relations. The effects of age on change in friendship choice was small, possibly because there was little variation in age within the classrooms.

It is possible that the racial effects on friendship choice found in this study are peculiar to schools with a large black majority. Preliminary analysis of a more extensive data set recently collected by the same researchers supports some of the findings on racial effects found in the previous study (Hallinan & Tuma, 1979). Sociometric data were collected from forty-eight classes that varied in racial composition from all black to all white. Descriptive analyses of these data revealed that black children were considerably more friendly toward same-race and other-race peers than whites, regardless of the racial composition of the classroom.

Effects of situational variables on friendship choice

A recent study investigated friendship patterns in open and traditional classrooms (Hallinan, 1976). It was hypothesized that in open classrooms characterized by fairly unrestricted student interaction a less hierarchical distribution of friendship choices would be found than in traditional classrooms where student interaction was constrained. Frequent interaction in open classrooms was also expected to accelerate the formation of mutual friendships and to foster their stability. Cross-sectional and longitudinal data were collected using the modified ranking technique. The cross-sectional data were obtained from fifty-one classes of fifth- to eighth-grade students in fourteen schools. Twelve of the classes were classified as open, twenty-five as semiopen, and fourteen as traditional, based on Walberg and Thomas's (1972) scheme. The longitudinal data were gathered at six points over a school year from nine classes of fourth- through sixth-grade students. Three of these classrooms were classified as open, four as semiopen, and two as traditional. The data were analyzed first by comparing the hierarchy in each group to the distribution of choices in a random baseline model (Coleman, 1964), controlling for friendliness, or the number of choices given. The average duration of mutual friendship choices was obtained by estimating the parameters of a continuous-time Markov model.

The findings showed that friendship patterns consistently observed in traditional classrooms are modified in settings with less restricted interaction. The distribution of popularity in the traditional classrooms was highly skewed, but, as expected, it was considerably more uniform in the open classrooms. Fewer social isolates and fewer sociometric stars were found in the open classrooms. This result suggests that opportunities to become known and liked through interaction increase the probability of a child's receiving some friendship choices. Contrary to expectation, a significantly larger number of mutual choices was found in traditional classes than in the other types of classrooms, although mutual friendships were more stable in open classrooms. It may be that the exposure of students to a large number of potential friends in an open classroom leads them to be more selective in choosing their friends, resulting in a small number of actual friends. On the other hand, increased interaction may make students more realistic in selecting friends and lead them to choose only those peers with whom they expect to establish an enduring relationship. Children in traditional classes gave and received more friendship choices than those in open classrooms. If these results are generalizable, they present a dilemma to educators. Although open classrooms tend to decrease the number of social isolates, foster a more uniform distribution of popularity, and support the stability of friendship choices, traditional classrooms seem to promote a large number of friendships. Thus the study shows that both environments have advantages and disadvantages for children's social development.

Hypotheses about effects of grouping patterns on friendship were tested by Hallinan and Tuma (1978) in the sociometric data from eighteen classes described earlier. Two measures of opportunity to interact were employed: whether students had the same reading teacher, and percent of instructional time students spent in small groups. Similarity effects were measured by within- and between-group task homogeneity and by percent of time the membership of reading groups was based on student choice. The data were analyzed using a linear multiple regression model with a categorical dependent variable (P's choice of O as best friend, friend, or nonfriend). The model controlled for individual effects of sex, race, age, academic achievement, and O's choice of P at a previous time point. The findings showed that interaction opportunities – assignment to the same teacher and to small groups for instruction – had statistically significant positive effects on the formation and stability of friendship choices. Percent of time spent in small groups for reading had greater predictive power than any other classroom characteristic in the study. This result is particularly interesting, because it provides strong evidence that small-group interaction promotes close friendships and impedes the dissolution of friendships. The effect of task similarity within groups was positive but weak. Between-group task homogeneity as measured by students working on the same material and on the same tasks had a strong positive effect on increased friendliness. Finally, the more students were permitted to determine the membership of instructional groups, the greater the stability of close friendships and the greater tendency of students' choices of others to become friendlier.

This study has a number of important implications. First, the results show that teachers play a major role in the social development of students through decisions they make about methods of classroom instruction. The findings suggest ways instructional groups might be used to foster close interpersonal relationships. This policy implication is consistent with Moreno's initial intent that sociometry be used for therapeutic purposes (Moreno, 1953). The study also suggests a basis for evaluating classroom innovations. The conceptual framework and methodology employed here may be used to examine the effects of classroom innovations involving organizational change on children's friendship relations.

The effects of class size on friendship choices was examined by Hallinan (1979b) in cross-sectional sociometric data on the fifty-one groups described earlier. The study revealed that class size has a strong effect on children's friendships. The mean number of friendship choices given (friendliness) and received (popularity) increased significantly with class size. Fewer social isolates were found in large classes than in small classes. The number of cross-sex friendship choices decreased as class size increased. The findings show that large classes provide children with certain advantages in making friends. Nevertheless, sex was a greater deterrent to friendship choice in large classes.

Hallinan and Tuma (1979) examined the effects of classroom racial composition on children's friendliness in data from the forty-eight classes described above. The results showed that when the greater friendliness of blacks was taken into account, the proportion of cross-race friendships made by blacks and whites was approximately the same regardless of the racial composition of the classroom. While the same-race friendship choices of blacks and whites increased over a school year, the proportion of cross-race friendship choices remained fairly constant. Same-race friendliness increased with the number of same-race peers in a class, whereas friendliness toward members of another race increased with the number of students of that race in the class. In four racially balanced classrooms, whites made a slightly higher percentage of cross-race friendship choices than blacks, and whites' friendliness increased over time. In general, this study showed that neither blacks nor whites discriminated more on the basis of race in the selection of friends. It suggests that efforts to improve race relationships among children are likely to be more successful in large desegregated classrooms with significant numbers of black and white students than in smaller classrooms or those containing a small number of students of one race.

Network studies

A number of researchers have examined the effects of network structure on friendship choice. In a recent study, Hallinan (1979a) raised questions about the effect of dyadic structure on friendship. Longitudinal sociometric data from five fourth-, fifth-, and sixth-grade classes were examined to determine the relative stability of asymmetric and mutual friendship dyads and the nature of change in asymmetric dyads over time. A continuous-time stationary Markov model was used to analyze the data. The findings showed that unreciprocated friendship choices were less stable than reciprocated choices, a result that supports one of the propositions of balance theory. Moreover, unreciprocated choices tended to be withdrawn rather than reciprocated over time. Children's mutual friendships were found to be twice as stable as their unreciprocated friendship choices, but they endured on the average only about three months. This study shows that friendship is a dynamic interactive process in which change occurs frequently. The friendship choices of sixth-graders lasted

considerably longer than those of the younger children, suggesting that
friendships become more stable as persons grow older, or that the importance of friendship changes with age. On the other hand, older students
may simply have more opportunities to nurture their friendships outside
the classroom than younger children.

Models recently formulated by Wasserman (1979) permit estimation of
the effects of reciprocity and popularity on change in friendship choice in
dyads. The models can determine to what extent being chosen by a classmate affects a student's choice of that classmate and how receiving a large
number of choices from group members influences a person's tendency to
choose members of that group as friends. Wasserman tested these models
in an analysis of secondary data from Newcomb (1961) and Katz and
Proctor (1959). The results demonstrated significant positive effects of
reciprocity and popularity on choosing friends over time.

Sørensen and Hallinan (1976) examined structural effects on change in
friendship choices within triads. It was hypothesized that asymmetric
dyads and intransitive triads are unstable and tend to change quickly to
restore balance or transitivity. This hypothesis was tested on longitudinal
sociometric data from a sixth-grade class by estimating the parameters of
a continuous-time Markov model. The results strongly supported the prediction. Intransitivity and asymmetry were found to be major sources of
change in a social network. Friendship choices were quickly initiated or
withdrawn in order to restore structural balance. The study also showed
that progress toward cohesive group relations requires periods of intransitivity and asymmetry. These latter structural forces were seen to act as a
deterrent to the development of more cohesive networks.

Rarely have studies examined how individual or organizational characteristics interact with structural effects on friendship choice. Eder and
Hallinan (1978) looked at the effects of sex differences in the tendency of
a dyad member to select a third person in the group as a friend. It was
argued that girls are socialized to prefer smaller social groups than boys,
which should lead girls to be more exclusive in their friendship choices.
Girls who were mutual best friends were expected to be less likely to
initiate a friendship with a third person than boys in a best-friend dyad.
These relationships were examined in longitudinal sociometric data from
four sixth-grade and one fifth-grade class. The results provided clear support for the hypothesis. Comparisons of change in friendship choices over
time in triads containing a mutual best-friend dyad showed that the dyadic
friendships of girls were significantly more exclusive than those of boys.
The findings have important implications for sex differences in the development of children's social skills and for the ability of new students to
gain acceptance and establish friendships in a class.

An example of a sociometric study that looks at organizational effects on network structure is found in Hallinan (1979b). In this study, the size and stability of friendship cliques were related to class size, classroom organization, and grade. Longitudinal data from eleven fourth-, fifth-, and sixth-grade classes and cross-sectional data from fifty-one sixth-, seventh-, and eighth-grade classes were analyzed using Alba's 1972 technique for identifying cliques. The technique identifies maximal complete subgraphs (groups of children all of whom are connected to each other by mutual friendship choices). It then merges those subgraphs that have two-thirds of their members in common. Both the maximal complete subgraphs and the merged graphs are regarded as cliques. The number of cliques was expected to increase with class size and grade. The increased interaction in open classrooms was expected to produce more stable cliques.

The incidence of within-class cliques was somewhat less than anticipated; 29 percent of the classes contained no cliques at all. The number and size of the cliques that did occur increased with class size. Classroom organization had little effect on clique structure. The largest cliques were found in the sixth grade, suggesting that seventh- and eighth-grade students are becoming more exclusive in their relationships. Most of the cliques were unstable over the school year, and clique membership fluctuated to some extent. Thus the study demonstrated that classroom characteristics have a modest effect on patterns of cliquing; they exert a small influence on clique formation and stability.

Conclusions

Recent developments in sociometry indicate a revival of interest in a somewhat ignored field. After an initial period of popularity in the 1940s and 1950s, sociometry lost favor and was viewed as adding little to the body of research on interpersonal attraction and friendship. However, recent attempts to conceptualize the friendship process and efforts to derive new methods of analysis have restored the vitality of sociometry. As a result, the nature and scope of sociometric studies have expanded considerably.

While the quality of sociometric studies has improved significantly over the past few years, shortcomings still persist in sociometric research. It is likely that these limitations will be the focus of work over the next few years. A fairly consistent omission in sociometric studies is an examination of age as a factor in the development of friendships. Data are usually collected in classrooms, where little variation in students' ages are found. While sociometric studies have been performed in every grade at the elementary-school level, it is difficult to compare the results of these studies to determine how age affects friendships patterns. The studies are too often characterized by different research methods, different independent variables, and even different dependent variables to allow for valid cross-age comparisons. Even the incidence of cross-sex friendships has not been systematically examined across grade or age in an elementary school. Moreover, certain age groups remain understudied by sociometricians. Friendship data are less often collected in schools with departmentalized instruction, because of the difficulty in defining the boundaries of a group. Because departmentalized instruction is popular at the junior-high and high-school levels, fewer sociometric studies of older children are available. As a result, sociometric studies as yet do not provide a clear understanding of how the maturation process affects children's friendship patterns or how individual level characteristics such as sex and ability interact with age to influence friendships.

An outstanding characteristic of the current body of sociometric literature is its preoccupation with studies in the classroom. An obvious reason for this concentration is that the classroom is believed to define a natural boundary for a group. If this assumption is not valid, sociometric questionnaires that restrict choices to within the classroom are likely to be a source of measurement error. Only a few studies have tried to examine open groups or to let the groups be defined by the sociometric data themselves. Children's neighborhood friends or friends from other classes have largely been ignored. Other formal or informal groups of children, such as activity groups, clubs, and even students who ride the same school bus, also deserve attention. The study of larger and more open groups than those previously examined would reveal the differential effects of interaction inside and outside the classroom on friendship formation and stability. This research would inform arguments about the importance of neighborhood schools or the effects of busing on children's social development.

The quality of any body of empirical work rests, of course, on the strength of the theories on which it is based. Recent work in sociometry has been more theoretically oriented than was previous research. Nevertheless, further conceptualization of the friendship process is needed to improve explanations of sociometric findings and to guide the selection of variables. For example, it is not clear which ascribed and achieved characteristics of children are associated with status, or how status and similarity interact to produce attraction. Nor is it known how status, as defined by a teacher's reward system, affects students' evaluations of their peers. A more powerful theoretical model is needed to integrate current findings on status and similarity effects and to describe how the personal characteristics of students that relate to status and similarity affect their friendship choices.

Recent developments in sociometry have been encouraging and have restored confidence in sociometry as an important body of knowledge about friendship, particularly children's friendships. These efforts now point to a need for a long-range program of research that is theoretically oriented, methodologically sophisticated, and systematic in its examination of the process of friendship formation and dissolution.

References

Abelson, R., Aronson, E., McGuire, W., Newcomb, T., Rosenberg, M., & Tannenbaum, P. (Eds.). *Theories of cognitive consistency: A sourcebook.* Chicago: Rand McNally, 1968.

Adams, R. S., & Biddle, B. J. *Realities of teaching: Explorations with videotape.* New York: Holt, Rinehart & Winston, 1970.

Alba, R. D. COMPLT – A program for analyzing sociometric data and clustering similarity matrices. *Behavioral Science,* 1972, *17,* 566–567.

Barker, R. G., & Gump, P. *Big school, small school.* Stanford, Cal.: Stanford University Press, 1964.

Blau, P. M. *Exchange and power in social life.* New York: Wiley, 1974.

Brophy, J. E. & Good, T. L. Teachers' communication of differential expectations for children's classroom performance. *Journal of Educational Psychology,* 1970, *61,* 365–374.

Cohen, J. Sources of peer homogeneity. *Sociology of Education,* 1977, *50,* 227–241.

Coleman, J. S. *Introduction to mathematical sociology.* New York: Free Press, 1964.

Coleman, J. S., Campbell, E. Q., Hobson, C. J., McPartland, J., Mood, A. M., Weinfeld, F. D., & York, R. L. *Equality of educational opportunity.* Washington, D. C.: Office of Education, U.S. Department of Health, Education, and Welfare. U.S. Government Printing Office, 1966.

Davis, J. A. Clustering and hierarchy in interpersonal relations: Testing two-graph theoretical models on 742 sociomatrices. *American Sociological Review,* 1970, *35,* 843–851.

Eder, G., & Hallinan, M. Sex differences in children's friendships. *American Sociological Review,* 1978, *43,* 237–250.

Elliott, G., & Hallinan, M. *An analysis of group structure by sociometric and multidimensional scaling techniques.* Unpublished manuscript, University of Wisconsin-Madison, April 1975.

Epstein, J. L., & McPartland, J. *The effects of open school organization on student outcomes.* Center for Social Organization of Schools, The Johns Hopkins University, April 1975 (Report No. 194).

Felmlee, D., & Hallinan, M. The effect of classroom interaction on children's friendships. *Journal of Classroom Interaction,* 1979, *14,* 1–8.

Festinger, L. *A theory of cognitive dissonance.* Evanston, Ill.: Row, Peterson, 1957.

Gibb, C. Leadership. In G. Lindzey, (Ed.), *Handbook of social psychology* (Vol. 2). Cambridge, Mass.: Addison-Wesley, 1954.

Glidewell, J., Kantor, M. B., Smith, L. M., & Stringer, L. A. Socialization and social structure in the classroom. In M. L. Hoffman & L. W. Hoffman (Eds.), *Review of child development research* (Vol. 2). New York: Russell Sage Foundation, 1966.

Hallinan, M. T. *The structure of positive sentiment.* New York: Elsevier, 1974.
  Friendship patterns in open and traditional classrooms. *Sociology of Education,* 1976, *49,*
  254–265.
  The process of friendship formation. *Social Networks,* 1979, 193–210. (a)
  Structural effects on children's friendships and cliques. *Social Psychology,* 1979, *42,* 43–
  54.(b)
Hallinan, M. T., & Sørensen, A. *Measuring transitivity in sociometric networks.* Working
  paper 73-19. Center for Demography and Ecology. University of Wisconsin-Madison,
  1973.
Hallinan, M. T., & Tuma, N. Race differences in children's friendliness. *Sociology of Edu-
  cation,* 1978, *51,* 270–282.
  Classroom effects on change in children's friendships. Mimeographed paper, Department
  of Sociology, University of Wisconsin-Madison, 1979.
Harary, F., & Ross, I. A procedure for clique detection using the group matrix. *Sociometry,*
  1957, *20,* 205–215.
Hargreaves, D. H. *Interpersonal relations and education.* Boston: Routledge & Kegan Paul,
  1972.
Heider, F. *The psychology of interpersonal relations.* New York: Wiley, 1958.
Holland, P., & Leinhardt, S. A method for detecting structure in sociometric data. *Ameri-
  can Journal of Sociology,* 1970, *75,* 492–513.
  The structural implications of measurement error in sociometry. *Journal of Mathematical
  Sociology,* 1973, *3,* 85–112.
Homans, G. C. *The human group.* New York: Harcourt, Brace & World, 1950.
  Social behavior; its elementary forms. New York: Harcourt Brace & Jovanovich, 1974.
Hubbell, C. H. An input–output approach to clique identification. *Sociometry,* 1965, *28,*
  377–399.
Jennings, H. H. *Leadership and isolation.* New York: Longmans, Green, 1950.
Katz, L., & Proctor, C. The concept of configuration of interpersonal relations in a group
  as a time-dependent stochastic process. *Psychometrika,* 1959, *24,* 317–327.
Katz, L., Taguiri, R., & Wilson, T. A note on estimating the statistical significance of mutu-
  ality. *Journal of General Psychology,* 1958, *58,* 97–103.
Leinhardt, S. Developmental change in the sentiment structure of children's groups. *Ameri-
  can Sociological Review,* 1972, *37,* 202–212.
Maccoby, E., & Jacklin, C. *The psychology of sex differences.* Stanford: Stanford Univer-
  sity Press, 1974.
Moreno, J. L. *Who shall survive?* New York: Beacon House, 1953.
Newcomb, T. M. *The acquaintance process.* New York: Holt, Rinehart & Winston, 1961.
Peifer, M. R. *The effects of varying age – grade status of models on the imitative behavior of
  six-year-old boys.* Unpublished doctoral dissertation, University of Delaware, 1971.
St. John, N., & Lewis, R. Race and the social structure of the elementary classroom. *Sociol-
  ogy of Education,* 1975, *48,* 346–368.
Schachter, S. *The psychology of affiliation.* Stanford, Cal.: Stanford University Press, 1969.
Shatz, M., & Gelman, R. The development of communication skills: Modification in the
  speech of young children as a function of listener. *Monographs of the Society for Research in Child Development,* 1973, *38* (5, Serial No. 152).
Sherif, M., Harvey, O. J., White, B. J., Hood, W. E., & Sherif, C. W. *Intergroup conflict
  and cooperation: The robber's cave experiment.* Norman, Oklahoma: University of
  Oklahoma Book Exchange, 1961.
Singer, B., & Spilerman, S. Representation of social processes by Markov models. *American Journal of Sociology,* 1976, *82,* 1–54.

Singleton, L. C., & Asher, S. R. Peer preference and social interaction among third-grade children in an integrated school district. *Journal of Educational Psychology*, 1977, *69*, 330–336.

Sørensen, A., & Hallinan, M. T. A stochastic model for change in group structure. *Social Science Research*, 1976, *5*, 43–61.

Thelen, M. H., & Kirkland, K. D. On status and being imitated: Effects on reciprocal imitation and attraction. *Journal of Personality and Social Psychology*, 1976, *33*, 691–697.

Thibaut, J. W., & Kelley, H. H. *The social psychology of groups*. New York: Wiley, 1959.

Tuma, N., & Hallinan, M. T. The effects of sex, race and achievement in school children's friendships. *Social Forces*, 1979, *57*, 1265–1285.

Walberg, H. J., & Thomas, S. C. Open education: An operational definition and validation in Great Britain and the United States. *American Educational Research Journal*, 1972, *9*, 197–208.

Wasserman, S. *Analyzing social networks as stochastic processes*. Mimeographed paper, Department of Applied Statistics, University of Minnesota, 1979.

White H., Boorman, S. A., & Breiger, R. L. Social structure from multiple networks to blockmodels of roles and positions. *American Journal of Sociology*, 1976, *81*, 730–780.

5   Social skills and group acceptance

Martha Putallaz and John M. Gottman

Introduction

A fair number of preschool and elementary school children fail to acquire any friends or have only a few friends at best. Gronlund (1959) reported that approximately 6 percent of third- through six-grade children in one school system had no classroom friends and an additional 12 percent of these children had only one friend, as measured by a sociometric questionnaire. A recent study by Hymel and Asher (1977) reported similar results – 11 percent of the children studied received no friendship nominations and another 22 percent received only one. They attributed their slightly higher percentages to the methodological difference that their subjects were limited to a fewer number of peer nominations than Gronlund's subjects.

There is some evidence that there are negative consequences of having few friends or of not being enthusiastically accepted by one's friends (see Asher, Oden, & Gottman, 1977). Although there are numerous methodological problems in this literature, the results are provocative and may suggest that measures of peer acceptance are good indices of psychological risk. For example, unpopular children are more likely to be low achievers in school (Bonney, 1971; Buswell, 1953), to experience learning difficulties (Amidon & Hoffman, 1965), and to drop out of school (Ullmann, 1957) than their socially accepted peers. As Asher et al. (1977) pointed out, however, the consequences of low peer acceptance may go beyond academic problems. Childhood unpopularity predicts the incidence of such behavior problems as juvenile delinquency (Roff, Sells, & Golden, 1972) and such other selected indices of behavior problems as bad-conduct discharges from the military service (Roff, 1961), the occurrence of emotional and mental-health problems in adulthood (Cowen, Pe-

We would like to acknowledge the assistance of Blair Sheppard, who provided statistical advice and insightful comments on an earlier draft of this chapter.

116

derson, Babigian, Izzo, & Trost, 1973), adult schizophrenia (Strain, Cooke, & Appolloni, 1976), neuroses (Roff, 1963) and psychoses (Kohn & Clausen, 1955; Roff, 1963).

The majority of the studies previously cited, however, rely on sociometric data to establish a connection between poor peer relations during childhood and later adverse consequences. Although the sociometric technique is generally an excellent measurement procedure with high indexes of reliability and validity (Gronlund, 1959), used by itself, it has some shortcomings. These concern the nature of hypothesis generation. While sociometric tests are useful for describing a social structure in an intact group and for the clinical identification of problems such as social isolation, they do not supply any information that would aid in the identification of the origin of the problem or in the detection of those factors currently maintaining the problem. Thus the factors primarily responsible for causing or contributing to a child's sociometric status remain largely unidentified at this time. It is the purpose of this chapter to investigate some of these factors and organize them into a coherent theory that has an empirical basis.

Asher et al. (1977) have suggested that a number of personal characteristics of a child may exert an influence on subsequent peer relations. It appears, for example, that the commonness of a child's first name bears a relationship to popularity and that social risk seems to accompany uncommon names (McDavid & Harari, 1966). Physical attractiveness may also affect social status, as more attractive children also appear to be more socially accepted by their peers (Young & Cooper, 1944). Further, children appear to use race and sex as criteria for selecting friends, as there seems to be a tendency for them to establish same-race and same-sex friendships (Criswell, 1939; Singleton & Asher, 1977).

In addition, a variety of situational factors also appear to affect children's popularity levels (Asher et al., 1977). Although the mobility of children from school to school does not seem to influence popularity (Roistacher, 1974; Young & Cooper, 1944), pupil turnover rate in a school does (Roistacher, 1974). Size of school population also appears to affect peer acceptance, because students attending smaller schools have greater opportunities for participation in school activities and social interaction (Gump & Friesen, 1964; Wicker, 1969). Similarly, size of classroom seems to be influential in determining the number of opportunities for social interaction, the smaller classes giving children more chances (Dawe, 1934). Reinforcement by the teacher or peers for engaging in friendship-making behavior also appears to influence popularity (Blau & Rafferty, 1970), as does academic achievement (Gronlund, 1959).

Supplementing the research focusing on the personal and situational factors that influence popularity, a second line of research in this area has been more behavioral in orientation, searching for possible behavioral concomitants of sociometric status. This research direction has an innate appeal. Clearly, an attempt to alter some of the physical or situational characteristics described previously in an effort to increase a child's popularity or level of peer acceptance would be extremely difficult if not impossible. An intervention attempt would not appear so futile, however, if research indicated that knowledge or performance of certain behaviors or social skills seemed to be the essential element required to attain the minimal level of peer acceptance necessary to avoid psychological risk.

Toward this end, an ethological approach, particularly characterized by an inductive research strategy and an emphasis upon behavioral description is useful for generating hypotheses. Ethological methodology typically involves the observation of behavior as it occurs in natural settings (McGrew, 1972). Behavior in these settings is labeled, described, and defined as objectively as possible. The quantitative analysis of observational data has usually involved the derivation of frequencies of behavior in a descriptive coding system as the major dependent variable for investigation. Unfortunately, the summary of observational data using only rates or relative frequencies of various behaviors leaves much to be desired in accomplishing the tasks of description and hypothesis generating. Recently, however, ethologists have applied information theory to the study of sequences of behaviors over time. Applied to the study of social behavior, information theory involves a mathematical definition of communication. The definition is that the behavior, X, of organism A has specific communicative value with respect to behavior Y of organism B if a knowledge of this behavior X reduces uncertainty in predicting behavior Y (Wilson, 1975). Stated mathematically, this means that the conditional probability $p\ (Y/X) > p\ (Y)$. Statistical tests have recently been discussed by Bakeman (1978), Gottman and Bakeman (1978), Gottman and Notarius (1978), Gottman (1979), and Sackett (1977). Information theory thus makes it possible to study patterns over time and sequences quantitatively, which is important for comparing groups of subjects.

The potential contribution of an observational methodology that employs sequential analysis is that it may be capable of discovering a theory that explains the social structure captured by sociometric methods in social interaction patterns. Currently there are no known consistent behavioral concomitants of sociometric status.

The search for a behavioral theory of sociometric status

The search for behavioral concomitants of sociometric status has had a long history. For example, Marshall and McCandless (1957a) found that the observed degree of the preschool child's friendly social interactions was positively related to the child's sociometric status, while that of hostile play interactions was not. In a second study, these authors observed that adult dependency in preschool children had a negative relationship to sociometric status: Dependence on adults accompanied relatively low social status (Marshall & McCandless, 1957b). Similarly, Moore and Updegraff (1964) examined the relationship between sociometric status and observed nurturance giving and dependency. Although no significant correlations were obtained, they reported that the relationship between high sociometric status and a child's degree of nurturance giving and dependence on other children approached significance. Dependency on adults, however, was negatively related to popularity in the youngest nursery school group but was uncorrelated in the two older nursery school groups.

A study by Charlesworth and Hartup (1967) prompted later researchers to examine sociometric status using the metaphor of reinforcement in social interaction rather than employing a personality trait orientation. Behavioral observations of preschool children dispensing and receiving positive "reinforcement" were taken along four dimensions: giving positive attention and approval, giving affection and personal acceptance, submitting to another's wishes, and giving things to another. The word reinforcement is in quotation marks in the preceding sentence because it was never demonstrated that these events altered the unconditional probability of a behavior by the peer. A better descriptive term might be "positive interactional style." It was found that the older nursery school children were positive to their peers at a significantly higher rate than the younger ones, and that the amount of positiveness given was related to the amount received. The sociometric status of the children was not examined in this study. However, Hartup, Glazer, and Charlesworth (1967) did consider the relationship between peer "reinforcement," both positive and negative, and sociometric status in two nursery schools, and thus considered their study a revision and extension of the Marshall and McCandless work. Their results confirmed those of Marshall and McCandless (1957a) that social acceptance is significantly correlated with the frequency of being positive to peers but not with the frequency of being negative. On the other hand, Hartup et al. (1967) found that social rejection was significantly correlated with being negative to peers but not with giving positive "reinforcement."

The detection of behavioral differences between popular and unpopular children seems to be more difficult when elementary-school rather than preschool children are studied (Asher and Hymel, in press). Gottman, Gonso, and Rasmussen (1975) correlated peer acceptance of third- and fourth-graders with their social interaction patterns in the classroom and with their knowledge of social skills as reflected by their performance on several tasks. Specifically, these tasks encompassed labeling emotions in facial expressions, referential-communication accuracy, perspective-taking tasks, blindfolded-listener tasks, knowledge of how to make friends, and ability to give help. It was found that popular and unpopular children differed in their knowledge of how to make friends and in their perform-ance on the referential-communication task. Consistent with the report of Hartup et al. (1967), it was found that popular children initiated and re-ceived more positive interaction with peers than unpopular children.[1] Gottman et al. expanded the observational categories used by Hartup et al. to include verbal and nonverbal behavior and examined behavioral differences between the children who enrolled in a working-class school as opposed to those who were attending a middle-class school. The results indicated that popularity in the middle-class school correlated with positive verbal interaction, while in the working-class school popularity was related to engagement in positive nonverbal interaction. Middle-class children who engaged in positive nonverbal behavior tended to be more disliked. A more complicated picture of popularity and its correlates is presented here than in the preschool literature. It appears that the particu-lar environment affects what kinds of behavior will lead to acceptance or rejection.

A further complication emerges when the study by Oden and Asher (1977) is considered. The coaching procedure used in this study signifi-cantly increased the sociometric ratings of the coached children com-pared to the ratings of the two control groups and resulted in maintenance of these gains at the time of a one-year follow-up assessment. However, a gain in the observed positive social behavior of these coached children, which one would predict would accompany their gain in sociometric status, was not found. More troubling, no behavioral differences were detected between popular and unpopular children prior to the interven-tion program. It is possible, as the authors suggested, that the particular task orientation (on-task, off-task) and social orientation (peer-oriented/ support, task-oriented, uncooperative/rejecting, other) coding categories were not specific enough for frequency differences to emerge. It was also suggested that these observations should have been made in the classroom, where behavior might more closely parallel the behavior that peer ratings were based upon, rather than out of the classroom as they were in this study.

In a replication attempt, Hymel and Asher (1977) took heed of these suggestions and changed the behavioral observation technique employed. Pre- and postintervention observations were made of the three low-status children participating in the coaching program as well as of the two most popular children in each of the eight classrooms included in the study. The children were thus involved in regular classroom activities during the observations. Observers recorded the duration of time each child was either alone, observing peers, interacting with the teacher, or interacting with peers. When the child was involved with peers, frequencies were noted for cooperative behavior, showing affection, noncompliance behavior, derogation, and attack. Thus, attempts were made to correct for some of the possible problems inherent in the behavioral observation method used in the Oden and Asher study. Again, however, behavioral observations were not found to discriminate between popular and unpopular children. A recent study by Ladd (in press) that used a modification of the coaching procedure and observational methods did find behavioral differences between coached and control children but did not observe popular children.

The overall picture of behavioral correlates is thus somewhat unclear. Results have also been limited in two major ways. First, interaction rates and not sequences are used; second, there is no analysis of by whom and toward whom on a sociogram an observation occurs. Neither the Hartup et al. (1967) nor the Gottman et al. (1975) studies coded initiating and receiving positive interactions with peers. In both studies, the popularity of only one of the children (called the target child) in any social interaction was considered. These shortcomings leave many possible interpretations of the correlation between popularity and positive peer interaction. For example, it could be that unpopular children are in effect laying gifts at the feet of their popular peers rather than that the positively oriented popular children are graciously dispensing their favors to their less popular peers.

Benson and Gottman (1975) conducted an observational study designed to obtain the same observational information as the Gottman et al. 1975 study in addition to information about the sociometric status of both the target child and the child with whom he or she is interacting. Because this study is unpublished and germane to the discussion, it will be summarized briefly in this chapter. A detailed report is available upon request from the second author.

The Benson and Gottman study

The subjects were 114 children from four classrooms in a working-class school: a kindergarten classroom, a first-grade classroom, a third-grade classroom, and a fourth-grade classroom. A sociometric measure using photographs taken of every child in each classroom was administered individually to each child following the procedure outlined by Hartup et al. (1967), except that children could pick any number of their peers as their best friends, a modification used in Gottman et al. (1975). Popularity was the total number of choices a child received from his classroom peers.

Classroom observations were made following the Gottman et al. (1975) modification of the Hartup et al. (1967) coding system. The observer watched each child for ten consecutive six-second intervals, coded the child's behavior each interval on a standard form, recorded the name of the child with whom the interaction took place, and then moved to the next child on the classroom list. Observations were sampled equally from the following situations: (a) lecture or demonstration; (b) seat work; (c) free play or unstructured activity *within* the classroom; (d) free play or unstructured activity *outside* the classroom.

The relationships between popularity and the observation categories were examined in a 2 × 2 × 4 multivariate factorial analysis of variance with the frequency of the twelve observational categories as the dependent variables. There were two levels of popularity (high and low, split at the classroom's median), two levels of sex, and four levels of grade. There was a significant popularity main effect, and no significant interaction effects of other factors with popularity. Popular children received more positive contact from peers and received more neutral contact from peers than did unpopular children. There were no differences between popular and unpopular children in the initiation of peer contact. These results could suggest that classroom popularity may be reflected in the behaviors of others toward the popular child and not in the behaviors initiated by the child.

Benson and Gottman then asked the question, "From whom are popular children receiving more positive and neutral contact?" A more detailed analysis of the distribution of peer interaction was undertaken to determine with whom (as a function of popularity) popular and unpopular children interacted. The same peer-observation category variables were recalculated depending upon whether the peer interaction was with a popular or an unpopular peer. A significant main effect was again found for the popularity factor, again with no significant interaction effects. Popular children were significantly more likely to initiate positive interactions with other popular children than unpopular children were. Popular children also received significantly more positive interactions from other popular children than unpopular children did. No significant differences were found in the negative-interaction categories. However, there was a tendency for the negative interactions of popular children to be with other popular children, and for the negative interactions of unpopular children to be with other unpopular children. Also, popular children initiated more neutral interactions with other popular children than unpopular children did. Popular children also initiated fewer neutral interactions with unpopular children than unpopular children did.

The finding that popular children are receiving their neutral and positive interactions from other popular children suggests a membership-group interpretation of these results: Popular children appear to form their own social subsystem, initiating and receiving positive and neutral interactions primarily within the group. Similarly, unpopular children initiate significantly more neutral interactions to other unpopular children than they do to popular children, again supporting a membership-group interpretation. Increasing a child's popularity may thus not be a simple matter of increasing the frequency of a child's positive interactions to peers but may involve a shift in membership groups. We do not yet understand the nature of these groups.

Support for the findings of the Benson and Gottman study is offered by Vaughn and Waters (1978). Following a suggestion by Chance and Jolly (1976), these investigators studied dominance patterns in a group by searching for asymmetries in visual gaze; the subordinate child should look at the dominant child more than vice versa. The attention-dominance hierarchy of a class of eighteen nursery school children was constructed by ranking the children in terms of the number of looks and glances each child received. Different ways of constructing the dominance hierarchy did not correlate. However, this attention measure was found to correlate highly with the sociometric data of the class, suggesting that the two were measuring much the same thing. This serendipitous result was studied by examining the relationship between each child's rank in the attention hierarchy and the distribution of his or her attention to peers; it was found that children tended to look at higher-ranking peers more than would be expected by chance. In other words, there seemed to be a distribution of attention upward in the attention hierarchy; thus there was a consensus of attention. Each child's attention seemed to be drawn to the child to whom his or her peers also paid the most attention. Vaughn and Waters further reported a greater tendency for the high-ranking children in the attention hierarchy to look at other high-ranking children than for the low-ranking children to look at the high-ranking children, although the analyses presented in the paper were incomplete and so do not provide enough information for the reader to draw this conclusion independently. There does appear to be evidence, then, to support the findings of the Benson and Gottman study that there exist distinct interactional social groups within the classroom that differ with respect to sociometric status.

Intervention studies

Another source of hypotheses about the relationship between sociometric status and social behavior has come from clinical-intervention studies. This method has involved the creation and evaluation of intervention programs designed to overcome low peer acceptance by either increasing the sociometric status of socially isolated children or increasing their rate of peer interaction, depending upon the investigator's definition of social isolation. There are two definitions of social isolation, one based on low rates of peer interaction and one based on low sociometric status, or peer acceptance. Three general types of intervention programs have emerged in the literature: shaping, modeling, and coaching (Asher et al., 1977).

Typically, shaping programs have been characterized by the use of reinforcement in the form of social praise or tangible rewards in order to increase the frequency of isolated children's peer interactions. Studies have demonstrated that such procedures can effect such an increase (Allen, Hart, Buell, Harris, & Wolf, 1964; O'Connor, 1972). However, the children's interaction patterns tend to return to baseline levels once the reinforcement has been terminated (O'Connor, 1972).

The second type of intervention program utilizes the principle of modeling. In the best-known study of this type (O'Connor, 1969; 1972), socially isolated children viewed a film consisting of eleven scenes of children receiving positive reactions following their approach and interaction with peers. After the film, the children studied showed a subsequent increase in their own rate of peer interactions that continued to be maintained at the time of a follow-up assessment several weeks later. However, a study by Gottman (1977a) that replicated only the follow-up assessment of the O'Connor study with added controls failed to demonstrate that either an increase in peer interaction rates or an increase in sociometric status results from the modeling film.

Even when shaping and modeling programs increase interaction rates, these gains do not necessarily include gains in peer acceptance, because sociometric data have typically not been collected in studies designed to increase interaction rates. As Asher et al. (1977) suggested, it is conceivable that a child's rate of peer interaction might increase without an accompanying increase in peer acceptance. It is conceivable that, given certain styles of interaction (e.g., domineering), increasing an isolate's contact with peers may be detrimental to increasing acceptance. In support of the lack of connection between the two dimensions, both Gottman (1977b) and Hymel and Asher (1977) failed to find a significant relationship between sociometric status and rate of interaction. Also, in a cross-age pairing study, Furman, Rahe, and Hartup (1979) found significant rate of interaction increases for relatively low interaction rate children (less than 33 percent peer interaction time was the criterion), but there were no changes in sociometric measures for these children, nor did they differ initially from higher rate of interaction children on the sociometric measure (Rosén, 1979).

Coaching studies tend to use sociometric measures to obtain a direct assessment of peer acceptance. Typically, in these programs children with low sociometric status have been explicitly instructed in specific rules or strategies of social behavior relevant to making friends. A small *N* study by Gottman, Gonso, and Schuler (1976) employed one such intervention program. The therapy involved coaching children on initiating an interaction with other children, learning a sequence of behaviors that would facilitate making friends, and practicing referential communication skills. Increased sociometric ratings resulted for the coached children, whereas those of the control group remain unchanged.

Oden and Asher's (1977) intervention program was perhaps the most important in the literature. Its results, particularly its generalization effects on sociometric measures on one-year follow-up, were impressive. The coaching program included: (1) instructions relevant to friendship initiation (participation, cooperation, communication, and validation–support); (2) opportunities for practice of these strategies with peers; and (3) postpractice review sessions with the coach. Pretest–posttest sociometric assessment of the four-week training indicated that the coached group increased on play sociometric ratings significantly more than did the two control groups. A greater, although not significant, gain was also shown with respect to the number of friendship nominations received. A one-year follow-up assessment indicated continued progress in sociometric ratings for the coached children. A later study failed to replicate the effectiveness of this coaching program (Hymel & Asher, 1977), but a more recent replication attempt by Ladd (in press) was successful.

Nonetheless, the problem of social isolation cannot be considered solved, although coaching seems promising as an intervention strategy. Coaching programs tend to include content about initiating and maintaining friendships. Perhaps the mixed success of these interventions can be attributed in part to the lack of a solid, descriptive knowledge base from which the skills taught to the isolated children have been selected. Few of the intervention programs arrived at their choice of skills on the basis of observed differences between socially isolated and nonisolated children in situations relevant to the coaching or modeling. The interventions have had to be designed on the basis of logic, reviews of nonprogrammatic investigations, studies of behavioral correlates, or intuition and armchair speculation. Unfortunately, those programs designed from reviews of research have had to be derived from vague and global findings.

Therefore, most intervention programs concentrate on teaching social isolates strategies designed to help them become included in already existing peer groups. For example, the modeling film used by O'Connor (1969) in his intervention program consisted of eleven episodes featuring children's attempts to enter groups of children. These scenes were graduated from what were considered low-threat situations (low-vigor social activities and small groups) to supposedly high-threat situations (high-vigor play activities and large groups). A narrative track accompanying the film explicitly described each child's entry actions, thus drawing the audience's attention to the relevant behaviors. One of these episodes was narrated as follows: "Now another child comes up close to watch. She wants to play too. She waits for them to see her. Now she gets a chair and she sits down with them so they will play with her. She starts to do what they are doing so they will want to play with her . . ." Clear strategies for entry were given to the audience. As Gottman (1977a) pointed out, O'Connor's entry strategies, as well as those taught in other intervention programs, have not been based upon any empirical knowledge of how nonisolated children at a particular developmental level gain entry into groups, but rather upon the adult author's intuition and speculation. Children's entry style may, in fact, differ considerably from that used by adults or from what adults imagine children's entry strategies to be.

An empirical examination of children's entry behavior is crucial to the development of a successful intervention program if it can be demonstrated that initial ability to be included in a peer group is predictive of later social acceptance. A study by Ziller and Behringer (1961) suggests that this may indeed be the case. In a longitudinal study that continued over eleven weeks, in examining the assimilation of twenty-eight newcomers to different elementary schools they found that between the two points in time the mean popularity of the newcomers declined; their mean popularity during the eleven-week period investigated assumed the form of a U-shaped function. However, the newcomers' popularity during the first afternoon in the classroom and their popularity eleven weeks later, as determined by a sociometric questionnaire, were substantially correlated. This suggests that something that the children were doing during their first attempts at entry into the classroom group was predictive of their ultimate social acceptance by peers.

Descriptive information about children's behavior during their attempts to be included by their peers is needed both for an understanding of the processes of social acceptance by peers and for the sound design of interventions. What children typically do during the entry process or even what behaviors constitute an entry sequence is unknown. There is only a small body of literature relevant to the topic of children's entry behavior. The reasons for studying entry behavior and thus the specific aspects or correlates of entry that have been examined have varied across studies. The major source of information concerning entry comes from newcomer research, which focuses on the assimilation of strangers into groups.

Newcomer studies

The findings from this literature support the notion that a common series of events is associated with the assimilation of all newcomers. From her study of preschoolers, Washburn (1932) proposed that regularity exists in the assimilation process, beginning with a period of inhibition induced by the novel situation, followed by a release of this inhibition. She suggested that the newcomer's behavior progressed as follows: Initially there was a period of alert but passive observation by the child, followed by a period of active exploration of either the setting or some particular object. Vocalization was usually found to be the final activity to emerge.

Washburn's observations have been examined in greater depth and elaborated upon, but basically they have been supported. McGrew (1972), for example, studied the entry of newcomers to nursery school and found a similar pattern of entry to emerge. McGrew described the newcomers on their first day to be initially "inhibited and shy." All twelve children studied were reported to display a great deal of "automanipulation" (e.g., thumbsucking, playing with one's hair or clothing), and all but one of them showed immobility during the first few minutes of entry into the novel situation. Passive exploration of the novel surroundings and of the other children occupied much of the newcomer's time. Typically, the newcomer sat or stood in one location and watched the activities of others but seldom entered into any of them. A few children were described as playing with the first toy given to them by the teacher for the remainder of the morning. McGrew also noted that a tendency to avoid performing conspicuous behavior patterns was also evident, as was a preference for quiet locations that the newcomer vacated if other children came near (McGrew & McGrew, 1972). Newcomers refused requests and queries by silently moving away and avoided competitive or quarrelsome situations. McGrew (1972) summarized the behavior of newcomers as being "the antithesis of aggressive: arms kept down and close to the trunk, face and eyes averted, movements slow, silent" (p. 138). McGrew (1972) described the new children as being conspicuously silent, speaking softly and answering many questions with head nods and shakes. Loud vocalizations such as yelling or squealing were not observed among the newcomers.

A similar pattern to that of the newcomers described by McGrew was reported by Jormakka (1976), who found this pattern to emerge among the fourteen pairs of unacquainted 6- and 7-year-old children who were studied but not among the fourteen pairs of acquainted children studied. Each pair of children was observed and their speech recorded as they played freely for twenty minutes in a room equipped with a sand box, a blackboard, and an assortment of toys.

The initial encounter of the unacquainted children was described as usually beginning with gazes directed at the other child's face, in contrast to the pairs of acquainted children, who hardly looked at each other but instead looked around the room. Jormakka concluded that looking played an important role in establishing contact between strangers as it seemed to function as an indication of a willingness to interact with the other child. At the same time, a high rate of intermittent gaze avoidance and turning one's back to the other among the unacquainted pairs seemed to reflect their ambivalence concerning the situation. This uncertainty about establishing contact was also reflected by the higher incidence of nonverbal nervous behavior among the stranger pairs than the acquainted children. Immobility and automanipulation were reported as frequent among the stranger pairs at the initial stage of encounter. As might be expected, walking was reported as more frequent among the acquainted children than the unacquainted pairs.

Differences in verbal behavior were also found between the acquainted and unacquainted pairs of children. Silence and whispering, which decreased over time, were typical of the initial behavior of unacquainted children. The silence that marked the beginning of the meeting tended to be longer among strangers as well. Not surprisingly, Jormakka found a smaller total verbal output for the unacquainted children than for the acquainted children. Laughing was common among acquainted children and in time increased in frequency among unacquainted children.

Some interesting differences between groups also emerged with respect to the content of speech. Description of play, attempts to influence or control the other child (suggestions, advice, commands), and negative reactions (resistance, blame, criticism) were more frequent among acquainted children at the initial stage of meeting. It seemed as if the stranger pairs were more cautious and restrained in their interactions than the acquainted pairs. Questions about the other child and giving information about oneself were more common among unacquainted children throughout the session. This type of personal talk was especially characteristic of unacquainted girls. In contrast, acquainted children seldom discussed personal subjects during the session. Asking for clarification ("What did you say?"; "You mean this?") and answering this type of question also comprised a larger portion of speech among stranger pairs than it did among acquainted pairs. The unacquainted children did not display any preference for a particular strategy for initiating a conversation. Half began the interaction with such questions as "What is your name?" or "Have you been here before?" The others, as well as the acquainted children, started with remarks about the equipment or with play suggestions. No mention was made as to which proved to be the most successful strategy with respect to initiation of the conversation. It does seem, then, that the behavior of pairs of children meeting for the first time as described by Jormakka is quite similar to the behavior of newcomers to a group (McGrew, 1972).

The newcomer hypothesis

The fearful, shy, withdrawn behavior that McGrew (1972) and Jormakka (1976) have described as typical of a child initially meeting another child or a group of children has also been observed by Gottman (1977b) in children who were rated low on peer acceptance. A linear typal analysis of the behavioral observations of 113 preschoolers when they were alone, interacting with peers, or interacting with their teachers resulted in the identification of five different types of children. Of these types, two groups of children were characterized as sociometrically neglected by their peers. One type had a profile elevation for negative teacher interaction. The other had a high behavioral rate of being "tuned out": that is, being alone and off task, daydreaming, or staring out into space. This latter group of children was significantly less accepted by their peers than was the teacher-negative group. Both types, however, were described by Gottman as exhibiting a high rate of the set of behaviors described by McGrew (1972) and Jormakka (1976). Gottman referred to these fearful, shy behaviors as "hovering."

In order to understand better the hovering behavior exhibited by children low on peer acceptance, Gottman conducted a small *N* study that would allow hovering and the role it plays in inclusion or rejection by peer groups to be examined more closely. It seemed logical from the newcomer literature that a situation requiring a child to attempt to gain entry into a group of children would maximize the probability of hovering occurring. It was common in the particular second-grade children that Gottman used in his study for the teacher to take certain children aside for individual instruction and then to tell them to join a particular group of children already at work in another area of the classroom. Gottman used this naturally occurring entry situation to study hovering.

Entry pilot study

The total number of positive sociometric peer nominations received was calculated for each of the twenty-three children in the class. A cutoff of five choices was used to dichotomize the children as being either popular or unpopular. Four triads were then formed, two that were composed of two unpopular and one popular child and two that were composed of two popular and one unpopular child. In addition, two popular and two unpopular children were selected to attempt entry into the triad groups. Thus four conditions, each having an *N* of one, were created – a popular child entering a mostly popular or mostly unpopular group and an unpopular child entering a mostly popular or mostly unpopular group. When the fourth child attempted to enter the group, each triad was in the process of playing a word game commonly used in the classroom.

The verbal and nonverbal behavior of the entry child was coded according to the following codes: (1) hovering (pleading and whining behavior, especially if the voice tone was halting, unsure, or tense); (2) assertive (definite statements of intent to join group play); and (3) exchanging "kibs" (chanting, glee, teasing, support, kibbitizing about the play of the game). The group's response to the child was coded as ignores, includes, rejects, or exchange kibs.

The data were analyzed using transition probability matrices that showed the probability of particular group responses for specific antecedent behaviors of the entry child. Thus, the transition probability matrices were 3 × 4 matrices with three possible entry strategies (hover, assertive, exchange kibs) and four consequent group responses (ignore, reject, exchange kibs, and include).

Gottman first examined peer play among the triads for possible behavioral differences between popular and unpopular children. It was found that unpopular children behaved more negatively to each other than the popular children did to one another. Unpopular children in unpopular groups tended to direct more of their behavior and attend to the popular child and be quite negative to each other. In contrast, popular children in popular groups addressed more of their behavior to each other and tended to ignore the unpopular child. It appeared, then, that the interactional style of the groups varied as a function of sociometric status.

The response of each of the groups to the entering child was examined next. Popular children who were assertive were most likely to be included in the group, regardless of the popularity of the group they entered. This was not true, however, for unpopular children. When the unpopular child who attempted entry into the unpopular group behaved assertively, he or she was ignored by the group. The most successful entry behavior for the unpopular child was hovering, closely followed by exchanging kibs. The unpopular child entering the popular group was never permanently included in the group. The children in the popular group switched the rules of the game temporarily in order to reject the unpopular child from the play. This child displayed no instances of assertive behavior but was instead high on hovering.

Gottman used a membership-group theory to interpret the data. Hovering was most likely to occur when children attempted entry into groups different from their own levels of popularity. In contrast, children entering groups of similar popularity to their own were more likely to be assertive and more likely to exchange kibs than those entering groups differing in popularity from their own. Gottman suggested that territoriality might be associated with sociometric structure.

Summary of literature review

Sociometric indexes of peer acceptance are important measures for identifying children at some risk for later psychological problems. Sociometric data need to be supplemented with observational data to clarify the social processes that underlie group acceptance. Observational data might be made more useful by employing detailed coding systems and sequential analytic techniques.

In the observational research that has searched for behavioral concomitants of sociometric status there is support for the conclusions that: (a) popular children and unpopular children interact in two distinct social groups; that is, a median split on sociometric measures provides a rough cut of what may be more complex social clique structures; and (b) popular children tend to have more positive and neutral interactions with their peers than do unpopular children.

Intervention programs for unaccepted and withdrawn children focused primarily on teaching children how to gain entry into groups of their peers, which suggests that research on the assimilation of newcomers is germane to our topic. The newcomer studies provide some support for the contention that initial sociometric scores are predictive of later acceptance by peers and also suggest a consistent behavioral profile of the new-comer. Newcomers tend to act tentatively or shyly and to engage in a complex set of behaviors that Gottman called "hovering." This hovering behavior appears to serve a functional purpose for the newcomer. When initially attempting entry into an unfamiliar group, it is unlikely that the newcomer would know a priori the norms and values held by that group. The newcomer thus acts tentatively rather than risk violating these un-known norms by behaving too definitively and thereby evoking the group's rejection. Hovering seems to decrease over time as the newcomer becomes increasingly familiar with the group's norms and is gradually assimilated into the group.

The Gottman (1977b) study identified a group of children low in peer acceptance who were characterized by a profile elevation in hovering be-havior. Taken together, our review of the newcomer literature suggested the hypothesis that unaccepted children may be behaving as if they were still newcomers. A pilot study by Gottman found evidence for this hy-pothesis.

A study of the separate social systems of popular and unpopular chil-dren would provide a context for the entry situation. Second, a study of entry and the group's response to varying styles of entry would provide a more rigorous test of the newcomer hypothesis and perhaps would ex-plain why unaccepted children act as if they were newcomers.

Entry study

Toward this end, a second, more comprehensive study was conducted with added controls correcting for the methodological weaknesses inher-ent in the pilot study (see Putallaz & Gottman, 1979, for a detailed report of this study). Second- and third-graders participated in the study. The total number of positive peer nominations was calculated for each of the sixty children; these calculations provided a means of determining each child's degree of popularity. The children in each of the five classes stud-ied were dichotomized into either popular or unpopular groups according to whether they scored above or below the median number of choices for their particular class. In all, twenty dyads were formed, ten popular pairs and ten unpopular pairs, homogeneous by sex and sociometric status. With the addition of an entry child of varying sociometric status to each dyad, four conditions were created. These conditions involved the entry of a popular child into either a popular or unpopular group and the entry of an unpopular child into similarly composed dyadic groups. Each dyad was videotaped playing a new word game in a research trailer for ten minutes. Fifteen minutes of additional videotaped data were then obtained on the attempts of the third child to enter the group.

Verbatim transcripts were made from the videotapes and were coded using the behavioral codes developed by Gottman and Parkhurst (1980). Space limitations prevent a detailed description of these codes. Briefly, this coding system consists of four double codes and sixteen content codes designed to describe children's conversations exhaustively and to facilitate the study of the social processes thought by the authors to be relevant to friendship. As is necessary for sequential analysis, the generalizability coefficients in the present research were extremely high. The Cronbach alpha values for the nonentry coding system ranged from .782 to 1.000, with a mean value of .962, and for the entry coding system from .872 to .989, with a mean of .953. Similarly, the computed Cohen's kappas, which control for agreement by chance, were .914 and .789. (For a discussion of reliability and generalizability issues, see Gottman & Parkhurst, 1980; Putallaz & Gottman, 1979.)

Dyadic interaction

First, we asked whether the styles of dyadic interaction prior to the entry of a third child differed as a function of the popularity composition of the dyad. To initially examine this issue, the ratio of agreement to disagreement was assessed for each dyad. This ratio provides an index of the overall positiveness-to-negativeness of the interaction, a higher value being indicative of greater positiveness. In other research on social interaction, it has been perhaps the most consistent discriminator between distressed and nondistressed families (Riskin & Faunce, 1970) and between distressed and nondistressed couples (Gottman, Markman, & Notarius, 1977). For popular dyads, the mean ratio was 2.86, while for unpopular dyads, it was 1.28. The frequencies of the agreement and disagreement codes, as used by the two types of dyads, were compared by means of a 2 × 2 chi-square analysis. This analysis showed that popular children agreed more and disagreed less than unpopular children.

Perhaps the higher incidence of disagreement within unpopular dyads can be attributed to differences in the consequences of disagreement in the two types of dyads. For example, it may be that disagreement is more likely to continue or escalate in the unpopular dyads than in the popular dyads. Using sequential analysis to test this possibility (see Gottman & Bakeman, 1978), we found that continued disagreement and escalation to squabbling were more likely in unpopular dyads than in popular groups.

Is there some way of understanding the mechanism for the lower likelihood of both continued disagreement and escalation to squabbling in popular dyads? Are popular dyads doing something else when they disagree that is different from what unpopular children do? A detailed sequential analysis and a reexamination of the content of the transcripts revealed that popular and unpopular children were very different in the manner in which they disagreed. When popular children disagreed, one child would typically cite a general rule as the basis for their disagreement and then provide an acceptable alternative action for the other child. An example of such a pattern was:

No, you ain't. You ain't supposed . . . you ain't supposed to use this first. You're supposed to pick one of these.

Thus, a popular child not only told the other child what he or she could not do, but also what was permissible. In contrast, an unpopular child would typically express disagreement by stating a prohibition very specific to the previous act of the other child without providing an alternative action for that child. An example of this type of disagreement was:

No. Can't say "bank" again (after the child had used the word "bank" on a previous turn at the game).

An unpopular child would tell the other child quite specifically what he or she could not do and would not suggest any alternative action for that child.

To summarize: (1) the interaction in unpopular dyads is more disagreeable and less agreeable; (2) disagreement in unpopular dyads is more likely to continue and escalate; and (3) the reasons given for disagreement in unpopular dyads are less likely to be general or to provide a constructive alternative action for the other child than is the case in popular dyads. The pattern of results that describes unpopular children's dyadic social interaction might thus be summarized as "contrary" and "bossy," because disagreement is followed by a command that prohibits a course of action without providing a constructive alternative. Thus disagreement is likely to continue or escalate into squabbling. This interactional style has been described anecdotally by Asher (personal communication).

Predictions concerning entry behavior

In order to understand an entering child's behavior, the relationship between a child's bids for entry and the possible outcomes of those bids need to be considered. From what we know thus far, let us reason logically through the consequences of the entry situation. The entering child may be either accepted, rejected, or ignored by the group. The entering child's "behavioral strategy" can be empirically derived by determining which of these three outcomes best predicts the entry child's response hierarchy preference. The probabilities of the set of bids for entry can be correlated with their probabilities of producing an accept, reject, or ignore response from the group. Multiple correlation analysis can then be used to determine the relative weight of the three outcomes in predicting the response hierarchy of the entering child.

This empirical method of assessing an entering child's behavioral strategy, in combination with the membership-group findings from the Benson and Gottman study, can be applied to aid in the prediction of a child's style of entry into a group. With no knowledge of the membership group of the entering child (that is, no knowledge of the child's popularity), a child entering a group would logically be expected to act to maximize the probability of acceptance and minimize the probability of rejection. However, if the child entered a group that was not his membership group, the newcomer hypothesis predicts that the child would be tentative in the way a newcomer would: The child might also secondarily act to maximize the probability of being ignored rather than risk violating the group's unknown norms by behaving too definitively and thus evoking the group's rejection. This possibility could be assessed by examining the relative weights of the multiple regression equation.

Now consider the implications of our knowledge of the unpopular child's dyadic interactional style. Because the dyadic social context in the unpopular membership group is disagreeable and bossy, it may further follow that this membership group would be quite likely to reject any child attempting to join its ranks regardless of the quality of the entry strategy exhibited. Thus, it may be that the unpopular child entering even his own membership group may also act such that he will be ignored rather than risk this high likelihood of rejection by drawing the group's attention to himself. The fact that Gottman (1977b) found hovering to be used most by unpopular children lends support to this contention. The unpopular child's entry even into his own membership group may thus resemble the entry behavior of a newcomer. If this is the case, then the response hierarchy preference of the unpopular child's entry into an unpopular group might best be described by the conditional probability of being ignored by the group. This predictability of ignore should be enhanced when unpopular children enter cross-membership groups, as they would be even less familiar with the norms of such groups and thus less certain of how to act so as not to evoke the group's rejection.

Entry of a third child

Terminology

The terminology used in connection with the entry portion of this study will be briefly discussed in order to facilitate an understanding of these results. First, a child was considered to have gained *entry* into the group once the child actually began to play the game. Using this definition, all children did eventually secure entry by the end of the observational session. An *entry bid* refers to each of the entering child's attempts to enter and become integrated into the group. The group's responses to these entry bids were coded as either *accepting* (responding positively to the entering child and his attempts at entry), *rejecting* (responding negatively to the entering child and his attempts at entry), or *ignoring* (failing to respond to the entering child and instead ignoring his bids for entry). All entering children were accepted, rejected, and ignored by the group at some point during their entry attempt. It is important to remember that an acceptance does not necessarily imply that the entering child has gained entry but merely that the group has responded to the child positively. With this terminology in mind, the results of the entry portion of the study will now be discussed.

Bids and time required for entry

We first considered whether it required more bids and therefore more time for unpopular children to gain entry. This was indeed the case with respect to bids. Popular children used an average of 15.89 bids and unpopular children used an average of 22.82 bids. Further, unpopular children did require more time to gain entry ($\overline{X}$ = 273.6 seconds versus $\overline{X}$ = 146.2 seconds) and also took more time to make their first bid at entry ($\overline{X}$ = 16.91 seconds versus $\overline{X}$ = 7.67 seconds) than popular children. This latter finding offers support for the hypothesis that unpopular children hover, or behave as if they were newcomers, when attempting to enter groups of their peers. Rather than initially draw the group's attention to themselves by speaking, they remain silent for longer periods of time than popular children in the same situation.

We next examined how the popularity of the group entered affected the number of bids and the amount of time the children required for entry. Popular children entered a popular group (their membership group) using fewer bids ($\overline{X}$ = 11.67) and in less time ($\overline{X}$ = 83.30 seconds) than any other group of entering children. In contrast, unpopular children entering a popular group (cross-membership entry) required both more bids ($\overline{X} = 24.57$) and more time ($\overline{X} = 293.70$ seconds) to secure entry than any of the other entering groups. Popular children were not very different from unpopular children with regard to entering an unpopular group. The popular children took slightly fewer bids ($\overline{X} = 18.00$ versus $\overline{X} = 19.75$) and slightly less time ($\overline{X} = 209.11$ seconds versus $\overline{X} = 253.50$ seconds) to enter than did the unpopular children.

Thus, popular children entered groups faster and with fewer bids than unpopular children. It was easier, in terms of time and bids expended, for both groups of children to enter their own membership groups and more difficult for them to enter cross-membership groups. Contrary to our expectation, however, it was comparable, if not somewhat less difficult, for popular children to make cross-membership entry than it was for unpopular children to enter their own membership groups.

Group response to entry attempts

Next we considered whether it was indeed the case, as would seem likely from the results found thus far, that unpopular children were rejected and ignored more and accepted less than popular children, thereby making entry into groups more difficult for them to attain. A log-linear analysis (Fienberg, 1978) was performed, using the procedures proposed by Bock (1974), on the number of times each child was accepted, rejected, or ignored by the group. A significant main effect was found for both the popularity of the entering child and the popularity of the group entered. Both the entering children's popularity and the popularity of the group entered affected the resulting probability that the children would be either rejected or ignored by the group. An examination of these main effects showed that popular children entering a group were as likely as unpopular children to be rejected, more likely than unpopular children to be accepted, and less likely than unpopular children to be ignored. Further, popular dyads were both less rejecting and less accepting than unpopular dyads in response to any entering child; they also differed from unpopular dyads by ignoring entering children more. Thus, unpopular dyads responded more emotionally to the entering child (i.e., either accepting or rejecting) than did popular dyads.

Examination of response repertoires

In order to better understand why unpopular children experienced more difficulty than popular children when entering a group, we examined whether popular and unpopular children had similar response repertoires for entry. First, we considered whether both popular and unpopular entering children displayed the particular entry strategies studied, thus allowing us to ascertain if unpopular children had an entry-skills deficit. Specifically, the following eight entry behaviors were examined: self-statements, demands, feeling statements, information statements, agreements, disagreements, informational questions, and an "other" category consisting of the remaining, less frequently used, entry bids. The evidence did not support a skills-deficit hypothesis, however, because both groups of children displayed all entry strategies studied. Furthermore, we found that the probabilities that describe the entry response hierarchy preference for each entry behavior for popular and unpopular children correlated significantly. The children, then, used each entry bid with moderately similar probabilities, regardless of popularity. Thus, if we examine response hierarchy preference, we must conclude that unpopular children have all the entry behaviors of popular children in their repertoires with only subtle differences in the ordering of their response hierarchies.

Comparative effectiveness of entry bids

We next considered why unpopular children experienced more difficulty entering groups and had to exert more effort to do so despite using the same entry behaviors in roughly the same ordered response hierarchy as popular children. Perhaps the bids most preferred by the unpopular children were not those that would be most effective in gaining them entry. To test this possibility, we computed a cost/benefit score for each entry behavior as used by popular and unpopular children by calculating the probability of the bid leading to acceptance of the user by the group minus the probability of the bid leading to nonacceptance (that is, the user being either rejected or ignored by the group). Thus, a high positive score would be indicative of an entry bid that had a high probability of leading to acceptance and a low probability of leading to the group rejecting or ignoring the user, while the converse would be true of a high negative score. Next, the correlation between the probabilities of each entry bid and its cost/benefit score was computed. This correlation would allow us to ascertain whether the entry bids which had the highest probability of occurring corresponded to those which had the most favorable cost/benefit score. For popular children, this correlation was .74, $p < .025$ for entry into popular groups and .51, $p < .10$ for entry into unpopular groups. For unpopular children, this correlation was $-.06$ for entry into unpopular groups and $-.13$ for entry into popular groups; neither of the latter two correlations was significant. This was a remarkable result. Popular children acted to maximize their benefits and minimize their costs, unlike unpopular children. Popular children acted in accordance with the likelihood of being accepted rather than being rejected or ignored by the group, unlike unpopular children. We are not implying that unpopular children were deliberately intending to be ignored or rejected when attempting to enter groups, but, rather, that this was the net effect of their behavior.

How are we to understand this result? Why would unpopular children not act in what appears to be their best interests? To examine this question, the correlations between the probabilities of each entry behavior and the separate likelihoods of the group's accepting, rejecting, or ignoring this bid for entry were studied. The purpose of these analyses was to determine empirically the criteria used by entering children in organizing their response hierarchy for entry, rather than relying on the cost/benefit score. To determine the criteria used by entering children in their response hierarchy ordering, a procedure similar to stepwise multiple regression was followed. First, the zero-ordered correlations between the hierarchy (H) and each of the three consequences, accept (A), reject (R), and ignore (I), were computed, and the highest of these correlations was taken as the first criterion. Second, the partial correlations were computed, and the highest of these was taken as the second criterion. In all cases, a statistical significance criterion of $p < .10$ was employed.

First, we will discuss the entry of children into their own membership group. For popular children, the first criterion for entry was maximizing the probability of being accepted and the second criterion was minimizing the probability of being ignored. For unpopular children, the first criterion clearly was maximizing the probability of being ignored, and, remarkably, the second criterion was maximizing the probability of being rejected. The newcomer hypothesis was thus supported by the finding that being ignored was the first criterion for the ordering of the entry-response hierarchy of unpopular children into their own membership group. Furthermore, this strategy was also highly ineffective in avoiding rejection.

We predicted that the newcomer effect would be enhanced when children entered cross-membership groups. For popular children entering unpopular groups, we found that the first criterion was maximizing the probability of acceptance but the second criterion was now maximizing the probability of being ignored. There is thus evidence of a newcomer effect for popular children when they enter cross-membership groups. When unpopular children enter popular groups the first criterion is still maximizing the probability of being ignored. However, there is no second criterion, because neither partial correlation coefficient approached significance. Thus, being ignored must be considered the only criterion for organizing the entry-response hierarchy of unpopular children entering a popular group.

There is clear evidence in these results that unpopular children act like newcomers. Their response hierarchy is organized such that the probability of being ignored by groups is maximized. When unpopular children enter their own membership group, this organization also has a high probability of leading to rejection. In other words, when the probability of being ignored is controlled for, unpopular children are doing just what they would have to do if their goal were to be rejected. Here then is a dynamic that maintains the social rejection of unpopular children.

Examination of entry behaviors

What specifically were unpopular children doing during entry that led both groups to ignore or reject them? After examining the entry-response hierarchies of both groups of children, it was evident that the hierarchies of unpopular children did differ from those of popular children in several ways. First, the computed agreement-to-disagreement ratio was 2.17 for the entering popular children in contrast to .89 for the entering unpopular children, a finding consistent with the previous analysis of the dyadic pre-entry data. Thus, even when entering, unpopular children were more disagreeable than popular children.

Unpopular children also were more likely to ask questions for information, say something about themselves, disagree, and state their feelings than were popular children. These four strategies appear to share at least one commonality: They all attempt to call the group's attention to the user. That is, unpopular children seem to try to exert control and divert the group's attention to themselves rather than attempt to integrate themselves into the ongoing conversation of the group. They introduce new conversational topics abruptly and direct the conversation to themselves by making self-statements, stating their feelings and opinions, and disagreeing with the group members more than popular children. When used by children, these strategies have a high probability of resulting in the group's ignoring or rejecting them. This point can best be illustrated by several instances from actual transcripts. The following transcript illustrates one unpopular child's attempts to call the group's attention to herself by repeatedly stating her feelings. It also illustrates the manner in which she was repeatedly ignored by the group. The name of the entering child is marked with an asterisk.

> Janet: Okay, I want this one again.
> Terry:* This is fun, ain't it?
> Janet (to Vera): Do you want this one again?
> Vera: I want this one.
> Terry:* This is a nice room, ain't it?
> Janet (to Vera): You can have this one. Here.
> Terry:* This is a nice table, ain't it?

As can be seen, this unpopular child repeatedly tried to divert the group from their ongoing activity of choosing playing pieces to a discussion concerning how much fun the game was, how nice the room was and, finally, even how nice the table was, to no avail. The group members simply continued to ignore her.

The following transcript is an example of another unpopular child's similar attempts to join the group's conversation by drawing the group's attention to himself. Rather than talk about the game the group members are engaged in, he tries to direct the conversation to an incident that involved only him during recess. Again, however, this strategy has the same result of being ignored by the group.

> Tom: M. Um . . . um . . .
> Eric:* Oh, you know . . . (David makes a face and they laugh) . . . you know I was playing with Glen. I hope you don't get mad at me. We're playing out there and Glen, he started to wrestle. I told him no so . . .
> Tom: Monkey. Monkey. Hey, um monkey. Monkey. Um, move ahead three spaces. It's your turn dumdum.
> David: Hey, um M. Monkey.
> Eric:* Uh, Glen . . . I poked, I poked his eye. I accidently poked Glen's eye and then he . . . he said he wouldn't take my apology, so Brian started getting mad at me so . . . and there I . . . Glen can see now . . . he said he couldn't see. Now he could see.
> David: I like this game.
> Tom: Okay. Okay.

In contrast, the next transcript illustrates the strategy of a popular child as he attempts to join a group. Rather than try to draw the group's attention to himself, he joins in the group's ongoing conversation by contributing relevant comments about the game the group is playing. This strategy proved quite successful, as the child was not only accepted but finally invited to join in the play of the game.

> Sam: Animals.
> Craig: What'd you get . . . B?

Matt:* What'd you go and pick?
Sam: Take another turn.
Matt:* Bear.
Sam: Gorilla. Thank you, Matt.
Matt:* Let's see . . .
Sam: Move ahead . . . (inaudible)
Matt:* Your turn.
Craig: Animals. Bear.
Matt: Hey. Mix these up.
Craig: I know. Okay, hold it. Yeah, do that. I got move ahead 3. Ooh. How
        lucky can you get. 1, 2, 3. Your turn, Matt.

In summary, then, unpopular children used four particular entry strategies – self-statements, feeling statements, disagreement, and informational questions – more than did popular children, and these strategies
were generally unsuccessful, often leading to the child's being either rejected or ignored by the group. These findings are clear if we invoke the
notion that unpopular children are behaving as if they were newcomers.
Consider the following parallel in the behavior of unpopular children and
the behavior of newcomers. After studying the process of assimilation of
newcomers into groups of 6- and 7-year-old children, Phillips, Shenker,
and Revitz (1951) proposed that the new child's most successful strategy
for integration was first to determine the "frame of reference" common to
the group members (e.g., activities, goals) and then to establish himself or
herself as sharing in this frame of reference. Specifically, the child should
first attempt to join the group's activities by imitating the actions or words
of a child in the nucleus group. This would account for the apparent success in the present study of entry bids involving agreement and exchanges
of information with group members and for the pronounced failure of disagreement when employed as an entry strategy. Phillips et al. proposed
that only later should the newcomer attempt to initiate, direct, or otherwise influence group activities. Unfortunately, the present research found
that unpopular children frequently used entry strategies that attempted to
influence the ongoing group activity by directing the group's attention to
themselves in one of four specific ways: making self-statements, stating
their feelings, asking information questions not relevant to the group's
activity, and disagreeing with group members. Phillips et al. further suggested that the premature use of such strategies would lead to the child
being ignored by the group, a finding well supported by this study.

Summary and conclusions

This chapter proposed a set of relationships between sociometric status
and group acceptance. First, in the Benson and Gottman study, sociometrics were found to provide a useful division of social groups into two

interactive cliques or membership groups, popular and unpopular. Second, in the literature, unpopular children's interaction was found to be more negative than that of popular children. In the study reported in this chapter, an analysis of dyadic interaction showed that, specifically, compared to popular children, (1) unpopular children were less agreeable and more disagreeable; (2) they were less likely to provide a general reason for disagreeing or to suggest a constructive alternative when criticizing a peer; and that (3) their disagreements were more likely to continue and to escalate into squabbling. We suggested that the interaction of unpopular children might be summarized as disagreeable and bossy and that they were unable to keep disagreements from escalating. This interactional climate provides the context for the entry situation.

We then discussed the implications of this social context and the membership group result of the Benson and Gottman study for the newcomer hypothesis. The newcomer hypothesis states that unpopular children are behaving as if they were newcomers: They "hover" when they enter groups of their peers. In our entry study we found evidence that unpopular children were indeed less likely to be accepted and more likely to be ignored by groups they enter. We also found that unpopular children waited longer before making a first bid, used more bids, and took more time for entry than popular children did.

Furthermore, unpopular children's response hierarchy preference was not predictable from a cost/benefit model that assumes that the entering child acts in such a way that the probability of being accepted is maximized and the probability of being ignored or rejected is minimized, whereas popular children's response hierarchy was predictable from this cost/benefit model. A more detailed analysis showed that unpopular children acted in such a way that the probability that they would be ignored was maximized, whereas the behavior of popular children maximized the probability that they would be accepted. There was also evidence for the newcomer hypothesis in popular children's entry into cross-membership groups; their second criterion after acceptance was maximizing being ignored. The entry of unpopular children into their own membership groups also resulted in the derivation of maximizing rejection as a second criterion.

We then asked how, specifically, unpopular children acted during entry such that the probabilities of being ignored and rejected were maximized. An analysis of the specific entry bids showed that during entry, unpopular children tended to disagree more than popular children did; they also attempted to call attention to themselves by stating their feelings and opinions, making self-statements, and asking informational questions, which only resulted in their being ignored.

We are proposing that the negative interactional style of some children causes them to affiliate with one another because the more agreeable children do not affiliate with them, but that they respond on a sociometric assessment by indicating that they would prefer to affiliate with the more agreeable children. Thus we suggest that dyadic interactional style creates two distinct membership groups that are identified by the sociometric nomination technique. Furthermore, we propose that once the two membership groups are established, the two different interactional contexts contribute to differences in entry response hierarchies. Specifically, the entry response hierarchies of popular children, regardless of the status of the group they attempt to enter, are ordered such that the probability of being accepted by the group is maximized while the probability of being ignored or rejected is minimized. It is not surprising that this is the case when popular children attempt to enter their own membership group, because they are not only familiar with the group's norms and expectations but also the interactional style typical of this group appears to be positive and agreeable in nature. Although the second criterion for the ordering of the entry response hierarchies of popular children when they attempt cross-membership group entry is to be ignored, giving some support to the newcomer hypothesis, the first criterion still is to be accepted. This may be because popular children are fairly adept at quickly discerning these unfamiliar norms. Thus, they can secure cross-membership group entry with minimal difficulty, reducing their need to behave like newcomers for extended periods of time. The present research offered support for this hypothesis, as results indicated that the entry of popular children into unpopular groups (cross-membership entry) was comparable, with respect to amount of time and bids expended, to the entry of unpopular children into their own membership group, whose norms unpopular children should know.

Unlike popular children, the entry response hierarchies of unpopular children are ordered such that the probability of being ignored by groups they attempt to enter is maximized. It is not unreasonable that the cross-membership group entry attempts of unpopular children would resemble those of newcomers, as they are unfamiliar with the norms of popular groups and perhaps are conscious of their lower status as well. It is surprising, however, that the entry behavior of unpopular children when entering their own membership group continues to resemble that of newcomers despite their presumed familiarity with the norms of their own membership group. One possibility is that the negative interactional style of the unpopular membership group makes being ignored by the group a desirable outcome. It may also be the case that the continual interaction with other socially unskillful children, caused by the split between the popular and unpopular membership groups, prevents unpopular children from acquiring appropriate entry response hierarchies. Also, this split between popular and unpopular membership groups may be responsible for unpopular children's insensitivity to the norms of the group they are entering. In any case, unpopular children act as if they were newcomers, regardless of the status of the group they attempt to enter; That is, they behave in a way that results in their being ignored and rejected. The entry-response hierarchy of unpopular children thus serves to maintain and possibly increase membership group differences.

Implications for intervention

The findings of the present research have several implications for intervention programs designed to increase the popularity of socially unaccepted children. First, on the basis of a review of the literature, a coaching format seems to be the most promising for intervention; it should be coupled with sociometric measures to evaluate outcomes. On the basis of our work, we would suggest that one aim of the intervention should be to decrease the tendency of unpopular children to act as if they were newcomers (in a way that results in their being ignored by the group). Specifically, they should be coached to reduce their initial hovering behavior by verbalizing their entry bids earlier when they attempt to join a group. Coaching should also be aimed at reduction in the unpopular children's use of entry strategies that draw attention to themselves, such as talking about themselves and stating their feelings, and that have a high probability of resulting in the group ignoring the child. Instead, unpopular children should be encouraged to determine the group's frame of reference by asking relevant questions and then to establish themselves as sharing in this frame of reference by agreeing and exchanging information with the group members.

Another facet of the intervention should involve a reduction in the frequent display of disagreement or disagreeableness by unpopular children when they interact with their peers as well as when they attempt entry. Similarly, it would be helpful to teach these children ways of preventing disagreement from continuing or escalating. Specifically, they can be coached in strategies employed by popular children. Unpopular children should be encouraged to cite a general rather than a specific reason for disagreement and then to provide an alternative action for the other child.

It must be remembered, however, that even popular children have a somewhat difficult time entering cross-membership groups. Our study found that in this situation even popular children were rejected or ignored 30 percent of the time. This would suggest that even if unpopular children were to behave just like popular children when attempting to join groups, the probability of their being rejected or ignored by the group would still remain high. It is thus crucial that intervention programs in some way "innoculate" unpopular children against being rejected or ignored when they try to enter groups. It would further seem essential to add a component to the intervention program that would provide a mechanism for increasing the group's likelihood of accepting new members. Establishing some form of incentive for the group members to accept other children might be one way to accomplish this goal.

Note

1 A more recent study by Butler (1979) also examined the relationship between popularity and social interaction patterns in the classroom. Although a different sociometric measure (the Bower class play) was used to determine the popularity of the children, the results obtained were consistent with those found by Gottman et al. (1975). Specifically, popular children were found to initiate and receive more positive interaction with their peers than unpopular children.

References

Allen, K. E., Hart, B., Buell, J. S., Harris, F. R., & Wolf, M. M. Effects of social reinforcement of isolate behavior of a nursery school child. *Child Development,* 1964, *35,* 511–518.

Amidon, E. J., & Hoffman, C. Can teachers help the socially rejected? *Elementary School Journal,* 1965, *66,* 149–154.

Asher, S. R. *Personal communication,* 1978.

Asher, S. R., & Hymel, S. Assessment of socially isolated and rejected children. In J. Wine and M. Smye (Eds.), *Social Competence.* New York: Guilford Press, in press.

Asher, S. R., Oden, S. L., & Gottman, J. M. Children's friendships in school settings. In L. G. Katz (Ed.), *Current topics in early childhood education* (Vol. 1). Norwood, N.J.: Ablex, 1977.

Bakeman, R. Untangling streams of behavior: Sequential analysis of observational data. In G. P. Sackett (Ed.), *Observing behavior (Vol. 2): Data collection and analysis methods.* Baltimore: University Park Press, 1978.

Benson, C. S., & Gottman, J. M. *Children's popularity and peer social interaction.* Unpublished manuscript, Indiana University, 1975.

Blau, B., & Rafferty, J. Changes in friendship status as a function of reinforcement. *Child Development,* 1970, *41,* 113–121.

Bock, R. D. *Multivariate statistical methods in behavioral research.* New York: McGraw-Hill, 1974.

Bonney, M. E. Assessment of efforts to aid socially isolated elementary school pupils. *Journal of Educational Research,* 1971, *64,* 345–364.

Buswell, M. M. The relationship between social structure of the classroom and the academic successes of the pupils. *Journal of Experimental Education,* 1953, *22,* 37–52.

Butler, L. J. *Social and behavioral correlates of peer reputation.* Paper presented at the biennial meeting of the Society for Research in Child Development, San Francisco, 1979.

Chance, M. R. A., & Jolly, C. *Social groups of monkeys, apes, and men.* New York: Dutton, 1976.

Charlesworth, R., & Hartup, W. W. Positive social reinforcement in the nursery school peer group. *Child Development,* 1967, *38,* 993–1003.

Cowen, E. L., Pederson, A., Babigian, M., Izzo, L. D., & Trost, M. A. Long-term follow-up of early detected vulnerable children. *Journal of Consulting and Clinical Psychology,* 1973, *41,* 438–446.

Criswell, J. H. A sociometric study of race cleavage in the classroom. *Archives of Psychology,* 1939, No. 235, 1–82.

Dawe, H. C. The influence of size of kindergarten upon performance. *Child Development,* 1934, *5,* 295–303.

Fienberg, S. E. *Analysis of cross-classified categorical data.* Cambridge, Mass.: M.I.T. Press, 1978.

Furman, W., Rahe, D. F., & Hartup, W. W. Rehabilitation of socially-withdrawn preschool children through mixed-age and same-age socialization. *Child Development,* 1979, *50,* 915–922.

Gottman, J. M. The effects of a modeling film on social isolation in preschool children: A methodological investigation. *Journal of Abnormal Child Psychology,* 1977, *5,* 69–78(a).

Toward a definition of social isolation in children. *Child Development,* 1977, *48* 513–517(b).

Detecting cyclicity in social interaction. *Psychological Bulletin,* 1979, *86,* 338–348.

Gottman, J. M., & Bakeman, R. The sequential analysis of observational data. In M. Lamb, S. Suomi, & G. Stephenson (Eds.), *Methodological problems in the study of social interaction.* Madison: University of Wisconsin Press, 1978.

Gottman, J. M., Gonso, J., & Rasmussen, B. Social interaction, social competence and friendship in children. *Child Development,* 1975, *46,* 709–718.

Gottman, J. M., Gonso, J., & Schuler, P. Teaching social skills to isolated children. *Journal of Abnormal Child Psychology,* 1976, *4,* 179–197.

Gottman, J. M., Markman, H., & Notarius, C. The topography of marital conflict: A sequential analysis of verbal and nonverbal behavior. *Journal of Marriage and the Family,* 1977, *39,* 461–477.

Gottman, J. M., & Notarius, C. Sequential analysis of observational data using Markov chains. In T. Kratochwill (Ed.), *Strategies to evaluate change in single subject research.* New York: Academic Press, 1978.

Gottman, J. M., & Parkhurst, J. T. A developmental theory of friendship and acquaintanceship processes. In W. A. Collins (Ed.), *Minnesota symposia on child psychology* (Vol. 13). Hillsdale, N.J.: Lawrence Erlbaum, 1980.

Gronlund, N. E. *Sociometry in the classroom.* New York: Harper and Brothers, 1959.

Gump, P. V., & Friesen, W. V. Participation in nonclass settings. In R. G. Barker & P. V. Gump (Eds.), *Big school, small school: High school size and student behavior.* Stanford, California: Stanford University Press, 1964.

Hartup, W. W., Glazer, J. A., & Charlesworth, R. Peer reinforcement and sociometric status. *Child Development,* 1967, *38,* 1017–1024.

Hymel, S., & Asher, S. R. *Assessment and training of isolated children's social skills.* Paper presented at the biennial meeting of the Society for Research in Child Development, New Orleans, 1977 (ERIC Document Reproduction Service No. ED 136 930).

Jormakka, L. The behavior of children during a first encounter. *Scandinavian Journal of Psychology,* 1976, *17,* 15–22.

Kohn, M., & Clausen, J. Social isolation and schizophrenia. *American Sociological Review,* 1955, *20,* 265–273.

Ladd, G. W. Effectiveness of a social learning method for enhancing children's social interaction and peer acceptance. *Child Development,* in press.

Marshall, H. R., & McCandless, B. R. Relationships between dependence on adults and social acceptance by peers. *Child Development,* 1957, *28,* 413–419. (a)
A study of prediction of social behavior of preschool children. *Child Development,* 1957, *28,* 149–159. (b)

McDavid, J. W., & Harari, H. Stereotyping of names and popularity in grade school children. *Child Development,* 1966, *37,* 453–459.

McGrew, P. L., & McGrew, W. C. Changes in children's spacing behavior with nursery school experience. *Human Development,* 1972, *15,* 359–372.

McGrew, W. C. *An ethological study of children's behavior.* New York: Academic Press, 1972.

Moore, S., & Updegraff, R. Sociometric status of preschool children related to age, sex, nurturance-giving and dependency. *Child Development,* 1964, *35,* 519–524.

O'Connor, R. D. Modification of social withdrawal through symbolic modeling. *Journal of Applied Behavior Analysis,* 1969, *2,* 15–22.
Relative efficacy of modeling, shaping, and the combined procedures for modification of social withdrawal. *Journal of Abnormal Psychology,* 1972, *79,* 327–334.

Oden, S., & Asher, S. R. Coaching children in social skills for friendship making. *Child Development,* 1977, *48,* 495–506.

Phillips, E. L., Shenker, S., & Ravitz, P. The assimilation of the new child into the group. *Psychiatry,* 1951, 14, 319–325.

Putallaz, M., & Gottman J. *An interactional model of children's entry into peer groups.* Unpublished manuscript, University of Illinois, Urbana, 1979.

Riskin, J., & Faunce, E. E. Family interaction scales, III: Discussion of methodology and substantive findings. *Archives of General Psychiatry,* 1970, *22,* 527–537.

Roff, M. Childhood social interactions and young adult bad conduct. *Journal of Abnormal and Social Psychology,* 1961, *63,* 333–337.
Childhood social interaction and young adult psychosis. *Journal of Clinical Psychology,* 1963, *19,* 152–157.

Roff, M., Sells, S. B., & Golden, M. M. *Social adjustment and personality development in children.* Minneapolis: University of Minnesota Press, 1972.

Roistacher, R. C. A microeconomic model of sociometric choice. *Sociometry,* 1974, *37,* 219–238.

Rosén, L. *Sociometric effects of a peer-interaction therapy for social isolation.* Unpublished honors thesis, University of Minnesota, 1979.

Sackett, G. P. The lag sequential analysis of contingency and cyclicity in behavioral interaction research. In J. Osofsky (Ed.), *Handbook of infant development.* New York: Wiley, 1977.

Singleton, L. C., & Asher, S. R. Peer preferences and social interaction among third-grade children in an integrated school district. *Journal of Educational Psychology,* 1977, *69,* 330–336.

Strain, P. S., Cooke, T. P., & Appolloni, T., *Teaching exceptional children.* New York: Academic Press, 1976.

Ullmann, C. A. Teachers, peers, and tests as predictors of adjustment. *Journal of Educational Psychology,* 1957, *48,* 257–267.

Vaughn, B. E., & Waters, E. Social organization among preschool peers: Dominance, attention, and sociometric correlates. In D. R. Omark, F. Strayer, & D. Freeman (Eds.),

Peer-group power relations: An ethological perspective on human dominance and submission. New York: Garland Press, 1978.

Washburn, R. W. A scheme for grading the reactions of children in a new social situation. *Journal of Genetic Psychology,* 1932, *40,* 84–99.

Wicker, A. Cognitive complexity, school size, and participation in school behavior settings: A test of the frequency of interaction hypothesis. *Journal of Educational Psychology,* 1969, *60,* 200–203.

Wilson, E. O. *Sociobiology: The new synthesis.* Cambridge, Mass.: Harvard University Press, 1975.

Young, L. L., & Cooper, D. H. Some factors associated with popularity. *The Journal of Educational Psychology,* 1944, *35,* 513–535.

Ziller, R. C., & Behringer, R. D. A longitudinal study of the assimilation of the new child in the group. *Human Relations,* 1961, *14,* 121–133.

6   Friendship between mentally retarded and nonretarded children

Jay Gottlieb and Yona Leyser

This chapter is concerned with the nature of relationships between educable mentally retarded (EMR) and nonhandicapped children. Our intent is to review some of the literature on this topic, evaluate the theoretical foundation on which most of the research is based, and suggest ways to improve the quality of retarded children's social involvement in school life. Our assumption in approaching the issue of mentally retarded children's interpersonal relationships is that there are few qualitative differences between retarded and nonretarded school children's social behavior. The differences between the two groups are matters of degree rather than of substance.

It may be useful first to provide some background information about retardation. A population of individuals exists in society that possesses few special talents or abilities. One of the defining characteristics of this population is that it has poor cognitive abilities (Grossman, 1973), which are usually first noted during the school years. These children are labeled as mentally retarded, and by definition occupy the lower 2 to 3 percent of the distribution of IQ scores. Some children are mentally retarded as a result of organic pathology acquired prior to, during, or soon after birth. The majority suffer from no known organic insult, but are labeled as mentally retarded primarily because they fail in school and may misbehave. These children are usually referred to as psychosocially retarded and represent approximately 85 percent of all diagnosed cases of mental retardation (MacMillan, 1977).

In addition to poor cognitive abilities, another defining feature of mentally retarded people is that they exhibit poor adaptive behavior (Grossman, 1973). Although the term "adaptive behavior" has cognitive components, it is used in the definition of mental retardation to refer to skills that are not usually associated with traditional intelligence tests, such as self-help and interpersonal skills. In recent years, considerable emphasis has been placed on the adaptive behavior component of the definition, pri-

150

marily to reduce the likelihood that a child will be labeled as mentally retarded solely on the basis of an IQ score that may not be culturally appropriate. Consequently, children who are defined as mentally retarded are also deficient in adaptive behavior, of which social interaction skills are one aspect.

Professionals concerned with the education of mentally retarded individuals are aware of their poor social skills and the adverse consequences these have on their vocational and social adjustment. Goldstein (1964), for example, concluded from his detailed review of the literature that mentally retarded people's poor interpersonal skills were the primary cause of their job-related problems; poor intellectual ability resulted in fewer difficulties.

The response of special educators to the limited social and academic capabilities of mentally retarded youth was to educate them in segregated classes where specially trained teachers could concentrate on their academic and social deficiencies. The classrooms in which mentally retarded children were educated contained fewer children than did regular classrooms. Teachers were especially trained to educate these children. The curriculum was tailored to their educational needs, and, in general, on a per capita basis, more resources were expended in educating mentally retarded children than nonretarded children.

Segregated education for mentally retarded children accomplished a number of purposes. Possibly its most important achievement was the shielding of mentally retarded children from the frustration resulting from inability to compete academically with nonretarded peers. In the view of the present discussion, the important point is that segregated education also avoided the common situation in which retarded children in regular classes were socially rejected by their classmates. Within a reference group composed exclusively of similar-ability peers, the segregated mentally retarded child was more often a sociometric star (Jordan, 1959) and generally made a better social adjustment than children of comparable IQ who remained in the regular classroom (Kirk, 1964).

But the accomplishments of the special class vis-à-vis retarded children's social adjustment and friendships were also counted as their greatest liability. Segregated classes were said to isolate mentally retarded children from the nonretarded children with whom they had eventually to compete. Also, segregated education denied nonretarded children experiences with mentally retarded children that might promote greater tolerance for and understanding of the enormous variability in human abilities. Further, it was argued that segregated classes prevented mentally retarded children from observing appropriate modes of social interaction as exhibited by nonretarded children, thus preventing them from modeling appropriate interpersonal behaviors necessary for effective interaction (Kaufman, Gottlieb, Agard, & Kukic, 1975).

Because of the disenchantment with segregated education voiced by the professional community and the failure of research to indicate the academic superiority of special classes (Guskin & Spicker, 1968), as well as a variety of social and legal factors (Semmel, Gottlieb, & Robinson, 1979), segregated education for mentally retarded children is on the wane. Public law 94-142 (the Education for All Handicapped Children Act of 1975) stipulates that all handicapped children in the United States regardless of the severity of their handicap, are to be educated with nonhandicapped peers to the maximum extent appropriate to their individual needs. Although guidelines do not yet exist regarding the defining features of a least restrictive environment, legal analyses of the law lead to the following conclusions: (1) Most mildly retarded children are to be educated mainly in regular classrooms, with appropriate educational support; and (2) most moderately and severely retarded children are to be educated in regular school buildings, although in segregated classrooms (Gilhool & Stutman, 1978).

Thus, educators will soon face the prospect of having to provide a free and appropriate public education for mildly retarded children in the mainstream of the school. They will also face the prospect of establishing segregated classrooms for a population of severely retarded children who historically have been closeted in institutions away from the public eye. There is no uncertainty regarding the intent of the law as it pertains to the education of mentally retarded children in contact with nonhandicapped peers. As Senator Hubert Humphrey, one of the law's chief sponsors, stated, "The time has come when we can no longer tolerate the invisibility of the handicapped in America" (118 Congressional Record, 525).

It is against this legal background of education for the mentally retarded that we must consider a number of issues related to the effects of physical proximity on both retarded and nonretarded children. Possible consequences of the forthcoming interaction between retarded and nonretarded children must be carefully considered in order to provide the information that will enable educators to serve better the clients for whom they are responsible.

Fortunately, as we begin a new era in the education of handicapped children, we are not totally ignorant of the likely course of social relationships between retarded children and their nonretarded classmates. Research has been done that pertains to a number of relevant concerns, especially the social status of mentally retarded children in regular-class mainstreamed settings.

Social aspects of educating mentally retarded children in the mainstream – a brief introduction

Although the term "mainstreaming" pervades the special education literature today, the concept itself is not new, nor do we lack information on how mainstreaming is likely to affect the social relations of educable mentally retarded (EMR) children. Thirty years ago, Johnson (1950) studied the sociometric position of academically retarded children in regular classes. Results indicated that children whom he labeled as mentally retarded were socially rejected almost four times as frequently as nonhandicapped children. Nonhandicapped children, on the other hand, were sociometrically accepted almost twice as often as the retarded children. Johnson's study was the first to investigate, in detail, the sociometric status of EMR children in regular classes, and the data from the study were used throughout the 1950s and early 1960s as justification for removing retarded children from the regular grades.

An examination of the procedures Johnson used can shed light on some aspects of friendship choices between retarded and nonretarded children in regular classes. In order to obtain sociometric ratings of mentally retarded children, Johnson first had to identify the mentally retarded children, because neither of the two communities he studied had any organized system of special classes. Johnson initiated a four-step process. First, he asked classroom teachers to name children in their classes who were exceptionally slow in their ability to grasp new things and who were academically retarded. Next, he administered group IQ tests in classes where the teacher identified one or more children as being slow. Then, he administered an individual IQ test to children who scored poorly on the group test. Finally, he identified children as EMR if they attained a test score of less than 70. The thirty-nine identified children (5.6 percent of the sample initially tested) were socially rejected almost four times as frequently as the other children.

When considering the socially rejected status of the thirty-nine children, two points must be considered. First, because none of the thirty-nine children were identified by the school prior to the study, they were never labeled as mentally retarded. Consequently, the variance in social rejection attributable either to the mentally retarded label or to special class placement did not enter into the findings. It is conceivable that the rejection rate would have been higher had the children been labeled as mentally retarded prior to the study.

The second point that must be considered is that the final sample of thirty-nine children was probably not representative of children who would have been in special classes had such classes been available. Usually, classroom teachers refer children for special-class placement when the children are academically retarded and they misbehave. Johnson did not allow teachers to refer children who only exhibited misbehavior. Because misbehavior is more closely associated with social rejection than academic retardation is (Gottlieb, Semmel, & Veldman, 1978), the rate of rejection Johnson obtained is probably an underestimate of the true rate of rejection of school-identified EMR children.

That EMR children in regular classrooms (mainstreamed children) are socially rejected considerably more often than nonretarded children is not suggested by Johnson's study alone. Several later investigations reported similar results (e.g., Heber, 1956; Kirk & Johnson, 1951; Miller, 1956). Taken in total, the data on the sociometric status of EMR children in regular classes do not portray a favorable picture; EMR children are rejected more and accepted less than nonretarded classmates. Yet, despite these data, special educators maintained that placing retarded children in regular classes would improve the extent to which they would be known, and, it was to be hoped, accepted by their nonretarded classmates (e.g., Christoplos & Renz, 1969). Contact between retarded and nonretarded children, it was asserted, would result in favorable social outcomes for the retarded child.

Contact hypothesis and mental retardation

One of the principal arguments advanced in support of the movement to integrate retarded people into the mainstream of society is that contact between retarded and nonretarded people will produce beneficial consequences, such as reducing strangeness between the retarded and nonretarded. This contact hypothesis was strongly advocated as a reason for mainstreaming retarded children who had been placed in self-contained special classes (see Christoplos & Renz, 1969). According to the contact hypothesis, as retarded children were enrolled in regular classes, normal children would become more familiar with them and would like them better as a result.

We conducted a series of studies to test this hypothesis. In the first study, Goodman, Gottlieb, and Harrison (1972) compared the sociometric status of ten EMR children who attended regular classes in a nongraded elementary school and eight EMR children who remained in a special class in the same school. We hypothesized that non-EMR children would rate the mainstreamed EMR children more favorably than they would rate the segregated children, because the mainstreamed children were more familiar to their non-EMR peers as a result of their contact with them in school. A forced-choice sociometric scale was administered to forty non-EMR children who rated the integrated and segregated EMR children and a randomly selected sample of other non-EMR children. The non-EMR raters were asked whether they liked, tolerated, didn't like, or didn't know each child whose name appeared on a list of their schoolmates. Results indicated that nonretarded children occupied a more favored social status in the peer hierarchy than either integrated or segregated retarded children, and that male raters rejected integrated EMR children whom they knew significantly more frequently than they rejected segregated EMR children whom they also knew. Ratings of female raters did not differentiate between integrated and segregated EMR children. These results failed to support the contact hypothesis that mainstreamed placement promotes the social acceptance of retarded children by providing greater opportunity for contact between retarded and nonretarded children.

In a subsequent study, Gottlieb and Budoff (1973) continued investigating whether increased contact between nonretarded and retarded children is accompanied by lower social status of the latter group of children. These investigators administered the same sociometric measure used in the previous study to 136 nonretarded elementary school pupils. Children provided sociometric ratings of a randomly selected group of nonretarded peers, twelve partially integrated EMR children, and twelve segregated EMR children who attended the same schools as the raters. Both the integrated and segregated EMR children were enrolled in one of two schools: The first school building was traditional in that it contained classrooms accommodating approximately twenty-five to thirty children; the second school building did not contain any interior walls, and as a result, all children, including the retarded children, were at least somewhat visible to all other peers. The segregated EMR children in the no-interior-wall school occupied a corner of the building and were the least visible children in the school. Still, they were more visible than the segregated EMR children in the traditional school building.

Two specific hypotheses were advanced. The first hypothesis was that, regardless of placement, EMR children in the no-interior-wall school would have lower social status than EMR children in the traditional school, because the former group of EMR children was more visible to their peers. The second hypothesis was that partially integrated EMR pupils would receive less favorable ratings than segregated EMR pupils regardless of the school they attended, because integrated EMR children were more visible to their peers than segregated EMR pupils. Results supported these predictions: Integrated pupils had lower social status

than segregated pupils regardless of the school in which they were enrolled, and EMR children were more rejected in the no-interior-wall
school than the traditional school. This study also confirmed the finding
of Goodman et al. (1972) that non-EMR children as a whole enjoy more
favorable social status than either partially integrated or segregated EMR
children.

Results of studies employing nonsociometric measures also seem to
contradict the contact hypothesis. For example, Gottlieb, Cohen, and
Goldstein (1974) assessed attitudes of 399 nonretarded elementary-school
pupils toward retarded children, using an adjective rating scale. The study
consisted of two independent replications employing children of different
socioeconomic levels. Children were drawn from three different types of
elementary schools: a no-interior-wall school where visibility of EMR
children was maximized, a traditional school with both integrated and
segregated EMR pupils, and a school in which there were no special-education pupils. For both the lower-class and affluent samples, attitudes
toward EMR children were found to be most favorable in schools with no
special-education pupils.

In a behaviorally based social-choice experiment by Gottlieb and Davis
(1973), nonretarded children in the intermediate grades were asked to
choose either a nonretarded child or an EMR pupil as a partner with
whom to play a ringtoss game. Results indicated that non-EMR children
almost invariably selected another non-EMR child when given the choice
between an EMR and a non-EMR child: A nonretarded child was selected
as the preferred partner twenty-seven out of twenty-eight possible times
in the first two treatment conditions. In the third treatment condition,
when the non-EMR subject was asked to choose either a segregated or an
integrated EMR child, there was no statistically significant difference in
the choice distribution – integrated EMR children were selected by eight
of fourteen non-EMR subjects. Thus neither of these studies supports
the notion that greater contact between retarded and nonretarded children
is accompanied by an increase in the social acceptance of retarded
children.

Only one investigation appears to be inconsistent with the previous
studies. Sheare (1974) administered a questionnaire measuring attitudes
toward special-class pupils to 400 nonretarded junior high school pupils,
half of whom were randomly assigned to classrooms with no EMR pupils
and half of whom were assigned to classrooms with partially integrated
EMR pupils. Results indicated that non-EMR adolescents who had the
opportunity to interact with EMR students expressed significantly more

favorable attitudes toward special-class pupils than did non-EMR pupils who did not have EMR pupils in their classes. This finding, however, was not supported in another study of adolescents' attitudes toward EMR children (Rucker, Howe, & Snider, 1969).

With the exception of Sheare's 1974 study, research has failed to support the proposition that integration into regular classrooms, with its resulting contact between retarded and nonretarded children, improves the social status of EMR children. Although effects of integrated placement may reflect factors other than contact (for example, removal of the ''mentally retarded'' label), integrated placement does provide greater opportunities for non-EMR children to observe the behavior of retarded children. Several studies have examined the effects of no-interior-wall schools on acceptance of retarded pupils (e.g., Gottlieb & Budoff, 1973; Gottlieb et al., 1974). When viewed in this way, results of studies of integration and architecture are often generally consistent: Retarded children whose behavior is more visible to their nonretarded peers occupy a social position that is lower than that of their less visible retarded peers.

Although class placement and architectural structure affect the extent to which peers can observe the behavior of EMR children, the amount of time that retarded children are actually exposed to nonretarded children during the school day was not directly studied in any of the previous investigations. Given the findings of studies of placement and architecture, as well as the findings of earlier studies that retarded children are rejected because they are perceived to misbehave (Baldwin, 1958; Johnson, 1950), one could speculate that the more time retarded children are visible to their nonhandicapped peers, the more they are likely to occupy an unfavorable social position. In other words, one might hypothesize that a negative linear relationship exists between a retarded child's social status and the amount of time he or she is integrated into regular classes.

This hypothesis was tested by Gottlieb, Semmel, and Veldman (1978), who assessed the relative contribution of perceptions of classroom behavior and academic ability, as well as the amount of time integrated, to acceptance and rejection of retarded children. Subjects were 300 elementary-school EMR children who were integrated with nonhandicapped peers for different amounts of time during the school day. Sociometric status was measured by the forced-choice sociometric instrument in which non-EMR raters indicated whether they liked, tolerated, didn't like, or didn't know each child in their class. Rejection and acceptance were the dependent variables in two commonality analyses in which the predictor variables were peers' and teachers' perceptions of EMR pupils' academic ability and aggressive behavior and the linear and quadratic components of the number of hours of academic integration per week. Results indicated that teachers' and peers' perceptions of EMR children's misbehavior were significantly related to social rejection scores. Teachers' and peers' perceptions of EMR children's academic competence, although not related to rejection, were significantly correlated with social acceptance scores: Children who were perceived as competent were better accepted. Length of contact did not contribute a significant percent of unique variance in social acceptance or rejection scores. This study revealed, then, that the amount of time for which a retarded child is integrated has little effect on his social status. These results supported findings of previous research that indicated that mere contact between normal and retarded children does little to improve attitudes toward retarded children. Rather, this study suggests that behavior that the retarded child is perceived to display has a greater influence on others' attitudes toward the child than exposure does.

The implication of our research, then, is that contact between retarded and normal children will not produce positive attitude change unless the retarded children can be taught to exhibit behavior that conforms to the standards expected by their nonretarded peers. In other words, placement of retarded children with nonretarded children must follow or coincide with efforts to modify the retarded children's inappropriate behavior patterns, assuming that retarded children are more apt to be accepted by their nonretarded peers when their behavior meets an acceptable standard of appropriateness or competence.

This speculation has received empirical support in a controlled laboratory study by Strichart and Gottlieb (1975) that examined the extent to which normal children will imitate a retarded child as a function of the latter's competence on a rigged task. As predicted, the more competent the retarded child, the more often the child was imitated. Furthermore, the more competent the retarded child, the more frequently the child was selected as a play companion on a future game task. This study demonstrated that the more competent the behavior displayed by retarded children, the more their social acceptance by nonretarded peers is likely to improve.

The literature reviewed suggests that contact alone is not likely to generate positive attitudes toward mentally retarded children. Other variables, such as the competence that the retarded child displays, must also be considered. However, a demonstration of appropriate behavior is only one of several factors that were initially hypothesized to intervene between contact and positive intergroup attitudes. Few of these additional factors were systematically considered when mainstreaming programs were being introduced.

The contact hypothesis reconsidered

The preceding review of research concerning the effects of contact on the sociometric choices of nonretarded children toward mentally retarded peers indicated that the majority of studies did not find that contact results in acceptance of the mentally retarded. The question arises as to whether the initial expectation of favorable attitudes toward the mentally retarded was justified. Did we have sufficient reason to believe that mentally retarded children would become better liked by nonretarded children when the two groups had opportunity to interact with each other? An answer to this question requires that we consider the provisions that are necessary for contact to result in more favorable attitudes by the majority group toward members of a minority.

The "contact hypothesis," which special educators borrowed to base their predictions regarding the positive effects of mainstreaming, was originally advanced by Allport (1954) to explain the nature of racial prejudice and ways to ameliorate it. Allport never suggested that the relationship between contact and attitudes was a simple one. He did state that in order to determine the effect of contact on attitudes a variety of variables must be investigated both singly and in interaction. Among the many variables that required study were the personality of the individuals experiencing the contact, the areas of contact, and the role and status aspects of the contact (Allport, 1954). The varied ways that contact could occur and differentially affect attitudes were also described by other theorists (e.g., Cook & Sellitz, 1955; Sherif & Sherif, 1953).

In a major review of the contact hypothesis as it concerns intergroup attitudes, Amir (1969) examined the role of contact under a number of headings, many of which are relevant for a discussion of the effects of contact on attitudes toward retarded persons. Amir listed, among other topics, opportunities for contact, equal-status contact, contact with high-status representatives of a minority group, and institutional support as issues related to the nature of contact that could affect interpersonal relations. The possible influence of these variables on attitudes and friendship choices toward mentally retarded children must be studied if we are to begin to understand the effects of contact between retarded and nonretarded children.

Opportunities for contact

There is little doubt that a regular classroom provides greater opportunities than a segregated classroom for the retarded child to interact with nonretarded children. However, regular class placement per se does not guarantee that interaction will occur. Although we are unaware of research that has systematically compared the rate of social interaction of retarded and nonretarded children in regular classes, our informal observations suggest that many retarded children in regular classes are isolated from the activities of their classmates. Retarded children in such circumstances are physically integrated but socially and psychologically isolated. Unless the classroom teacher actively works to involve the retarded child in the class routine, it cannot be assumed that interactions will occur. However, when the necessary steps are taken and retarded children are made to be integral members of the class, their sociometric status improves significantly, as is evident from the results of studies that have used this approach and that are reviewed later in this chapter.

However, close examination of the attitude change studies suggests that in addition to promoting opportunities for contact, the investigations also structured situations that allowed the retarded child to compete on relatively even terms. This aspect of the treatments leads us to consider a second factor in the contact hypothesis: equal-status contact.

Equal-status contact

Allport (1954) originally pointed out that in order for contact to reduce racial prejudice, the contact must involve equal status between the majority- and minority-group members. That is, one member of the group must not occupy a clearly subordinate role to the other. Support for the equal-status principle is available in a study by Mannheimer and Williams (1949), which reported that soldiers in racially integrated platoons were more apt to favor integrated companies than soldiers who were attached to racially segregated platoons.

The need for equal-status contact poses many problems when we attempt to apply this principle to improving attitudes toward mentally retarded children. As long as academic proficiency remains a valued trait in society, it is doubtful that retarded children will attain equal status in school. Although situations can be structured that minimize the academic demands that are placed on all children, such as the studies that attempt to improve the sociometric status of retarded children (e.g., Ballard et al.,

1977), these situations are artificial. Regular class activities invariably stress academic material and situations that minimize these activities do not represent the vast majority of classes. As long as the need to feel competent remains a critical element of the socialization process (Campbell, 1964) and continues to be the central concern that schools try to impress on children (Dexter, 1964), it is doubtful that mentally retarded children will be able to compete on equal-status grounds.

Mentally retarded children also are disadvantaged in general communication skills that are crucial in influencing interpersonal relationships. Lack of such skills may preclude equal-status interaction. Mentally retarded children exhibit developmental lags in speech and language. As Semmel (1966) noted, delayed language development is one of the earliest and most significant symptoms of mental handicap. Most often, the magnitude of retarded children's deficiencies on these overt tasks is so severe that differences between retarded children and their nonretarded classmates cannot be concealed for an extended period of time, as studies of aptitude change attempt to do (e.g., Ballard et al., 1977).

To reiterate, the contact hypothesis predicts intergroup attitude improvement when equal-status contact between the majority- and minority-group members is possible. In the case of mentally retarded children, equal-status contact in the regular classroom is unlikely. Retarded children display a variety of obtrusive disabilities in areas that are valued by society. Although it is possible to construct situations that enable the retarded child to compete on an equal status in novel situations, these novel situations lack generalizeability. An even greater lack of generalizeability occurs when we attempt to assess yet a different set of conditions that Allport suggested: contact with a high-status minority person.

Contact with high-status representatives of a minority group

Several studies have indicated that friendly contact between members of a majority group and high-status representatives of a minority group tends to reduce prejudice toward the entire minority group. In the realm of mental retardation, there are few high-status children, although some do exist. For the most part, the characteristics of high-status retarded children are not known, although children who do not misbehave are far more likely than misbehaving children to be included among the high-status group (Gottlieb, Semmel, & Veldman, 1978).

Whether or not contact with a high-status retarded child tends to improve nonretarded children's attitudes toward other retarded children is presently an unanswered question – one that will be difficult to answer. Unlike black children, for example, who are known to belong to an identifiable minority group, mentally retarded children in the mainstream of education are not identified to their classmates as mentally retarded, and most cannot be identified simply by sight. Therefore, when nonretarded children enjoy an interaction with a high-status retarded child, their attitudes may not generalize to other retarded children, because the nonretarded children may not know that the person with whom they had contact is a member of a minority group. They may know the child is a poor achiever or cannot communicate well either verbally or orally, but they probably do not know that the child was labeled by the school as mentally retarded. In the absence of a label that targets a child as a member of a distinctive group, there is little reason to expect attitudes toward that child to generalize to others of the group. An exception to this statement would occur when the classroom teacher, as a representative of school authority, identifies the child to the other children as retarded and treats him or her especially well.

Institutional support

Institutional support can come from any authority that is accepted by the interacting groups. In the case of mental retardation, institutional support for mainstreaming must come from teachers and administrators. Unfortunately, there is little evidence that school professionals favor the practice of mainstreaming (Baker & Gottlieb, 1980). Most regular classroom teachers feel poorly equipped to teach handicapped children in their classes (Gickling & Theobold, 1975).

The teacher is an important influence on the nature of the retarded child's friendships. Evidence among high-school students indicates that the instructor is able to influence students' sociometric choices (Flanders & Havumaki, 1963). Among younger children, Gottlieb et al. (1978) found that teachers' ratings of retarded children's behavior explained more variance in the EMR children's sociometric status than nonretarded children's ratings of behavior did, even though the nonretarded children provided the sociometric choice data.

The data regarding teachers' attitudes toward mainstreaming retarded children are fairly clear: Most teachers do not express positive attitudes toward mainstreaming, and after a year's experience with retarded children, an even greater majority of regular class teachers are opposed to mainstreaming (Shotel, Iano, & McGettigan, 1972). Furthermore, most regular class teachers do not alter their classroom practices to accommodate retarded children. To the extent that retarded childrens' progress in regular class depends upon the willingness of regular classroom teachers to develop an appropriate academic and social milieu, there is little reason to expect retarded children to prosper.

In sum, the mainstreaming movement was predicated on the assumption that mentally retarded children would be less stigmatized and better accepted if they were not placed in segregated classrooms. Today, approximately twelve years after the movement away from self-contained classes began, there is little evidence that mainstreaming operates to the social or academic advantage of retarded children. The friendships with nonretarded children that were supposed to result from mainstreaming have, for the most part, not developed. The contact hypothesis that formed the philosophical underpinnings for much of the mainstreaming movement did not take into account the many variables that affect intergroup relations. Opportunities for contact were provided, but not nearly enough. Equal-status contact is difficult if not impossible to achieve for more than a brief period of time. High-status retarded children are few in number. Finally, institutional support from teachers and administrators has been slow in coming.

Despite the rather bleak portrait of the intergroup relations between retarded and nonretarded children, two facts are apparent. First, as a group, retarded children's mean social acceptance scores are approximately ¾ of a standard deviation below that of nonretarded children before an experimental treatment is imposed, and approximately ½ a standard deviation below after an effective experimental intervention (Ballard et al., 1977). Such data suggest that interventions designed to improve the social acceptance are successful in securing some improvement, although the improvement does not render retarded children comparable in status to nonretarded children. The second fact that persists is that the intent of federal legislation is for handicapped children to be educated with nonhandicapped peers. As part of our obligation to provide an appropriate education in the mainstream of the school, we must take every possible step to ensure that retarded children are not socially rejected by their peers. Taken together, these two facts mandate that we continue our efforts to design intervention strategies to improve the sociometric position of retarded children. However, before presenting a review of interventions, we will first indicate briefly some cognitive and motivational characteristics of mentally retarded children that must be considered in the design of interventions.

Characteristics of the mentally retarded

Indexes of cognitive dysfunctions

Overall, the literature indicates that mentally retarded persons are inefficient learners (MacMillan, 1977; Robinson & Robinson, 1976). As Mercer
and Snell (1977) have noted, "Slowness and inefficiency in the acquisition
of knowledge and skills (learning) are primary factors which are consistently used to describe mentally retarded individuals" (p. 313). Investigations of the learning processes of mentally retarded people have indicated
difficulties in input organization, attention, memory, and incidental learning.

Spitz's work (1963, 1966) has suggested that, compared to normals,
mentally retarded individuals have more difficulty in organizing input material. Spitz suggested that the major difficulty is with the spontaneous
use of categorization strategies. The performance of mentally retarded
persons may be hampered by either an inefficient organizational strategy
or by an inability to organize input. Spitz (1966) offered the following
learning sequence within which the difficulties of the mentally retarded
learner could be postulated: (a) arouse (person is alerted); (b) attend (attention is given to a specific stimulus); (c) input (file into appropriate
"hold" area); (d) hold; (e) recall (retrieve material from temporary file if
necessary); (f) store (put into appropriate permanent file); and (g) recall
(retrieve material from permanent file if necessary). According to Spitz,
the major difficulty of the mentally retarded is in area c.

Zeaman and House (1963) concluded that the mentally retarded
are deficient in attention. They suggested that the difficulty of the
retarded learner is that of paying attention to the relevant stimuli in
discrimination tasks. Nonretarded subjects, on the other hand, are more
likely to attend to dimensions that have been critical to solving similar problems in the past and to ignore those dimensions that are irrelevant.

The work of Ellis (1963, 1970) suggested that the mentally retarded are
deficient in short-term memory. Ellis identified this difficulty as one that is
due to a failure to use active rehearsal strategies spontaneously. It involves both acquisition and retrieval strategies. Retarded subjects do not
appear to use either strategy spontaneously (Robinson & Robinson,
1976). Training the mentally retarded to rehearse leads to improved performance. However, several problems in training have been noted. First,
the effects of training typically dissipate rapidly. Second, training individuals in the various components does not guarantee that they will be joined

together properly unless the overall sequence itself is explicitly trained (Robinson & Robinson, 1976).

Motivational characteristics

In addition to the many cognitive limitations of mentally retarded children that could prevent them from benefitting from interventions, a number of motivational difficulties also complicate training attempts. For our brief overview, the motivational difficulties of mentally retarded children can be centered around two interrelated concerns: expectancy to fail and internal–external orientations.

The retarded individual experiences more failure than children with average or above average intelligence and therefore tends to develop a greater generalized expectancy for failure (Cromwell, 1963). As a result of their repeated failure experience, mentally retarded children are thought to be motivated by a fear of failure rather than by a motivation to succeed. When presented with a new task, the child often expects to fail even before attempting the task. This high expectancy of failure lowers the overall performance of the mentally retarded below the level one would expect based on intellectual capacity alone (Cromwell, 1963). Moss (1958) characterized the mentally retarded as "failure avoiders" who are sensitive to cues associated with impending failure; because of their preoccupation with failure cues, they are not alert to cues that are relevant to successful solutions. However, mentally retarded people are alert to cues provided by other people in their environments; that is, retarded people are outer-directed (Zigler, 1966).

Studies have suggested that a disproportionate number of mentally retarded people function from an external orientation (Lawrence & Winschel, 1975). That is, they do not view their own efforts as being instrumental in obtaining rewards; the efforts of others dictate consequences. Therefore, retarded children often look to others to guide their actions.

In the context of the present discussion, the fact that mentally retarded children are often externally oriented suggests the hope that they will focus on the cues provided by other children in their environment. Thus, for example, if we want to change retarded children's behavior by having them model others' behavior, we have reason to expect that they will attend at least initially to the behavior modelled by the other people.

As we now review a variety of intervention techniques that have been applied to nonretarded children, it is important to bear in mind some of the cognitive and motivational characteristics that typify many retarded children so that we may tailor interventions appropriately.

Interventions

Over the last fifty years, many general procedures have been developed to cope with the problems of the socially rejected and isolated child in the classroom. Although most of these interventions do not deal directly with the mentally retarded child, they have implications for dealing with the socially rejected mentally retarded pupil.

A brief review of several types of intervention will be offered in this section. However, we would like to suggest a note of caution: Many of these interventions have been reported by individual teachers working solely within their own classes and lack adequate experimental designs. Although it is difficult to draw conclusions from these types of reports, they may provide some practical suggestions for other classroom teachers. They may also offer ideas for research to the interested investigator. We will begin with sociometric grouping since this strategy has been the most popular with EMR children.

Sociometric grouping

One of the early strategies for helping socially rejected children is that of sociometric grouping or the "sociometric placement technique" (Moreno, 1953). This technique requires that the classroom seating arrangement, work groups, or play groups be rearranged based on the results of sociometric testing. The idea behind regrouping is that pupils with low status will have an increased opportunity to be in closer physical and (it so hoped) psychological proximity to high-status children. From a theoretical view, it may be suggested that: (a) the high-status child will serve as a model whose behavior will be imitated by the low-status child, and (b) the high-status pupils will change their attitudes toward the low-status children after interacting with them. These two assumptions underlaid several studies that used sociometric grouping patterns with EMR children.

In the first study, Chennault (1967) attempted to improve the social acceptance of special-class EMR children through interaction, in organized group activities, with the most popular children in their classes. Low-status junior-high-school EMR children participated in a dramatic skit with high-status retarded children for two fifteen-minute periods weekly over a five-week period. Sociometric testing after the skit was performed revealed that the isolates who participated in the skit improved their social position scores significantly more than the rejected EMR children who did not participate.

McDaniel (1970) employed a similar approach to improve the social status of EMR adolescents by having them engage in square dancing and basketball over a six-week period. Sixteen EMR adolescents of comparable chronological age and IQ who participated only in the usual classroom activities constituted the control group. At the end of every week, experimental and control subjects were asked to indicate with whom they would like to sit and play and with whom they would not like to sit and play. The experimental group obtained higher social acceptance scores. For some retarded children, contact with other retarded children resulted in a greater number of rejections.

It has been demonstrated that it is sometimes possible to improve the social status of EMR children by having them interact with other retarded children who provide the sociometric ratings. How durable is the change? Do formerly rejected children revert to their original social positions when the opportunities for social interaction are removed? Rucker and Vincenzo (1970) extended Chennault's investigation by having the two least accepted special-class pupils interact in carnival preparation activities with the most popular members of their special class. The authors predicted that the low-status special-class children who participated in the planning would improve their social acceptance scores significantly more than a control group but that the gains would not persist one month after the completion of the treatment. Both predictions were supported. Immediate sociometric improvements did result, but they were not maintained on the post-posttest.

Lilly (1971) incorporated various refinements in the nature of experimenter and peer interactions that might contribute to improved social status and relate to the permanence of improved social acceptance by nonretarded classmates. Lilly had two low-sociometric-status, low-achieving children participate with two other children in making a film to be shown to the class. Depending on the treatment conditions, the other children were either high or low status, and the experimenter participated either fully or minimally. The investigator observed that all treatments were equally effective in improving social acceptance one week following the completion of the treatment, but that the gains were lost on the post-posttest six to seven weeks following the initial posttest. Like Chennault (1967), McDaniel (1970), and Rucker and Vincenzo (1970), Lilly did not analyze his data to reveal whether there were differential changes in the sociometric scores assigned to the rejected children by the children with whom they interacted, as opposed to the remaining nonparticipating classroom members.

The most recent investigation of attitude improvement toward main-streamed EMR children was conducted by Ballard, Corman, Gottlieb, and Kaufman (1977). These investigators identified one EMR child in each of thirty-seven classrooms. Twenty-five of the classrooms were marked for experimental intervention while the remaining twelve were designated as the control group. Each experimental classroom consisted of several groups of four to six children, one of which contained the EMR pupil. Children in a group participated together to produce and present a multimedia project, such as a slide show or skit. The experimental treatment, which lasted for eight weeks, was designed to maximize the extent of cooperation and constructive interchange among pupils in a situation that minimized the salience of the retarded child's limited abilities. Results of the experiment revealed that EMR pupils in the experimental classrooms had significantly higher posttreatment acceptance scores than did the EMR pupils in the control classes. In this investigation, the post-testing was conducted two to four weeks after the end of the experimental treatment and represents the first indication in the literature that so-ciometric improvement is durable for at least this amount of time.

Studies of attitude change indicate that it is possible to effect at least temporary improvement in attitudes toward EMR children when opportu-nities for contact between majority- and minority-group members are de-veloped from sociometric grouping techniques. However, when we con-sider use of this intervention paradigm with the rejected mentally retarded child, two cautions should be noted. First, only in one study has it been reported that the mentally retarded child will imitiate desired social be-havior as a result of interaction with socially accepted pupils (Gampel, Gottlieb, & Harrison, 1974). No evidence exists that any of the EMR subjects in the sociometric intervention studies improved their social be-havior. Second, it is possible that during these interactions the socially accepted children may become even more aware of the cognitive and so-cial incompetence of the mentally retarded child, and therefore will reject the retarded child more than they previously did.

At present, we do not know the precise reasons why the social status of EMR children improved after the children were paired for several weeks with high-status nonhandicapped children. The most likely explanation is that the contact opportunities between retarded and nonretarded children did not allow the latter to display academic incompetence because the tasks were of a nonacademic nature. An alternative is that the task struc-ture allowed for cooperative behavior between the retarded and nonre-tarded children that led to rewards for the entire group. If either of these explanations is valid, the social status of retarded children might be improved by alteration of environmental variables: Changes in the quality of retarded children's behavior need not occur.

Role playing

Publications on role playing have suggested that it has several unique advantages in the classroom (see Chesler & Fox, 1966; Furness, 1976; Shaftel & Shaftel, 1967). Role playing allegedly helps students to: (1) develop increased self-understanding and awareness of their own feelings, (2) express feelings without fear of embarrassment or retaliation, (3) develop empathy for and insight into other people, (4) try out new behaviors and experiment with new roles, (5) learn and practice new social skills, (6) improve psychomotor skills, (7) improve creativity and imagination, and (8) enhance subject-matter learning (Roark & Stanford, 1975). Role playing as a teaching methodology has also been found to be useful with mentally retarded persons (Buchan, 1972; Katz, 1972; Moreno, 1953, Sarbin, 1957). However, few definitive conclusions can be drawn since the research either lacked control groups (Taba & Elkins, 1950) or used only a single subject (Cartenson, 1955; Solt, 1962). Other studies of a more carefully controlled and generalizable nature did not support the notion that role playing is effective for improving the acceptance of socially rejected or isolated pupils (Leyser, 1979; Long, 1957; Sourwine & Conway, 1953).

Several reasons can be noted for the limited effectiveness of the reported role playing interventions. First, it is possible that a child who is widely rejected and poorly accepted has highly visible personality characteristics and manifests inappropriate social skills to such an extent that he or she is invulnerable to short role-playing treatments, especially when conducted in a group. Second, there has been no indication as to the rejected subject's actual involvement in the role playing. It is possible that they were mainly observers to the role playing rather than role players themselves.

Counseling

Counseling has been used to help socially rejected children get a better insight into and understanding of their situation and to promote a willingness to change. For example, Kranzler, Mayer, Dyer, and Munger (1966) used counseling in four fourth-grade classrooms to help socially rejected pupils gain in peer status. Subjects were the five lowest children in each classroom based on the results of a sociometric test (Moreno type). Children were randomly assigned to one of three conditions: a counseling condition, in which pupils received individual and group therapy using a client-centered approach, a teacher-guidance condition in which low-status pupils were assigned tasks and given praise, and an untreated control condition.

A sociometric test was administered five months after the start of the treatment. Results showed that the counseled group differed significantly from the teacher-guidance and control groups. The latter two groups did not differ significantly from each other. In the second posttest seven months later, the difference between the counseled and the control group was still significant. The authors noted the long-term effects of counseling but were also aware of their inability to determine whether it was the group counseling, the individual counseling, or the fact that the children were removed from the classroom and given special attention that made the difference.

The authors attempted to improve on the Kranzler et al. (1966) study in a later investigation (Mayer, Kranzler, & Matthes, 1967) involving 265 low-status fifth- and sixth-grade children and employing the same conditions. However, no significant differences among groups were detected when the sociometric posttest was administered two months later. In attempting to explain the lack of significant findings, Mayer et al. (1967) pointed out that the treatment program was much shorter than the program used in the 1966 investigation, and concluded that short-term counseling is not effective in changing social status.

It has been suggested that successful counseling has several prerequisites. These include the person's concern about the problem, such as concern about having poor peer relationships; and a willingness or motivation to change. Furthermore, as Kranzler et al. (1966) noted, although progress during the counseling session was similar to progress that takes place during counseling sessions for adults, the children in the study did not seem able or willing to set or enforce limits for the group and seemed less interested in the problems of others. The authors also questioned the effectiveness of group counseling with a group composed entirely of socially rejected pupils, because these children have not only been rejected by peers but have also been rejected by each other.

Questions can be raised as to the effectiveness of group or individual counseling with mentally retarded children as well. Evidence from research (Miller, 1956) indicates that mentally retarded rejected children may not be aware of their low social status and therefore may not be ready to change. Furthermore, because counseling is highly verbal, it may not be the most useful method with this population.

Other techniques that may be used with children require many fewer verbal and abstract abilities. Robinson and Robinson (1976) noted that contemporary approaches to counseling that are broader and more flexible than traditional psychotherapy can be used with the mentally retarded with some modifications. For example, the difficulty in verbal ability that many mentally retarded experience can be overcome by reducing the verbal component. Also, the tendency of the mentally retarded to remain passive in learning and memory situations may require more active strategies. A number of nonverbal techniques (i.e., play therapy, music therapy, art therapy), as well as several verbal techniques have been used with the mentally retarded and are reviewed by Robinson and Robinson (1976), who note that at the present time few definitive statements can be made about their effectiveness.

Positive reinforcement

Several studies have demonstrated the effectiveness of positive reinforcement in increasing the sociometric status of children. For example, in a study by Lott and Lott (1960), third- and fifth-grade children were divided into three-member groups for participation in a board game called Rocket Ship. Groups were composed of children who had not chosen each other on a sociometric measure. The experimenter arranged to have some children succeed and others fail in playing the game. Prior to the game, the experimenter decided how many children in each group would be rewarded during the game: zero, one, two, all. Shortly before the close of the school day, the classroom teacher administered the sociometric test. Results from this test indicated that the proportion of play group members chosen as friends by successful, or reinforced, children was significantly greater than the proportion chosen by nonsuccessful children.

Blau and Rafferty's 1970 study was also built around the idea that when children are reinforced jointly, each member of the pair becomes a cue for reinforcement for the other and thus has a concomitant effect on the evaluation of the friendship status. Furthermore, they speculated that the greater the amount of reinforcement, the more intense the friendship. Friendship in this study was operationally defined by scores obtained on the picture sociometric technique.

Subjects were forty-eight children from preelementary schools, who were divided into dyads to work on a cooperative button-pressing task. Pairs received either continuous reinforcement for cooperative responding, fixed-ratio twenty reinforcement, fixed-ratio forty reinforcement, or no reinforcement (control). Tokens that could be exchanged for candies, balloons, and pennies were used as reinforcers. At the conclusion of the experiment, children were administered picture sociometric posttests. Findings revealed significant increases in sociometric ranks from pretest to posttest for all experimental children but not for the nonreinforced group. The study failed to confirm the hypothesis that there was a differential effect based on reinforcement schedules. Nonetheless, as the authors noted, the importance of reinforcement in relation to friendship status was demonstrated.

The two studies just reported were conducted in a setting outside the classroom. The effect of teacher reinforcement on the sociometric status of children has been evaluated in several classroom studies. Flanders and Havumaki (1963) reported that verbal praise offered by a teacher–trainer to certain students in the group for their contribution to the discussion was effective in increasing the social acceptance of the individually praised students. On the other hand, praise given to the group as a whole was not effective in changing social status.

Retish (1968) investigated the effects of reward or verbal reinforcement given by classroom teachers to socially rejected pupils in grades two and five. Two of the four rejected pupils in each of twenty classrooms were assigned to the experimental condition and two to the control condition. Teachers were instructed to reinforce the pupils in the experimental condition for their positive academic or affective behavior in front of the class. Findings revealed that students in the reinforcement group made significantly greater gains in their social acceptance scores than did the control-group subjects. Alden, Pettigrew, and Skiba (1970) also reported a significant increase in the positive attitudes of peers toward the least-chosen children as a result of individual contingent group reinforcement, in which the teacher combined verbal reinforcement to the low child with some extra credit to the whole class following the low child's correct answer.

The studies reviewed in this section suggest that classroom teachers might become effective agents of change in children's social status. Offering positive reinforcement to low-status pupils in front of their peers seems to be valuable in helping them gain peer recognition. These studies were not conducted on mentally retarded children, however, and problems must be recognized in adapting the procedure for this population. If the predominant norms of the classroom focus on academic subjects, and if competitive and high performance in reading and arithmetic is highly valued, then the mentally retarded child integrated into the regular classroom is less likely to have opportunities to be reinforced. However, if a wide range of performance is recognized, the mentally retarded may have more opportunities to invite reinforcement. Furthermore, the teacher may have to use tangible rewards in addition to verbal reinforcement, given that retarded children particularly benefit from tangible reinforcers (MacMillan, 1977).

Changing the patterns of interaction between the teacher and rejected pupils may be another method of producing changes in social status. For example, Semmel, Ballard, Sivasailam, and Olson (1976) attempted to increase the quality and frequency of interaction between the teacher and rejected pupils in order to change social status. The authors used a Computer Assisted Teacher Training System (CATTS) that enabled them to offer teachers feedback about their interaction with rejected pupils. The authors hypothesized that the feedback would produce significant changes in three major teacher behavior categories – making statements, giving positive reinforcement, and asking questions. They also hypothesized that positive changes in the sociometric status of the rejected pupils would occur as a function of the feedback given to the teachers.

Sixteen elementary school teachers and thirty-two low-status, low-achieving pupils in grades one through six, formed the target population. Students were identified by a sociometric test, "How I Feel Toward Others" (Kaufman, Agard, & Semmel, in press), at the beginning of the study. Teachers were asked to emphasize three social facilitation skills during their interactions with the target pupils. These included: (1) asking more questions, (2) calling on the target pupil by name, and (3) answering the target pupil's questions and positively reinforcing appropriate behavior. Postsession feedback was provided to teachers in the form of computer printouts that were profiles of the teacher interactions with the low-status pupils. Three weeks after the postsession feedback had been terminated, posttesting took place. Significant increases in the social status of the rejected pupils from pre- to posttesting periods were revealed. Data also revealed that teachers significantly increased the frequency with which they provided positive reinforcement and asked questions. A stepwise multiple regression analysis showed that increase in posttest scores for the rejected pupils was significantly related to the increases in teacher interactions with them.

Coaching

The idea that children can acquire new social behavior through direct instruction is another viable alternative for teaching social skills. Asher, Oden, and Gottman (1977) suggested that teachers and peers can become coaches who verbally transmit rules of social behavior. They included three components in the coaching technique: (1) providing a rule or standard of behavior, (2) providing opportunities to rehearse or practice the behavior, and (3) providing opportunities for feedback in which the child's performance is discussed and suggestions for improvement made.

Oden and Asher's 1977 investigation was aimed at assessing coaching as a method for training isolated children in social skills in order to increase their peer acceptance. The three lowest-rated children in each of eleven classrooms were randomly assigned to one of the three conditions: coaching, peer pairing, and control. Subjects in the coaching condition were verbally instructed in social skills. They were then provided with an opportunity to practice their social skills by playing with a peer and, finally, they had a postplay review session with the coach. In the peer pairing condition, the isolated child was paired with partners and played the same games as the children in the coaching condition, but received no coaching. In the control condition, the experimenter took each child out of the classroom with another child, but the children played solitary games. Sociometric ratings for playmate, workmate, and best friend were used, in addition to a behavior assessment. Results from the sociometric test revealed that, following treatment, children in the coaching condition were rated significantly higher by peers on the play measure compared to the other two conditions. Interestingly, coached children were rated higher as a playmate both by children who had served as partners and by those who had not. No significant differences were found, however, on the ratings for workmate and best friend. Also, no significant gains on positive social behaviors were noted. On a follow-up one year later, using the "playmate" sociometric rating, the coached children's improvement continued. Scores revealed that the formerly isolated children were only somewhat below their classroom mean at the follow-up.

The idea of using coaching with mentally retarded children is very attractive. A mentally retarded child may not have learned the necessary social skills for making friends, because of problems in incidental learning, poor attention, poor language skills, or any of a number of other difficulties, such as exhibiting inappropriate interpersonal behavior. Direct instruction may be a useful alternative to relying on incidental learning. When providing direct instruction, emphasis should be given to factors such as overlearning, rehearsal, and reinforcement, which are often necessary for the instruction of retarded children (Mercer & Snell, 1977). This process may require more time than was allowed by Oden and Asher (1977).

Modeling

The effectiveness of modeling in modifying the social interaction patterns of socially isolated and withdrawn children has been evaluated in a number of investigations. These studies use a different selection criterion for social isolation than the earlier studies reported in this chapter. Rather than defining rejection and isolation on the results of sociometric tests, these studies identify social isolation by means of pupil behaviors. Social isolation is determined by means of objective observations of withdrawn or isolated behavior.

O'Conner's 1969 experiment was designed to evaluate the effectiveness of symbolic modeling as a treatment to increase the amount of social behavior in preschool isolates. Teachers in nine nursery-school classes were asked to identify the five most socially withdrawn children in their classrooms. These children were then observed and their behavior was scored in terms of five response categories, which included physical proximity, verbal interaction, "looking at," "interacting with," and size of group involved in any interaction. Thirteen subjects who met the two criteria of teacher nomination and extremely low observed interaction with peers were selected and randomly assigned to the modeling or the control conditions. Another group of twenty-six nonisolated children were also observed, to furnish an additional comparison group. Children in the experimental group viewed a film portraying a sequence of eleven scenes in which children interacted in a nursery-school setting. The interactions were followed by positive consequences. A narrative soundtrack emphasized the appropriate behavior of the models. The control group viewed a film depicting twenty minutes of the acrobatic performance of Marineland dolphins. Immediately after being shown their respective films, children were returned to their classroom and observed. Statistical analysis of the data revealed significant increases in social interaction for the children in the modeling treatment as compared to the children in the control groups. No follow-up observations were made in that study.

In another study, O'Connor (1972) compared the effectiveness of modeling with shaping and also included a six-week follow-up assessment. Results indicated that shaping produced significant increases in the subjects' interactions. Highly significant differences were found in the follow-up. The high levels of social interaction achieved in the modeling and modeling-plus-shaping conditions remained stable over time. However, the effects of the shaping condition alone were no longer evident at the time of the follow-up assessment. The modeling and the modeling-plus-shaping groups did not differ significantly in the follow-up assessment.

In another study, Evers and Schwarz (1973) evaluated the effectiveness of modeling and teacher praise in modifying social withdrawal in preschoolers. Subjects were thirteen social isolates. Half of the subjects were assigned to a modeling group and viewed the O'Connor film. The remaining subjects viewed the film but also received two days of teacher praise contingent on the subjects' peer interaction in the classroom. Teachers were instructed to ignore isolate play and reinforce the children as group members after they interacted with peers. The teacher also approached the isolated children and guided them into interaction with other children. Results were congruent with O'Connor's (1972) findings: The "modeling plus praise" condition was not significantly different from "modeling only" for the children's social interactions. Both groups showed a significant increase in their social interactions between pre- and posttests. Continued improvement for both groups was also noted during the follow-up four weeks later.

Ross, Ross, and Evans (1971) used a "modeling plus guided participation" procedure with a 6-year-old boy who exhibited extreme fear and avoidance of interpersonal relations. The use of general modeling procedures was not feasible, because the prerequisite that the child attend to the stimulus presentation could not be met. The procedure of modeling and guided participation was therefore used. In this procedure, the model leads the subject through a hierarchy of increasingly difficult tasks using demonstration, practice, and joint participation until the subject successfully performs the desired response without fear.

Social interaction measures and avoidance behavior measures were taken before and after treatment, which lasted over a period of seven weeks with one ninety-minute session per week. Treatment was conducted by a female psychologist, and a male undergraduate acted as the model. The treatment was effective in significantly increasing the child's social interactions to approximate those of a comparison group of socially competent children. The avoidance behavior had almost completely disappeared. Tests of generalization of treatment effects conducted two months later on the playground revealed that the boy was able to interact effectively with children with no adult intervention.

The studies reviewed in this section lead us to conclude that modeling is an effective technique for teaching isolated children social interaction skills. As has been reported by Bandura (1969), "Observational learning entails systematic coding and central organization of modeling stimuli, their representation in memory in verbal and imaginal codes, and their subsequent transformation from symbolic forms to motor equivalents" (p. 127). Bandura also noted that the absence of modeling effects may result "from either failure in sensory registration due to inadequate attention to relevant social cues, deficient symbolic coding of modeled events into functional mediators of overt behavior, retention decrements, motor deficiencies or unfavorable conditions of reinforcement" (p. 202). As has been shown in the brief review of the major learning and behavioral characteristics of mentally retarded children, many demonstrate some deficiencies in these subprocesses that may mitigate against the use of observational learning as an intervention. However, evidence seems to suggest strongly that modeling and imitation techniques can be effectively used with the mentally retarded (MacMillan, 1977; Mercer & Snell, 1977; Robinson & Robinson, 1976).

The extensive review of the literature on modeling and mental retardation by Mercer and Snell (1977) suggests that numerous variables influence the modeling process in the mildly retarded. The reader is directed to Mercer and Snell (1977) for a detailed description of these variables.

Conclusions

Research on the friendship choices of nonretarded and retarded children indicates that mentally retarded children usually occupy the lower positions in the social-status hierarchy of their peer group, although not all retarded children are socially rejected. The initial rationale for placing mentally retarded children in mainstreamed regular classes was not empirically based. The contact hypothesis, on which the mainstreaming philosophy was predicated, was mainly concerned with providing increased opportunities for retarded children to interact with nonretarded peers. Quality of the contact was deemphasized. The principles of equal-status participation with high-status members of a minority group and the availability of institutional support, which had both been theorized to be important elements for enabling contact to improve attitudes, were not incorporated into initial ideas about the social effects of mainstreaming.

Despite the fact that the majority of data suggest that mainstreaming per se does not result in increased numbers of friends for mentally retarded children, several factors require us to continue our efforts to develop interventions to improve the social status of mainstreamed retarded pupils. First, the fact that nonretarded children like many of their retarded classmates indicates that the ability to make friends is partly determined by individual traits and behaviors rather than by assignment to an identifiable group. Presumably, the traits or behaviors that are responsible for retarded children's inferior social status can be modified with appropriate intervention. We must recognize, however, that we may have to modify intervention strategies that were developed to improve the social status of normally intelligent children in order to apply them to mentally retarded children.

In addition, we cannot forget that federal legislation mandates that we educate all handicapped youngsters in the least restrictive environment. Although the defining characteristics of the "least restrictive environment" are not yet fully established, doubtless the intent of the law was to ensure that handicapped children would be educated with their nonhandicapped peers. Consequently, we can expect a variety of pressures designed to enforce the integration of handicapped children into regular classes. Given a host of data that indicate that retarded children are likely to be socially rejected in regular classes, we must attempt to reverse this fact. If we do not, handicapped children will not be receiving the most appropriate education.

References

Alden, S. E., Pettigrew, E., & Skiba, E. A. The effects of individual contingent group reinforcement on popularity. *Child Development,* 1970, *41,* 1191–1196.

Allport, G. W. *The nature of prejudice.* Cambridge, Mass.: Addison-Wesley, 1954.

Amir, Y. Contact hypothesis in ethnic relations. *Psychological Bulletin,* 1969, *71,* 319–342.

Asher, S. R., Oden, S. L., & Gottman, J. M. Children's friendships in school settings. In L. G. Katz (Ed.), *Current topics in early childhood education* (Vol. 1). Norwood, N.J.: Ablex, 1977.

Baldwin, W. K. The educable mentally retarded child in the regular grades. *Exceptional Children,* 1958, *25,* 106–108; 112.

Ballard, M., Corman, L., Gottlieb, J., & Kaufman, M. T. Improving the social status of mainstreamed retarded children. *Journal of Educational Psychology,* 1977, *69,* 605–611.

Baker, J. L., & Gottlieb, J. Attitudes of teachers toward mainstreaming. In J. Gottlieb (Ed.), *Educating mentally retarded persons in the mainstream.* Baltimore: University Park Press, 1980.

Bandura, A. *Principles of behavior modification.* New York: Holt, Rinehart & Winston, 1969.

Blau, B., & Rafferty, J. Changes in friendship status as a result of reinforcement. *Child Development,* 1970, *41,* 113–121.

Buchan, L. G. *Role playing and the educable mentally retarded.* Belmont, Cal.: Fearon Publishers, Education Division, 1972.

Campbell, J. D. Peer relations in childhood. In M. L. Hoffman & L. W. Hoffman (Eds.), *Review of child development research* (Vol. 1). New York: Russell Sage Foundation, 1964.

Cartenson, B. The auxiliary chair technique: A case study. *Group Psychotherapy,* 1955, *8,* 50–56.

Chenault, J. Improving the social acceptance of unpopular mentally retarded pupils in special classes. *American Journal of Mental Deficiency,* 1967, *72,* 455–458.

Chennault, J. Improving the social acceptance of unpopular mentally retarded pupils in special classes. *American Journal of Mental Deficiency,* 1967, *72,* 455–458.

Christoplos, F., & Renz, P. A critical evaluation of special education programs. *Journal of Special Education*, 1969, *3*, 371–379.

Cromwell, R. L. A social learning approach to mental retardation. In N. R. Ellis (Ed.), *Handbook of mental deficiency*. New York: McGraw-Hill, 1963.

Cook, S. W., & Sellitz, C. Some factors which influence the attitudinal outcomes of personal contacts. *International Sociological Bulletin*, 1955, *7*, 51–58.

Dexter, L. A. *The tyranny of schooling*. New York: Basic Books, 1964.

Ellis, N. R. The stimulus trace and behavioral inadequacy. In N. R. Ellis (Ed.), *Handbook of mental deficiency*. New York: McGraw-Hill, 1963.

Memory processes in retardates and normals. In N. R. Ellis (Ed.), *International review of research in mental retardation* (Vol. 4). New York: Academic Press, 1970.

Evers, W. L., & Schwarz, J. C. Modifying social withdrawal in preschoolers: The effects of filmed modeling and teacher praise. *Journal of Abnormal Child Psychology*, 1973, *1*, 248–256.

Flanders, T. Z. & Havumaki, S. The effect of teacher–pupil contacts involving praise on the sociometric choices of students. In J. M. Seidman (Ed.), *Education for mental health*. New York: Thomas Y. Crowell, 1963.

Furness, P. *Role-play in the elementary school: A handbook for teachers*. New York: Hart Publishing Co., 1976.

Gampel, D. H., Gottlieb, J., & Harrison, R. H. Comparison of classroom behavior of special-class EMR, integrated EMR, low IQ, and nonretarded children. *American Journal of Mental Deficiency*, 1974, *79*, 16–21.

Gickling, E. R., & Theobold, J. T. Mainstreaming: Affect or effect. *Journal of Special Education*, 1975, *9*, 317–328.

Gilhool, T. K., & Stutman, E. A. Integration of severely handicapped students toward criteria for implementing and enforcing the integration imperative of PL 94-142 and Section 504. In *Developing criteria for the evaluation of the least restrictive environment*. Washington, D.C.: Department of Health, Education, and Welfare, 1978.

Goldstein, H. Social and occupational adjustment. In H. A. Stevens & R. Heber (Eds.), *Mental retardation*. Chicago: University of Chicago Press, 1964.

Goodman, H., Gottlieb, J., & Harrison, R. H. Social acceptance of EMRs integrated into a nongraded elementary school. *American Journal of Mental Deficiency*, 1972, *76*, 412–417.

Gottlieb, J., & Budoff, M. Social acceptability of retarded children in nongraded schools differing in architecture. *American Journal of Mental Deficiency*, 1973, *78*, 15–19.

Gottlieb, J., Cohen, L., & Goldstein, L. Social contact and personal adjustment as variables relating to attitudes toward EMR children. *Training School Bulletin*, 1974, *71*, 9–16.

Gottlieb, J., & Davis, J. E. Social acceptance of EMRs during overt behavioral interaction. *American Journal of Mental Deficiency*, 1973, *78*, 141–143.

Gottlieb, J., Semmel, M. I., & Veldman, D. J. Correlates of social status among mainstreamed mentally retarded children. *Journal of Educational Psychology*, 1978, *70*, 396–405.

Grossman, H. J. (Ed.). *Manual on terminology and classification in mental retardation*. Washington, D.C.: American Association on Mental Deficiency, 1973.

Guskin, S., & Spicker, H. H. Educational research in mental retardation. In N. E. Ellis (Ed.), *International review of research in mental retardation* (Vol. 3). New York: Academic Press, 1968.

Heber, R. F. The relation of intelligence and physical maturity to social status of children. *Journal of Educational Psychology*, 1956, *47*, 158–162.

Johnson, G. O. A study of social position of mentally handicapped children in the regular grades. *American Journal of Mental Deficiency*, 1950, *55*, 60–89.

Jordan, A. M. Personal social traits of mentally handicapped children. In T. Thurstone (Ed.), *An evaluation of mentally handicapped children in special classes and regular grades*. Washington, D.C.: U.S. Office of Education Cooperative Research Program, Project #OE-SAE-6452. Chapel Hill: University of North Carolina, School of Education, 1959.

Katz, E. Job role playing in the classroom. *The Journal of Special Education of the Mentally Retarded*, 1972, *8*, 152; 167.

Kaufman, M. J., Agard, J. A., & Semmel, M. I. *Mainstreaming: learners and their environments*. Baltimore: University Park Press, in press.

Kaufman, M., Gottlieb, J., Agard, T., & Kukic, M. Mainstreaming: Toward an explication of the construct. In E. L. Meyer, G. A. Vergason, & R. J. Whelon (Eds.), *Alternatives for teaching exceptional children*. Denver: Love Publishing Co., 1975.

Kirk, S. A. Research in education. In H. A. Stevens & R. Heber (Eds.), *Mental retardation*. Chicago: University of Chicago Press, 1964.

Kirk, S. A., & Johnson, G. O. *Educating the retarded child*. Boston: Houghton-Mifflin, 1951.

Kranzler, G. D., Mayer, G. R., Dyer, C. O., & Munger, P. E. Counseling with elementary school children: An experimental study. *Personnel and Guidance Journal*, 1966, *44*, 944–949.

Lawrence, E. A., & Winschel, J. F. Locus of control: Implications for special education. *Exceptional Children*, 1975, *41*, 483–490.

Leyser, Y. Role playing – path to social acceptability. *Elementary School Journal*, 1979, *79*, 157–166.

Lilly, M. S. Improving social acceptance of low sociometric status, low achieving students. *Exceptional Children*, 1971, *37*, 341–347.

Long, N. J. *An exploratory study of the relationship between the growth of the whole child and an attempt to improve the social power of sociometrically rejected elementary-school children*. Unpublished Ph.D. dissertation, University of Michigan, 1957.

Lott, B. E., & Lott, A. J. The formation of positive attitudes toward group members. *Journal of Abnormal and Social Psychology*, 1960, *61*, 297–300.

MacMillan, D. L. *Mental retardation in school and society*. Boston: Little, Brown, 1977.

Mannheimer, D., & Williams, R. M. Jr. A note on Negro troops in combat. In S. A. Stouffer, E. A. Suchman, L. C. DeVinney, S. A. Starr, & R. M. Williams, Jr. (Eds.), *The American Soldier* (Vol. 1). Princeton, N.J.: Princeton University Press, 1949.

Mayer, G. R., Kranzler, G. D., & Matthes, W. A. Elementary school counseling and peer relations. *Personnel and Guidance Journal*, 1967, *46*, 360–365.

McDaniel, C. O. Jr. Participation in extracurricular activities, social acceptance, and social rejection among educable mentally retarded students. *Education and Training of the Mentally Retarded*, 1970, *5*, 4–14.

Mercer, C. D., & Snell, M. E. *Learning theory research in mental retardation: Implications for teaching*. Columbus, Ohio: Charles E. Merrill, 1977.

Miller, R. V. Social status and socioempathic differences. *Exceptional Children*, 1956, *23*, 114–119.

Moreno, J. L. *Who shall survive?* New York: Beacon House, 1953.

Moss, J. W. *Failure-avoiding and success-striving behavior in mentally retarded and normal children*. Ann Arbor, Mich.: University Microfilms, 1958.

O'Connor, R. D. Modification of social withdrawal through symbolic modeling. *Journal of Applied Behavior Analysis*, 1969, *2*, 15–22.

Relative efficacy of modeling, shaping, and the combined procedures for modification of social withdrawal. *Journal of Abnormal Psychology*, 1972, *79*, 327–334.

Oden, S., & Asher, S. R. Coaching children in social skills for friendship making. *Child Development*, 1977, *48*, 495–506.

Retish, P. *The effect of positive overt teacher verbal reinforcement on peer acceptance.* Unpublished doctoral dissertation, Indiana University, Bloomington, Indiana, 1968.

Roark, A. E., & Stanford, G. Role playing and action methods in the classroom. *Group Psychotherapy, Psychodrama, and Sociometry,* 1975, *28,* 33–49.

Robinson, N. M., & Robinson, H. B. *The mentally retarded child: A psychological approach* (2nd ed.). New York: McGraw-Hill, 1976.

Ross, D. M., Ross, S. A., & Evans, T. A. The modification of extreme social withdrawal by modeling with guided participation. *Journal of Behavior Therapy and Experimental Psychiatry,* 1971, *2,* 273–279.

Rucker, C. N., Howe, C. E., & Snider, B. The participation of retarded children in junior high academic and nonacademic regular classes. *Exceptional Children,* 1969, *35,* 617–623.

Rucker, C. N., & Vincenzo, F. M. Mainstreaming social acceptance gains made by mentally retarded children. *Exceptional Children,* 1970, *36,* 679–680.

Sarbin, T. R. Spontaneity training of the feebleminded. In C. L. Stacey & M. F. DeMartino (Eds.), *Counseling and psychotherapy with the mentally retarded.* Glencoe, Ill.: The Free Press, 1957.

Semmel, M. I. *Language behavior of mentally retarded and culturally disadvantaged children.* Fifth Annual Distinguished Lecture Series in Special Education. School of Education, University of Southern California, Los Angeles, 1966.

Semmel, M. I., Ballard, E. V., Sivasailam, C., & Olson, J. *The improvement of social status among rejected pupils through the modification of teacher behavior using the computer-assisted teacher training system (CATTS): An in-service training application of CATTS.* Bloomington, Ind.: Center for Innovation in Teaching the Handicapped, 1976.

Semmel, M. I., Gottlieb, J., & Robinson, N. M. Mainstreaming: Perspectives on educating handicapped children in the public schools. In D. Berliner (Ed.), *Review of research in education* (Vol. 7). Washington, D.C.: American Educational Research Association.

Shaftel, F. R., & Shaftel, G. *Role-playing for social values: Decision-making in the social studies.* Englewood Cliffs, N.J.: Prentice-Hall, 1967.

Sheare, J. B. Social acceptance of EMR adolescents in integrated programs. *American Journal of Mental Deficiency,* 1974, *78,* 678–682.

Sherif, M., & Sherif, C. W. *Groups in harmony and tension: An integration of studies in intergroup relations.* New York: Harper & Row, 1953.

Shotel, J. R., Iano, R. P., & McGettigan, J. F. Teacher attitudes associated with the integration of handicapped children. *Exceptional Children,* 1972, *38,* 677–683.

Solt, M. Z. George wanted in. *Childhood Education,* 1962, *38,* 374–376.

Sourwine, A. H., & Conway, K. L. The effects of role playing upon the social atmosphere of a small group of sixth-grade children. *American Psychologist,* 1953, *8,* 439.

Spitz, H. H. Field theory in mental deficiency. In N. R. Ellis (Ed.), *Handbook of mental deficiency: Psychological theory and research.* New York: McGraw-Hill, 1963.

The role of input organization in the learning and memory of mental retardates. In N. R. Ellis (Ed.), *International review of research in mental retardation* (Vol. 2). New York: Academic Press, 1966.

Strichart, S. S., & Gottlieb, J. Imitation of retarded children by their nonretarded peers. *American Journal of Mental Deficiency,* 1975, *79,* 506–512.

Taba, H., & Elkins, D. *With focus on human relations: A story of an eighth grade.* Washington, D.C.: American Council on Education, 1950.

Zeaman, D., & House, B. J. The role of attention in retardate discrimination learning. In N. R. Ellis (Ed.), *Handbook of mental deficiency: Psychological theory and research.* New York: McGraw-Hill, 1963.

Zigler, E. Mental retardation: Current issues and approaches. In L. W. Hoffman & M. L. Hoffman (Eds.), *Review of child development research* (Vol. 2). New York: Russell Sage Foundation, 1966.

7 Self, social group, and social structure: surmises about the study of children's friendships

Vernon L. Allen

Friendship is a source of endless fascination. Studying its origin and development may lead to a better understanding of social relationships among children. These five chapters vary widely in the nature of the research questions posed, the methodological tools marshalled to attack these questions, the theoretical perspectives from which the data are interpreted, and the characteristics of the samples of children studied. Yet, at the same time, these studies have complementary and convergent conclusions and implications and exemplify broad common themes.

It is easy to become lost in the abundant data from research reports and fail to see some of the more obvious but important facts about friendship. In order to avoid too much concentration on specific research studies, I shall attempt to organize comments around a few general issues to which the individual research reports in this section can be related.

A comment about the term "group processes" is in order before I proceed. A great deal of children's behavior does take place in interaction with or in the presence of other people. But what do we mean by the term "group"? First, how many persons are necessary to make up a group? Certainly one person is not a group. But what about two, three, four, or more? Because the usual definition of a group concerns interdependence among persons, perhaps two persons should be considered a group. Research on behavior as a function of group size has shown, however, that there is a sharp discontinuity between two-person interactions and interactions involving three or more (Cartwright & Zander, 1968). This suggests that qualitative differences exist between two-person relationships

This chapter was written while the author was a Fellow at the Netherlands Institute for Advanced Study in the Humanities and Social Sciences. Appreciation is expressed to Patricia S. Allen for helpful comments.

and relationships among a larger number of persons. Moreover, certain phenomena are possible in groups of three or more that are not possible in two-person interactions: for example, coalition, rejecting a deviant, majority pressure.

Whether psychological processes based on two-person interactions are applicable to larger social entities such as groups or social organizations is an empirical question. Many psychological theories assume that generalization from two-person processes to large groups is possible (e.g., Thibaut & Kelley, 1959). Nevertheless, we should stay alert to the possibility that results of studies of dyads may not always be applicable to group social interactions. And certainly we should not forget that new psychological phenomena arise in groups that may not occur in two-person interactions; social identity based upon group membership is a case in point, as are the group-level phenomena that were mentioned earlier. Friendship is usually thought of as a relationship between two persons, but, the chapters in this section suggest, it is profitable to examine friendship as it develops and is manifested in the context of the social group and to explore the critical contribution of ingroups (especially ascribed or unchosen groups) to the perception and evaluation of self by the individual and by other persons who belong to outgroups.

Intragroup and intergroup processes

The groups a child belongs to play an important role in friendship formation. At the very least, the group provides the opportunity for close friendships to develop as a result of frequent contact with other persons who are similar in some way. In discussing the role of one's membership group in friendship, it is important to distinguish among various types of social groups, several of which are discussed in the five preceding chapters in the "Group Processes" section. Groups such as Little League baseball teams (Fine's chapter) are informal social groups that a child can join and leave more or less at will. In contrast, membership in groups based on ascribed criteria such as race, sex, or intellectual ability is not determined by the individual's free choice. Even within the two broad categories of achieved (chosen) and ascribed (unchosen) groups, distinctions can be made that are important for friendships. It is clear, as discussed in Schofield's chapter, that not all ascribed membership groups have the same implications for the individual. Group memberships based upon race and sex differ in both future implications and cultural and historical background. Likewise, various types of achieved groups differ along the dimensions of transient – permanent and formal – informal organization and in terms of purpose or task.

Entry

Negotiating entry into a group such as those studied by Putallaz and Gottman and Corsaro may be different from attaining entry into a more formal and longer-lasting group, such as the Little League baseball teams described by Fine. In the latter instance, the question of acceptance or rejection is clear cut – one is either a member of the team or one is not. Acceptance by other group members in a more temporary group (or near-group) is less determinate, and there is more uncertainty on the part of the newcomer about whether he or she is accepted. Formal, longer-lasting groups are likely to have a formal structure of leadership, division of labor, roles, and so forth that facilitates a newcomer's adjustment to the group. In the entry (newcomer) study reported by Putallaz and Gottman, the child seeking entry faced an uncertain, ambiguous, and, accordingly, a stressful situation. In a formal group such as a Little League club, would the same situation confront a newcomer, and might the consequences of certain entry tactics differ?

An important determinant of the success of the newcomer's attempts at entry is the relationship among members of the existing group. The sequential analysis Putallaz and Gottman used to study the success of entry attempts may be useful for studying a variety of types of social behavior. In general, research on social behavior has paid too little attention to sequential relations over time. For example, one wonders about the eventual impact of unsuccessful entry attempts. Dissonance theory (Festinger, 1957) predicts that the greater the effort a person exerts to become a member of a group the more the newcomer will value the group and like the members. Hence, one might predict that the unpopular child who found it very difficult to gain acceptance by a group would like the others better when finally accepted than would a newcomer who was accepted quickly. This prediction points out the importance of investigating the newcomer's reactions to the group as a function of his or her behavior and the group's response to it.

It is important to distinguish between knowledge of and performance of certain social techniques for gaining entry to the group, as described in Putallaz and Gottman's chapter. One way of separating knowledge about social skills from performance of the skills is to compare behavior in a role-playing setting with behavior under spontaneous conditions. For example, we found differences in the nonverbal behavior of high- and low-achieving children when they listened to lessons that they did and did not understand (Allen & Atkinson, 1978). Yet when these same children were instructed to role-play both understanding and not understanding a lesson, no differences in their nonverbal behavior were found. Both high- and low-achieving children understood equally well what the appropriate nonverbal behavior was, but they differed in their use of these cues in a spontaneous situation.

The study of entry techniques might have important implications for the initiation of cross-group relationships such as those between black and white or normal and retarded children. Preexisting stereotypes about the outgroup and the possibility of rejection by outgroup members presumably make the entry problem a critical stage in potential cross-group relationships. It would also be interesting to conduct research investigating children's use of entry techniques and the degree of success attained by ingroup and outgroup members. A research paradigm similar to that employed in Putallaz and Gottman's study might be profitably applied to the study of ingroup – outgroup relations.

The problem of entry of the newcomer suggests the interesting complementary problem that might be called the "exit problem." How does a child leave an unwanted group with the least amount of unpleasantness? In a more general form, this is the problem of the dissolution or diminution of friendships. In adulthood, formal arrangements have been established to help facilitate such transitions from close to distant friendship status – one form is called "divorce." Complementary to the entry problem or the establishment or building up of friendships, then, is the opposite process – disengagement, or the reduction of friendship ties among children.

Group goal

There are numerous types of social groups that differ in purpose or goal. Discussion of social interaction and friendship in a group would be incomplete without a consideration of the group task: Social interaction and friendship usually occur in the context of some type of joint activity directed toward a goal or task. The Little League baseball team studied by Fine is a good example of a group with an explicit task that requires a division of labor and coordination among members; the task provides a context for social interaction and the development of friendships. Directing more attention to the group's goal or task may contribute to a better understanding of children's friendships. A typology of group tasks has been suggested by Steiner (1972). The type of task determines to a great extent the nature of the social interaction that occurs among children.

In Fine's chapter on Little League baseball teams, the symbolic inter-actionist view is used as a theoretical framework. This perspective has many positive qualities. It makes explicit the central role of the self (or social identity) in social interaction and friendship and focuses our attention on the instrumental value of friendship. But the theory is highly abstract and thus difficult to test in a particular situation. Further, many of the functions that Fine discusses might be interpreted more parsimoniously within the framework of social comparison theory (Festinger, 1954). From the many interesting examples given in the chapter, it seems that much of the time the boys were engaged in evaluating self (attitudes, beliefs, abilities) in relation to peers.

Fine argues that friendship in the group serves three functions: a staging arena for behavior, explicit training, and display of appropriate self-images. Any list of functions of friendship must remain highly arbitrary, however. Why should three functions be chosen instead of four, five, six, or more? Although Fine's use of participant observation must be applauded for the richness of data it yields, there is a need for quantitative evidence to support the conclusion that friendship serves only these three functions. What is the frequency of occurrence of behaviors that fall into these three categories? Explanations in terms of function have been popular in sociology, but such theories present many problems. It is possible to propose latent functions as well as obvious ones, which is an even more slippery concept. The types of behaviors that friends in a group manifest are likely to depend very much upon the nature of the group and the children participating in it. Nevertheless, the symbolic-interaction analysis Fine employs is useful in identifying concepts that are undoubtedly of central importance in social development and that should not be neglected in the study of children's friendships.

Internal processes

It may be useful in research on group processes in children's friendships to take a broad view of the internal processes of the group. Some research has suggested that a small group can be viewed as an ongoing system operating to maintain internal stability and to attain the group's goal. Viewing the group as a system will help us interpret friendship and popularity in terms of consequences for the group as a whole. The presence of a highly unpopular child might have beneficial consequences for the group, in spite of the unpleasant consequences for the unpopular child. Thus an unpopular child (a deviant) helps other group members see more clearly the boundaries of unacceptable behavior in the group; also, a scapegoat may improve the effectiveness of the group and increase friendship among other group members. I use this extreme example to suggest that friendship usually exists in the context of a broader group and therefore might be better understood by taking as the level of analysis the group as a whole.

A classroom seems to have many of the dynamic characteristics of a small group. Differences among classrooms might provide clues for understanding friendships in groups. It may be that differences in the personality of classroom teachers produce variations in the group's atmosphere, which may be more or less conducive to the development of friendships among children because of specific variables. Group atmosphere can be characterized in terms of its several psychological dimensions, as Moos (1979) has demonstrated. Research in this area might provide useful information about differences in the nature of children's friendships in groups.

The group also plays an important role in providing normative definitions of friendship and in specifying the obligations of friendship. The importance of such norms is particularly clear in informal teenage groups and in organized groups such as boys' gangs. The chapters by Fine and Schofield, which deal with boys' athletic teams and with racial groups, respectively, indicate clearly that normative factors are operating in these settings.

Intergroup relations

Trying to understand the relationship between a child and other group members is a complex task, but even greater complexities are introduced when other groups must be taken into account. All the problems associated with the ingroup – outgroup relationship arise. Relationships between ingroup and outgroup members have long interested psychologists. As Schofield indicates in her chapter, one of the most important effects of group membership is its contribution to the person's social identity. Before I discuss between-group friendship relations in more detail, it should be noted that a reciprocal relation often exists between the affective reactions toward ingroup members and toward outgroup members. This problem deserves further study in children's groups.

Research has confirmed what most of us know from observing political affairs and international relations. The presence of a real or supposed external enemy increases the cohesiveness (mutual attraction) among members of a group. Thus, friendship among members of a group is strongly influenced by the relationship that exists with the outgroup. An interesting example is found in Sherif's "Robber's Cave" study, in which a series of win – lose competitions between two groups of boys at a summer camp resulted in strong hostility between the groups. One consequence of the intergroup conflict was the increase in sociometric status of the lowest-status boy by other ingroup members (Sherif, Harvey, White, Hood, & Sherif, 1961). Aside from the general increase in cohesiveness produced by hostility toward an outgroup, intergroup conflict may provide an opportunity for engaging in behavior that would alter the relative status among ingroup members: For example, bullying may be valued if it is expressed as daring behavior directed toward the outgroup.

The separation of people into different groups can be based on a wide variety of personal characteristics, such as sex (boy/girl), race (black/white), and intelligence (normal/retarded). Numerous other personal characteristics can be used as the basis of group membership, such as language (French/English in Canada), ethnic background, and religion (Protestant/Catholic in Northern Ireland). Once categorized as a member of a particular group, a great deal of a person's consequent behavior will be influenced by group membership. Membership in a group seems to carry with it a set of feelings, beliefs, and behaviors that are directed toward pertinent outgroups. As is well known, group members tend to view their own group more favorably than they do outgroups.

Recent research has interpreted the existence of such ingroup (positive) bias as due to the operation of basic cognitive processes (Tajfel, 1978). The mere categorization of persons into ingroup and outgroup members is sufficient to produce behavior that favors the ingroup at the expense of the outgroup. Even when persons are divided into two different groups on the basis of such a trivial response as preference to paintings, results show that persons favor the ingroup when given the opportunity to award points to an ingroup and an outgroup member (Tajfel, Flament, Billig, & Bundy, 1971). It is important to note that this favoritism toward the ingroup member occurs even in the absence of any negative attitudes (prejudice) toward outgroup members: There was no previous history of hostility and conflict between the members of the ingroup and outgroup in the experiments. These studies indicate, then, that the impact of group membership on behavior may stem from very basic cognitive processes. Pitted against these basic forces as they are, teachers and school administrators should not be surprised to find that it is difficult to prevent negative intergroup attitudes and behavior. Contributing to the difficulty of promoting positive intergroup relations are the natural consequences of categorization and such other "normal" cognitive processes as "illusory correlations" (Hamilton & Gifford, 1976), which serve to prevent friendships and positive behavior from developing between members of ingroups and outgroups.

Among the antidotes offered for the lack of friendships and positive relations between ingroup and outgroup members is the contact hypothesis. Especially in the area of race relations, this hypothesis has been popular, and it has been examined in other contexts as well (for example, in Gottlieb's chapter on the mainstreaming of retarded children). The implicit theory of friendship underlying the contact hypothesis seems to be the similarity of attitude-belief-value theory. Research has found that people do tend to assume the existence of a dissimilarity in attitudes and beliefs between ingroup and outgroup members (Allen & Wilder, 1979). According to similarity theory, therefore, if members of two different groups could experience social interaction under favorable conditions, they would discover that they are not so different from each other and would like each other and might become good friends. Under conditions that do not meet the similarity assumption, we would not expect contact alone to produce friendship. This expectation seems to be borne out in retardate – normal contact and to some extent in cross-race and cross-sex contact between children as well. If the outgroup members are found to possess characteristics that lead to dislike, then contact between groups will not lead to more friendship but will further exacerbate a poor relationship between the groups. Consistent with this prediction, experimental research has shown that an initially disliked stimulus will become even more strongly disliked after repeated exposure (Perlman & Oskamp, 1971). Likewise, increased contact may confirm negative stereotypes and it sometimes does, as research by Schofield (this volume) and others (Triandis & Vassiliou, 1967) indicates. It is obvious that contact can lead either to an improvement or to a deterioration of the relationship between members of different groups; contact alone will not automatically lead to better relations. We have all met persons whom we increasingly dislike as we get to know them better.

Compounding the problems caused by racial group membership in the research reported in Schofield's chapter is the difference in social class between the black and white children, which seems to have been the source of much of the difficulty. Race, a much more salient characteristic of group members, was probably erroneously assumed by the children to have been the basis of problems that could have been more accurately accounted for by social-class differences.

Though the ingroup–outgroup categorization is often inimicable to cross-group friendships, still it need not be an insurmountable barrier. Some cross-group friendships do occur, and the school can employ certain techniques to encourage cross-group cooperation among children. For instance, several techniques have been developed for use in the classroom to encourage cooperation among members of a small group composed of children differing in race and sex (Slavin, 1978). "Superordinate" groups (Sherif et al., 1961) serve to deemphasize one aspect of group membership and stress instead the children's common group membership on other, more general, criteria. An athletic team that represents the school as a whole is a good example of this type of group. We need not be too pessimistic about the value of contact in promoting cross-group friendships. Children who experience close and extensive contact with outgroup members for the first time after several years in school may already have developed attitudes, friendship patterns, and other behaviors that are not easy to change. Cross-group interaction in the school at earlier ages might have salutary effects (Singleton & Asher, 1977).

Finally, the relationship between groups (or between subgroups or cliques) need not be viewed as an all-or-none phenomenon. An interesting issue for research is linkages between groups of children: the extensiveness of the linkages, the nature of the children who provide the linkages, and overlapping group membership. As a case in point, Fine mentions one boy who had acquired more advanced knowledge than other group members about girls and sexual matters from his association with boys outside the Little League group. It seems there was a two-step flow of communication from sources outside the group through this group member to other group members.

The sociocultural milieu

The school

Friendships among children exist within a broad societal and cultural context. For instance, the centrality of the school and the educational values that it promotes influence the nature of friendship in a number of ways. Values of intellectual achievement promoted by the school become means of gaining prestige among one's classmates (assuming that children accept the school's values). By contrast, in cultures where cooperation rather than competition is valued (e.g., Indians in the American Southwest), achieving at a higher level than one's schoolmates could decrease prestige and popularity. Differential academic performance by blacks and whites in desegregated schools and by normals and retardates in mainstreamed schools becomes a source of friction for cross-group friendships, because the norms of school and society at large place a high value on achievement.

We might expect that the cleavage between normal and retarded children in terms of friendship choice would be greatly vitiated if intellectual competence were a less important value in the society or if lack of intellectual ability were taken as an indication of the possession of other valued characteristics (e.g., intuition or spiritual power). In sum, we must realize that children's friendships exist within the structure of the values and norms of the adult society. Children's choices of friendships are affected by these pervasive values and institutions such as the school often make these desired characteristics salient and explicit to children.

Ecology

The ecological specificity of children's friendships is an important issue. Research questions on friendship are often asked in relation to a specific group of children who interact within a particular behavioral setting, such as the school. Other behavioral settings also exist in the child's environment, however, and friendships may well change across these different ecologies. One might compare a child's "best friends" in a Little League team with best friends in school. Not only is it likely that friendships will differ in the two settings – simply because different children are present – but the nature and basis of the friendships may differ as well. In Part II of this book, Corsaro concludes that nursery-school children's friendships are highly situationally specific. We should be alert to the role of ecological factors in friendship formation and in determining the nature of friendships in older children as well as in nursery-school children. Physical proximity facilitates friendship formation by increasing the likelihood of social contact among people, and frequency of social contact is strongly correlated with liking and the formation of friendships (Festinger, Schachter, & Back, 1950). The child's living arrangement, then, influences the extent of the availability of other children and thus influences the amount of contact that takes place with other persons in the course of day-to-day life. Hence, the nature of the community and the residential area (demography, apartments or single-dwelling units, etc.) affects the structure and outcomes of a child's friendships.

How do the friendships of a child in the community at large differ from friendships in school and in other institutionalized behavioral settings such as athletic teams, clubs, and other adult-sponsored or adult-approved social settings? A particularly important difference is that friendships in the community at large are likely to be less homogeneous with respect to age than friendships in school. Same-age friendships are promoted and cross-age friendships are discouraged by institutional arrangements such as the age-differentiated school. By contrast, in the community there are ample opportunities for a child to engage in social interaction with older and younger children.

The extreme degree of segregation by age that is currently found in our society has not always existed (Ariès, 1962). Prior to the late Middle Ages there was considerable mixing among children of widely different ages and also between children and adults. In the course of their working day as apprentices and in their social life as well, children interacted freely with other people of widely heterogeneous ages. Commonly, a single class in a school prior to the seventeenth century would be comprised of students representing a wide range of ages. Ariès (1962) cites data from one seventeeth-century school that indicate that students from the ages of 9 to 24 were together in one class. The age-segregated classrooms that are now typical serve to prevent the development of heterogeneous-age friendships. Ariès maintains that the concept of childhood as a separate stage of life arose only at the end of the sixteenth century. Cross-age friendships are discouraged by historico-cultural factors such as the conception of childhood as a stage of innocence during which younger children should be protected from older children.

That cross-age friendships are not unusual under favorable circumstances is indicated by our study of one-room schools, many of which still exist in some western states in the United States (Allen & Devin-Sheehan, 1976). Data from this study (N = 1405) indicated that a considerable number of children nominated as their "best friend" children who were older or younger than the respondent by one year or more. In grades one through three, a total of 82 percent of the children chose as best friends other children who were not the same age (mostly older); in grades four through six, the corresponding result was 67 percent for cross-age nominations as best friends; and in grades seven and eight, 60 percent of the children chose either a younger or older child as best friend. Consistent with these data, 76 percent of the students stated that it was easy to be friends with children of all different ages. Admittedly, these cross-age friendships are determined to a considerable extent by the constraints that the situation imposes: the limited number of same-age children available in a one-teacher (one-room) school. In much the same way, the high degree of homogeneous-age friendship in age-differentiated schools is also determined by the lack of opportunity the environment affords for interaction with cross-age schoolmates. At the very least, the data from the one-room school study indicate that children are not adverse to forming close friendships with older or younger children. The environment of the one-room school, in contrast to that of age-differentiated schools, suggests the importance of external or ecological factors in social interaction and friendship formation.

History and culture

Historical influences on children's friendships are illustrated vividly by research on cross-race friendships (blacks and whites). Children have not lived their lives in a cultural vacuum; at an early age they are aware of intergroup conflicts, both present and past, that involve their own membership group. The overt racial conflicts of recent years in the U.S., as well as the long history of less than ideal race relations in this country, cannot fail to influence children's perceptions of the relationship between the ingroup and outgroup. Research shows that children have a sense of racial identity at an early age (Harding, Proshansky, Kutner, & Chein, 1969) and that young children hold stereotypes with a remarkable degree of consensus. Chapter 3 suggests that racial stereotypes influence a child's inclination to seek friendship with a child of another race; stereotypes also sometimes influence the interpretation of behavior in such a way as to decrease the likelihood that an initial interaction will lead to friendship. As a case in point, Schofield's data suggest white students in the desegregated school sometimes seemed to misinterpret typical behavior (for example, minor "hassling") of the lower-class blacks as being aggressive responses directed toward them personally. Likewise, the black children seemed to misinterpret the academic achievement of the whites and their offer to help the blacks with schoolwork as "arrogance" or "snobbery."

Misinterpretation of the behavior of cross-race peers is reminiscent of accounts of cross-cultural misunderstandings. Numerous descriptions have been given of persons from one culture who reached an erroneous conclusion about the meaning or the intention of the behavior of other persons because of lack of understanding of the other culture. Well-controlled experiments have helped clarify the psychological basis of these errors (Detweiler, 1975). Such errors in inferring the intentions of another seem also to occur in the case of persons from different subcultural backgrounds – and in the United States it is not unreasonable to construe race as subculture. Research has shown differences in the "subjective cul-

ture" of blacks and whites lead to mistakes about the behavioral intentions and mistaken evaluations of the behavior of persons from a different
race (Triandis, 1976; Triandis, Weddon, & Feldman, 1974).

It should be possible to reduce the difficulties caused by differences
between persons' subjective cultures by providing appropriate training.
This approach has been undertaken with some evidence of success in an
effort to improve the interaction among persons from different cultures.
For example, one strategy entailed the development of self-administered
programmed materials called the "culture assimilator" (Fiedler, Mitchell,
& Triandis, 1971). This technique has also been extended to use in black–
white interaction in the job setting (Triandis, 1976). Why not extend such
cross-cultural training techniques to the problem of the relationship between black and white children? To the extent that lack of friendship
across races is due to cultural differences that contribute to misunderstanding, critical situations could be identified and incorporated into a
cross-race "culture assimilator" for children. If explicit training can improve social skills that are important for establishing and maintaining
friendships in general (as research in this book suggests may be true), then
training on cross-race problems due to differences in subjective cultures
should likewise be amenable to explicit training.

In summary, it is clear that children's friendships exist within a broad
ecological, societal, cultural, and historical context that cannot be ignored
if we are to attain a satisfactory general understanding of friendship in
childhood.

Children's friendships or children's *friendships*

Studying children's friendships poses a thought-provoking problem that is
usually not made explicit but that has interesting consequences for research strategy. A researcher who investigates children's friendships may
place relatively more emphasis on the first word (*children's* friendships)
or on the second (children's *friendships*). In other words, one may be
primarily concerned with understanding relationships among children, of
which friendship is an important part, or one may be primarily concerned
with investigating friendship, with the particular age of the persons studied being of secondary importance. Psychologists who have developed
general theories of friendship and liking have tended not to emphasize the
age of the persons studied. In a logical continuation of this research tradition, children might be used as subjects because of convenience, not because of any inherent interest in friendships among children. Researchers
who are interested in *children's* friendships would probably be dissatis-

fied with research directed toward a general theory of friendship, because their basic effort seems to be to understand more about children's social behavior and the way it develops.

Several tacit assumptions underly the choice of the relative emphasis. If a researcher studies friendship in children rather than in adults, he or she implicitly assumes that there are important differences between children and adults in the nature of their friendships and the critical variables involved. But if one gives a relatively greater amount of emphasis to the study of friendship per se, one assumes an underlying generality in theoretical accounts of friendship that cut across adults and children. To state the issue succintly: Do theories of friendship pertain to human relationships in general (with perhaps only small or quantitative differences between children and adults)? I have formulated this question for purpose of discussion and do not intend to imply that there are no differences between the friendships of adults and of children. Yet I do not mean to say that theory may not be applicable to friendships in general, as long as appropriate adjustments are made for different types of persons (children, adults, retarded, etc.).

The reports of researchers in the field imply the existence of ambivalence or uncertainty on this question. On the one hand, some investigators state that general theory and basic variables should be applicable to children, subject only to quantitative adjustments; the use of the contact hypothesis and cognitive consistency theory by authors in this section are cases in point. Yet one senses a reluctance to follow through on the implications of the general applicability of theories of friendship, as indicated by research designs and the type of concepts used. Two different groups of psychologists – social and developmental – have been actively working on the problem of friendship without much communication or mutual intellectual assistance. Investigators who study friendship from each of these perspectives – developmental psychologists who are interested in *children's* friendships and social psychologists who are interested in children's *friendships* – could doubtless learn a great deal from each other.

The role of theory

Examining the research on children's friendships leads one to the conclusion that theory in the area is underdeveloped and that too little effort has been devoted to theoretical work. Perhaps the paucity of satisfactory theory is due to investigators' desire not to attempt theoretical formalization before devoting time to observation and description of the phenomenon under study. Much can be said in defense of careful observation, but eventually attention must be devoted to attempts at providing explanatory constructs and developing general theory to account for the accumulated data. It would not be incorrect to say at this time that theory dealing with friendships in childhood is in its infancy.

To what extent do the psychological processes underlying social relationships differ at various points in the life-span? Not many researchers who deal with children's friendships seem to have employed developmental factors as central variables. But as the chapter by Fine on the Little League suggests, the nature of friendships at certain periods of childhood (in this case, preadolescence) is likely to differ in important ways from that at other periods. This raises the need for a developmental theory for friendships of children – that is, a theory that takes into account ontogenetic changes in children's social behavior that are analogous to age-related changes in cognitions about interpersonal relations. In sum, the development of theory in the study of children's friendships should be a high priority in the field, and existing theories of interpersonal attraction should be explored for their potential theoretical utility for children's friendships (Duck, 1977; Huston, 1974; Murstein, 1971).

Friendship as attitude

A number of theoretical issues revolve around the nature and meaning of the concept of "friendship." Studies have usually allowed respondents to define the term for themselves and most persons probably would agree about the commonsense meaning of the term. Since "friendship" refers to an orientation toward an external object – another person – it may be useful to think of friendship as an attitude. Although "friendship" may contain elements distinct from other types of attitudes, conceptualizing it as an attitude illuminates several characterisics that may be useful in the study of friendships (McGuire, 1969). In particular, it is generally agreed that attitudes are comprised of three components: cognitive (beliefs), affective (positive – negative feelings), and behavioral (overt responses). Just as in other attitudes, it is useful to remember that all three components are present in friendship. Moreover, it is well known that these components will not always be consistent. In particular, it has often been observed that inconsistency may exist between behavior and the other components; a person's overt response does not always agree with his or her verbal report of affect and cognitions concerning an object (Wicker, 1969). This finding is not surprising, because there are many determinants of a person's overt behavior other than affective-cognitive responses. Social norms or any of a variety of situational exigencies influence one's overt behavior. This is not to say, however, that consistency between overt behavior and the cognitive-affective components of an attitude is rare. On the contrary, overt behavior can often be predicted from knowledge of a person's cognitive-affective responses. With reference to friendship, an attitude-theory analysis suggests that we should not be surprised if frequency of social interaction does not always accord with sociometric data. It can also be suggested that theoretical and empirical work on attitude structure, attitude formation, and processes of attitude change might profitably be applied to the friendships of children.

Construing friendships as attitudes also points to the continuity of the underlying dimension of affective responses to an attitude object. It suggests that it might be useful to think of friendship not only in terms of discrete, qualitative states ("best friend"), but also in terms of the relative degree of positive reactions to other persons. This approach would force us to look in a more detailed and explicit way at different levels of liking with a view toward determining whether there are important cognitive-behavioral concomitants of different degrees of affective response to other persons. This approach also suggests that it might be valuable to study all levels of intensity of affective response to other persons rather than concentrating on the positive end of the affective continuum. Thus, it might be instructive to study "enemyship" as well as friendship.

Methods

The chapters in Part I (and in Part II as well) represent diverse methodological approaches to the study of friendship; in part, the variety of approaches stems from the different disciplinary backgrounds of the investigators. It can only be a healthy scientific state for an area to be subjected to empirical investigation by a variety of methods. Sociometric techniques, participant observation, and controlled experiments arc all represented. The sophistication of some of the quantitative techniques currently being developed is very high and holds the promise of producing analyses that were not possible previously. In particular, the use of regression techniques for the analysis of sociometric data and the use of sequential analysis for investigating the contingency of responses should yield useful results. It is clear that the standard sociometric technique is still useful, as demonstrated by research in the chapter by Hallinan. By using children's repeated responses and analyzing cliques instead of a single target, complex and interesting results were obtained. It would be important to know whether the results for changes over time and for the structure of smaller subgroups are reflected in a corresponding change in the behavior among the children in question.

The increasing sophistication of measurement and statistical techniques in this chapter seems not to be matched by a concern for identifying the processes that underlie observed relationships between variables. We still see variables that have been extensively investigated in the past being used, variables that can only be considered to be ersatz measures for the unknown psychological processes that account for results. The independent variables used in traditional sociometric research, such as sex, race, SES, constitute a mixed bag of psychological factors; it is difficult if not impossible to know what is actually being assessed. It is necessary to go beyond such static or status characteristics of subjects. What do these variables mean for friendship? What are the psychological or social processes that relate friendship to these static variables? Might it be advisable to try to develop a better theoretical understanding of the active underlying psychological or social processes and then investigate them directly?

A technique not represented in the research is the long-term longitudinal or longitudinal – cross-sectional methodology. Given the cost and practical difficulties of conducting longitudinal research, one can understand the lack of data on developmental trends in children's friendships over a period of years. Still, it is to be hoped that such research will be initiated in the future. Longitudinal research would permit examination of differences between long-term and short-term friendships and in the social interaction that might differentiate between the two types. Further, longitudinal research could examine the pattern of a child's friendships. Are some children typically involved in many short-term friendships whereas other children predominantly engage in a few long-term friendships?

As in any area of research, it is desirable that the methodology used in the study of children's friendships avoid both uncontrolled looseness and premature precision. Much can be said in praise of both free observation and controlled experimentation. The appropriateness of a method for obtaining answers to the question being asked should be the final criterion in choice of a method, rather than any strictures about methods in general. The observational technique, as illustrated in the chapters by Fine and Schofield, is particularly useful in the hypothesis-finding or theory-generating stage of a research program. But as precise hypotheses are formulated, better-controlled methods are likely to provide more convincing data. It might be useful in research on children's friendships to gather observational data in an informal way in the early stages and to move at later stages to better-controlled methods designed to answer specific questions. The better part of methodological wisdom would seem to be diversity: "Let a hundred flowers bloom."

Intervention and its assumptions

The theme of intervention – intentional attempts to bring about behavioral change – is either explicit or implicit in many of the chapters in this volume. Techniques include manipulating physical proximity to bring about greater contact and interaction between different groups of children and various methods of direct teaching (coaching, modeling, etc.). Intervention research directed toward attempts to improve the sociometric status of a target child is an extremely valuable technique for improving our understanding of children's friendships. By exposing existing knowledge to the rigorous test of producing behavioral change in real-life situations, a great deal can be learned about the relative effects of the many factors that contribute to friendship.

Barriers to change

Formidable obstacles are arrayed against the possibility of a successful outcome of intervention programs designed to enhance the friendship status of unpopular children. And it is not unfair to state that, at this time, such behavioral engineering efforts have had mixed outcomes at best. Considering the massive forces opposing behavioral change, it is not surprising minor attempts at change have had such slight impact. The effectiveness of the technique of increasing contact by proximity is often neutralized by the strength of ingroup norms and prevailing stereotypes. Coaching directed toward improving unpopular children's social skills must contend with the role expectations the child has developed over a long period of time in interaction with other children. Role expectations concerning a child do not exist in social isolation; the role is a part of an extensive social network and hence is difficult to change without simultaneously changing the responses of those in complementary roles. Once a child has been enacting a role or is given a label (e.g., nickname), even if training produces a change in his or her behavior the other children's behavior will still be greatly influenced by the prior role expectations or label. Therefore, their behavior and attitudes toward the target child will remain stable. Lack of reinforcement for the target child's new behavior means that the new responses will be slowly extinguished. In the case of increase in contact produced by proximity between races (or between any ingroup and outgroup), role expectations contribute to the forces resisting change.

Anchored in the preexisting and ongoing social system of the group or classroom, informal social roles attain great stability. It might thus be predicted that attempts to produce a change in the social status of an unpopular child would have a greater chance of success if the target child were removed from his or her group and existing social network. Suggestions offered earlier for ways of improving cross-group (e.g. race) friendships need not be repeated here. One additional suggestion seems warranted, however. Research indicates that unpopular children are often low achievers; low achievement of blacks relative to whites seems to be one of the sources of difficulty in cross-race friendships. Therefore, it may be reasonable to approach the problem of improving popularity and friendship status through an indirect route, such as by devising programs to improve the achievement level of target children or groups of children in their schoolwork or in other areas of competence that will be positively evaluated by peers. This suggestion is not so far-fetched. Results of experimental studies of cross-race interaction reveal that a white student's liking for a black co-worker was greater when the relative competence of the black child had been enhanced by prior training on the task (Freese, 1969).

The difficulties that unpopular children experience in making and sustaining friendships may well be only a part of a much more complex set of problems in personality and interpersonal relationships. These psychological problems are likely to exist within a larger network of family problems. Results of a large longitudinal study in Sweden by Magnusson, Duner, and Zetterblom (1975) support this suggestion. In that study, male and female children who were high, moderate, or low in popularity were selected. (The three groups did not differ in intelligence, parental education, or other factors.) Data were obtained from parents about personal relationships in the family and attitudes on a variety of issues. The results disclosed interesting differences among the parents as a function of popularity of their children. In the families of the low-social-status children, the home atmosphere was characterized by conflict between parents and between parents and the child, and the parents were more dissatisfied with life and with their upbringing of the child than were parents of popular children. Unpopular children appear to be unpopular even with their parents; the parents themselves would not seem to be good candidates for winning a popularity contest. Results of the Magnusson et al. (1975) study revealed, then, a strong correlation between the emotional relationship existing in the home and the child's adjustment to peers: Popular and unpopular children seem to participate in different kinds of home environments. Thus, much of the behavior of unpopular children may be anchored in one of the most powerful of primary groups – the family. Programs attempting to change the behavior of unpopular children should give some attention to techniques for overcoming this source of resistance to change.

Implicit goals

It seems to be an underlying assumption of intervention studies that friendship is without question a desirable goal. Consistent with this assumption are data indicating a correlation between lack of friendship and psychological maladjustment. But it must be remembered that causation cannot be inferred from correlational data; perhaps psychological problems are a cause of unpopularity rather than the reverse. Aside from empirical evidence, however, there seems to be a value judgment involved: Unpopularity in childhood is an undesirable condition that should be ameliorated if possible. This value judgment should not escape close scrutiny. At the least, we should consider the nature of an interpersonal relationship and not presume to equate quantity with quality. One very good friendship may be preferable to being popular with a large number of persons. Should intervention research aim toward increasing the breadth or the depth of friendships? This question requires the answer to another: What are the sequelae of these types of changes?

It would follow that teaching a child the skills needed for popularity may be less desirable than teaching discriminative skills – those skills needed to differentiate among other persons on the basis of their friendship-worthiness. This skill goes beyond the tactics that would be taught in a child's edition of *How to Win Friends and Influence People*.

Furthermore, there may be subtle or remote consequences of unpopularity that are highly desirable to the individual and society. The unpopular child might be inclined to cultivate his or her cognitive capacities to a much greater extent than would have been possible when caught in the whirl and web of social life. Will the work of psychologists who attempt to increase the popularity of the unpopular child result in depriving the world of valuable creative contributions? I must confess that I am skeptical about my skepticism. At the same time, it might be wise to pause before initiating any program of behavioral change to examine thoroughly the possibilities for negative consequences being produced even from the best of intentions.

References

Allen, V. L., & Atkinson, M. L. The encoding of nonverbal behavior by high- and low-achieving children. *Journal of Educational Psychology*, 1978, *70*, 298–305.

Allen, V. L., & Devin-Sheehan, L. *Cross-age interaction in one-teacher schools*. Working Paper No. 161, Wisconsin Research and Development Center for Cognitive Learning, University of Wisconsin, Madison, 1976.

Allen, V. L., & Wilder, D. A. Group categorization and attribution of belief similarity. *Small Group Behavior*, 1979, *10*, 73–80.

Ariès, P. *Centuries of childhood* (R. Balkick, Trans.). New York: Knopf, 1962.

Cartwright, D., & Zander, A. *Group dynamics: Research and theory* (3rd ed.). New York: Harper & Row, 1968.

Detweiller, R. A. On inferring the intentions of a person from another culture. *Journal of Personality*, 1975, *43*, 591–611.

Duck, S. W. *Theory and practice in interpersonal attraction*. London: Academic Press, 1977.

Fiedler, E., Mitchell, T., & Triandis, H. C. The culture assimilator: An approach to cross-cultural training. *Journal of Applied Psychology*, 1971, *55*, 95–102.

Festinger, L. A theory of social comparison processes. *Human Relations*, 1954, *7*, 117–140. *A theory of cognitive dissonance*. Stanford, Cal.: Stanford University Press, 1957.

Festinger, L., Schachter, S., & Back, K. *Social pressures in informal groups*. New York: Harper, 1950.

Freese, L. *The generalization of specific performance expectations*. Unpublished doctoral dissertation, Stanford University, 1969.

Hamilton, D. L., & Gifford, R. K. Illusory correlation in interpersonal perception: A cognitive basis of stereotype judgments. *Journal of Experimental Social Psychology*, 1976, *12*, 392–407.

Harding, J., Proshansky, H., Kutner, B., & Chein, I. Prejudice and ethnic relations. In G. Lindzey & E. Aronson (Eds.), *Handbook of social psychology* (2nd ed., Vol. 5). Reading, Mass.: Addison-Wesley, 1969.

Huston, T. L. (Ed.). *Foundations of interpersonal attraction*. New York: Academic Press, 1974.

Magnusson, D., Duner, A., & Zetterblom, G. *Adjustment: A longitudinal study*. New York: Wiley, 1975.

McGuire, W. The nature of attitudes and attitude change. In G. Lindzey and E. Aronson (Eds.), *Handbook of social psychology* (2nd ed., Vol. 3). Reading, Mass.: Addison-Wesley, 1969.

Moos, R. *Evaluating educational environments*. San Francisco: Jossey/Bass, 1979.

Murstein, B. I. (Ed.). *Theories of attraction and love*. New York: Springer Publishing, 1971.

Perlman, D., & Oskamp, S. The effects of picture content and exposure frequency on evaluations of Negroes and whites. *Journal of Experimental Social Psychology*, 1971, *7*, 503–514.

Sherif, M., Harvey, O. J., White, B. J., Hood, W. E., & Sherif, C. W. *Intergroup conflict and cooperation: The robber's cave experiment*. Norman, Okla.: University of Oklahoma Book Exchange, 1961.

Singleton, L. C., & Asher, S. R. Peer preferences and social interaction among third-grade children in an integrated school district. *Journal of Educational Psychology*, 1977, *69*, 330–336.

Slavin, R. E. *Cooperative learning*. Report No. 267, Center for Social Organization of Schools, The Johns Hopkins University, Baltimore, 1978.

Steiner, I. D. *Group productivity*. New York: Academic Press, 1972.

Tajfel, H. (Ed.). *Differentiation between social groups: Studies in the social psychology of intergroup relations.* London: Academic Press, 1978.

Tajfel, H., Flament, C., Billig, M. G., & Bundy, R. F. Social categorization and intergroup behavior. *European Journal of Social Psychology,* 1971, *1,* 149–177.

Thibaut, J. W., & Kelley, H. H. *The social psychology of groups.* New York: Wiley, 1959.

Triandis, H. C. (Ed.). *Variations in black and white perceptions of the social environment.* Urbana, Ill.: University of Illinois Press, 1976.

Triandis, H. C., & Vassiliou, V. Frequency of contact and stereotyping. *Journal of Personality and Social Psychology,* 1967. *7,* 316–328.

Triandis, H. C., Weddon, D. E., & Feldman, J. M. Level of abstraction of disagreement as a determinant of interpersonal perception. *Journal of Cross-Cultural Psychology,* 1974, *51,* 59–79.

Wicker, A. Attitudes versus actions: The relationship of verbal and overt behavioral responses to attitude objects. *Journal of Social Issues,* 1969, *25,* 41–78.

Part II

Social-cognitive processes

8 Friendship in the nursery school: social organization in a peer environment

William A. Corsaro

Introduction

The discovery of friendship is a major step in the child's acquisition of social knowledge. Before children make friends, their social bonds are primarily between the child and parents or other adult caretakers. This is not to say that children do not influence caretakers or actively construct concepts of social relations within the family by participating in interactive events. Within the family, however, children have relatively little opportunity for negotiation; they must recognize, accept, and adapt to their relationships with parents and siblings. Young children's social knowledge is built around these significant others, who introduce them to cultural values and norms and to interpretive procedures that connect abstract values and norms with specific interactive demands (Cicourel, 1974). When children first move outside the family unit, they discover a range of options in the selection of interactive partners. Through interaction with peers, children learn that they can negotiate social bonds on the basis of their personal needs and social contextual demands. They also learn that their peers will not always accept them immediately; often a child must convince others of his or her merits as a playmate, and sometimes he or she must anticipate and accept exclusion.

Although few sociologists have treated friendship as a specific topic of inquiry (Hess, 1972), many studies of elementary-school children and adolescents (Bowerman & Kinch, 1959; Coleman, 1961; Dumphy, 1963; Eder & Hallinan, 1978; Eisenstadt, 1956; Fine, this volume; Hallinan, this volume) and adults (Babchuk, 1965; Gans, 1961, 1967; Lazarsfeld & Merton, 1954; Liebow, 1967; Whyte, 1955) have shown that friendship and

I wish to acknowledge the helpful comments of Donna Eder, Vickie Renfrow, and Sheldon Stryker and the editorial assistance of Carolyn J. Mullins. I also wish to thank Alicia Dailey for help with data analysis and coding. This research was supported by grants from the Spencer Foundation and the National Institute of Mental Health (Grant No. 1 F22 MH01141-01 and No. 1 R03 MH2895-01).

peer relations serve important socialization functions. There have been no sociological studies of how young children develop conceptions of friendship, however. Futhermore, except for the theoretical work of Cicourel (1974) and Denzin (1977), sociologists have all but ignored the social development of young children (see Corsaro, 1979a). Denzin (1977, p. 1) claimed that "there does not exist, nor has there ever existed, a sociology of childhood."

Denzin may have overstated the situation; nevertheless, few sociologists have studied either the social worlds of young children or children's acquisition of social knowledge. In contrast, psychology and anthropology have a growing literature on childhood culture and the development of interactive skills and social knowledge. Developmental psychologists have been interested in peer relations and the social development of young children (e.g., Glick & Clarke-Stewart, 1978; Lewis & Rosenblum 1975, 1977; Richards, 1974). Some of the research, an outgrowth of earlier work on language acquisition, has focused on language and communicative skills. The recent work on children's language reflects the general trend in theories of language development toward greater concern for semantics, social context, and the functional aspects of speech in social interaction (Bates, 1976; Bruner, 1975; Ervin-Tripp & Mitchell-Kernan, 1977; Halliday, 1975; Ochs, 1979). The central findings of research on children's communicative skills (Garvey, 1974, 1975, 1977; Keenan, 1974, 1977; Keenan & Klein, 1975; Shatz & Gelman, 1973) have challenged Piaget's categorization of children's speech as egocentric and have stimulated interest in peer interaction and play as important aspects of children's social and cognitive development.

A second research area within psychology has focused on young children's development of social knowledge (Damon, 1977; Selman, 1976; Shantz, 1975; Turiel, 1978a). Specifically, researchers have attempted to identify levels of development of social concepts such as friendship (Damon, 1977; Selman, 1976, and this volume; Youniss, 1975), positive justice (Damon, 1977), authority relations (Damon, 1977), and social conventions (Damon, 1977; Turiel, 1975, 1978a). Most of this research has been heavily influenced by cognitive developmental theory. The work of both Selman (1976, and this volume) and Damon (1977) rests on the hypothesis that physical, logical, and social concepts are interrelated; both theorists hold that logical and physical operations as outlined by Piaget (1950) are the basis on which children develop social concepts. Although Turiel (1978a, 1978b) also is a cognitive developmental theorist, he has argued that logical, physical, and social concepts are not necessarily interrelated. Instead, "thought is organized (and changes sequentially) within a domain and not necessarily across domains" (1978b, p. 4). Arguing that a fundamental task of theorists of social development is to identify different domains of social knowledge, Turiel (1978a) used this perspective to distinguish social convention and morality as discrete conceptual and developmental domains.

Although these two research areas within psychology differ in substance, both emphasize the importance of social context. Unfortunately, this shared recognition rarely has inspired the direct study of young children's behavior in peer environments.[1] The basic reason may be the conception of socialization embodied in major theoretical approaches. As Speier (1973, p. 141) has so aptly put it, "traditional perspectives have overemphasized the tasks of describing the child's developmental process of growing into an adult at the expense of the direct consideration of what the events of everyday life look like in childhood."

The process of development to adulthood is important, but researchers also need to understand better the features of children's social environments from the children's perspective at different ages. Social knowledge, regardless of level of development, emerges in response to the demands of specific interactive situations. To understand the development of social knowledge at different ages, several things are necessary. First, we must identify features in the content of social knowledge that remain stable over time; second, we must discover how individuals recognize the appropriateness of a specific type of knowledge; third, we must discover how they use that knowledge to produce social behavior. If the acquisition of social knowledge results from the child's interaction with the environment, as many developmental theorists believe, then we need to investigate not only developmental features of children's cognitive and communicative skills and the structure of social concepts, but also the features of objects, events, and patterns of interaction that make up the world of children.

Anthropology has a long history of research on features of childhood culture. In addition, the renewed interest in peer relations and play has been accompanied by several recent sociolinguistic studies of peer interaction in natural settings. In an excellent review of anthropological studies of play, Schwartzman (1976) classified ethnographies by whether they emphasized play texts, contexts, or texts within contexts. Play texts refer to the content of the play or game (descriptions of what the children say and do in play); contexts of play refer to the social, psychological, or environmental correlates of the play event (see Sutton-Smith, 1974).

The work of Opie and Opie (1959, 1969), among the most widely known studies of play texts, involved direct observation and interviews of young children as a basis for describing and categorizing children's lore (see evaluation by Schwartzman, 1976). Studies of this type are important because they describe features of childhood culture that do not exist in adult culture and that have been transmitted informally over time within children's play groups. However, the researchers did not go beyond description to address the possible social and interpersonal functions of these activities in the everyday lives of young children.

Many studies of play contexts compare and emphasize variations in the functions of play across age, sex, cultural, and ethnic groups (Schwartzman, 1976). Again, the emphasis is on the function of play as preparation for adult roles (Lever, 1978; Smilansky, 1968) and not on the functions of play within the immediate context of peer culture. Finally, several studies of play contexts have stressed the effects of ecological context on the nature and types of play (Barker & Wright, 1966; Gump, Schoggen, & Redl, 1963; Parten, 1933; Shure, 1963), but most do not describe play texts extensively, and they seldom document variations in children's use of language across different types of play.

Ethnographic studies of children's play that emphasize the analysis of texts within context focus on communication and language as an organizing mechanism. These studies build on the theoretical work of Bateson (1972) and Goffman (1974) or on the recent work on contextualization in children's speech by Cook-Gumperz and Gumperz (1976). Cook-Gumperz and Gumperz have a dynamic view of context as an achieved and negotiable part of any social interaction. According to this view, participants have a "notion" of the activity they believe they are engaged in, and they communicate this notion to their interactive partners. The notion of the activity then serves as a framing device to limit the search for an interpretation of any referential item or gestural/kinesic schema. Therefore, contextual information (including propositional content of syntactic strings; elements of speech style such as formal or informal speech; paralinguistic cues including pitch, stress, intonation, and rhythm; extralinguistic cues such as gestures, manipulation of objects in the setting; physical movement; and background knowledge of participants and the setting) is both coded as semantic information and signaled as part of the interaction by means of the process of contextualization. According to Cook-Gumperz and Gumperz, "the signalling of context makes the context available to the participants as a potentially shareable cognitive construct which frames the range of possible interpretations both in terms of the relevance of presuppositions and as a guide to further action" (1976, p. 12).

Ethnographic research in nursery schools (Cook-Gumperz & Corsaro, 1977; Corsaro, 1979a, 1979c; Corsaro & Tomlinson, 1980; Newman, 1978) has illustrated the importance of peer play for the development of communicative skills, including the children's ability to use contextual information to organize and sustain interactive events.

This chapter reports a year-long ethnography of peer interaction whose purpose was to discover nursery-school children's concerns and perceptions of their everyday worlds. Identification of these concerns and careful examination of communication between peers revealed features of children's developing social knowledge about friendship, peer and adult norms, and authority relations and their cognitive strategies for linking this knowledge to the demands of specific interactive events. From these findings, several hypotheses were generated about children's emerging conceptions of friendship and the socioecological demands of the nursery school as a peer environment.

Method: ethnographic setting and procedures

Setting and population

The nursery school, part of a child-study center, was staffed and operated by a state university for educational and research purposes. The teaching methods, curriculum, and schedule allowed for substantial periods of self-selected activities and peer play. There were two groups of children at the school. In the morning group there were twenty-four children (eleven boys and thirteen girls), ranging in age from 2 years, 11 months (2.11) to 3 years, 11 months (3.11). In the afternoon group there were twenty-six children (fifteen boys and eleven girls), ranging in age from 3 years, 9 months (3.9) to 4 years, 10 months (4.10). Because all but two of the children in the afternoon group had attended morning sessions at the school the year before the research, children in the morning group were less experienced with the setting than those in the afternoon group. Although minority groups (blacks, Mexican-Americans, and Asians) were represented in the school, the proportion was less than that in the city in which the school was located. The occupational background of parents ranged from blue collar to professional, but most of the children came from middle- and upper-class families. Because there were no significant differences across the morning and afternoon groups regarding any of the findings in this report, I have, in all but one instance, collapsed the data across the two groups.

Field entry and data collection

I have described field entry and data collection in detail elsewhere (Corsaro, in press). In this section I briefly outline the phases of data collection and analysis. The first phase of data collection, involving monitoring activities in the school from a concealed observation area, began at the start of the school year in October and was followed three weeks later by three months of participant observation. Near the end of the fourth month of the research, the video equipment was introduced into the setting. With the aid of an assistant, I videotaped episodes of peer interaction twice a week and continued participant observation on other days until the end of the school year in June.

I collected observations of episodes that occurred in all areas of the school, that involved a range of activities, and that included all the children in both age groups. In later phases I sampled peer interactive episodes that allowed me to estimate the consistency of patterns that I had identified in the initial analysis of field notes.

Sampling unit

In naturalistic research, specimens of behavior are recorded as they occur in the setting under study. Later analysis depends upon the consistent sampling of these specimens into units with specified boundaries throughout the research process. In this study the sampling unit is called the "interactive episode." Most episodes involved two or more children. In these cases I defined an interactive episode as sequences of behavior that begin with the acknowledged presence of two or more interactants in an ecological area and end with the physical movement of interactants from the area, which terminates the originally initiated activity.[2] I observed few instances of solitary play. For these cases I sampled the episodes until the child left a specific ecological area of play and joined a play group or until the child was joined by one or more other children.

Use of the interactive episode as a sampling unit has the important advantage of providing contextual information for all behavior that occurs during the episode. Using units of short (one- to two-minute) sequences (or slices) of behavior drawn from longer episodes hinders valid interpretation of the meaning of specific behaviors, which often depend on preceding and subsequent activities. Using the episode as a sampling unit has the disadvantage of demanding major investments of time to collect data for all children across a range of activities. Overall, I collected a total of 633 episodes in field notes and 146 episodes in twenty-five hours of videotape data.

Analytic procedures

The analyses of the data can be divided into three distinct phases. I will briefly outline these phases here and discuss findings in each phase in the analysis section of the chapter. During the first phase, I used field notes from the first three months of school to identify what most mattered to the children in the nursery-school setting. The analysis of field notes revealed that the children were most concerned with (1) gaining access to play groups when they found themselves uninvolved; and (2) resisting the access attempts of other children when they were participants in play groups. The analysis of field notes was followed by the examination of videotaped episodes that occurred over the last five months of the school term. The analysis of the video data resulted in the discovery of a basic pattern involving the relationship among the children's strategies for gaining access to play groups, justifications for the resistance of access attempts, and references to friendship while attempting or resisting access. This pattern is discussed at length in the analysis section.

During the second phase of analysis, I examined the structure of social contacts (who played with whom) in the videotaped episodes. My aim was to find out whether the structure of social contacts was consistent with the pattern discovered in the first phase of analysis regarding the relationship between access attempts, types of resistance to access, and references to friendship.

The third phase of analysis involved a search of the data for all spontaneous discussions of friendship. The analysis of discussions of friendship led to the discovery of patterns consistent with findings in the earlier phases of analysis and led to additional hypotheses about children's conceptions and use of friendship when they interact with peers.

In the presentation and interpretations in the analysis section I rely on representative cases (Denzin, 1971) from field notes and videotaped episodes and on what Becker (1970) and Lazarsfeld and Barton (1955) have termed quasi-statistics. Quasi-statistics are the enumeration and analysis of frequency distributions for a given phenomenon that help researchers determine whether initial findings hold for the group and environment under study. The quasi-statistical method also allows ethnographers to estimate the consistency of patterns in field data over time. It should be remembered, however, that this was a hypothesis-generating study. Any inferences drawn from quasi-statistics demonstrate the strength of a given pattern as a basis for a hypothesis and not as a statistical test of the hypothesis.

Analysis

Protection of interactive space and friendship

Patterns in field notes. My initial aim was to discover (1) the basic dimensions of the nursery school as a peer environment and (2) consistent strategies of communication that the children used to produce and sustain peer activities. Because I wished to discover stable features of the school as a peer environment from the children's perspectives, I felt it essential to identify what most mattered to the children in everyday activities with peers and teachers.

To identify the children's central concerns, I examined the field notes from the first three months of daily participant observation. The field notes revealed that the children shared two major, interrelated concerns involving social participation and the protection of ongoing interactive episodes. First, the children rarely engaged in solitary play; children who found themselves alone[3] consistently tried to gain entry into one of the ongoing peer episodes. Second, children who were participating in ongoing episodes protected the interaction by resisting children who wanted to join in. In most of these instances, the children were not attempting to maintain control over objects (play materials) or territory, but rather were protecting *interactive space* (the ecological area in which the interactive episodes were unfolding). These two patterns, which were the source of recurrent conflict, reveal a great deal about the social order of the school, solidarity among peers, and the children's conception and use of friendship. For example, in the following sequence drawn from field notes, Linda (3.8) attempts to gain access to an ongoing episode involving Barbara (3.0), Nancy (3.1), and the researcher (R). Barbara (B) and Nancy (N) had been playing with toy animals and building blocks for around ten minutes when Linda (L) attempted to gain entry. Linda watched at a distance for one minute, then entered the block area, sat next to Barbara, and began playing with the animals.[4]

> B–L: You can't play!
> L–B: Yes I can. I can have some animals too.
> B–L: No, you can't. We don't like you today.
> N–L: You're not our friend.
> L–BN: I can play here, too.
> B–N: No, her can't – her can't play, right N?
> N–B: Right.
> L–R: Can I have some animals, Bill?
> R–L: You can have some of these. ((R offers L some of his animals.))

B–R: She can't play Bill, cause she's not our friend.
R–B: Why not? You guys played with her yesterday.
N–R: Well, we hate her today.
L–All: Well, I'll tell teacher. ((L now leaves but then returns with a teaching assistant (TA).))
TA–BN: Girls, can L play with you?
B–TA: No! She's not our friend.
TA–B: Why can't you *all* be friends?
B–TA: No!
N–B: Let's go outside, B.
B–N: Okay. ((B and N leave. L remains shortly and plays with animals then moves into juice room.))

In pursuing the relationship among access attempts, protection of interactive space, and references to friendship illustrated in the above sequence, I will first present data from the field notes that specify how often access attempts were resisted and the range of types of resistance. I will then examine the video data regarding the frequency of types of resistance and present a micro-sociolinguistic analysis of an access–resistance sequence to capture the processual, negotiated features of this peer behavior.

In the field notes sixty-nine (53.9 percent) of the 128 episodes involving access attempts included initial resistance. In addition to resistance, several other features of peer interaction relate to the concerns of gaining entry and protecting interactive space. First, most of the episodes were of relatively short duration. In field notes, 51.4 percent of all peer episodes lasted less than five minutes, and 32.5 percent lasted less than ten minutes. Because peer episodes normally lasted less than ten minutes during the two-hour free-play period in both the morning and afternoon sessions, the children were often confronted with the need to enter a new play group. Furthermore, the children had to be prepared for the breakdown of interaction at any time, because playmates often simply left a play area and terminated the activity without a formal, verbal marker (see Corsaro, 1979c). As a result, peer interaction was fragile in that termination could occur without warning at any time, and the predominant mode of leave taking (physical movement from a play area) most often precluded any possible negotiation to continue the activity. Therefore, the children often found themselves with playmates one minute and alone the next, in which case they could choose from a range of options that included solitary play, entry into teacher-directed activity,[5] or attempts to gain access to an ongoing peer episode. If they tried to gain access to a peer episode, they frequently encountered initial resistance.

One important question regarding initial resistance to access attempts is whether it occurred for all children who attempted access. In all the peer episodes in field notes for the first three months there were no instances in which certain children were consistently either accepted or excluded. Only four children were initially accepted or resisted more than three times. For each of these children the frequencies of initial acceptance and resistance were nearly identical.[6] There was one pattern related to sexual makeup of groups, sex of the child attempting access, and rate of resistance. The rate of resistance was approximately 50 percent for access attempts by boys and by girls to all-girl groups and mixed groups and for boys' access attempts to all-boy groups; however, the rate of resistance was 75 percent for girls' access attempts to all-boy groups.[7]

Aside from the pattern involving the resistance of all-boy groups to girls' access attempts, initial acceptance or resistance did not seem to be attributable to individual characteristics (general popularity, age, sex, etc.). However, it may be that interactive history – who plays with whom over an extended period of time – is important. Therefore, when I present patterns of social contacts in the video data, I will extend the analysis and include consideration of interactive history.

To this point I have used the term "initial resistance," because attempts to gain access did not always result in permanent exclusion. On many occasions, children were able to overcome initial resistance (Corsaro, 1979c). Of the sixty-nine cases of initial resistance in field notes, thirty-five (50.7 percent) led to permanent exclusion. Clearly, the children discovered that initial resistance could be overcome and that exclusion was a negotiated process. The complexity of this process is especially clear in the videotaped data; I will present a detailed analysis of a videotaped sequence of attempted access, initial resistance, and eventual acceptance in the next section. Given the frequency of initial resistance and the fact that it is overcome nearly 50 percent of the time, the children encounter an ambiguous interactive situation. There is no clear choice regarding either strategies for gaining entry or protecting interactive space. The expectation of initial resistance is tempered by the knowledge that the resistance can be overcome. This ambiguity or uncertainty regarding access to ongoing episodes in turn leads to conflict and to a central concern on the part of the children not only to resist intrusion but also to seek access to ongoing events when they are uninvolved.

In an earlier paper I discussed at length the nature of children's access rituals (Corsaro, 1979c); in this report I focus on children's resistance strategies and justifications for exclusion. Analysis of all episodes recorded during the first three months of participant observation revealed five types of resistance. Verbal resistance with no justification occurred only as the first reaction to an attempt at access. When a child persisted in trying to gain access, this strategy was dropped in favor of one of the four described below. The following example shows this type of resistance:

Laura (L), age 4.1, Daniel (D), age 4.4, and Lenny (Le), age 3.9, are playing house in the climbing bars. Jonathan (J), age 4.9 approaches:

> J–D: I'll be the daddy.
> D–J: Okay.
> L–J: No, you won't! No! N–O spells NO! No!
> Le–J: No! Get out of here!

J leaves and is followed by D, while L and Le continue playing.

A second type of resistance is reference to arbitrary rules which involves justification of exclusion on the basis of arbitrary rules. The rules generally relate either to the excluder's immediate needs and desires or observable characteristics of the intruder (e.g., sex, size, dress). The following example shows this type of resistance:

Linda (L), age 3.8, and Jack (J), age 3.8, have lined up wooden boxes to make a train. Bill (B), age 3.10, and Denny (D), age 3.5, approach. B and D are barefoot:

> B–L: What is this? Is it a city? Is this your train?
> L–B: You can't play with bare feet!
> J–B: Yeah, go away!
> B–D: It's a train!

B and D leave area and run towards climbing bars.

A third type of resistance involved specific claims of ownership of objects or areas of play. These justifications for resistance were not arbitrary but were based on temporal aspects of possession ("I had that first"), school rules, or social rules of role play. The following example shows this type of resistance:

Denise (D), age 4.1, and Eva (E), age 4.7, are playing in the climbing bars. Brian (B), age 4.4, approaches. B is pretending to be a wild animal and has a tail stuck in back of his pants:

> B–ED: That's my house.
> E–B: We were living here first.
> B–D: Well – remember I was up there before.

D climbs down behind B and pulls his tail.

> B–D: You're bad.

B now chases D around the yard, then moves inside school; D returns to bars with E.

In a fourth type of resistance, which I termed justification with reference to space or number of people, the children's justifications for exclusion demonstrated a recognition that interaction can break down when a play area becomes overcrowded. This type of resistance differs from claims of ownership; here the children go beyond claims of ownership to justify exclusion on the basis of the ecological constraints of the school. Use of this type of resistance shows children's awareness of and sensitivity to the social organizational features of this peer environment. In the following example, two children are allowed to enter an ongoing episode before one child, Laura, discovers the negative effects on stability of interaction of the large number of playmates. This discovery then serves as a basis for an attempt to exclude; the result is conflict and eventual breakdown of the activity.

Laura (L), age 4.1, and Sue (S), age 3.11, are playing in the upstairs playhouse and are pretending to prepare a meal. Antoinette (A), age 4.1, moves up the stairs, and S goes to head of stairs to block her entry:

L–S: She can come in.

S lets A enter and all three children continue to prepare the meal. Now Alice (Al), age 4.3, comes upstairs.

Al: Can I play?
L–Al: No!
Al–A: A, A can I play?
A–Al: Okay.

Al enters and stands next to A:

L–Al: This is only for girls.
Al–L: Okay.
Al–A: Can I be a little baby?
A–Al: Yeah, you can be a little baby.
L–A: No, she can't. We can only have one baby.

Al and A now play near table while L and S continue cooking. Then L walks over to table:

L–AAl: Now what are you guys messing around for?

At this point Allen, age 3.9, enters.

L: Oh, we're having so many people!
L–Allen: Get out of my house! Get out of my house!
Allen–L: No it's my house!
L–Allen: No!

At this point a teacher intervened and told the children to clean up the house and come downstairs.

A final type of resistance involved the denial of friendship. My first example, in which Barbara and Nancy resisted Linda's access attempt, showed that children use friendship to differentiate defenders from intruders. Although the denial of friendship and accompanying expressions of dislike may seem cruel to adults, they are often qualified temporally ("We don't like you *today*"). This type of resistance must be evaluated in terms of the children's conceptualization of friendship at this age (Damon, 1977; Selman, 1976; Youniss, 1975) and the demands of the interactive setting. Consider the following example:

Denny (D), age 3.5, and Leah (L), age 3.2, are running and pretending to be lions. Joseph (J), age 3.2, watches from a distance. Glen (G), age 3.9, who had been playing with D earlier, approaches D and L. J follows closely behind G:

D–G: Grr–Grr. We don't like you.
L–G: Grr–Grr.
G–D: You were my friend a minute ago.
D–G: Yeah.
G–D: Well, if you keep going "grr" you can't be my friend anymore.
J–D: Yeah.
D–G: Well, then I'm not your friend.
L–GJ: Yeah. Grr–Grr.

L and D now run off toward climbing bars; G moves into sandpile with J and they begin digging.

In this example, when Glen encountered initial resistance, he reminded Denny that only a short time ago they were friends. Denny agreed, but continued to resist and was not dissuaded by Glen's threat to end the friendship. In fact, Denny decided that, at least at this point in time, he was no longer Glen's friend. In this sequence the references to friendship are bound to the particular interactive situation. Denny used denial of friendship as a device to protect the interactive space and ongoing activity (playing lion with Leah). In contrast, Glen used the threat of denial of friendship as a strategy to overcome Denny's resistance.

According to cognitive developmental theory the source of development of social concepts is the child's actions in dealing with the objects and events in his environment. The preceding example demonstrates the complexity of contextual features of a peer environment in which children must actively construct social concepts (such as friendship) through their actions upon the environment and at the same time connect these concepts with specific interactive demands. In this example the children were not only learning about the concept of friendship but also were attempting to use the developing notion as a device to justify and overcome exclusion.

Protection of interactive space in the video data. In this section I will further investigate the relevance of the patterns isolated in field notes by examining the frequency of types of resistance in the video data and by presenting a micro-sociolinguistic analysis of a videotaped access–resistance sequence.

The videotaped data were collected over the last four months of the school term. A total of 129 peer episodes were videotaped, of which seventy (54.3 percent) included attempts to gain access. Of these seventy episodes, thirty-four (48.6 percent) included initial resistance to access attempts. The pattern of resistance to around half of the attempts to gain access, which was isolated in field notes, appears again in the video data.

Table 8-1 shows the frequency of types of initial resistance in the video data. References to ownership and overcrowding were the two most frequent types of resistance (46.8 percent and 17 percent respectively). This finding suggests that the children have gained knowledge of the organizational features and rules of the school. The use of these types of justifications, especially references to overcrowding, also suggests that the children are aware of the tenuous nature of peer interaction in this setting and of the disruptive effects of allowing additional playmates to join a peer episode once it is underway.

Finally, there were also several instances (12.8 percent of the total) in which the denial of friendship was used as a basis for exclusion. Although the percentage is relatively small, it is in line with the pattern in field notes regarding the relationship between protection of interactive space and conceptions of friendship.

The videotaping of instances of conflict stemming from resistance to access attempts allowed for the micro-sociolinguistic analyses of the children's use of access rituals (see Corsaro, 1979c) and their strategies for the protection of interactive space. Micro-sociolinguistic analysis allows the researcher to go beyond static frequency distributions of certain types of behavior (e.g., types of access attempts and initial resistance) to capture the dynamic, negotiated features of social interactive processes. The access and resistance strategies (as well as the developing conceptions of friendship) children carry into interactive episodes are, in Cook-Gumperz and Gumperz's (1976) terms, just a few of the multiple informational cues that the children use in the contextualization process. Micro-sociolinguistic analysis goes beyond the identification of developing social concepts and other contextual information (or cues) and focuses on how the information is used in the interactive process.

In examining the videotaped episodes, I found that the children's acceptance of peers into ongoing episodes often followed a four-stage

Table 8-1. *Frequency of types of initial resistance to attempts to gain access*

Type of resistance	N	%
Verbal without justification	7	14.9
Reference to arbitrary rules	4	8.5
Claim of ownership of object or play area	22	46.8
Reference to overcrowding	8	17.0
Denial of friendship	6	12.8
Total	47	100.0

process: (1) an attempt at access; (2) initial resistance; (3) repeated access attempts followed by further resistance with the eventual agreement among defenders of an area to let others enter; and (4) the assignment of positions (e.g., policeman, mother, baby, friend) to the new members. In the following example I present a micro-sociolinguistic analysis of a sequence of behavior that contained this four-stage process. The analysis demonstrates that acceptance of others into a play group is a negotiated process involving the use of a wide range of contextual information.

Steven (S), age 4.10, and Jonathan (J), age 4.9, are on the climbing bars when Graham (G), age 3.11, approaches the bars and attempts to enter. S and J had been playing "police" for some time before G's attempt to gain access.[8]

		Transcription	Description
(1)	S–G:	No, you can't get in! You can't get in! You can't get in! You can't get in!	S is in bars and moves near where G is trying to enter and shouts down. Volume increases with each repetition.
(2)	G–S:	Yes, we can!	G begins climbing up board which is slanted against bars.
(3)	S–G:	It's only for police! It's only for policemen!	
(4)	S–JG:	He's gonna have it, policeman. He's gonna have it.	S climbs down bars toward G. S is referring to J with the title "policeman."
(5)	J–G:	You're gonna have it, dum-dum!	S is now standing on ground next to G. As he says "dum-dum" J jumps to ground and pushes G down. The push was just hard enough to knock G off his feet.
(6)	G–J:	You are!	G gets up and moves toward J, who backs off. S then moves in

222   W. A. CORSARO

Transcription	Description
	front of G and they exchange threatening karate chops, but there is no physical contact. Tommy (T), age 4.3, now enters area and stands near G.
(7) G–T: T, get them! Grab them! Grab them, T.	G moves behind T, pushing him forward toward J and S.
(8) T–G: Kick'em?	
(9) G–T: No, grab them. Grab them, quick!	T moves toward J and S, who are now climbing back onto the bars.
(17) T–G: Come on let's go.	T turns and moves away from bars.
...	
(18) G–T: Yeah.	G follows T away from bars.
(19) J–S: Good! We got the run of *our* policehouse.	J moves higher in bars near S.

S's first utterance to G was a direct warning for him to stay out. S used several types of contextual information here (physical movement, the second-person pronoun, repetition, heavy stress, and increasing volume) to make his utterance a clear defense of the play area. G not only realized that his attempt at access was being resisted, but that S was very serious about his intent to defend the area. In line 3, S offered a justification for excluding G based on arbitrary rules. There was no way G could be a policeman; he could only be a policeman if he had been playing from the start of the episode. The first three utterances also demonstrate how access attempts and resistance get strung together in an initiation–response sequence. G's initial strategy was to move into the area. This attempt was resisted by S with no justification. G persisted, and in turn S offered a justification for exclusion based on arbitrary rules. This pattern of stringing together types of resistance by the defender of an area occurred in all cases in which there were persistent access attempts. In this case there was a movement from a simple type of resistance (resistance with no justification) to a more complex type (justification based on arbitrary rules) as the negotiation process progressed.[9]

S's utterance in line 4 marked an important shift in the interaction, in that it involved his fellow "policeman," J, in the protection of interactive space and also marked solidarity in the dyad. Instead of calling J by name (or assuming J heard his threats to G), S used a different contextual cue, the title "policeman," to threaten B through speech directed to J. As a result, S's one utterance performed multiple functions. J took up the threat to G (line 5) and jumped down from the bars to push G to the ground. G then enlisted help from T, and the dispute continued until T recommended leaving and G agreed (line 18). At this point the children had moved through the first two stages of an attempt at access and initial resistance.

The dispute did not end at line 19, however, because G returned shortly thereafter to renew his attempt to gain access. Upon his return he first enlisted aid from a girl (Antoinette, age 4.1) and then from a teaching assistant. In negotiation with G, A, and the teaching assistant, both S and J first used resistance based on ownership, claiming they had been on the bars first. The teaching assistant, however, invoked a higher-order rule – that the bars were a public place that had to be shared – and G and A were able to move onto the bars. At that point J decided to let them play and tried to persuade S to agree to the new arrangement.

(195)	J–S:	We want to talk about it, so--ah--let-let-S why don't we cooperate and why don't you agree to be a nice policeman?	J is standing in bars next to S. G and A are also in bars.
(196)	S–J:	O--o--ok.	S stretches out "OK" and seems unhappy but resigned to the agreement.
(197)	J–S:	Here, shake hands.	J reaches over bar and extends his hand to S. S and J shake hands while A and G watch from the other end of the bars.
(198)	J–S:	Hey! I shook it from over this bar.	
(199)	S–J:	We have to get those robbers.	S points to A and G.
(200)	A–G:	Come on. We--come on, let's go, G.	G and A climb higher in bars, while S moves toward them.
(201)	S–J:	We have to get the robbers who stole the jewels.	

Beginning with J's request to "talk about it," the sequence moved into the third stage, in which the defenders negotiated the possibility of allowing the other children to enter into the activity. This stage is often marked (as it was here) by a shift from communication between defenders and intruders to communication between defenders. In this example, the end of the negotiation process was marked by an extralinguistic cue (the handshake) between the defenders (S and J). Once agreement was reached there was direct movement into the last stage, which involved the integration of the new members into the ongoing activity (S's utterance at line 199).

Although this is a lengthy example and I have focused on only a few of the contextual cues involved, it illustrates the importance of micro-sociolinguistic analysis. Micro-sociolinguistic analyses capture processes (such as the nature of access–resistance strings and stages in the process of accepting peers into ongoing episodes) that are difficult to detect when one relies only on frequency distributions of coding schemes. Even sequential analysis of codes is often insufficient for identifying processual features, because no coding system is sensitive enough to capture all of the contextual information that social actors routinely employ in communicative processes.

Summary. In this section I used field notes from the first three months of the school term to identify the children's basic concerns and to isolate social organizational features of the nursery-school setting. I then further explored the patterns in field notes by examining access–resistance sequences in the video data.

The analysis of field notes revealed that the nursery school has definite organizational features that affect the children's concerns and behavior. The school is an example of what Goffman (1961) called a "multi-focused" setting. In such a setting, the "persons immediately present to each other can be parceled out into different encounters" (Goffman, 1961, p. 18). In addition to the multifocused nature of the setting, the children are also faced with the knowledge that interactive episodes can be terminated at any moment without formal marking or opportunity for negotiation. Furthermore, once an episode ends, the children then must deal with the threat of resistance to their attempts to gain access to other ongoing peer episodes.

Given these features of the nursery-school setting, the children develop two conflicting concerns: (1) to gain access to ongoing episodes when they are uninvolved, and (2) to protect interactive space from the intrusion of others when they are participants in ongoing episodes. These concerns are manifested most clearly in the children's strategies for gaining access and the nature and frequency of resistance to access attempts. Patterns in access–resistance sequences in the videotaped episodes suggest that the children are aware that peer interaction is fragile, that acceptance into ongoing episodes is often difficult, and that entry of others into ongoing episodes is potentially disruptive.

Finally, the children at times used the denial of friendship as a basis for exclusion. The use of this type of resistance to access attempts suggests that the children's developing conceptions of friendship may be tied to the organizational features of this peer environment. Friendship may be used as a device for protecting interactive space from potential disruptions that occur routinely in peer interaction in this setting. I will pursue these working hypotheses in the next two sections of the chapter, in which I focus on the structure of social contacts apparent in the video data and on the children's spontaneous references to friendship in peer interaction.

The structure of social concepts

If, as the data reported on in the last section suggest, the children are aware of the fragility of peer interaction, the difficulty of gaining access into play groups, and the potentially disruptive effects of the entry of peers into ongoing episodes, then the structure of their social contacts should reflect this awareness. Specifically, if the children are aware of these contextual demands, they will try to distribute their social contacts in such a way as to maximize their options for dealing with the demands. For example, by playing with several (four to seven) peers regularly, as opposed to concentrating social contacts around one or two playmates, children increase their chances of successful access to play groups. Thus, an examination of the structure of social contacts in the two nursery-school groups is necesssary.

In previous studies of peer relations and friendship among preschool children (Challman, 1932; Green, 1933; Koch, 1933; Marshall & McCandless, 1957; Parten, 1932), friendship has been defined in terms of frequency of contact or ranking of sociometric choices. If recent work on early conceptual levels of friendship is correct (Damon, 1977; Selman, 1976, this volume; Youniss, 1975), then an association may indeed exist between conceptions of friendship and frequency of contact. However, there is some question about the nature of such a relationship.

Young children probably do view frequent playmates as friends, but, contrary to what earlier researchers have claimed, they may not perceive frequent playmates as best friends. The notion of "best friends" or of degrees of friendship implies a recognition of personal qualities upon which the concept is based. Best friends, according to this argument, are differentiated from other friends because they possess these personal qualities. However, a recognition of personal qualities may not be part of most preschool children's conceptions of friendship (Damon, 1977; Selman, 1976). Instead of concentrating only on degrees of friendship with children of this age, it may be more fruitful to analyze the overall structure of play contacts. Such analyses may provide support for recent theories about conceptual levels of friendship (Damon, 1977; Selman, 1976; Youniss, 1975) and serve to further investigation of hypotheses about the influence of social context on children's peer relations.

Procedure. I used videotaped episodes for the analysis of the structure of social contacts because (1) the quality of the data allowed for repeated micro-sociolinguistic analysis in making decisions regarding social contacts; and (2) the data had been collected during the last four months of the school term when interactive patterns had been stabilized. Of the 146 videotaped episodes, seventeen involved teacher-directed activities and were not included in the analysis. For the remaining 129 episodes I coded instances of social contacts for all children in each group.

I coded as a social contact an instance in which the children involved engaged in associative play at some point during the course of an episode. Following Parten (1932), I defined "associative play" as an instance in which the children were engaged in and mutually aware of common activity and interest.[10] In this coding procedure no child could have more than one social contact with any other particular participant in a given episode.[11] Prior ethnographic work, as well as the advantage of multiple viewing of the data, greatly enhanced the stability and consistency of coding decisions. Although the coding decisions may seem simple (associative play or no associative play), there were numerous instances of peer play for which both multiple viewings and background knowledge of participants were necessary to determine if all the children participating in a given episode were really playing together.

The sequence of peer interaction in the following example demonstrates features of the coding process. This sequence began with two children, Ellen and Leah, playing alone in one corner of a playhouse in the school. A third child, Glen, entered shortly thereafter. There had been no prior interaction between Glen and the two girls on this day. Although all but one of Ellen's reactions to Glen's behavior were negative, I coded both Ellen and Leah as involved in associative play with Glen.

Glen (G), age 3.9, Ellen (E), age 3.4, Leah (L), age 3.2, and Barbara (B), age 3.0, are downstairs in the playhouse with other children. E is the master of L who is pretending to be a baby kitty. G moves around the house pretending to eat everything in sight. B is outside the playhouse and is mainly involved with other children who are pretending to be her kitties, but she often enters the activity in playhouse with G, E, and L.

Transcription		*Description*
(1)	E–G: That's my kitty's.	L crawls into corner followed by E. G comes over and pretends to eat pans.
(2)	E–G: You're in my kitty's little bed and she hates you.	G continues to eat.
(3)	L: Yucky!	
(4)	E–G: Yucky. Go away!	G eats another pan.

Transcription	Description
(5) E–G: Go away	E hits at G with pan lid. G takes lid from E and eats it.
(6) E–G: Go away. We don't want you.	G moves from corner to table in center of playhouse.
(7) L–E: He's messing up my room!	
(8) E–L: He ate your food. Oh, too bad.	E says this with high pitch and endearing intonation similar to adult baby talk. G now takes plate from table, pretends to eat it and then drops it to the floor. E moves over near table and picks up the plate. G moves toward bed at far end of playhouse from corner where L still sits.
(9) E–G: Go away!	E comes up behind G, taps him with plate, and then runs back to corner with L and is pursued by G.
(10) E–G: Don't eat this food!	G grabs hat off rack in corner and begins eating it. E takes hat from G.
(11) E–G: No! That's hers.	E means that the hat belongs to L. E places hat back on rack while G grabs and eats a plate, which E then takes away from him.
(12) E–G: G, we don't need you.	G now moves toward telephone near front of playhouse.
(13) E–L: I washed my hair, baby.	G meanwhile eats phone. E comes over and takes phone away and pretends to make a call while G moves back toward corner.
(14) E–G: We don't need you, get out of our house.	E grabs hat before G can get it from rack. B now enters and attempts to take tinker toy G has been carrying. G pulls away from B and now grabs and pretends to eat the coat rack. After finishing rack G licks his lips.
(15) E: Ha! Ha! a piece of candy!	E is laughing and seems to be referring to G's apparent enjoyment of the coat rack. G and B now struggle over the tinker toy G has in his hand. A teacher intervenes, and B

Transcription	*Description*
	moves outside the house. G now wanders out of house briefly, then returns back to the corner.
(16) E–G: Go away!	G now eats a wig he finds on the floor and then moves to center of playhouse and attempts to eat the table. E now begins to gather all things in corner away from G. But G moves to corner and grabs a belt and eats it.
(17) E–L: We don't need him.	E says this as she pushes G away. G now moves back toward phone and eats it again.
(18) E: Go away out of our house! I don't need G.	G moves back toward corner but is distracted by B's asking researcher about microphone.
(19) E–L: (I don't know where) he went. I'll see.	G now leaves and goes to upstairs playhouse. E and L are in corner. G is upstairs eating things as another child, Nancy, watches. E now comes upstairs and takes a blanket near where G is sitting. G grabs blanket from E, eats it and gives it back. E then moves downstairs and G follows, and eating routine continues until episode ends with clean-up time.

As I noted earlier, I coded both Ellen and Leah as involved in associative play with Glen in this sequence. I coded no social contacts between Barbara and either Glen, Ellen, or Leah. My decision to code associative play was first anticipated around utterance 9 when Ellen seemed to lure Glen back to the corner. It was all but settled by line 15, where she genuinely appreciated his enjoyment in eating the coat rack as if it were candy; and the decision was finalized when Ellen followed Glen upstairs on the pretense of needing a blanket. It was necessary to observe the entire development of this spontaneous peer event to see that rejection itself ("We don't want you") had become a game that these children were playing together.[12]

The use of the episode as the sampling unit, the multiple viewing of the videotape, and prior ethnography of these children in the nursery school were all important factors in making these decisions regarding associative play. If, for example, I had relied on time sampling of sequences of one minute or so, I could not have captured the contextual richness of this event. Even using the episode as the sampling unit, the final decisions regarding associative play were based on multiple viewings and careful examination of both verbal and nonverbal information and temporal features of the unfolding event. Prior ethnography was also important, in that I had witnessed Glen pretending to be a monster on two previous occasions. I was also skeptical of Ellen's desire to be rid of him, because she had been a participant (frightened child) in one of the earlier instances.

After I coded the entire sample of peer episodes for associative play, I selected a subsample of forty-two episodes that were then coded independently by a research assistant.[13] There was over 92 percent agreement between me and the assistant for the coding of associative play in these episodes.

After the reliability coding, I tabulated the number of playmates and the total number of social contacts for each child in both groups. Because I was concerned with the overall structure of social contacts for each child rather than with merely the identification of the most frequent playmates, I also computed the mean number of contacts, the standard deviation of contacts (s.d.) and the coefficient of variation (V) for each child. The s.d. is a way of estimating how widely each child spreads his or her social contacts across the number of possible playmates. A low s.d. indicates that contacts are spread out over playmates, and a high s.d. means that contacts are clustered around a few specific playmates. The coefficient of variation (V) (Freund, 1952; Mueller, Schuessler, & Costner, 1977) controls for the number of contacts and is computed by $V = \text{s.d.}/\overline{X}(100)$. A V score of around 90 or above indicated clustering of social contacts around a limited number of playmates; a score of near 50 or below indicated little or no clustering. A V score between 51 and 89 indicated clustering around several playmates.

Findings. The mean V score for the morning group was 70.2 (s.d. = 19.6), and the mean V score for the afternoon group was 66.6 (s.d. = 19.9). The difference was not significant: t (46) = .62.[14] In the morning group, the V scores for most of the children fell within the range of 51 to 89. Only four children had V scores of 90 or more, and only three children had V scores of less than 51. There were no significant differences by sex or age within the morning group. For boys the mean V score was 67.8 (s.d. = 12.8); for girls the mean V score was 71.8 (s.d. = 24.1); t (21) = .48. For children who ranged in age from 2.11 to 3.4, the mean V score was 64.6 (s.d. = 14.0); for children from 3.5 to 3.11 years the mean V score was 75.7 (s.d. = 27.1); t (21) = 1.16.

The pattern of distribution of V scores in the afternoon group was similar to that of the morning group. Only three children had V scores of 90 or more, while three other children had scores of less than 51. Again, there were no significant differences by sex or age. The mean V score was 70.5 (s.d. = 19.4) for boys and 60.8 (s.d. = 15.17) for girls; t (23) = 1.28. The mean V score for children ranging in age from 3.9 to 4.3 was 62.9 (s.d. = 24.0); it was 69.5 (s.d. = 15.3) for children from 4.4 to 4.10 years; t (23) =76.

In addition to computing V scores, I also compared each child's distributions of social contacts in both the morning and afternoon groups with a random distribution using the Kolmogorov-Smirnov test (Hays and Winkler, 1971). For both groups each of the children's observed distributions differed from the random distributions at less than the .01 level, except for one child in each group. For these two children the observed distributions differed significantly from the random distributions at less than the .05 level.

Overall, these findings show that most of the children in each group play more often with some children than with others but do not concentrate their social contacts around one or two playmates. This pattern corresponds with my earlier findings regarding the children's awareness of organizational features of the nursery school and suggests the following hypothesis: Because interaction is fragile and acceptance into ongoing episodes is often difficult, the children may develop stable relations with several playmates as a way of maximizing the probability of successful access.[15]

To this point I have investigated the relationship between social organizational features of the school and patterns in peer interaction. In the final section of this chapter, I will try to demonstrate the linkage between this relationship and children's conceptions of friendship by examining the children's spontaneous references to friendship in peer interaction.

Functions of spontaneous references to friendship

Hartup (1975) has argued that "a differentiated analysis of the functions of language in the ontogeny of friendship is a high priority need" (p. 23). Thus far, the data show that the children mention friendship when they protect interactive space from intruders. However, the children also refer verbally to friendship in other interactive situations. Examination of the fifty-one spontaneous references to friendship in field notes and video data resulted in the identification of six categories of talk about friendship.

Of the fifty-one references to friendship, twenty-three occurred in situations involving attempts at access or exclusion. Several of the earlier examples showed that friendship was often tied to exclusion. The following example shows an instance in which a child referred to friendship following a successful attempt to gain access.

Martin (M), age 2.11, and Dwight (D), age 3.1, are playing in the climbing box. Denny (De), age 3.5, runs by and M yells:

M–De: Denny!
De–M: Martin!

Denny climbs in box next to Martin.

M–De: Dwight is here.
De–M: Can I come?
M–De: Yeah, you can come.
De–M: Yeah, cause I'm your friend, right?
M–De: Cause I'm your friend.

In this example Denny ties his acceptance to friendship. The notes and videotapes include other instances in which the children began attempts to gain access with phrases such as, "We're friends," and "We're friends, right?"

Twelve references to friendship occurred within the course of ongoing events, and often signified that the children were now friends because they were playing together. For example:

Richard (R), age 3.11, and Barbara (B), age 3.0, are building with blocks while Nancy (N), age 3.1, sits nearby.

R–B: We're playing here by ourselves.
B–R: Just – ah – we friends, right?
R–B: Right.
R–B: Go over there. ((Points to a block.)) Get that block behind you.

The children's references to friendship in examples like the one above are in line with Selman's (1976; this volume) findings on early conceptions of friendship. According to Selman, at the earliest level friendship is based on physical-geographical space or bonds formed by temporary action. At this level friends often are people with whom you happen to be playing now. We saw in an earlier example that the children did, at times, qualify the denial of friendship by making it temporary ("You're not our friend today").

A third type of verbal reference to friendship, which occurred on three occasions in the data, marked competition within and possible segmentation of play groups. The following example shows this type of reference.

Five children are playing with water in the outside sandbox. Each child has an individual hose. The children are Peter (P), age 4.6, Graham (G), age 3.11, Frank (F), age 4.9, Lanny (L), age 4.9, and Antoinette (A), age 4.1.

L: Hey, we made the best waterfall, see?
F–L: Yeah.
P–L: That's not a waterfall.
L–P: Yes, it is –
P–L: L's can't. L's isn't.
L–F: I did the – a waterfall, right F?
F–L: Yeah.
A: F's is.
F–L: Don't L. L!
L–F: Yes. Mine is, isn't it, F?
F–L: It's mine.
L–F: It's both of ours, right?
F–L: Right and we made it ourselves.
L–F: Right.
P–G: G, we're not gonna be F's and L's friend, right?
G–P: I am.
F–P: I'm gonna throw water on you if you don't stop it. And tell all the teachers.

On four occasions (two in each group) the children used references to friendship as an attempt at social control.

Peter (P), age 4.6, tries to get Graham (G), 3.11, to move over and play next to him.

P–G: Graham – if you play over here where I am, I'll be your friend.
G–P: I wanna play over here.
P–G: Then I'm not gonna be your friend.
G–P: I'm not – I'm not gonna let – I'm gonna tell my mom to not let you –
P–G: All *right*, I'll come over here.

The previous two examples are interesting because in both instances the main participants, Peter and Graham, were two of the three children in the afternoon group who confined most of their social contacts to each other and one other child. The examples demonstrate that Peter may be trying to protect this relationship as he and Graham participate in a larger play group.

A fifth category of references to friendship, which occurred five times, involved the specification of personal characteristics of friends or non-friends. In one example, Barbara told her playmate, Rita, "I'm not your friend" after Rita had taken a doll Barbara had been playing with. Barbara then told me that Rita was "a naughty girl." In all five cases, the references (positive or negative) were tied to preceding actions of playmates and did not imply enduring characteristics.

On four occasions the children referred to friendship in the course of expressing concern for the welfare of playmates. All but one of these references were tied to the recognition of a child's absence from school. For example:

Anita (A), age 4.6, and Vickie, age 4.9, were frequent playmates and had referred to each other as friends on several previous occasions. Today Vickie is absent from school and Anita is sitting on a box near the sandpile. Mark (M), age 3.10, approaches:

M–A: Are you playing with Brian, A?
A–M: No – I'm waiting for Vickie.

Vickie was absent from school for the second day in a row.

M–A: Oh.
A–M: But I don't think she's coming here.
M–A: Maybe she's sick.
A–M: Yeah, maybe.
A–M: Or maybe she quit –
M–A: Well, maybe she has a babysitter.
A–M: Well, anyway I'm busy.

A now goes to have juice, and M runs to climbing bars and joins Brian.

Finally, on one occasion recorded in the video data, two children showed a mutual concern and referred to each other as best friends.

Jenny (J), age 3.8, and Betty (B), age 3.7, are climbing in a large wooden box. B has just returned to play with J after being away for some time on this morning. Ellen (E), age 3.4, approaches and offers pieces of paper to B and J.

E: Do you guys want – do you guys – want a ticket?
J–E: No, we don't!

E now moves to other end of the box.

B–J: I do like you. J, my ( ). I do.
J–B: I know it.
B–J: Yeah. But I just ran away from you. You know why?
J–B: Why?
B–J: Because I ( ) –
J–B: You wanted to play with Linda?
B–J: Yeah.
J–B: I ranned away *with* you. Wasn't that funny?
B–J: Yes.
J–B: 'Cause I wanted to know what happened.
B–J: I know you wanted – all the time – you wanna know because you're my best friend.
J–B: Right.

These two children not only use the term "best friend" but discuss friendship at a fairly abstract level. From the discussion it is apparent that the children feel they are best friends because they care about each other. They show an awareness of how their actions affect each others' feelings: This awareness is clearest in Betty's explanation of why she ran away and Jenny's expression of her need to know what happened to Betty. In Damon's (1977) synthesis of work by Selman and Youniss on developmental progressions in children's conceptions of friendship, he argues that at the most advanced level "friends are persons who understand one another, sharing with each other their innermost thoughts, feelings and other secrets; therefore, friends are in a special position to help each other with psychological problems (loneliness, sadness, loss, fear, and so on) and must, in turn, avoid giving psychological pain or discomfort to each other" (pp. 161–162). This level of friendship was found only among 11- and 12-year-olds in Damon's (1977) and Selman's (1976) research, which was based on clinical interviewing. Betty and Jenny are, of course, considerably younger. However, both had high V scores (98.8 and 136.1, respectively), and they consistently played together over the entire school term. This finding suggests that children who develop intensive, long-term peer relations may acquire complex conceptions of friendship at an early age.

Summary and conclusions

In this chapter I have emphasized the important effects of social organizational features of the nursery school on the children's social relations and conceptions of friendship. Field notes from the first three months of participant observation revealed important organizational features of the school. The field notes and later video data showed that the children rarely engaged in solitary play and that when they found themselves alone they consistently tried to gain entry into ongoing peer activities. However, because of their recognition of the fragility of peer interaction and the multiple sources of disruption in the nursery school, children who were participating in peer activities often protected the interaction by resisting children who attempted to gain access. These two patterns led to recurrent conflict. In these conflict situations, the children occasionally used claims of friendship in attempts to gain access and the denial of friendship as a basis for exclusion. The patterns in field notes and the video data suggested two hypotheses: (1) The children construct concepts of friendship and at the same time link these concepts to specific organizational features of the nursery-school setting; and (2) the children's developing knowledge of friendship is closely tied to the social-contextual demands of this peer environment.

Analyses of the overall structure of social contacts in the videotape data showed that most of the children in both age groups played more often with some children than with others but did not concentrate their social contacts on one or two playmates. This pattern was in line with the earlier findings and hypotheses and suggested a third hypothesis: (3) Through peer interactive experience in the nursery school the children come to realize that interaction is fragile and acceptance into ongoing activities is often difficult, and therefore develop stable relations with several playmates as a way to maximize the probability of successful entry.

These three hypotheses were supported by the examination of access attempts and the protection of interactive space in peer episodes that were videotaped during the second half of the school term. I found, for example, that the children's justifications for exclusion reflected an awareness of the organizational features and rules of the nursery school. In addition, micro-sociolinguistic analyses of the videotaped episodes demonstrated the complexity of the negotiation process in the children's development of social knowledge and communicative skills. The negotiation process often led to the increased solidarity of small (dyadic and triadic) play groups and provided the children with experience in accommodating the social needs and rights of others who wish to join the group.

Although examination of children's spontaneous references to friendship resulted in the identification of six categories of talk about friendship, the majority of the references (thirty-five of fifty-one) fell into two categories. In support of the earlier hypotheses, the children often referred to friendship as a basis for both inclusion into and exclusion from play groups. In addition, many of the children's references to friendship occurred in the course of ongoing events and signified that the children were now friends because they were playing together. In the nursery school, references in this context signaled growing solidarity within the play group and were often followed by plans to protect the emerging, shared activities. When children referred to friendship during access attempts or during the course of ongoing events, the relation between the social contextual demands of the nursery school and the conception and use of friendship was apparent. These findings suggest a fourth hypothesis: (4) For these children, friendship often serves specific integrative functions in the nursery school, such as gaining access to, building solidarity and mutual trust in, and protecting the interactive space of play groups, and is seldom based on the children's recognition of enduring personal characteristics of playmates.

When generating hypotheses, the researcher must be concerned with how well they are grounded in the data. There is seldom perfect fit between data and hypotheses, and exceptions to general patterns in the data should not contradict major claims of the hypotheses. In the present data several of children's spontaneous references to friendship displayed personal concern for the welfare of playmates, and in the case of one dyad a mutual intimacy approaching best-friend status was evident. However, these children were also exceptions in the overall structure of their social contacts. Unlike the majority of the children in the school, these children concentrated their social contacts on one or two playmates. In short, there were exceptions to specific hypotheses, but the exceptions were in line with the general emphasis of the set of hypotheses on the relation between contextual demands of the nursery-school setting and the development and use of social knowledge.

The study detailed here was exploratory, but the hypotheses regarding features of children's conceptions of friendship concur with recent research on children's development of social knowledge (Damon, 1977; Selman, 1976, this volume; and Youniss, 1975) and may be extended generally to preschool children. Selman (this volume), for example, found preschool children's conceptions of friendship (which were elicited in clinical interviews) to be generally based on "thinking that focuses upon propinquity," and that for young children, "a close friend is someone who lives close by and with whom the self happens to be playing with at the moment."

The primary goal of Selman's work is to build and validate general developmental models of social knowledge. What ethnographic studies of children's social worlds add to the work of cognitive developmental theorists (such as Selman) is insight into the importance of social context in the development of social concepts and the way in which children use social concepts to meet social-contextual demands in everyday activities.

Social knowledge is acquired and used in the various contexts that make up children's worlds. The present research provided an intensive examination of one such context. There is a need for further ethnographic work across a range of social settings with children at different stages of development. The recent work of Gottman and Parkhurst (1980) on spontaneous play among best-friend dyads in the home setting demonstrated the complexity of friendship processes among young children in these situations. Many more such studies are needed. We know little, for example, about the role played by parents and other adults in young children's exposure to social knowledge in the home setting.[16] Regarding older children, the work of Fine in informal peer-group settings and Schofield in a junior high school reported in this volume demonstrates the importance of ethnographic approaches for studying the socialization process. Fine's work tells us a great deal about friendship among preadolescent boys and is a contribution to a much-neglected area. However, there has been little, if any, ethnographic research of this type on preadolescent girls.

If children construct social knowledge—including conceptions of friendship—by acting upon the environment, then we need to examine those actions within their situational contexts. The many practical problems associated with such research should not dissuade us from discovering how children are exposed to, acquire, and use social knowledge in their everyday world.

Notes

1 Several studies of children's language have involved observations of young children in natural settings (Halliday, 1975; Keenan, 1974, 1977; Shatz & Gelman, 1973). Garvey's work (1974, 1975, 1977), although carried out in a laboratory setting, involved previously acquainted children.

2 Cook-Gumperz and Corsaro (1977) discuss the implication of this definition for the study of interaction in natural settings.

3 In field notes, ten episodes (1.6 percent of the total peer episodes) included solitary play. The 129 videotaped peer episodes included three (2.3 percent) instances of solitary play. Other researchers (Barnes, 1971; Parten, 1932; Rubin, Maioni, & Hornung, 1976) have found higher rates of solitary play. It is difficult to compare the findings in these studies with the present research because of the differences in data collection techniques. In the other studies the researchers worked with more structured sampling strategies in which they observed each child for one minute for a set number of times. I have previously discussed the advantages of using the interactive episode as the sampling unit. Sampling by interactive episodes ensures the contextual richness of naturalistic data. Although the issue cannot be pursued at length here, I believe that time sampling of sequences of behavior of short duration (one to five minutes) may, in part, affect the level of solitary play recorded. This effect seems most apparent regarding what Parten (1932) has termed "onlooker/unoccupied" behavior, which is a type of solitary play. An observational study of adults at a cocktail party using one-minute time sampling techniques would probably reveal a high level of such behavior and would fail to capture (as it does with children in the nursery school) the functions of such behavior for access attempts into ongoing activities (Corsaro, 1979c). In short, different methods of sampling specimens of behavior from ongoing interaction in natural settings make comparisons of findings difficult if not impossible.

4 Pseudonyms are used in all examples drawn from field notes and videotapes. Words enclosed in double parentheses are descriptions of nonverbal behavior.

5 Unfortunately, I recorded only a few episodes (five in field notes and seventeen on video tape) of teacher-directed activities. The behavior of the children who participated in these episodes followed no consistent pattern, but the sample was small and it is not possible to draw any conclusions about the children's use of this option.

6 For the four children involved, the difference between initial acceptance and resistance were as follows: Debbie, four cases of initial acceptance and three of initial resistance; Denny, two cases of initial acceptance and four of initial resistance; Tommy, five cases

of initial acceptance and six of initial resistance; and Brian, five cases of initial acceptance and three of initial resistance.

7 The raw data regarding sexual makeup of groups and the percentage of cases of resistance to children attempting access is as follows: boy(s) attempting access to all-boy
groups, 46.4 percent resistance in twenty-eight attempts; girl(s) attempting access to
all-girl groups, 58.8 percent resistance in seventeen attempts; boy(s) attempting access to
all-girl groups, 53.3 percent resistance in fifteen attempts; girl(s) attempting access to
all-boy groups, 75.0 percent resistance in twenty-four attempts; boy(s) attempting access
to mixed-sex groups, 45.0 percent resistance in twenty attempts; girl(s) attempting access to mixed-sex groups, 52.2 percent resistance in twenty-three attempts.

8 The following symbols are used in all examples that come from transcripts of videotaped
episodes:

(   )   Words inside parentheses were not clearly heard and should be regarded as
          probable translations. When blank, no translation was possible, but word or
          words of about the indicated length occurred.

Italics   Marks a child's stress on certain words or phrases.

((   )) Words enclosed in double parentheses are descriptions of nonverbal behavior.

------   Denote pause in speech. At the end of an utterance, this symbol signifies that the
          speaker has been interrupted.

9 In the video data, ten of the thirty-four episodes that contained resistance to access
included multiple resistance. Of these ten episodes, nine fit the pattern of movement
toward a more complex type of justification for resistance (i.e., a movement from either
resistance without justification or resistance with justification based on arbitrary rules to
one of the other three types of resistance).

10 If all but one child left an area, and the one remaining engaged in solitary play, I sampled
this behavior as a new episode.

11 This is caused by the decision to code social contacts by episode. For example, if three
children (A, B, and C) are involved in associative play and B leaves but the episode
continues with A and C involved in play, then should B return during the course of the
same episode and begin playing with A and C the renewal of play was not recorded as an
additional social contact. B's leaving is seen as a temporary withdrawal from the earlier
play and his or her return is not a new contact.

12 Although Glen (or any of the other children) did not refer to his behavior as similar to that
of Cookie Monster on the children's television show *Sesame Street*, this sequence may
indeed be based upon shared knowledge about this character. I have consistently found
that it is not always necessary for the children to connect emerging activities overtly with
underlying shared knowledge and expectations in childhood culture (see Cook-Gumperz
& Corsaro, 1977).

13 This subsample included all transcribed episodes and was not random. The episodes
were representative of the children involved, activities, and areas of the school and over
time.

14 One child from each group was not included in the analysis because these children dis-
continued attendance during the fifth month of the school term.

15 These data still do not explain why five children in the two groups clustered around one
or two playmates or why six children had no distinct pattern of clustering. An explanation would require data on (1) the frequency with which these children participated in
teacher-directed activities as opposed to peer activities, (2) their reactions to initial resistance to access attempts, and (3) the stability and duration of episodes in which they
were participants. Unfortunately, I have data only on the latter two points and have not
yet completed the analyses. However, the present data still suggest that these children
may have quite different developmental histories with respect to companionship and

affection in peer relations. Some of the data on the children's spontaneous discussions of friendship are important in this regard.

16 As I have discussed in a previous research report (Corsaro, 1979b), adults continually expose children to the normative order by the way they talk to them in everyday interactive situations. Sheldon Stryker (personal communication) notes that caretakers' proscriptions may partially structure children's "discovery" of friendship and other social concepts and related normative criteria (e.g., "See who's come over to play with you, it's your friend Tommy," "You must share, he's your friend"). There is a need for systematic ethnographic studies of discussions of friendship in the home to specify the caretaker's role in the child's acquisition of this social concept.

References

Babchuk, N. Primary friends and kin: A study of the associations of middle-class couples. *Social Forces*, 1965, *45*, 501–507.

Barker, R., & Wright, H. *One boy's day*. Hamden, Conn.: Archon Books, 1966.

Barnes, K. Preschool play norms: A replication. *Developmental Psychology*, 1971, *5*, 99–103.

Bates, E. *Language and context: The acquisition of pragmatics*. New York: Academic Press, 1976.

Bateson, G. *Steps to an ecology of the mind*. New York: Ballantine, 1972.

Becker, H. S. *Sociological work: Method and substance*. Chicago: Aldine, 1970.

Bowerman, C., & Kinch, J. Changes in family and peer orientation of children between the fourth and tenth grades. *Social Forces*, 1959, *37*, 206–211.

Bruner, J. The ontogenesis of speech acts. *Journal of Child Language*, 1975, *2*, 1–19.

Challman, R. Factors influencing friendships among preschool children. *Child Development*, 1932, *3*, 146–158.

Cicourel, A. *Cognitive sociology*. New York: Free Press, 1974.

Coleman, J. *The adolescent society*. New York: Free Press, 1961.

Cook-Gumperz, J., & Corsaro, W. Social-ecological constraints on children's communicative strategies. *Sociology*, 1977, *11*, 411–434.

Cook-Gumperz, J., & Gumperz, J. Context in children's speech. In J. Cook-Gumperz & J. Gumperz (Eds.), *Papers on language and context*. Working Paper #46, Language Behavior Research Laboratory, University of California, Berkeley, 1976.

Corsaro, W. Young children's conception of status and role. *Sociology of Education*, 1979, *52*, 46–59. (a)

Sociolinguistic patterns in adult – child interaction. In E. Ochs (Ed.), *Developmental pragmatics*. New York: Academic Press, 1979. (b)

We're friends, right?: Children's use of access rituals in a nursery school. *Language in Society*, 1979, *8*, 315–336. (c)

Entering the child's world: Research strategies for field entry and data collection in a preschool setting. In J. Green & C. Wallat (Eds.), *Ethnographic approaches to face-to-face interactions*. Norwood, N.J.: Ablex Publishing, in press.

Corsaro, W., & Tomlinson, G. Spontaneous play and social learning in the nursery school. In H. Schwartzman (Ed.), *Play and culture*. West Point, N.Y.: Leisure Press, 1980.

Damon, W. *The social world of the child*. San Francisco: Jossey-Bass, 1977.

Denzin, N. The logic of naturalistic inquiry. *Social Forces*, 1971, *50*, 166–182.

Childhood socialization. San Francisco: Jossey-Bass, 1977.

Dumphy, D. The social structure of urban adolescent peer groups. *Sociometry*, 1963, *26*, 230–246.

240	W. A. CORSARO

Eder, D., & Hallinan, M. Sex differences in children's friendships. *American Sociological Review*, 1978, *43*, 237–251.

Eisenstadt, S. *From generation to generation*. New York: Free Press, 1956.

Ervin-Tripp, S., & Mitchell-Kernan, C. (Eds.), *Child discourse*. New York: Academic Press, 1977.

Freund, J. *Modern elementary statistics*. Englewood Cliffs, N.J.: Prentice-Hall, 1952.

Gans, H. *The urban villagers*. New York: Free Press, 1961.

The Levittowners. New York: Random House, 1967.

Garvey, C. Some properties of social play. *Merrill-Palmer Quarterly*, 1974, *20*, 163–180.

Requests and responses in children's speech. *Journal of Child Language*, 1975, 41–63.

The contingent query: A dependent act in conversation. In M. Lewis & L. Rosenblum (Eds.), *Interaction, conversation, and the development of language*. New York: Wiley, 1977.

Glick, J., & Clarke-Stewart, A. (Eds.), *Studies in social and cognitive development*. New York: Gardner Press, 1978.

Goffman, E. *Encounters*. Indianapolis: Bobbs-Merrill, 1961.

Frame analysis. New York: Harper & Row, 1974.

Gottman, J. M., & Parkhurst, J. T. A developmental theory of friendship and acquaintanceship processes. In W. A. Collins (Ed.), *Minnesota symposia on child psychology* (Vol. 13). Hillsdale, N.J.: Lawrence Erlbaum, 1980.

Green, E. Friendships and quarrels among preschool children. *Child Development*, 1933, *4*, 237–252.

Gump, P., Schoggen, P., & Redl, F. The behavior of the same child in different milieus. In R. Barker (Ed.), *The stream of behavior*. New York: Appleton-Century-Crofts, 1963.

Halliday, M. *Learning how to mean: Explorations in the development of language*. London: E. Arnold, 1975.

Hartup, W. The origins of friendship. In M. Lewis & L. Rosenblum (Eds.), *Friendship and peer relations*. New York: Wiley, 1975.

Hays, W., & Winkler, R. *Statistics: Probability, inference and decision*. New York: Holt, Rinehart & Winston, 1971.

Hess, B. Friendship. In M. Riley, M. Johnson, & A. Fonner (Eds.), *Aging and society: A sociology of age stratification* (Vol. 3). New York: Russell Sage Foundation, 1972.

Keenan, E. Conversational competence in children. *Journal of Child Language*, 1974, *1*, 163–183.

Making it last: Repetition in children's discourse. In S. Ervin-Tripp & C. Mitchell-Kernan (Eds.), *Child discourse*. New York: Academic Press, 1977.

Keenan, E., & Klein, E. Coherency in children's discourse. *Journal of Psycholinguistic Research*, 1975, *4*, 365–380.

Koch, H. Popularity in preschool children: Some related factors and a technique for its measurement. *Child Development*, 1933, *4*, 64–75.

Lazarsfeld, P., & Barton, A. Some functions of qualitative analysis in sociological research. *Sociologica*, 1955, *1*, 324–361.

Lazarsfeld, P., & Merton, R. Friendship as a social process: A substantive and methodological analysis. In M. Berger, T. Abel, & C. Page (Eds.), *Freedom and control in modern society*. Princeton, N.J.: Van Nostrand, 1954.

Lever, J. Sex differences in the complexity of children's play and games. *American Sociological Review*, 1978, *43*, 471–483.

Lewis, M., & Rosenblum, L. (Eds.), *Friendship and peer relations*. New York: Wiley, 1975.

Interaction, conversation, and the development of language. New York: Wiley, 1977.

Liebow, E. *Tally's corner*. Boston: Little-Brown, 1967.

Marshall, H., & McCandless, B. A study in prediction of social behavior of preschool children, *Child Development*, 1957, *28*, 149–159.

Mueller, J., Schuessler, K., & Costner, H. *Statistical reasoning in sociology*. Boston: Houghton-Mifflin, 1977.

Newman, D. Ownership and permission among nursery-school children. J. Glick & A. Clarke-Stewart (Eds.), *Studies in social and cognitive development*. New York: Gardner Press, 1978.

Ochs, E. (Ed.), *Developmental pragmatics*. New York: Academic Press, 1979.

Opie, I., & Opie, P. *The lore and language of school children*. New York: Oxford University Press, 1959.

Children's games in street and playground. Oxford, Eng.: Clarendon Press, 1969.

Parten, M. Social participation among preschool children. *Journal of Abnormal and Social Psychology*, 1932, *27*, 243–269.

Social play among preschool children. *Journal of Abnormal and Social Psychology*, 1933, *28*, 136–147.

Piaget, J. *The psychology of intelligence*. London: Routledge and Kegan Paul, 1950.

Richards, M. (Ed.), *The integration of a child into a social world*. London: Cambridge University Press, 1974.

Rubin, K., Maioni, T., & Hornung, M. Free play behaviors in middle- and lower-class preschoolers: Parten and Piaget revisited. *Child Development*, 1976, *47*, 414–419.

Schwartzman, H. The anthropological study of child's play. *Annual Review of Anthropology*, 1976, *5*, 289–328.

Selman, R. The development of interpersonal reasoning. In A. Pick (Ed.), *Minnesota symposia on child psychology* (Vol. 10). Minneapolis: University of Minnesota Press, 1976.

Shantz, C. The development of social cognition. In E. M. Hetherington (Ed.), *Review of child development research* (Vol. 5). Chicago: University of Chicago Press, 1975.

Shatz, M., & Gelman, R. The development of communication skills: Modifications in the speech of young children as a function of listener. *Monographs of the Society for Research in Child Development*, 1973, *38* (5, Serial No. 152).

Shure, M. Psychological ecology of a nursery school. *Child Development*, 1963, *34*, 979–992.

Smilansky, S. *The effects of sociodramatic play on disadvantaged preschool children*. New York: Wiley, 1968.

Speier, M. *How to observe face-to-face communication: A sociological introduction*. Pacific Palisades, Cal.: Goodyear, 1973.

Stryker, S. *Personal communication*, April, 1979.

Sutton-Smith, B. Toward an anthropology of play. *Association for the Anthropological Study of Play Newsletter*, 1974, *1*, 8–15.

Turiel, E. The development of social concepts: Mores, customs and conventions. In D. DePalma & J. Foley (Eds.), *Moral development: Current theory and research*. Hillsdale, N.J.: Laurence Erlbaum Associates, 1975.

The development of concepts of social structures: Social conventions. In J. Glick & A. Clarke-Stewart (Eds.), *Studies in social and cognitive development*. New York: Gardner Press, 1978. (a)

Social regulations and domains of social concepts. In W. Damon (Ed.), *New directions for child development, Vol. 1: Social cognition*. San Francisco: Jossey-Bass, 1978. (b)

Whyte, W. F. *Street corner society*. Chicago: University of Chicago Press, 1955.

Youniss, J. Another perspective on social cognition. In A. Pick (Ed.), *Minnesota symposia on child psychology* (Vol. 9). Minneapolis: University of Minnesota Press, 1975.

9   The child as a friendship philosopher

Robert L. Selman

Prologue

Field notes from the author's observations during lunch in the cafeteria of a day-school for troubled children (October, 1978):

Throughout lunch, Marvin, age eight, has been playing with a new Battlestar Galactica rocket. Joey, age nine, is manifesting an intense interest in using Marvin's rocket.

> Joey: Marvin, let me play with your rocket and I'll do anything you want.
> Marvin: Get me another dessert.
> Joey: (returning with a second orange) Now can I play with your rocket?
> Marvin: Nope.
> Joey: If you let me use your rocket, I'll be your . . . Let me use it because I *am* your friend.
> Marvin: (matter-of-factly) You're not my friend.
> Joey: (losing control, screaming until red in the face) Yes, I am! I *am* your friend! Yes, I *am*! Yes, I *am*! I'll *blast* you if you say I'm not your friend!

The philosophy and psychology of friendship concepts

In 1968, Lawrence Kohlberg wrote a short article for the popular magazine *Psychology Today* titled "The Child as a Moral Philosopher" (Kohlberg, 1968). Although at that time American psychologists were becoming well acquainted with Piaget's methods and data, they still tended to view and assess his approach primarily from a psychological perspective, despite Flavell's earlier clear-cut articulation of Piaget's epistemological philosophy (1963). Kohlberg's article, although simplistic by de-

Support of the preparation of this chapter was facilitated by a Career Development Award –KO2-MH00157-02 – to the author from the National Institute of Mental Health. The research described was supported in part by a grant from the Spencer Foundation. Parts of this chapter have been adapted to appear in a book by the author, *The Growth of Interpersonal Understanding: Developmental and Clinical Analyses*.

sign, accomplished two things. First, it demonstrated to a large audience how Piaget's cognitive-developmental approach might be applicable to social psychology. Second, it reemphasized that social philosophy and social psychology are not distinct and unrelated disciplines – that ontogenetic changes in individuals' social philosophies are valid and interesting topics for psychological study.

Like moral philosophizing, philosophizing about friendship is not a new endeavor. In the *Nicomachean Ethics,* Aristotle proposed a typological theory of friendship composed of three distinct functions: (1) the friendly behavior of pleasant but momentary interactions; (2) the provision of kind actions or isolated aid to unknown persons or slight acquaintances; and (3) the ideal of mutuality and commitment. Cicero contributed certain perceived situational parameters to the analysis (in Hunt, 1914). True friendship, he observed, meaning Aristotle's third type, could occur only among those of equal and symmetrical status, with neither holding a claim of authority upon the other.

If Cicero was correct in claiming that only an ideal and equal friendship was a true friendship, we must then ask whether it makes sense to speak of close personal relationships among children who have not yet achieved this highest level as "true" friendships. Should we say that they have imperfect friendships? An alternative approach is Piaget's epistemological philosophy, which would have us examine the child's understanding of friendship ontogenetically: in other words, directly study the more primitive conceptions of friendship manifested in growing children, both as a road to understanding the developmental psychology of intimate relationships and as a means to understanding the philosophical concept of friendship itself.

Although philosophizing about the nature of friendship is an old tradition, it is only in the last several years that psychologists have become interested in the study of children's friendship philosophizing and children's theories about what makes a good friendship. Recently, five reviews that touch upon this area have been written (Bigelow & LaGaipa, in press; Damon, 1977; Hartup, 1978; Rubin, 1980; and Serafica, 1978). However, although we are suddenly long on reviews, we are still remarkably short on empirical data. The literature on developmental aspects of friendship conceptions is restricted to a handful of studies (Bigelow & LaGaipa, 1975; Bigelow, 1977; Berndt, 1978; Gamer, 1977; Hayes, 1978; Reisman & Shorr, 1978; Selman, 1976; Serafica, 1978; Youniss & Volpe, 1978). Nevertheless, the data that are coming in from these and ongoing studies are remarkably similar, even if the frameworks within which the data are presented are not.

It is one of the aims of this chapter to provide an explanation for the commonalities observed in the findings thus far. To do so, I will examine results as well as the methods used for collecting and categorizing responses made by children at different ages to simple and straightforward questions such as "What makes someone a close friend?"

In addition, in studying conceptions of friendship and, more generally, social cognition and its development, I am especially interested in exploring a particular methodological question and its implications: namely, how and at what point in the analysis does the psychologist decide to impute meaning to the child's responses? In social-cognitive psychology, it is as difficult to reliably and validly develop meaningful and clear-cut categories into which to code words and verbally expressed meanings as it is in social behavioral psychology to do so for verbally or nonverbally expressed actions. Other developmental studies of friendship concepts appear to be heavily weighted toward an empiricist approach. Although any research effort in this area must start with the researcher's own intuitive ideas of possible factors that make someone a close friend, seldom are these factors made explicit a priori. Instead, data are collected using commonsense questions and those psychological categories that the scorers can use to reliably code the bulk of responses. Those that show some developmental (age) variation are kept in the system. In the literature review that follows, I will show that this research strategy has produced results that are remarkably consistent. I will then suggest a common organizing principle in these findings and contrast this research strategy with my own.

Bigelow and LaGaipa (1975) analyzed the written responses of Canadian children in grades one through eight. Their charge to subjects was to write an essay about what children expect of their best friend that is different from their expectations about people who are not best friends. From their data analysis and their own understanding of friendship, Bigelow and LaGaipa developed a set of twenty-one original dimensions to code the content of each child's essay. Subsequently, Bigelow reported a cross-cultural validation of the study's results with 480 Scottish children (1977). In both these studies, Bigelow reported that eleven of the originally anticipated dimensions were used increasingly by older children: help (friend as giver) (2), [1]common activities (2), propinquity (3), evaluation (3), acceptance (4), incremental prior interactions (4), loyalty and commitment (5), genuineness (6), intimacy (7), common interest (7), and similarity in attitudes (7).

Two dimensions prevalent in the responses of the younger children declined in use with age: sharing (friend as receiver) and general play. Three other dimensions – reciprocity of liking, ego reinforcement, and sharing (friend as giver) – remained at about the same level of usage across the age range of the sample. Five categories increased in use with age in the first study but did not do so in the replication. These were stimulation value, organized play, demographic similarity, help (friend as receiver), and similarity in attitudes and values. Bigelow (1977) then went one step further. Using the statistical procedure of cluster analysis, he found that certain of the dimensions appeared to emerge together at certain ages. From this he inferred the existence of three loosely defined stages, or more precisely, he empirically observed clusters of categories that emerged at about the same age. During the second and third grades, a reward–cost stage emerged in which the children appeared to weigh the cost of their efforts in relation to gains from their friends. The predominant emergent dimensions were propinquity, common activity, and similar expectation. During roughly the fourth and fifth grades, dimensions of sharing – particularly of norms, values, rules, and sanctions – emerged in some synchrony (the normative stage). During the sixth and seventh grades, a third stage yielded dimensions of self-disclosure, intimacy, and personality dispositions as critical to the differentiation of friends from acquaintances. Hartup, in his review, called this an empathetic stage, whereas Serafica interpreted it as an emphasis on internal or psychological attributes.

More recently, Berndt (1978) studied children in kindergarten, third grade, and sixth grade using open-ended questions about best friends, nonfriends, and friendships breaking up. Berndt assigned the children's responses about best friends to seven substantive categories: (1) defining features (someone says he is your friend); (2) psychological attributions (has a good personality); (3) shared activity (we play football); (4) quality of interaction (he doesn't fight with me); (5) intimacy and trust (I can share problems with her); (6) faithfulness (he won't leave me); and (7) loyal support (she will stick up for me in a fight). Berndt reported that at all ages responses coded as shared activity and quality of interaction were most commonly mentioned. However older children mentioned quality of the interaction, psychological attributes, and intimacy and trust more often than younger children.

In a second study, Berndt applied the categories, with some modifications, to responses about friendship breakups, and fairly similar results were obtained. Older children more often than younger children mentioned quality of interaction, intimacy and trust, loyal support, and faithfulness as critical factors. However, because in both samples Berndt found few correlations among categories, he concluded, in contradiction to Bigelow, that it is unlikely that stages exist.

Nevertheless, Berndt's developmental descriptions appear largely concordant with Bigelow's. They are concordant with findings from a study by Gamer (1977), who used nine categories to code the responses of children aged 6 to 7, 9 to 10, and 12 to 13 to five open-ended questions about friends, best friends, and the importance of friends. Gamer also reported that older children used more categories than did younger ones. In addition to the questions, Gamer used a procedure in which children at each of the different age levels were shown a depiction of and/or read eight statements about what makes a best friend. The statements were: someone who shares things; someone who can understand your feelings; someone who can teach you new games or things to do; someone who helps you; someone who likes the same things you do; someone who can keep a secret, someone who always wants to play with you; someone who defends you. Each child was asked to pick from the list the most important statement about what makes someone a good friend. Whereas the younger children did not choose any one category more often than another, the older children were most likely to choose "someone who can understand your feelings." However, when Gamer looked at comparisons of choices across the age range, she found that the 6-to-7-year-olds were more likely than were the older children to choose "someone who helps you" or "someone who defends you."

The studies of Bigelow, Berndt, and Gamer focused on children's developing conceptions or expectations about another person who would fit the concept good or best friend. Youniss and Volpe (1978) studied the development of social cognition and social relations, such as acts of friendship, using the Piagetian construct of operativity. They asked children of different ages what actions (or operations) are necessary to demonstrate the establishment or maintenance of social relationships in general. For example, children were asked to provide examples of operations (actions) that "show that you like someone," "show that you are friends with someone," or "show someone that you are being kind to him." Like the other researchers, Youniss and Volpe found that the younger children associated friendship with sharing of material goods or overt fun activities, whereas the older children reported that the acts that demonstrate friendship or friendly behavior are sharing private thoughts and feelings out of a sense of mutual respect and affection. Youniss stressed that with development, mutuality involves an increased understanding of the interrelationship between interpersonal acts and personal psychological states. For example, older children more clearly understand that an act of friendship can transform a person from a lonely or sad state to a happy state.

Although the studies reviewed so far use a wide variety of categories to code verbally transmitted responses, there is remarkable agreement among their findings. As children grow older, they appear to have conceptions of friendship that rely increasingly on an understanding of the psychological interdependence between persons (people need each other), that view relations as systematic and coherent (friends stick by one another over time), and that imply an understanding of the potential depths and complexities of the thoughts, feelings, and personalities of individuals (a friend helps you know what kind of person you are). The question raised, given the commonalities found in the description of friendship concepts, is whether there is some underlying social-cognitive process that can be used to help explain or characterize the similarities across studies.

I believe that the developmental construct of levels of social perspective-taking, or social perspective coordination,[2] provides just such an organizational tool or principle, and I will devote much of the remainder of this paper to an attempt to demonstrate this point, first by reporting the procedure that I have used in describing the development of friendship concepts, and second by comparing my results with those of the studies already described.

At the outset I will mention a basic difference in strategy that distinguishes my work from the studies examined so far. In each of the other studies, the children's verbalized responses were categorized largely on the basis of a method that codes for the language used in a child's spontaneous orientation. For example, a child is asked what makes two people best friends, and if the response is "someone who sticks by you," it is then categorized as "loyal support" (Berndt) or "loyalty and commitment" (Bigelow), without any further in-depth probing or exploring of what the child may mean by "sticks by you" or by loyalty or trust. My assumptions dictate a different approach. I assume that spontaneous utterances alone will not necessarily give an adequate picture of a subject's thinking and level of understanding. I also assume that concepts like loyalty and trust or words like "sticks by you" themselves may have different meanings to children at different ages. For example, as previous studies have shown, it is unlikely that a 5-year-old will spontaneously mention the term loyalty as a condition for friendship. However, even if he or she did, it would be unlikely to mean the same thing as it would if used by a 12-year-old. This is not a trivial distinction; it would be easy enough to teach a young child to say that loyalty is important in a friendship, but even if this were done, I would assume that this conception of loyalty would most likely be assimilated to the structure of a 5-year-old's social understanding. For example, our research indicates that even among seventh-grade children who spontaneously profess loyalty as a crucial dimension of friendship, without a method that probes for underlying meaning we cannot be sure that one seventh grader's concept of loyalty means the same thing as the next.

The link between the developmental structure of children's deeper social understanding and their social concepts is the basis of our work. Describing a method for making that link is the aim of this chapter. This structural-developmental approach refers to a set of assumptions and research methodologies common to a number of theories of cognitive and social development. Although the approach finds its roots in the early interactionist writings of Baldwin (1906) and Mead (1934), the extensive theoretical and empirical work of Piaget provided much of the present impetus for research in this area. The hallmark of such research is an interest in describing an invariant sequence of cognitively based stages or qualitatively distinct ways of organizing and understanding a certain domain of experience through which all children are hypothesized to develop. In contrast to other approaches, the focus is on the structure rather than on the content of thought, on universal patterns rather than on individual or situational differences, and on patterns of thinking rather than on emotions or behavior.

In the last ten years, there has been an increasing interest in extending this approach to the study of the child's developing understanding of the social world. The structural-developmental approach to social development has been used to study a variety of areas, including moral judgment (Damon, 1977; Kohlberg, 1969), social customs and conventions (Furth, 1978; Turiel, 1978), and conceptions of self (Broughton, 1978). As in structural-developmental theory in general, the goals of such social-cognitive studies have been to define qualitatively distinct stages in the child's conception of various aspects of the social world and to focus on the form of the thinking and on universal patterns related to underlying cognitive structures rather than on affectivity or individual or group differences.

With these goals in mind, the Harvard–Judge Baker Social Reasoning Project[3] was established in 1973 to study the child's developing interpersonal conceptions and to analyze the social perspective-taking structures assumed to underlie them. "Social perspective-taking" refers to the process by which a child is able to take the perspective of another and relate it to his or her own. Developmentally, social perspective-taking is viewed as beginning at the level at which the child fails to distinguish the social viewpoints of self and other. It then develops in a series of qualitative steps: first, distinguishing the social viewpoints of self and other, and then relating them to each other in progressively more complex and integrated ways. (See Table 9-1A for a brief description of each level.) Our working expectation is that the description and delineation of developmental changes in interpersonal conceptions in four domains (individuals, friendships, peer-group relations, and parent–child relations) will reveal that conceptions and changes in conceptions can be shown to be logically related to levels of perspective coordination (perspective-taking). From this viewpoint, perspective-taking is assumed to be a basic underlying structure that can be used to analyze developing social conceptions such as friendship.

The other approaches I have reviewed collect data on the child's spontaneous language of friendship (Hartup, 1978) and then attempt, post hoc, to give it developmental meaning (as in Bigelow's initial attempt to define stages). Our approach starts with a general structural-developmental theory of social cognition and then attempts to see whether children's expressed conceptions, empirically observed, bear any reliable, valid, and useful relationship to our theory. While each approach has certain advantages, I believe that we must strive to view social-cognitive-developmental inquiry as the study of the expression of deeper meaning: the study of what is meant and understood rather than the study of what is said. With this stance, it becomes somewhat clearer why one would want to study the ontogenesis of friendship conceptions from a structural-developmental perspective and why a method that probes deeply into each subject's understanding and awareness of interpersonal relations is a necessary tool for this exploration.

Developing an ontogenetic model of the understanding of friendship

Our program of research has three phases within each social domain we study. These phases are: (1) initial descriptive model building using interview methods to tap reflective thought; (2) construct validation; and (3) application to other modes besides reflective thought through which interpersonal understanding is expressed. As is traditional, the initial phase consists of a developmental analysis (here using perspective-taking levels) of data to describe developmental patterns in reflective interpersonal understanding in the domain in question. Next, in the construct validation phase, we evaluate how well the perspective-taking analyses of the mode of reflective understanding and the levels established satisfy essential formal stage criteria of structural developmental theory (structured wholeness, invariant developmental sequence, and universality). In the third phase, the stage descriptions based on methods that elicit a child's reflective reasoning are applied to the analysis of children's understanding-in-use as expressed in a wider variety of naturalistic social contexts. This is the functional application phase. Table 9-2 summarizes this

Table 9-1. *Developmental levels and stages of friendship.*

A. *Developmental levels in the coordination of social perspectives (relation between perspectives of self and others)*

B. *Stages of reflective understanding of close dyadic friendships*

Level 0: Egocentric or undifferentiated perspectives. Although the children can recognize the reality of subjective perspectives (e.g., thoughts and feelings) within the self and within others, because they do not clearly distinguish their own perspective from that of others, they do not recognize that another may interpret similarly perceived social experiences or courses of action differently from the way they do. Similarly, there is still some confusion between the subjective (or psychological) and objective (or physical) aspects of the social world, for example, between feelings and overt acts, or between intentional and unintentional acts. (Roughly ages 3 to 7.)

Stage 0: Momentary physicalistic playments. Conceptions of friendship relations are based on thinking which focuses upon propinquity and proximity (i.e., physicalistic parameters) to the exclusion of others. A close friend is someone who lives close by and with whom the self happens to be playing with at the moment. Friendship is more accurately playmateship. Issues such as jealousy or the intrusion of a third party into a play situation are constructed by the child at Stage 0 as specific fights over specific toys or space rather than as conflicts which involve personal feelings or interpersonal affection.

Level 1: Subjective or differentiated perspectives. The child understands that even under similarly perceived social circumstances the self and others' perspectives may be either the same or different from each other's. Similarly, the child realizes that the self and other may view similarly perceived actions as reflections of disparate or distinct individual reasons or motives. Of particular importance, the child at Level 1 is newly concerned with the uniqueness of the covert, psychological life of each person. (Roughly ages 4 to 9.)

Stage 1: One-way assistance. Friendship conceptions are one-way in the sense that a friend is seen as important because he or she performs specific activities that the self wants accomplished. In other words, one person's attitude is unreflectively set up as a standard, and the "friend's" actions must match the standard thus formulated. A close friend is someone with more than Stage 0 demographic credentials; a close friend is someone who is known better than other persons. "Knowing" means accurate knowledge of other's likes and dislikes.

Level 2: Self-reflective or reciprocal perspectives. Children are able to reflect on their own thoughts and feelings from another's perspective – to put themselves in the other's shoes and to see the self as a subject to other. This new understanding of the relation between self and other's perspective allows children to consider their own conceptions and evaluations of others' thoughts and actions. In other words, children are able to take a second-person perspective, which leads to an awareness of a new form of reciprocity, a

Stage 2: Fair-weather cooperation. The advance of Stage 2 friendships over the previous stages is based on the new awareness of interpersonal perspectives as reciprocal. The two-way nature of friendships is exemplified by concerns for coordinating and approximating, through adjustment by both self and other, the specific likes and dislikes of self and other, rather than matching one person's actions to the other's fixed standard of expectation. The limitation of this Stage is the discontinuity of these reciprocal expectations. Friend-

Table 9-1 *(cont.)*

reciprocity of thought and feelings rather than a reciprocity of action. (Roughly ages 6 to 12.)

ship at Stage 2 is fair-weather – specific arguments are seen as severing the relationship although both parties may still have affection for one another inside. The coordination of attitudes at the moment defines the relation. No underlying continuity is seen to exist that can maintain the relation during the period of conflict or adjustment.

Level 3: Third-person or mutual perspectives. The subject at Level 3, aware of the infinite regress potential of the chaining of reciprocal perspectives, moves to a qualitatively new level of coordination, an understanding of the person's ability to step outside of an interpersonal interaction and coordinate simultaneously the perspectives of each party in the interaction. This ability to take the third-person perspective leads to the awareness of the mutuality of human perspectives and hence of the self–other relationship. (Roughly ages 9 to 15.)

Stage 3: Intimate and mutually shared relationships. At Stage 3 there is the awareness of both a continuity of relation and affective bonding between close friends. The importance of friendship does not rest only upon the fact that the self is bored or lonely; at Stage 3, friendships are seen as a basic means of developing mutual intimacy and mutual support; friends share personal problems. The occurrence of conflicts between friends does not mean the suspension of the relationship, because the underlying continuity between partners is seen as a means of transcending foul-weather incidents. The limitations of Stage 3 conceptions derive from the overemphasis of the two-person clique and the possessiveness that arises out of the realization that close relations are difficult to form and to maintain.

Level 4: Societal or in-depth perspectives. The subject conceptualizes subjective perspectives of persons toward one another (mutuality) to exist not only on the plane of common expectations or awareness, but also simultaneously at multidimensional or deeper levels of communication. For example, perspectives between two persons can be shared on the level of superficial information, on the level of common interests, or on the level of deeper and unverbalized feelings. Also, perspectives among persons are seen as forming a network or system. These perspectives become generalized – e.g., into the concept of society's perspective or the legal or moral point of view. (Roughly age 12 to adulthood.)

Stage 4: Autonomous interdependent friendships. The interdependence that characterizes Stage 4 is the sense that a friendship can continue to grow and be transformed through each partner's ability to synthesize feelings of independence and dependence. Independence means that each person accepts the other's need to establish relations with others and to grow through such experiences. Dependence reflects the awareness that friends must rely on each other for psychological support, to draw strength from each other, and to gain a sense of self-identification through identification with the other as a significant person whose relation to the self is distinct from those with whom one has less meaningful relations.

research process. Focusing on the friendship domain in particular, the primary aim of this paper is to describe the work during the initial constructive-descriptive phase of our research. These steps are specified in Table 9-2.

Phase 1: Constructing and describing the model

Step a: Pilot exploration. The goal of this step is to develop meaningful interviews to be used in Step b of this phase. To be meaningful, interviews must yield enough useful information for interviewers to get a reasonably good picture of conceptions in a given domain. Following a recommendation made by Flavell (1974), we predefined a set of issues that seemed to represent from an analytic perspective the differentiating or unique features that needed to be considered for each domain (Selman & Jaquette, 1978). For the friendship domain, the six issues described in Table 9-3 seemed particularly important. We used these issues as a conceptual starting point in open-ended pilot-exploratory interviews with forty-five children. Whereas the issues chosen were couched in adult or socially scientific terms (e.g., ''termination''), the assumption was that children of all ages have experiences that touch on these issues and that they therefore construct their own increasingly differentiated conceptions of each. For example, younger children understand jealousy only in the context of material possessions (''He has a nice toy''), whereas for older subjects both psychological (''He likes someone else more'') and material factors are understood to engender a jealous reaction. We also realized that younger children's thinking about these issues may not be naturally differentiated; nevertheless, the loosely structured interview process allowed us to see where there was fusion and where differentiation among issues had taken place.

At this point in the research process, these target categories or issues were kept loosely defined and flexible guidelines to devise a first approximation of the kind of interview questions that might most productively be asked of subjects. Our conceptual starting point was reshaped by application to the real-world substance of children's, adolescents', and adults' thoughts and ideas. Although we used many sources and media to probe and reshape this initial approximation (projective techniques, eavesdropping on conversations in school cafeterias and during recess, drawings, symbolization), the most frequently used and easily replicable method was the open-ended interview, in which we asked the individual to discuss and resolve a series of hypothetical interpersonal dilemmas. Each

Table 9-2. *Flow chart of research process for developing the model.*

Phase 1: Constructive-descriptive phase

  Step a: Pilot-exploratory. Through interviews, identify domains (e.g., friendship), issues (e.g., trust, conflict resolution), and questions for data collection.

  Step b: Formal data collection. Collect data on a broad-spectrum sample – subjects at different ages, sexes, social classes – using similar methods.

  Step c: Descriptive analysis. Analyze responses and describe levels. Construct a manual that provides examples of understanding of each friendship issue at each developmental stage.

Phase 2: Construct validation phase

  Evaluation 1: Structured wholeness. Do individuals generally understand all friendship issues consistently at a particular stage? (Factor analysis, correlations.)

  Evaluation 2: Invariant sequence. Do all individuals' understandings of friendship develop through each stage in the sequence? (Longitudinal study.)

  Evaluation 3: Universality. Does the descriptive stage sequence validly capture the understanding of individuals from different cultures or from atypical populations? (Cross-cultural, comparative study.)

Phase 3: Functional Application Phase

  Apply model to coding real-life reasoning and understanding.

  Relate understanding of a domain (e.g., friendship) with actual friendship relations, patterns, and interactions.

  Obtain repeated observations in natural settings to code and describe growth patterns in understanding and use of friendship conceptions.

Table 9-3. *Issues in the friendship domain.*

---

1. *Friendship formation.* Why (motives) friendships are important and how (mechanisms) friendships are made. Characteristics of an ideal person with whom to make friends.
2. *Closeness and intimacy.* The various types of friendships, what is an ideal friendship, and what factors make for intimacy. Difference between close and "everyday" friend.
3. *Trust.* What friends do for each other: reciprocity, commitment, obligations.
4. *Jealousy.* Feelings about intrusions into a new or established relationship; factors that engender jealousy between friends.
5. *Conflicts and their resolutions.* How friends resolve problems; the meaning of conflict in a friendship; positive as well as negative effects.
6. *Termination.* How and why friendships break up.

---

dilemma was focused on one of the four domains. For each of the domains under study, we produced two familiar dilemmas depicted by preadolescent or adolescent actors on six- to eight-minute sound filmstrips, each most appropriate in content and theme for children aged either 7 to 11 or 11 and over.

To study developmental changes in friendship concepts, we presented, in either filmstrip or verbal form, a dilemma in which a child of about the subject's age has been asked by a newcomer in town to go to a special event at a time that conflicts with a previous engagement with a longtime chum. In the preadolescent form of this dilemma, the heroine, Kathy, has been asked by the new girl to go to an ice-skating show the next afternoon. This conflicts with a previous date to plan a puppet show with her best friend, Debby. To complicate matters, the filmstrip makes it explicit that Debby, the old friend, does not like the new girl. In the adolescent version, the structure of the situation is similar (the need to choose between the old and new friend), but the content is different: the old friend has a personal problem about which she needs the heroine's advice. This change in the content of the dilemma is an important accommodation to naturally occurring changes in social concerns and interest from early childhood to adolescence that stimulates discussion.

In Phase 1, we were not highly concerned with methodological issues, such as whether the sex of the story protagonist matched that of the subject or whether the subject actually liked movies or puppet plays, because in this phase of the research our purpose, more like that of the developmental philosopher than the developmental psychologist, was to elicit a compendium of as many natural concepts from children and adults of different ages as possible. Testing a particular child, assigning that child to a particular developmental level, or obtaining sex or age norms in friendship concepts elicited under reflective interview conditions is premature if the initial descriptive groundwork, the social-cognitive mappings of conceptions, is not well established. On the other hand, to obtain a thorough library of responses, it was important to empirically sample the reasoning of individuals who varied widely in experience and upbringing. At the end of Step a, we had tried out a useful spectrum of issues and questions about the issues that concerned us on male and female subjects of various ages and backgrounds. We had learned which issues we should plan to pursue and which lines of questioning we should expect to be profitable.

Step b: Formal data collection. Following the general plan of the Piagetian *méthode clinique* (1926), we interviewed a broad range of subjects using a series of semistructured questions that permitted follow-up and probing of subjects' ideas. Our sample consisted of ninety-three subjects, both male and female, aged 3 to 34, black and white, and of the lower and middle class.

Each subject was interviewed on one friendship dilemma. As in Step a, the dilemma-interview procedure was not viewed as an assessment of a particular individual's social thinking capacity, but as an eliciting interview, a means of gaining more and more complete descriptive information about what developmental form concepts take. The dilemma and interview function as stimuli to thinking on the part of both interviewer and interviewee, so that together they can explore as thoroughly as possible each social relationship under examination.

Following the pilot findings of Step a, each of the preidentified issues was used as the basis for a series of intensive semistructured questions about the dilemma and about friendship. Each interview lasted up to forty minutes and generated up to twenty-five pages of transcript from some older subjects. For each issue we constructed an initial probe question related directly to some aspect of the dilemma. The response to this standard question normally required follow-up probes for clarification. Discussion of the hypothetical story was followed by an inquiry into the respondent's general understanding of the nature of the issue under examination. This, in turn, was followed by an exploration of the subject's application of the issue to his or her own personal experience.

For example, to explore thinking about the issue of conflict resolution, we referred the subject back to the hypothetical dilemma: "Suppose Kathy goes to the ice show with the new girl. If Debby (the old friend) and Kathy have a big argument over this problem, how would they work things out so they stay close friends?" Follow-up probes were used to test the subject's limits of friendship conceptions. The interviewer asked the subject to consider an alternative underpinned by higher-level reasoning; for example, "Could their friendship become better or stronger if they have an argument over Kathy's going to the ice show with the new girl?" The nature of conflicts between friends was then explored with a set of questions such as: (1) "What kinds of things do good friends sometimes fight about?"; (2) "What's a good way to settle arguments between friends?"; and (3) "Can good friends have arguments and still be friends?" Finally, to tap the reasoning children use when they consider their own personal experience with disagreements and fights between friends, we asked the children whether they would be willing to share with us any personal experience of this type that they felt was important to their understanding of this issue. After completing interviews on all issues with all ninety-three subjects, we moved to Step c.

Step c: Descriptive analysis. The last step in this initial phase was to develop a detailed description of levels of conception for each issue, which
resulted in the construction of an issue-by-stage manual for each domain.
The pilot subjects' transcribed interviews were used as the raw material
for this process. First, each interview was analyzed as a whole (across the
six issues) to evaluate the highest level of perspective-taking the subject
manifested. This procedure was undertaken in accordance with a previously developed procedure for assessing perspective-taking in both so-
cial- and moral-dilemma interviews (Selman, 1976). We then examined
the way in which a subject who demonstrated the capability for a given
level of perspective-taking actually conceptualized each issue in each domain. When a particular concept, explanation, rationale, solution, or
analysis seemed to be reported with some regularity (for example, if it
was mentioned in more than five protocols) we analyzed what level of
social perspective-taking seemed to be logically necessary for a subject to
generate such a social conception.

A concrete example of this process may be helpful. On the basis of an
overall reading of an entire interview about friendship relations, a subject
showed the capacity for using Level 3 social perspective-taking (whereby
the self is able to step outside a dyadic interaction and view self and other
from a third-person perspective). In rereading the subject's interview and
looking specifically for concepts dealing with the issue of conflict resolution, we found that the subject said, "I think fights are an important part of
close friendship. Nobody is perfect, and you're bound to get a close friend
angry at you once in a while. If you don't work it out things build up and
pretty soon the whole relationship is blown. In fact sometimes if you have
a real fight and find out you're still friends, then you've got something that
is stronger."

The above conception seems, theoretically, to rest strongly on the idea
that friendship is a *relationship*, a system made up of two people in interaction over time. This statement appears to manifest semantically a conception of conflict resolution logically based upon Level 3 perspective
coordination (see Table 9-1).

It is possible for a subject to manifest Level 3 perspective-taking at
some point in the course of an interview but not use conceptions of conflict resolution that appear to represent Level 3 structure. According to
the model that guides our work, each perspective-taking level is a deep
structure that is by definition logically necessary but not sufficient for the
actual observed manifestation of a structurally parallel social conception
about any specific issue (Selman, 1976).[4] In other words, children who
demonstrate understanding of friendship as a relation based on mutual

trust have by definition also demonstrated Level 3 perspective-taking. A central observation in our descriptive work was that the empirical analysis of the protocols indicated that multiple concepts about a given issue were often manifested at a given level. For example, other subjects' responses to questions about conflict resolution were coded at Level 3 if they suggested that a conflict between friends might be caused by a personality conflict between them or a personality conflict within one of the friends. These concepts not only seem to be based on Level 3 understanding, they also point out how conceptions about issues in one domain interrelate with conceptions about issues in another. In this case, conceptions about the issue "personality" in the domain of intrapsychic relations relate to conceptions about the issue "conflict resolution" in the domain of friendship. A subject who says, "A friendship must be based upon dependability" is clearly saying something about a conception of individuals as well as of friendship relations. Thus the procedure of using the deeper model of perspective-taking levels as analytic tools or organizing principles and moving within the same data to the relatively more surface concepts of individuals and friendship, peer-group, and parent–child relations, as well as moving back and forth among these social conceptual domains, provided a means of assigning levels to the various empirical conceptual responses obtained.

A library of responses at each level for each issue was then developed; these responses varied in length from a sentence or two to over twenty lines of transcribed discussion. This library of level-by-issue categorized responses became the raw material for the construction of an interview and scoring manual for each domain. Throughout the process, each issue within a domain at each level was characterized by a set of one or more social conceptions reflected in responses, which we called "aspects" or "themes." This procedure, repeated for each of the issues at each level, yielded a level-by-issue-by-theme description of conceptions about issues in the friendship domain (as well as the individual, peer-group and parent–child domains), with a varying number of themes at each level for each issue (Selman, Jaquette, & Bruss-Saunders, 1979). Table 9-4 summarizes the procedure.

The construction of such a detailed descriptive map was greatly facilitated by eliciting responses to the same questions from subjects at different ages and by using a technique that probed responses that sounded similar on the surface but whose underlying meanings were developmentally quite different. ("A good friend is someone who is close to you" means "a person who lives down the street" at age five and "a person you share a lot of the same values with" at age fifteen.) To make this

Table 9-4. *Flow chart of the descriptive analysis process in the friendship domain.*

Step	Process
1	Protocols of friendship interviews transcribed.
2	Each protocol given overall perspective-taking score.
3	Each protocol broken down into responses about various issues (e.g., conflict resolution, intimacy and closeness).
4	Spectrum (across subjects) of responses about each issue analyzed for level: all responses assigned to library on level-by-issue basis (*level*-by-issue manual).
5	For each issue, aspects or themes emerge from responses that characterize each level.
6	Stages of friendship conceptions described (*stage*-by-issue manual of friendship conceptions assembled). At each stage, various aspects of each issue characterize the given stage of conception of friendship.

process more explicit and concrete, I shall set out in some detail the developmental themes – the subjects' conceptions of how persons maintain friendships in difficult situations, the methods or procedures they use to rectify disagreements with friends, and the kinds of conflicts they believe are natural and expected in friendship – that emerged at each level for the issue we have been studying thus far: conflict resolution. This will also provide a sense of how overall stage descriptions are generated across issues at each level.[5] It should be noted that both "level" and "stage" refer to forms or structures of social reasoning (developmental, logically coherent, etc.) that correspond to given levels of perspective-taking. In this description, a certain type of thinking about a specific issue is designated as being at a certain level. That type of thinking, when consistent in an individual across all issues in a given domain, is designated as being at a certain stage. We use "stage" to refer to more complete conceptions across issues in domains, and "level" to refer to both underlying perspective-taking structure and less complete conceptions or responses about single issues.

Phase 1: Developmental themes in conflict resolution

At Level 0, children's suggestions of solutions for conflict between friends appear to be both momentary and physicalistic. Two frequently recommended aspects or themes have been identified: noninteraction and direct physical intervention. In the former case, the child's understanding of conflict resolution appears to be action oriented and lacking consideration of the psychological causes of the conflict or effects of the resolution (feelings, motives, attitudes) for either party. Two mechanisms are often articulated for dealing with conflict within this theme. The first is that one of the involved parties moves to another activity ("Go play with another toy"). The second is a physical separation for a time ("Go away from him and come back later when you're not fighting"). However, children coded at Level 0 seem to see their own suggested resolution-through-separation not as a time to cool off and reflect on the problem (as at Level 2) but as an out-of-sight–out-of-mind solution. In-depth probing suggests that these children believe that if two people do not physically interact (i.e., are separated) they cannot be in any conflict. Conflict does not appear to be seen as a disagreement of psychological perspectives.

The second conflict-resolving strategy often mentioned as an alternative to physical withdrawal is physical force, or, as one 5-year-old girl said when asked what to do when two friends argue over a toy, "Punch her out and take it." This is coded as Level 0 because no further amplification was elicited to indicate any concern for or understanding of the psychological effects on or attitudes of either party.

Level-1 reasoning is reflected in responses that indicate an understanding that the subjective or psychological effects of conflict are important, but with respect to only one of the individuals involved. Rather than view conflicts as existing between two individuals with subjective perspectives, children whose conceptions are at this level appear to view conflict as essentially a problem that is felt by one party and caused by the actions of the other. It is for this reason that we term these children's understanding of conflicts to be one way or unilateral; their resolutions are also one way. Essentially the child seems to say that it is important to reduce the psychological effects of the conflict on the identified recipient by reversing the effects of the conflict-producing activity. Two new themes emerge at this level. The first is negation of the perceived problem action, thereby appeasing the offended friend's subjective feelings ("Stop the fight and give him back what you took"; "Take back what you called him"). The second and related suggestion is the performance of positive action that will return a person who is experiencing psychological discomfort to a state of comfort or psychological calm ("Give him something nice that will make him feel better").

Advances in understanding coded as Level 2 reflect the subject's cognizance that both parties may participate psychologically in the conflict. One aspect of understanding at this level is that any satisfactory resolution of a conflict between two parties must be to the satisfaction of both. A second advance shown at this level is that of making a distinction between saying you're sorry and meaning it. In certain responses (coded at Level 1), simply saying appears to be understood to be sufficient; reasoning indicating this is inadequate underlies the second aspect of Level 2, that one must mean what one says. This insistence appears to require a Level-2 perspective-taking; the self needs to be aware that another self can judge one's beliefs and intentions as well as one's actions.

At Level 3, we find an understanding of several new aspects: (1) recognition that friendship conflicts may be due to conflicts of personality; (2) recognition that conflicts of a certain type may actually strengthen a relationship over time rather than weaken it; (3) recognition of the difference between superficial and deeper conflicts and methods for resolving them; and (4) a suggestion that talking things out is a good way to resolve differences, because it allows each party to express personal feelings. Perhaps the core reorientation at this level is the understanding that certain friendship conflicts reside within the relationship itself. To individuals coded as using Level 3, this conception appears to mean that some conflict resolutions cannot be arrived at solely through detente; each side must feel that both he and the other are truly satisfied with the resolution and would be satisfied if in the other's place. ("If you just settle up after a fight that is no good. You gotta really feel that you'd be happy the way things went if you were in your friend's shoes. You can just settle up with someone who is not a friend, but that's not what friendship is really about.") Talking things out appears to be the recommended mode of conflict resolution at this level.

Reasoning of subjects at Level 4 demonstrates how, with development, conceptions across domains (e.g., of friendships and of individuals), become more elaborately integrated in the subject's mind. For example, evident in the reasoning of subjects coded at this level is the understanding that intrapsychic conflicts – conflicts within an individual – can be a factor in conflicts between that individual and a friend. ("Sometimes when a person's got problems of his own, he finds himself starting fights with all his friends. The best thing you can do is try to be understanding.") The predominant suggestion for resolving conflicts between persons who are seen as having ever-deepening relations and commitments to one another (Level-4 friendships) is to keep the lines of communication open. By this, the subjects seem to mean keeping in touch with one's own deeper feelings as well as with the more personal and sensitive concerns of the friend and establishing a mode or operating procedure for communicating these feelings back and forth over time. In addition, coded as Level 4 is the understanding that actions as well as words can symbolize the resolution of a conflict within a relationship. For example, the interviewer might ask, "What is the best way for arguments to be settled between good friends?" and the Level 4 subject would respond, "Well, talk it out, but usually it fades itself out. It usually takes care of itself. You just act like it's all okay. You do something to let the other guy know everything is cool. But if not, then talk it out." Level 4, in this sense, captures what is meant by contemporary idioms such as "good vibes": unspoken communication that symbolizes agreement and resolution understood by both parties.[6]

From this brief journey through the development of conceptions of conflict resolution in friendship we can see both the importance of and the challenge to the structural-developmental approach of defining the meaning of social expressions. Subjects at all levels can suggest that the separation of conflicting parties is a useful strategy for conflict resolution. The difference is in how this is construed. If physical separation alone with no reference to its effect on either party is the resolution, the subject's suggestion is coded Level 0. If separation is seen as an opportunity for each party to work out his own feelings, it is coded as Level 2. If separation is explicitly described as a symbolic act that both parties understand to transcend the necessity for verbal communication, it is coded as Level 4. The technique that has been most effective to date in helping us to differentiate among superficially similar responses is to probe and follow-up subjects' initial responses for maximum explanation, clarification, and amplification.

The qualitative description of developmental aspects of the understanding of strategies for conflict resolution within the context of a friendship relation also suggests certain properties characteristic of the overall stage-by-issue analysis of friendship conceptions. First, some of the forms of understanding appear additive. For example, the idea that one should mean it when one says "I'm sorry" to a friend, an understanding emergent at Level 2, is certainly not rejected at higher levels but becomes integrated into higher-level concepts. Second, not all actual conflicts between friends require the use of the highest level of understanding for adequate resolution; thus, even an individual who has the capacity for higher-level understanding does not necessarily need to use it in discussing all situations. However, when one looks at each level across all of the issues in each domain, certain characteristics begin to emerge. These "stages," so called because they are composed of understandings of separate elements (issues) but defined by a logically common developmental structure (a perspective-taking level) are briefly summarized in Table 9-1B.

One useful way of distinguishing the stages of friendship conceptions is to ask both what individuals understand that they did not understand previously and what beliefs they now view as silly or childish that previously appeared to be important or central to their friendship philosophy. In attempting to assess a child's stage of friendship philosophizing according to their hierarchical model, the following guidelines are useful.

First, does the individual appear to understand that for friendly interactions to form or be maintained one must do more than demand that the potential play partner play with the self, or that one partner must do what the other says? If so, then the individual appears to have attained at least a Stage-1 understanding. If not, the subject is more likely functioning at Stage 0. At this lowest stage, the child appears to fail to understand the need to consider the will or interest of either child; friendly interactions are unreflectively designated as "getting what one wants"; "wants" are defined in material terms only, not in psychological terms.

But given that an individual has an understanding of the need to consider thoughts and feelings and not only actions, one can ask, "Does the individual understand the need to coordinate or at least consider the feelings or attitudes of both partners in making social plans and decisions? Are conflicts between persons understood to be resolved by means of each party gaining some satisfaction rather than only through meeting the needs of one of the parties?" If so, the individual appears to have attained at least a Stage-2 understanding. If not, the individual is most likely still functioning at Stage 1. At Stage 1, the individual appears to consider only the subjective concerns and needs of one of the parties, not both. The child at Stage 1 does not appear able to express or construct an understanding of how the multiple, reciprocal psychological perspectives, wants, and needs of the self and the other influence the formation and maintenance of friendly interactions.

But given that an individual does understand psychological reciprocity as a critical aspect of social relationships, one can ask, "Does the individual appear to conceptualize friendships as mutual dyadic systems – as relationships formed for interpersonally cooperative functions and goals rather than simply as reciprocally useful sets of interactions between individuals designed to meet the needs of each relatively independently of the other? Does the individual appear cognizant of the necessity for continuity and commitment in a friendship relation that underlies the context-specific or situational fluctuations of daily interpersonal life?" If so, then the individual appears to have attained at least a Stage-3 understanding. If not, then the individual is most likely still functioning at Stage 2. At Stage 2, friendships are still understood only as reciprocities of multiple subjective satisfactions. They are understood to be both dissolved and reconsti-

tuted with relative ease, and the major function of friendship is still understood to be the personal satisfaction of each separate self rather than
mutual sharing or gaining satisfaction from the satisfaction of one's partner.

Given the individual's understanding of mutual and not simply reciprocal coordinations as the basis for long-term friendship relations, one can
ask, "Does the individual understand that friendship relations are dynamic, changing, and open-ended rather than static, constant, and
closed? Does the individual understand how complex changes within individuals – for example, changes in personal interests and attitudes or
changes in personality – may relate to changes in the pattern of relationships between individuals? Is there evidence of an understanding of the
complex ways in which individuals can define themselves through their
friendships?" If so, then the individual appears well on his way to having
attained a Stage-4 understanding.

This hierarchical model suggests that once a child makes a reflective
discovery – for example, the importance of mutuality – he or she cannot
undiscover or forget this new principle. However, even making such a
discovery does not guarantee that the individual will always act accordingly or apply it in everyday life. Conversely, children who do not reflec-
tively understand mutuality, for example, may still happen to act in mutually coordinated ways with peers, even if they do not interpret their
actions as such.

I have attempted to describe explicitly how in this phase we impose a
structure on the interview data. Readers may ask whether the stages enu-
merated here represent a formal analysis only from the model builder's
perspective or whether they really exist in the reflective understanding of
our subjects. Not until we empirically tested the validity of this formal
model on new samples of subjects could we say that these stages were
generally evident in reflective understanding.

Phase 2: validating the model

The result of the first or constructive phase of research, then, is a formal
detailed level- or stage-by-issue descriptive model of reflective understanding in a given interpersonal domain derived from empirical research
and structural analysis. The goal of the second phase is to evaluate
whether children's naturally developing interpersonal understanding actually fits this model. To do this, more formally gathered data are evaluated to determine whether or how well children's interpersonal reasoning
meets the structural-developmental criteria of structured wholeness, in-

variant sequence, and universality. (For a brief expansion on these criteria, see Table 9-2.)

I have prepared a summary of findings to date (Selman, 1980). In general, the evidence supported the coherence and validity of the system when the analyses had been of data collected under reflective interview conditions (Selman, 1976; Selman & Jaquette, 1978). Considering the issue of structured wholeness, factor analyses and age-controlled correlations across domains indicate that subjects generally do manifest an understanding of interpersonal concepts at very close to the same level or stage across all issues and domains. With respect to universality, longitudinal comparisons of normal and emotionally disturbed samples (children with emotional difficulties severe enough to warrant special placement in two private day schools but with no clear-cut psychoses or organic difficulties) show that subjects' understanding develops in the same patterns and sequences, albeit with a two-to-three-year lag for the disturbed group. Pertaining to invariant sequence, in neither group did two- and five-year longitudinal follow-ups show stage regression.

These findings and others, although preliminary, lend support to the claim that perspective-taking analyses of reflective interview data yield a coherent picture of the child's developing interpersonal understanding. In any case, at this point validation results were sufficiently supportive that my research shifted its primary research question from whether stages exist (i.e., searching for further proofs) to whether stage analyses are useful ways of ordering data and findings. With this in mind, let us return to the developmental aspects of the other social-cognitive studies of friendship conceptions discussed earlier to see what use can be made of this framework for understanding their results.

This is the time to reemphasize certain methodological differences between our approach and those of the researchers whose work I reviewed earlier. Although there appears to be some similarity and overlap between our issues and other researchers' categories, they are derived and used quite differently. In the friendship domain, for example, we generated some potentially important issues and used preliminary interview findings to discover which of our predefined issues were important in children's spontaneously expressed notions about friendship at various ages, and which issues might be important across ages (might show developmental change). We then used these issues as sub-topics of the friendship domain and looked at a large sample for developmental change from level to level within each issue. In contrast, other investigators have obtained categories directly from subjects' spontaneous responses. Then, in a more-or-less purely quantitative way, they have scored responses at various ages for absence or presence of categories and thereby described friendship concepts or stages on the basis of frequency of use.

Nonetheless, as was noted in Hartup's 1978 review, there is a marked similarity, at least on the surface, between the stage descriptions that emerge from our logical–deductive analysis and conceptual clusters such as those Bigelow finds using a statistical method. Furthermore, our analysis can suggest meaning for unexplained findings. Perhaps Berndt does not find high correlations among categories because his coding is based on brief responses that sound alike (or different) on the surface but may have different (or similar) underlying meanings (Berndt, personal communication).

Similarly, consider the findings obtained by Gamer, who asked children to choose the most important of eight statements about what makes a best friend. Recall that Gamer found that only older children chose the statement "someone who can understand your feelings" with any regularity, and that when the younger and older groups were compared, the younger were more likely than the older to pick "someone who helps you" or "someone who defends you." One can speculate that the younger children did not understand the value of having a friend who "understands your feelings," because this concept is logically based on the Level-2 perspective-taking ability to look at the psychological aspects of the self from a second-person perspective. That the "help" and "defense" choices were more often chosen by the younger children than by older subjects coincides with the natural preoccupation at Levels 0 and 1 with physicalistic and body integrity concerns and the young child's lack of concern for or understanding of the importance of psychological integrity, at least in a reflective context.

Similarly, one can examine Bigelow's and Berndt's findings that not until sixth or seventh grade do children generally profess concepts of loyalty as basic to friendship expectations and speculate that the word-concept *loyalty* (although it may have a range of developmental meanings) when used in its natural sense generally implies a commitment based on an understanding of the mutual relation between self and other (rests upon a sense of mutuality), the base of which is a Level-3 coordination of perspectives.

All of the studies appear to find that certain concepts emerge at certain ages but that not all earlier concepts are necessarily rejected; this suggests a hierarchical developmental model. Such a hierarchical model stresses, for example, that beliefs such as the young child's notion that friends have to be physically together to be friends are grounded in reality. This reality

will be replaced, eventually, by a higher-level reality that reconceptual-
izes the function of physical contact in social relations.

Having developed fairly complete, reasonably well-validated descriptions of development in several domains of interpersonal reasoning,
our next step was out of the reflective interview and into the real
world.

Phase 3: applying the model

A major criticism of structural-developmental, social-cognitive research
and theory concerns its almost exclusive focus on reflective social reasoning and relative neglect of social behavior. Although we firmly believe
that assessing children's reflective social reasoning is a valid and important area of investigation, we also recognize the importance of subsequently studying understanding as expressed under real-life conditions
and studying the relation of both reflective and natural social reasoning to
other ways of observing social behavior. Our project's focus is to turn
from basic descriptive research about reflective interpersonal conceptions to an application of these developmental descriptions to the study of
actual interpersonal problem solving or functioning.

In line with this, our project members have been exploring whether our
formal model, derived from the analyses of reflective reasoning (conceptions-in-theory) can be used to analyze the interpersonal reasoning-in-
action (conceptions-in-use) that subjects use in naturally occurring social
situations. More specifically, we have begun to use the map of social-con-
ceptual stages (issues-by-levels) as a developmental coding scheme for
the analysis of spontaneous interpersonal problem solving during naturally occurring peer-group discussions (Jaquette, 1978; Lavin, 1979;
Selman & Jaquette, 1978; Selman, Lavin, & Brion-Meisels, 1978) and of dia-
logues that occur between therapists and children in psychotherapy
(Jurkovic & Selman, 1980). This move recapitulates Piaget's shift in orientation during the 1940s from a phase of research that focused on children's developing theories about (reflections on) physical reality to a later
phase focused on stage analyses (operations) seen to represent cognitive
activity or practical thought directly rather than reflection on activity.
Our own work in these areas, although still only beginning, has already
produced useful and intriguing results in several areas of application and
investigation. I will conclude this paper with two anecdotal case-study
examples of friendship that may demonstrate the importance of moving in
the direction of application.

The case of Tommy. The next step after using developmental levels to examine reflective reasoning or reasoning about a hypothetical situation is to apply these levels directly either to naturally occurring reasoning and problem solving or, even more directly, to the observed social-interaction strategies children use in making friends and solving conflicts among themselves. Both have proved to have considerable clinical utility in our work with children with a history of poor social relationships. As a first example, I will draw from our experience with Tommy (a pseudonym), a boy referred to a day school for troubled children in which we have ongoing research and clinical commitments.

When first admitted to the school at age 14, Tommy, who had a history of severe social deprivation and abuse, frequently hid under his desk out of fear of teachers and peers. Gradually, however, he began to form a close tie to his teacher; this tie was based, however, almost entirely on a one-sided "you-give-I-take" interaction, characteristic of Stage-1 understanding of the nature of friendships. By the end of his second year, Tommy formed his first real peer relationship.

Rather than being based on what is usually the source of an adolescent friendship – sharing feelings and establishing a common bond of trust (Stage 3) – Tommy's relationship was based on playing and sharing toy trucks with a younger child in his class. This relationship also exemplified a Stage-1, one-way notion of friendship, both a "do-what-I-want" orientation and a reciprocity limited to a give-and-take of activities and possessions. In his occasional attempts to make new friends, Tommy would approach the target child with a toy to share or would go up to other children and try arbitrarily to join in their play. If the other did not respond in kind, Tommy would become upset and leave, not realizing the effect of his own inadequate social strategies. The occasional child who attempted to form and maintain a friendship with Tommy in a more age-appropriate way – by more mutual sharing of ideas, feelings, or activities, for example – was not responded to, was rebuffed, and would give up the effort.

Tommy's story illustrates how it is possible to code some aspects of social interaction strategies in structural-developmental terms and demonstrates some functions of the similarities and differences that emerge within and across individuals when this comparative analysis is done. Tommy's behavior, for example, is consistently illustrative of one-way Stage-1 notions of friendship concepts, formation, and maintenance. When children who demonstrated a higher-level understanding of making friends approached him, Tommy was not able to respond in kind, and his low-level social approaches were rejected by same-age peers. Hence no relationships were formed. The exception was his friendship with a younger, less social-developmentally mature child who interacted in a way characteristic of Stage-1 reasoning. Our stage-by-issue map appears to be able to help us not only understand developmental patterns in reflective reasoning but place Tommy's behavior along a developmental continuum. It leads us to look at Tommy's social-interaction strategies and to see him not simply as overly angry, hostile, or unfriendly, but as a child whose way of making friends is developmentally lagging behind that of his peers.

Marvin and Joey. As a final example of applying the developmental map to real-life situations, let us turn to the cafeteria anecdote about Marvin and Joey in the prologue. Is Marvin, contrary to his own disclaimer, Joey's friend? Like many things in life, it depends on one's perspective. If one takes an adult definition of friendship, one might judge that no real friendship exists and that Joey has at best an incorrect conception of what friendship is or how friends are expected to behave toward one another. But we might also look at their relationship, with its daily companionship and shared activities, and decide that they are friends, although not at a very high developmental level. Joey considers himself to be Marvin's friend, even if Marvin disclaims any reciprocity. And repeated observations indicate that Marvin's concept of friendship would permit him to call Joey a friend again tomorrow. Both children are exhibiting and acting in accordance with a one-way orientation toward friendship. Although there is a certain appropriateness and charm to this orientation at the age of 5 or 6, if development to a more adequate understanding of friendship does not ensue, our reaction will change from amusement to concern. To be able to assess the level of social understanding represented by behavior or speech and to have rough norms for such development gives the researcher, educator, or clinician a clue to how a child is functioning and when concern is in order.

Conclusion

I have presented these two anecdotes to illustrate the application of the descriptive map to behavior. I believe they show useful directions to pursue in research and practice; they also highlight the paradoxical situation within which workers using a structural-developmental approach often find themselves. Some critics, who focus on methods of data collection, claim that people do not reason as adequately under real-life conditions as they do in reflective interviews and suggest that the reflective-interview approach assesses some inflated or maximum level of philosophical competence rather than a more behavioristically anchored psychological performance. Other critics, whose focus is on understanding the relationship between reflective and practical understanding, claim that reflective understanding is a residue of psychosocial structures of practical understanding already implemented in the child's practical understanding-action repertoire months or years earlier. They point out that, for example, children pass through periods of momentary playmateship or one-way assistance long before they can put these experiences into coherent thoughts and words (theories). To these critics, reflective methods of assessment underestimate rather than overestimate understanding, at least for very young subjects.

That both these criticisms may at times have some validity does not negate the power of a structural-developmental stage analysis of social cognition or its application to behavior. Perhaps we may resolve the seeming conflict between theory and method by remaining sensitive to the intricate relations between the theoretical model being considered and both the actual methods of assessment being used in its service and the real-life reasoning and behavior to which the model relates. If the descriptive stages generated by in-depth probing of reflective understanding can be put to use validly in applied contexts, the stage model has served its purpose well.

Therefore, rather than seeing the validity of this developmental model as standing or falling upon, for example, the observed degree of synchrony between levels of reflective and natural reasoning (one possible structural criterion), it might be better to observe empirically what the relation is, and then, using the observed relation as the dependent variable, use independent methods to see how individuals with various levels of functioning across modes actually get along in their social relations. I am suggesting a three-dimensional model of the growth of interpersonal understanding. The developmental (vertical) dimension is organized around levels of perspective coordination. The conceptual (horizontal) dimension is focused across the various intra- and interpersonal-relation domains (e.g., friendship) and the issues specific to each. The third dimension, orthogonal to the other two, is the mode of social-cognitive functioning, ranging from reflective reasoning (as in an interview), to natural reasoning (as in an argument), to behavior (as in social-interaction strategies). Interpersonal functioning may be at different levels in these different functional modes, and people's "observed" levels may transfer across modes easily or with difficulty. But in order to apply a developmental model to a range of interpersonal modes through which understanding is manifest, the underlying structure – the social-cognitive map – must first be adequately described and charted.

It is for this reason that I have stressed throughout this paper that, in its early phase, a social-cognitive approach must try to construct a developmental map using methods that will allow an observer to reliably assess the meaning of interpersonal concepts. If this goal is achieved, I believe a structural-developmental model will be useful for understanding many developmental aspects of social behavior and functioning.

Notes

1 Numbers in parentheses represent the grade in school at which the earliest onset of responses in each category occurred in the two samples.
2 Thanks are given to David Bearison for recommending "coordination of social perspective" as an alternative term to "social perspective-taking" to represent the process under examination.
3 The Harvard–Judge Baker Social Reasoning Project's past and present members, in addition to the author, include: Ellen Cooney, who has worked on differentiating and outlining the theoretical and methodological implications of reflective reasoning and initial orientation to interpersonal reasoning, and more recently has investigated patterns and processes of stage change; Diane Byrne, who has worked on the structural or perspective-taking component of interpersonal reasoning; Dan Jaquette, who has collaborated on broadening the interpersonal-understanding measurement system with respect to the peer group concept and who has devised a coding system for analyzing interpersonal reasoning-in-action; Debra Lavin, who has looked at the natural usage of perspective taking and peer feedback in small groups; Carolyn Newberger, who has begun studying interpersonal awareness in adults with a particular focus on parental awareness of children; Ellie Saunders, who has completed a developmental description of conceptions of the parent–child relationship; Carolyn Stone, who has begun research on developmental models for examining social influence strategies; and Steven Brion-Meisels, who is attempting to link this approach to educational practice.
4 Although the topic is too lengthy to take up in detail here, it must be stated that the relation between structures and concepts being considered here does not imply that levels of conception or social-cognitive structures are not manifested either earlier or later in time (age) under less verbal modes of expressing social understanding (see Selman & Jaquette, 1978). Verbal discussion under interview conditions is but one medium that allows us to look at concepts as they develop. We can then look at the same concepts as they are used under other conditions or in other modes of expression. At this phase, however, it is important that we use the same method (reflective interviews) to look for both perspective-taking level and social conceptions. Otherwise, methodological factors would provide unnecessary interference to the structural analysis.
5 The following descriptions are drawn from the 1979 version of our interpersonal-understanding manual. Copies are available from the author.
6 Although there may be more sophisticated levels of understanding than those expressed in our sample, Level 4 appears to capture adequately the upper bound of our adult sample; these expressed concepts are rarely used in our sample. Most subjects capable of expressing these concepts also found the lower levels adequate for discussing most of the issues in their consideration of friendship.

References

Baldwin, J. M. *Social and ethical interpretations in mental development.* New York: Macmillan, 1906.

Berndt, T. J. *Children's conception of friendship and the behavior expected of friends.* Unpublished manuscript, Yale University, New Haven, Connecticut, 1978.

Personal communication, January, 1979.

Bigelow, B. J. Children's friendship expectations: A cognitive-developmental study. *Child Development,* 1977, *48*, 246–253.

Bigelow, B. J., & LaGaipa, J. J. Children's written descriptions of friendship: A multidimensional analysis. *Developmental Psychology,* 1975, *11*, 857–858.

The development of friendship values and choice. In H. Foot, A. H. Chapman, & J. Smith (Eds.), *Childhood and friendship relations.* New York: Wiley, in press.

Broughton, J. Development of concepts of self, mind, reality and knowledge. In W. Damon (Ed.), *New directions for child development* (Vol. 1). San Francisco: Jossey-Bass, 1978.

Damon, W. *The social world of the child.* San Francisco: Jossey-Bass, 1977.

Flavell, J. H. *The developmental psychology of Jean Piaget.* Princeton: Van Nostrand, 1963.

The development of inferences about others. In T. Mischel, (Ed.), *Understanding other persons.* Totowa, N.J.: Roman and Littlefield, 1974.

Furth, H. Children's societal understanding and the process of equilibration. In W. Damon (Ed.), *New directions for child development* (Vol. 1). San Francisco: Jossey-Bass, 1978.

Gamer, E. *Children's reports of friendship criteria.* Paper presented at the meeting of the Massachusetts Psychological Association, Boston, May, 1977.

Hartup, W. W. Children and their friends. In H. McGurk (Ed.), *Issues in childhood social development.* London: Methuen, 1978.

Hayes, D. Cognitive bases for liking and disliking among preschool children. *Child Development,* 1978, *49*, 906–909.

Hunt, H. A. K. *The humanism of Cicero.* Cambridge, Mass.: Loeb Classical Library, 1914.

Jaquette, D. L. *Stage oscillation in social-cognitive abilities: A longitudinal analysis of interpersonal maturity in a group of disturbed preadolescents.* Unpublished doctoral dissertation, Harvard University, Cambridge, Massachusetts, 1978.

Jurkovic, G., & Selman, R. L. A developmental analysis of intrapsychic understanding: Treating emotional disturbances in children. In R. L. Selman & R. Yando (Eds.), *New directions for child development* (Vol. 7). San Francisco: Jossey-Bass, 1980.

Kohlberg, L. The child as a moral philosopher. *Psychology Today,* 1968, 2 (*4*), 24–30.

Stage and sequence: The cognitive-developmental approach to socialization. In D. Goslin (Ed.), *Handbook of socialization theory and research.* Chicago: Rand McNally, 1969.

Lavin, D. *Patterns of social reasoning in emotionally disturbed children under varying social contexts.* Unpublished doctoral dissertation, Harvard University, Cambridge, Massachusetts, 1979.

Mead, G. H. *Mind, self and society.* Chicago: University of Chicago Press, 1934.

Piaget, J. *The language and thought of the child.* New York: Harcourt Brace, 1926.

Reisman, J., & Shorr, H. Friendship claims and expectations among children and adults. *Child Development,* 1978, *49*, 913–916.

Rubin, Z. *Children's friendships.* Cambridge, Mass.: Harvard University Press, 1980.

Selman, R. L. Toward a structural analysis of developing interpersonal relations concepts: Research with normal and disturbed preadolescents. In A. D. Pick (Ed.), *Minnesota symposia on child psychology* (Vol. 10). Minneapolis: University of Minnesota Press, 1976.

The growth of interpersonal understanding: Developmental and clinical analyses. New York: Academic Press, 1980.

Selman, R. L., & Jaquette, D. Stability and oscillation in interpersonal awareness: A clinical-developmental analysis. In C. B. Keasey (Ed.), *Nebraska symposium on motivation* (Vol. 25). Lincoln: University of Nebraska Press, 1978.

Selman, R. L., Jaquette, D., & Bruss-Saunders, E. *Assessing interpersonal understanding: An interview and scoring manual.* Harvard-Judge Baker Social Reasoning Project, Cambridge, Massachusetts, September, 1979.

Selman, R. L., Lavin, D., & Brion-Meisels, S. *Developing the capacity for self-reflection: A look at troubled children's conceptions-in-theory and conceptions-in-use.* Paper presented to a Society for Research in Child Development study group: Social cognition in context. Ohio State University, Columbus, Ohio, July, 1978.

Serafica, F. C. *The development of friendship: An ethological-organismic perspective.* Unpublished manuscript, Ohio State University, Columbus, Ohio, 1978.

Turiel, E. Distinct conceptual and development domains: Social convention and morality. In C. B. Keasey (Ed.), *Nebraska symposium on motivation* (Vol. 25). Lincoln: University of Nebraska Press, 1978.

Youniss, J., & Volpe, J. A relational analysis of children's friendships. In W. Damon (Ed.), *New directions for child development* (Vol. 1). San Francisco: Jossey-Bass, 1978.

10 Children without friends: social knowledge and social-skill training

Steven R. Asher and Peter D. Renshaw

Introduction

Friendships serve important and diverse functions in children's lives. For example, friends promote social-skill development by providing children with regular access to play groups (Corsaro, this volume), facilitating complex forms of play (Gottman & Parkhurst, 1980), and giving direct instruction on such important concerns as the management of aggression and of sexual relationships (Fine, this volume; Hartup, 1978). Friends also serve emotional functions by providing children with security in various situations (e.g., Freud & Dann, 1951; Ispa, 1977).

Given the functions served by children's friendships, it is of concern that a considerable number of children lack friends in school. Research over the past four decades indicates that about 5 to 10 percent of elementary-school children are named as a friend by no one in their class (Gronlund, 1959; Hymel & Asher, 1977; Kuhlen & Lee, 1943). This is a large number of children, particularly since most elementary-school teachers regard the promotion of social development as one of their primary goals.

Children can be without friends for a variety of reasons. These include both personal characteristics, such as physical appearance, gender, or race, and situational factors, such as opportunities for participation and mobility of the peer group (Asher, Oden, & Gottman, 1977; Hartup, 1970). In addition to these factors, the child's social-skill repertoire may be an important contributor to children's difficulties in peer relationships. Indeed, the hypothesis can be advanced that children without friends are prevented from establishing effective peer relationships by their own lack of social skills. This social-skill deficit hypothesis has guided a considerable amount of research by developmental, clinical, and educational psychologists.

273

Our chapter is designed to examine in detail the social-skill deficit hypothesis. We will first discuss sociometric methodology, because it is the major approach used to identify children without friends. Next, we will consider evidence from both descriptive research and training studies regarding the influence of social skills on sociometric status. We will then outline a framework for conceptualizing the dimensions of social competence and discuss the way in which these dimensions may be influenced by social-skill training. Finally, we will discuss the need for a developmental perspective in this area of research.

Sociometric methods for identifying children without friends

Nomination and rating-scale measures

Sociometric methodology has been the primary means of identifying children without friends. The most commonly used variant of the methodology is the peer-nomination technique, adapted from Moreno (1934). Investigators most often use positive nominations, in which children are asked to name classmates who meet certain criteria (e.g., friend, play partner, work partner). A child's score is the number of nominations received from classmates. Negative nominations are sometimes included as well (e.g., Dunnington, 1957; Moore & Updegraff, 1964): Children are asked to name children they do not especially like or would not want as a friend or playmate.

A different type of sociometric technique is the rating-scale measure (Roistacher, 1974; Singleton & Asher, 1977; Thompson & Powell, 1951) in which children rate each classmate according to a particular criterion, such as how much they like to play or work with each peer. The child's score is the average rating received from the entire class, or, in cases in which there is considerable sex bias in children's ratings, the child's score can be based on the average rating received from same-sex peers (Oden & Asher, 1977). This type of sociometric method, in contrast to the nomination method, provides an indication of each child's perception of every classmate.

Children without friends are not a homogeneous group, and a combination of sociometric measures can be used for the purpose of identifying different types of low-status children. Using the positive- and negative-nomination methods together, children without friends can be divided into those who are neglected and those who are rejected. The neglected children receive few, if any, positive or negative nominations and appear as quiet and nontalkative to their companions (Gronlund & Anderson, 1957). The rejected children also receive few, if any, positive nominations but do receive many negative nominations, and they appear to be aversive to their companions (Gronlund & Anderson, 1957).

The positive-nomination method can also be used in combination with the rating-scale sociometric method. The number of positive nominations a child receives on a limited-choice sociometric instrument (e.g., "Name three children you especially like") can be viewed as an index of the number of friends a child has, and the rating a child receives in response to a question such as "How much would you like to play with (child's name)?" can be regarded as a measure of a child's overall acceptability or likability in the peer group. Several sources of evidence suggest the utility of this distinction between acceptance and friendship. Studies in desegregated schools have typically revealed strong race bias when the friendship nomination measure is used (Criswell, 1939; Shaw, 1973) but only slight bias when the rating-scale measure of acceptance is employed (Singleton & Asher, 1977, 1979). Apparently, children can generally accept cross-race peers even though they do not typically regard them as best friends. Furthermore, Asher and Renshaw (in preparation) have found that children who are low on both acceptance and friendship differ behaviorally, as measured by teacher ratings, from children who are low on friendship but are generally well-accepted by their classmates. In general, the former group demonstrated a lower level of social skillfulness than the latter group, although both groups appeared less skilled than children who were high on both measures. Finally, Oden and Asher (1977) found that coaching children in play skills led to increased acceptance as measured by the rating-scale sociometric technique but did not result in increased friendship nominations.

Reliability and validity

There is substantial psychometric evidence to recommend the reliability of sociometric measures. Test–retest reliability with elementary-school students has been extensively examined and is quite satisfactory for both nomination and rating-scale measures (e.g., Bonney, 1943; Gronlund, 1959; Oden & Asher, 1977; Roff, Sells, & Golden, 1972). For example, Oden and Asher found that reliability over a six-week period was .69 for a nomination measure, .82 for a play rating-scale measure and .84 for a work rating-scale measure.

Until recently, the reliability of sociometric measures with preschool children has been problematic. The picture-nomination sociometric measure especially developed for preschoolers (McCandless & Marshall, 1957) produces only moderate test–retest correlations (Hartup, Glazer, & Charlesworth, 1967; McCandless & Marshall, 1957; Moore & Updegraff, 1964). However, it seems that the rating-scale technique, when adapted for preschool children, does yield reliable scores. Asher, Singleton, Tinsley, and Hymel (1979) tested two classes of 4-year-olds, and over a four-week period the test–retest correlation was .81 and .74 for the rating scale, compared to .56 and .38 for the positive-nomination measure. The greater stability of scores with the rating-scale method probably is caused by the fact that a child's score is the average of ratings from a number of peers. If a single rater changes his or her perception of the child from one time to another, the score the child receives is not greatly affected.

In addition to good reliability, sociometric scores appear to have predictive validity. For example, children without friends are more likely, later in life, to drop out of school (Ullmann, 1957) and to become juvenile delinquents (Roff et al., 1972). It should be emphasized that the relationship of sociometric status to dropout rates and delinquent behavior is correlational and may not mean that poor peer relationships cause later problems. Furthermore, we need to know more about what types of peer-relationship problems predict to later adjustment difficulties. Nonetheless, these data suggest that sociometric measures can be used to select children who are at increased risk for later-life problems.

To summarize, sociometric methodology offers a reliable and valid basis for identifying children who are having difficulties forming friendships with other children. Moreover, the combined use of different sociometric techniques (e.g., positive-nomination and rating-scale sociometrics) provides a differentiated picture of the child's peer status. In the next two sections we will examine whether individual differences in social skillfulness underlie variations in sociometric status.

The social-skill hypothesis: (I) Evidence from descriptive research

Psychologists have persistently searched for the behavioral correlates of sociometric status. Since Koch (1933), regular attempts have been made to identify the behavioral characteristics of children who are either popular or unpopular in their peer group (e.g., Campbell & Yarrow, 1961; Gottman, Gonso, & Rasmussen, 1975; Gronlund & Anderson, 1957; Hartup et al., 1967; Lippitt, 1941). The obtained correlations between behavior and sociometric status in these studies have often been modest, yet the results do provide a consistent picture of the behaviors associated with peer popularity. In general, the accumulated evidence suggests that children who are well liked participate in peer activities, are cooperative and helpful, communicate effectively, and are friendly and supportive toward their peers (Asher et al., 1977; Hartup, 1970; Moore, 1967). Although these results suggest that unpopular children lack certain social skills, an alternative interpretation of the results can be proposed. It may be that low-status children are not deficient in social skills but have become trapped in the role of a marginal group member and are behaving accordingly (Campbell & Yarrow, 1961; Moore, 1967). That is, the behavior of low-status children may not reflect their true competence, because their behavior may be determined by their peer status.

To determine whether unpopular children are capable of effective social behavior, their social skillfulness needs to be assessed in a context that is independent of their current peer group. This could be done by collecting sociometric data in the child's current peer group and then assessing the child's interaction style with a new group of peers. To our knowledge, this type of study has not been done, perhaps because of the complexities of arranging interaction opportunities among previously unacquainted children. Another approach to independent assessment of children's social competence is to present children with hypothetical social situations and elicit their responses. Those children who have learned the appropriate social skills but are prevented by their marginal group membership from behaving in a socially skillful manner should be likely to reveal their true competence in such hypothetical situations. Research using this approach is reviewed in the next section.

Children's response to hypothetical situations

There are different ways of assessing social skills using hypothetical situations. Gottman et al. (1975) had children role-play their responses to certain problematic situations. Third- and fourth-grade children pretended that the experimenter was a new child in class and that the subject wanted to make friends with this new child. The children's role-playing responses were scored according to whether they offered a greeting, asked for information (e.g., "Where do you live?"), attempted to include (e.g., "Wanna come over to my house sometime?"), or gave information (e.g., "My favorite sport is basketball"). Results indicated that children of high sociometric status were much more skillful on the role-playing test than were low-status children.

A somewhat different approach is to present children with a hypothetical situation and have them tell what the protagonist could do in that situation. This strategy was used in a recent study by Ladd and Oden

(1979). Third- and fifth-grade children were asked to give behavioral solutions to hypothetical situations involving a child needing help (e.g., a child being teased by classmates; a child needing help on a school task). Children's ideas about how to help were coded into one of thirteen categories (e.g., console–comfort; solicit the aid of an adult). The major finding was that there was a negative correlation between children's sociometric status and their uniqueness of ideas. Children who were negatively perceived by their peers gave more unique responses (in that no one else suggested that category of response).

The uniqueness measure used by Ladd and Oden is a transituational measure in that it can be applied to separate situations or items and then summed across items. While the uniqueness measure has transituational applicability and requires prior content analysis of children's ideas, the measure by itself conveys no information about the types of strategies children suggest. We have begun to examine the actual content of children's ideas using the hypothetical-situations methodology. In addition, we have begun to exploit the opportunity the method provides for assessing children's responses in a wider range of situations than would be practical using real-life behavior assessment. By examining the content of children's strategies in a variety of situations the social-skill deficits associated with particular contexts can be determined more adequately.

We have used the hypothetical-situations technique in a study with sixty-five kindergarten children of high and low sociometric status (Asher & Renshaw, in preparation). A child was defined as high status if he or she received a large number of positive nominations and a high average play rating; a child was defined as low status if he or she was low on both measures. Children were individually shown nine hypothetical situations that required some communication or action by a protagonist. As each item was presented, the child was encouraged to give one and, if possible, additional ideas on what the protagonist could do. Three types of situations were selected, because of their relevance to making and keeping friends. One type concerned initiating social relationships with other children: for example, the problem of getting to know a new group of children, or the task of making a new friend. A second type concerned social-maintenance situations, such as how to maintain a conversation, how to help a friend in need, or how to play cooperatively with another child. A third type of situation concerned the management of conflict, such as how to respond when another child tries to take away a toy.

Responses to each situation were categorized according to the strategy the child suggested. Our initial analysis focused on whether children of high and low sociometric status differed in the types of strategies they suggested. The pattern of similarities and differences is complex. On the one hand, 70 percent of the three most common strategies given by the popular children to each item were also among the three most common strategies given by the unpopular children. This suggests that to a considerable extent high- and low-status children have similar ideas regarding how to behave in various social situations. On the other hand, where differences did occur between the groups, the social-skill deficit of the low-status group was highlighted.

We drew on two sources of data. First, we examined the strategies suggested exclusively by either the low- or high-status children. Those strategies that were suggested exclusively by the unpopular children were often inappropriately negative, whereas this was never the case among the popular children. For example, some low-status children suggested such ideas as "take the game" when we asked how the protagonist could play together with two peers who were engaged in a board game; or, when presented with a peer's statement that he or she had received a new puppy, some unpopular children responded "So?" In contrast, the strategies suggested exclusively by the popular group were often quite prosocial and sophisticated: In response to the game-entry situation, popular children suggested such ideas as waiting for the game to end and then asking to join the next game.

The second source of data comes from examining the strategies that best discriminated between the two groups in percentage of usage. On those items concerning the management of conflict, unpopular children were much more likely to suggest aggressive strategies. For example, when presented with the situation in which one child tries to take away another's toy, 12 percent of the unpopular children's responses were aggressive ("Punch him," or "She could beat her up"), whereas aggression was suggested in only 2 percent of the popular children's responses. On those items in which the task was to initiate new social relationships or to maintain ongoing social relationships, unpopular children were more likely to suggest vague ideas or to appeal to authority figures. Thus the unpopular children's responses indicate a lack of sophistication in handling the everyday social tasks of childhood.

This examination of the content of children's strategies provides insight into the nature of children's ideas about specific social situations. In addition, however, some general dimensions are needed to allow us to make statements that summarize the content of children's ideas across situations. As a preliminary step in this direction, judges who were blind to the children's sociometric status rated children's strategies on three dimensions: assertiveness, relationship enhancement, and effectiveness. An assertive response was defined as one that tended to be more active than passive and usually involved self-initiative. A relationship-enhancing response was defined as one that was likely to maintain or enhance a positive relationship between children. An effective response was defined as one that was responsive to the requirements of the situation and likely to solve the explicit or implied problem. Children were assigned scores for each scale based on the ratings given to each of their responses. The results indicated that popular and unpopular children did not differ significantly in assertiveness but that popular children's responses were rated as significantly more effective and relationship enhancing.

The data from this study show that even though there is considerable similarity between high- and low-status children's ideas about how to interact, the differences that do occur are crucial in predicting social status. These data, along with the findings of Gottman et al. (1975) and Ladd and Oden (1979), indicate that poorly accepted children exhibit less skillful social-interaction strategies even when the assessment is made independently of their peer group. This is not to say that children's responses to hypothetical situations provide a pure test of their social skills. There are undoubtedly potential constraints on children's performance aside from possible social-skill deficits. For example, the child's level of test anxiety, comfort with the interviewer, or interest in becoming engaged in the task influence performance. Still, these constraints differ somewhat from those that operate when children are observed interacting in their regular peer group. The fact that both observational data and hypothetical-situations data yield differences between children of high and low sociometric status supports the assumption that children's limited social skills contribute to their poor acceptance by peers.

The social-skill hypothesis: (II) Evidence from training studies

If low sociometric status is largely a function of lack of skills, then training children in social skills should lead to improvement in their status. That is, by increasing children's social skillfulness through appropriate teaching procedures, it should be possible to observe changes in behavior and concurrent changes in sociometric status. Experimental intervention thus provides a useful method for testing the social-skill hypothesis.

Although social-skill training has a long history, only recently have social-skill training studies used sociometric measures as outcome variables. Earlier studies examined a variety of behavioral outcomes, including both simple rate of interaction (e.g., O'Connor, 1969, 1972) and more qualitative measures of social interaction, such as the use of cooperative social strategies (e.g., Chittenden, 1942). Because we wish to provide historical perspective on the sociometric outcome studies, first we will briefly review the behavioral-outcomes literature.[1]

Behavioral-outcome studies: effects of direct verbal instruction

Using a training strategy to test the social-skill hypothesis requires effective teaching procedures. The history of child psychology shows that direct verbal instruction can be quite effective in changing the behavior of young children. In the 1930s and 1940s, there were several successful intervention studies in which children were directly instructed in various skills (e.g., Chittenden, 1942; Keister, 1938). The most sophisticated social-skill training study of this period was carried out by Chittenden (1942), who was interested in nursery-school children's strategies for being assertive. Chittenden's assumption was that children who used a high percentage of dominative strategies and a low percentage of cooperative strategies did so because they could not think of cooperative strategies for reaching their goal. Therefore, she provided a training procedure that enabled these children to appreciate the negative consequences of their dominative strategies and the positive consequences of cooperative strategies. The training procedure focused on what to do when there are limited resources available (e.g., a single toy). Two dolls were used to demonstrate the distinction between positive outcomes, such as sharing and having a good time, and negative outcomes, such as fighting. As the two dolls faced a variety of potential conflict situations, the experimenter and child discussed possible ways of resolving the conflicts and the child was asked what the dolls could do to play successfully. Posttest observations in a naturalistic play situation indicated that children who received training decreased significantly more than control children in their amount of dominative behavior and increased more than the control children in cooperative behavior, although not significantly.

Although early studies using direct verbal instruction to teach children social interaction skills were quite successful, very little social-skill training research was conducted over the next ten to fifteen years. When interest revived in the late 1950s and early 1960s, there was relatively little emphasis on verbal instruction and greater emphasis on the influence of contingencies, such as tokens or verbal praise, on children's social behavior (e.g., Azrin & Lindsley, 1956; Allen, Hart, Buell, Harris, & Wolf, 1964). It was not until the late 1960s that instruction again came to play an important role in the training procedures. In 1969, O'Connor reported a study in which preschool children who interacted infrequently with their peers were shown a modeling film designed to increase the children's rate of interaction. Although the study was interpreted by O'Connor and others as demonstrating that modeling high rates of interaction is effective in increasing children's frequency of interaction, the film also employed verbal instructions in teaching social skills. The film contained eleven modeling episodes, with a narrator describing the action in each episode. In each case the child-model is shown entering an ongoing peer activity and being well received. An analysis of the film's narration made by Gottman (personal communication) indicates its instructional content. On many occasions, the narrator called attention to the child's intentions to interact (eight utterances), described how to interact for positive consequences (twenty-seven utterances), gave descriptions of ongoing behavior (twenty-four utterances), and described the positive consequences of interaction (twenty-eight utterances).

Studies using this film have found significant increases in the children's rate of interaction immediately following viewing, and the data with regard to maintenance of change are generally positive. Two studies have reported maintenance of change four to six weeks later (Evers & Schwarz, 1973; O'Connor, 1972). One study (Gottman, 1977) failed to find any effects after eight weeks. Because this study did not have an immediate posttest, however, it is unclear whether training effects dissipated or were not produced originally. If effects were not obtained, it could be because of the particular sample employed. The children were enrolled in Head Start and may have been less verbally proficient than children in the nursery schools used in other studies using O'Connor's film.

A study by Zahavi and Asher (1978) relied exclusively on verbal instruction and discussion to teach social-interaction skills. The eight most aggressive children in a preschool were identified using a time-sampling observation procedure. The intervention consisted of a discussion between the teacher and the child in which three concepts were emphasized: (1) that aggression hurts another person and makes that person sad; (2) that aggression doesn't solve problems and only brings about the resentment of the other child; and (3) that sharing and taking turns are positive ways to solve conflicts. The discussion consisted of a question–answer format; thus the child participated to some extent in developing the concepts. Results of this study indicated that children who received this intervention decreased in aggressive behavior compared to a control group and increased in positive behaviors such as cooperative play or constructive individual play activity. Following the posttest observations, the control group received the intervention, and their aggressive behavior also subsequently decreased. Although a small sample was employed, this study provides evidence of the effect of a verbal instructional training strategy with very young children.

None of the behavioral-outcome studies that found improvement on a behavioral measure identified children based on sociometric status or examined the effects of social-skill training on children's acceptance by peers. Would the children in these studies have been initially low in sociometric status, and, if so, would sociometric status have been increased by the training? Three behavior patterns were targeted in the studies discussed above: dominative behaviors (e.g., Chittenden, 1942), aggressive behaviors (e.g., Zahavi & Asher, 1978), and rate of interaction without regard to the content of the interaction (e.g., O'Connor, 1969). It seems plausible that children who use dominative or aggressive strategies with peers would be less well liked, and that training in cooperative behavior would increase their social acceptance by peers. It is also plausible that children with extremely low rates of interaction (Walker, Greenwood, Hops, & Todd, 1979) may be experiencing peer-relationship problems. However, most investigators using the rate-of-interaction measure have selected children whose rates of interaction are rather high: O'Connor's (1969, 1972) criterion was 15 percent and other investigators have used higher criteria, such as 33 percent (Furman, Rahe, & Hartup, 1979), or 50 percent (Keller & Carlson, 1974). It seems implausible that children interacting near these levels are necessarily at risk or in need of special help. It also seems unlikely that increasing these children's rate of interaction, without regard to the quality of their interaction, would lead to increases in sociometric status.[2]

Social-skill training and sociometric status

We turn now to an examination of skill-training studies in which sociometric status was a criterion variable. Because these studies provide direct experimental tests of the social-skill-deficit hypothesis, they warrant close examination. The studies share two features. First, the training programs emphasize those abilities that previous research has found to correlate with sociometric status. For example, Gottman, Gonso, and Schuler (1976) taught less popular children how to distribute and receive positive interaction, how to make friends, and how to take the perspective of a listener, because these abilities had been shown in a previous study (Gottman, Gonso, & Rasmussen, 1975) to correlate with sociometric status. This approach to the selection of program content has been called the "competence-correlates" approach (Asher & Markell, 1979).

Second, the assumption is made that children, even very young children, can be directly taught social skills by adults. By direct instruction, the adult hopes to exploit the child's cognitive capacity both to grasp the ideas being conveyed and to provide specific examples of how to translate the ideas into practice. For example, in the coaching procedure devised by Oden and Asher (1977), the adult-coach introduces an idea, such as "cooperate," and encourages the child to think of specific behavioral examples. The child is taught to understand, in the terms of his or her own life experience, the meaning of the concept "cooperation." Thus, by adopting a coaching procedure, researchers assume that children can indeed modify their behavior both as a function of their knowledge of general interaction concepts and of their capacity to translate this knowledge into effective action.

The evidence from coaching studies for the social-skill-deficit hypothesis is strong. Of the four studies to be reviewed, three have shown long-term improvements in children's sociometric status as a result of training. In the first of these, Gottman et al. (1976) trained two unpopular third-grade girls on three skills – how to give and receive positive interaction, how to make friends, and how to take a listener's role. An attention-control procedure was included, in which control subjects interacted for an equal span of time as experimental subjects with the adult-coach but did not receive skill training. Control subjects appeared to enjoy their experience, but at a nine-week follow-up they remained at the same level on the sociometric measures. In contrast, the two trained children improved significantly on a play-rating measure, and one of the two trained children improved on a work-rating measure. Although the sample was small, the design of the study precludes easy dismissal of the results.

A subsequent study by Oden and Asher (1977), with a larger sample, also demonstrated long-term sociometric change following coaching. The training program consisted of coaching the children in four social-interaction concepts: participation, cooperation, communication, and validation-support. These concepts were chosen based on comprehensive reviews of the behavioral correlates of sociometric status (Asher, Oden, & Gottman, 1977; Hartup, 1970; Moore, 1967). Special attention was given to devising a coaching procedure that could be employed in a reasonably standardized way. The procedure had three components. First, children were individually instructed by an adult in certain social-interaction concepts. Next, children were given an opportunity to practice the ideas by playing with a classmate of the same sex. Finally, the adult and the child reviewed the ideas in light of the child's recent play experience. This three-step procedure took a total of about thirty minutes. The entire coaching program, conducted over a four-week period, consisted of an initial play session followed by five of the thirty-minute sessions.[3]

The Oden and Asher study was designed to test whether the verbal-instruction component of the intervention was the important factor. Therefore, in addition to the coached group of children, two comparison groups were employed: one group of children (peer-pairing group) was given the opportunity to play a game with a peer as many times as had the coached children, thereby controlling for peer-practice opportunities; another group (control) played the games alone, thus receiving neither verbal instruction nor peer practice. Three sociometric measures were administered: a play-with rating measure, a work-with rating measure, and a best-friends nomination measure. In addition, behavioral observations were made of the children in the coaching and peer-pairing conditions during their twelve-minute play sessions.

The results of this study indicated that coaching led to significant gains in peer acceptance on the play-rating measure. Nonsignificant trends were evident on the work ratings and best-friends measures. No change was shown on the behavioral-observation measures. Most encouraging were results from a one-year follow-up assessment, in which the play-rating sociometric measure was administered. Children in the coaching condition continued to increase in peer acceptance, children in the peer-pairing condition made modest gains, and children in the control condition continued at the same level as they had been the year before. These long-term follow-up data are striking in light of the resistance to long-term sociometric change demonstrated in studies that modify the social setting but do not directly teach social skills (see Gottlieb & Leyser, this volume, for a review). The data also indicate the stability of low status among peers for children who received no intervention. Most important, the study provided experimental support for the presumed relationship between certain social skills and peer acceptance: Children trained in particular skills increased in peer acceptance. Furthermore, training in a play situation led to significant increases on the play-with sociometric measure, but not on the work-with or best-friends measures. These are interesting findings, because the coaching procedure emphasized play skills in a play context. Presumably, somewhat different skills would have to be taught to affect the work-with and best-friends measures.

A puzzling finding in this study was that no behavioral changes were observed during the play sessions even though dramatic changes in sociometric status had occurred. One possibility is that there was an inexact match between the concepts taught and the behavioral coding system used. Ladd (in press), in a subsequent study, used a coding system that closely matched the concepts taught and found behavioral as well as sociometric change. Third-grade children who were low on the play-rating measure were coached on asking positive questions, offering useful suggestions or directions, and offering supportive statements. Eight coaching sessions, lasting forty to fifty minutes each, were conducted over a three-week period. The coaching procedure consisted of verbal instruction, rehearsal, and postrehearsal review. The review phase included coaching in self-evaluation skills.

Ladd included both an attention-control group and a nontreatment control group in his experimental design. The coaching group showed significant gains at posttest and at one-month follow-up on both questions and suggestions/directions. Both control groups remained at pretest levels on all behavioral measures throughout the experiment. Thus the coaching intervention influenced children's performance on two of the three designated target skills. It is especially notable that the coached group also demonstrated significant sociometric gains at posttest that were maintained on the follow-up assessment. Posttest sociometric gains were made by the attention-control group but were not maintained over four weeks. These results suggest a relationship between the trained skills and maintenance of sociometric status gains.

One study did not find that coaching was superior to a peer-pairing condition. Hymel and Asher (1977) assigned third-through fifth-grade unpopular children (children low on both the nomination and play-rating measure) to either a peer-pairing condition, a general coaching condition (the Oden and Asher procedure), or an individualized coaching condition. In the latter condition, an attempt was made to stress skills in which the child was particularly deficient. Results of this study indicated that children in both coaching conditions made gains and that gains were greater at six-month follow-up. However, children in the peer-pairing condition also made considerable gains, and there were no significant differences between the three conditions in the degree to which children changed in sociometric status. Because this study did not use a no-treatment control group, the increase for all three conditions may have been evidence of treatment impact or evidence of regression toward the mean. Given that control-group children in previous research (Gottman, Gonso & Schuler, 1976; Oden & Asher, 1977) have shown little change, the Hymel and Asher data probably are a case of all conditions being effective. Why the coaching conditions were no more effective in the study than the peer-pairing condition is unknown.

To summarize, three of the four coaching studies reviewed above demonstrate persuasively that coaching children in social skills can positively affect sociometric status. In each of these studies the use of appropriate control groups strengthened the inference that instruction in social skills accounted for the target children's gain in popularity. It is the Ladd study, however, that provides concurrent evidence of behavior change. This study suggests that it was indeed the specific social skills that were coached that mediated the increase in sociometric status. The only stronger evidence would be to demonstrate that the extent of change on behavioral measures is correlated with the degree of change on sociometric measures.

Explanations of the coaching effect

The experimental evidence supports the social-skill-deficit hypothesis. Children coached in social skills made gains in sociometric status. Reflection on the components of the coaching procedure, therefore, may be fruitful in helping to establish a fuller account of the dimensions of social skillfulness. Social skills are complex and multifaceted, and successful intervention attempts should target the important components of social skillfulness. Researchers who make intervention attempts with children often have assumed that inducing behavioral change is sufficient, but the coaching procedure assumes that certain types of cognitive processes should also be changed if social competence is to be enhanced. What is required, therefore, is an explication of the dimensions of social skillfulness that have been incorporated in the coaching process.

What are the components of social skillfulness and how might training influence the development of these components? One dimension of social skillfulness involves *children's knowledge of general interaction principles or concepts*. Oden and Asher focused on this dimension when they sought to teach children the meaning and importance of participating, cooperating, communicating, and being validating or supportive of the other child. The presumption here is that general concepts such as these can be used to guide behavior across a variety of situations. It may be that provision of these general concepts is central to the effectiveness of the coaching procedures.

A second and related dimension of social skillfulness involves *knowledge of the specific behaviors or behavioral sequences* that can be used to actualize the more general concepts or principles. Children's difficulties in a certain situation may come not from lacking a general concept of what is required but from not knowing precisely how that concept is to be put into action. For example, a child may know that he or she should communicate with a child who is new in the class, but the child may not know what to say in that specific situation. This aspect of social skillfulness also was of concern to Oden and Asher. As part of the coaching procedure, children were encouraged to think of specific behavioral examples for each of the general concepts, in the context of the particular games that were played.

Another aspect of social skillfulness concerns *the goals children set for themselves in particular situations*. Some children may construe situations in ways that lead to maladaptive goals. For example, most children probably define a game situation as one in which the goal is to win but also for both parties to have a good time. These children try to win, but not at the expense of both players' enjoyment of the game. Other children, however, might define the goal as defeating the opponent at all costs. These children try so hard to win that they ignore the relationship aspects of the game and decrease the likelihood that the other child will want to play again. Accordingly, the unpopular child's problem is not only a lack of knowledge of principles or specific behavioral strategies, but also a tendency to define interpersonal goals in ways that promote dysfunctional social behavior. The effectiveness of coaching may result in part from suggesting alternative interpersonal goals for children in play situations. In their coaching procedure, Oden and Asher linked use of interaction concepts to the goal of having fun playing with others. It may be that this encouraged children to change their focus from an exclusive emphasis on winning the game to the more complex goal of trying to win the game while ensuring that both players had a good time.

The processes we have been discussing have a cognitive basis. However, it is unlikely that children are usually aware or conscious of their selection of goals or their decisions about which behavioral principles to apply or which behavioral sequences best actualize those principles. Indeed, most social interactions take place automatically, without explicit deliberation or reflection. It is as if children and adults function on "automatic pilot" in most of their social interactions. Within a culture, people learn that situations often carry with them social conventions related to what the goals are, what general principles govern interactions, and what specific behavior patterns are appropriate. For example, imagine that a child is playing with a sled in the snow and the child's friend approaches without a sled. The convention governing friendship relations is for some joint activity to occur (the goal), by adopting a generally positive, sharing attitude (the principle), which leads to specific behaviors such as taking turns or using the sled together (the specific behavioral sequence). By staying within the conventional boundaries of behavior, the child establishes the conditions for a harmonious sequence of interaction.

The existence of social conventions thus makes it possible for children and adults to interact automatically or without self-consciousness much of the time. Nonetheless, occasions do arise when people must disengage their automatic pilot and engage in conscious deliberations about their next actions. Deliberate social planning often comes about when something has gone wrong – when one's expectations for a particular situation have not been fulfilled. This ability to engage in nonautomatic processing depends upon the individual's ability to monitor the impact he or she is having on others. How are children to adjust their behavior unless they can read the effects that their behavior is having on other children? Thus, we would posit another important dimension of social skillfulness: *the ability to recognize the kind of impact one is having on others*.

It is unlikely that coaching in previous research has been directly teaching this skill. However, it is quite possible that the procedures used have indirectly sensitized children to the need to engage in this process. One child whom Oden coached suggested this possibility. During one of the later sessions, the child spontaneously said, "You mean, what I do affects whether kids like me or not?" This child had realized that her behavior could affect others' behavior and feelings, and by implication, that she needed to pay attention to the kind of impact she might be having. There were elements in the coaching procedure that might have stimulated this realization. For example, after each play session the coach asked the child whether he or she had fun, whether the other child had fun, and whether the ideas they talked about earlier helped to make the game more fun to play. Thus a process of monitoring of social interaction was probably being encouraged.

To summarize, we are suggesting that coaching may have been effective because it influenced a number of dimensions of social skillfulness. These include the child's knowledge of general interaction principles or concepts, the child's knowledge of specific behavioral sequences that operationalize the concepts, the child's goal-construction process, and the child's ability to monitor his or her impact on others. In the next section we will examine the implications of this analysis for future investigations of the relationship of social skills to sociometric status.

Implications for assessment and training

The literature on the social-skill correlates of sociometric status has focused primarily on children's behavioral strategies, either as directly observed or as rated by peers or teachers. Our analysis indicates the way in which a focus on behavioral strategies can be integrated into a more complete framework of social skillfulness. Thus, in addition to assessing children's specific behavioral strategies, we need to measure the children's knowledge of social interaction principles, goal-construal processes, and ability to monitor the impact their actions have on others. Unpopular children may have deficits in one or more of these processes. Thus, in both correlational-descriptive studies and in experimental-intervention studies we need to develop and implement assessment procedures to measure each of these dimensions of social skill.

Our analysis of social skillfulness also has implications for social-skill training. To date, coaching research has explicitly focused on training general interaction principles and specific behaviors that exemplify those general principles. Yet our analysis has suggested that coaching could also be affecting children's goal-construal processes or self-monitoring skills. The importance of goal-construal and self-monitoring processes in sustaining effective social interaction suggests that training programs for unpopular children should directly target these processes. One advantage of targeting specific dimensions of social skillfulness is the potential it holds for furthering our theoretical understanding of the determinants of effective social interaction. A second advantage is the potential for increasing the effectiveness of social-skill training programs for children with different patterns of social-skill deficits.

The social-skill hypothesis: (III) The need for a developmental perspective

Research conducted from a social-skill-deficit perspective has produced insights into the reasons that some children lack friends. A neglected issue in the research literature that merits closer attention is whether there are developmental changes in the social-skill basis of sociometric status. It seems likely that the social skills required to form and maintain friendships change as children grow older. Research directed toward this question would provide a fuller account of the processes contributing to effectiveness with peers and would have implications for devising age-appropriate training programs.[4]

An independent literature on children's friendship expectations (Bigelow, 1977; Bigelow & La Gaipa, 1975; Damon, 1977; Selman, this volume) implies the possibility of developmental changes in the social-skill basis of peer relations. This literature implies that young children view friends as those with whom they have had frequent contact, positively interacted, and shared material resources such as toys. For older children, friendship is affirmed through helping and through the mutual sharing of thoughts, feelings, and interests. Older children do not negate the importance of simple forms of cooperation and sharing; however, they appreciate that friendship is terminated not simply by a decrease in contact or a lapse in positive interaction but by frequent displays of lack of understanding or disloyalty. These findings suggest that children of all ages need skills in sharing and cooperation to make friends but that older children, in particular, require skills in identifying shared interests, disclosing thoughts and feelings, and maintaining an atmosphere of trust.

Given the long history of research on the behavioral basis of sociometric status, why has a developmental perspective failed to emerge? Investigators may have been constrained from undertaking developmental research in this area by narrow vision with respect to the selection of methodology. Any behavior-assessment methodology must meet certain criteria if it is to be useful for studying developmental changes in the social-skill basis of sociometric status (Asher & Hymel, in press). First, it must be sensitive to the various behavioral dimensions that contribute to children's acceptance by peers at different ages. Behavior that is appropriate and effective for one age-group may be regarded as immature or deviant by another. The behavior-assessment methodology must also be sensitive to infrequently occurring but psychologically salient behaviors that can have long-term effects on how children are viewed by their peers. Furthermore, it must cover the variety of social contexts in which children interact with one another. This factor is important for a developmental framework, for as children grow older the contexts in which they interact become more diverse.

Although various methodologies exist for studying the social-skill basis of sociometric status (Asher & Hymel, in press), the methodology of choice for most investigators of the behavioral correlates of sociometric status has been naturalistic observation. This approach provides the most direct evidence about how children actually interact with their peers. Yet it is difficult to fulfill the criteria described above using naturalistic observation techniques. Although behavioral codes can be created for measuring observable behaviors such as cooperation or aggression, it is more difficult to assess more subtle, less observable dimensions, such as honesty or loyalty, that contribute to children's attitudes toward one another, particularly at older ages. In addition, it is costly in time and resources to detect infrequently occurring events, to study children in various contexts, and to study children at different ages. Even the costs of extensive observations of multiple age-groups in one context are considerable. Recent studies using naturalistic observation methodology to study the behavioral correlates of sociometric status have made a limited number of observations per child, have not stratified observations based on situa-

tional variables, and have not obtained large enough samples at various
ages to study developmental changes in the relationship of behavior to
sociometric status (e.g., Gottman, 1977; Gottman, Gonso, & Rasmussen,
1975; Hymel & Asher, 1977).

Clearly, then, comprehensive naturalistic-observation research is
needed. Attention should also be directed to other methodologies that
have been relatively neglected and that have distinctive strengths for developmental research. One promising method that has been underutilized
is direct observation of behavior in analogue situations rather than in the
child's everyday environment. This methodology can be used to evoke
events that may occur infrequently in the everyday environment but have
psychological importance. The research described by Putallaz and Gottman (this volume) indicates the utility of an analogue research strategy.
They used this methodology to study children's styles of entry into an
ongoing social interaction. This type of behavioral event would have been
far more difficult to study in a natural setting.

The hypothetical-situations technique is another relatively neglected
methodology. This technique, which was earlier shown to have utility for
assessing social knowledge across contexts, can also be used as a means
of investigating age-related changes in children's social knowledge. By
studying children's responses to situations such as initiating a friendship
or resolving a conflict, it is possible to identify what children at different
ages regard as effective and appropriate strategies and what strategies are
associated with high versus low sociometric status.

Finally, peers and teachers can be valuable sources of data on age appropriate behavior and can provide data about the influence of low-fre-
quency events on sociometric status. Techniques that exploit this data
base include open-ended descriptions, ratings, and nominations of children by their teachers and classmates. A study by Coppotelli and Coie
(1978) suggests the potential utility of peer-assessment methods for developmental inquiry. They used the "Guess Who" technique (Hartshorne,
May, & Maller, 1929) and had third-, fifth- and eighth-grade children indicate the names of classmates who fit various behavioral descriptions.
They found that the correlations between various behavioral traits, as
measured by the "Guess Who" technique, and sociometric status were
much lower in eighth grade than in third and fifth grade. This suggests
either that the behaviors leading to liking and disliking become more diverse over age or that other nonbehavioral factors (e.g., previous reputation, physical appearance) assume greater importance as children grow
older.

The current literature, therefore, provides some suggestions concerning the developmental changes in the social-skill basis of sociometric

status. Further research from a developmental perspective, using the various methodologies discussed above, will provide a fuller account of age-related changes and thereby increase the effectiveness of training programs with children of different ages.

Conclusion

In this paper we examined the hypothesis that social skillfulness is a crucial determinant of children's peer relationships. We demonstrated that the evidence from correlational and experimental studies converged to support the social-skill-deficit interpretation of low sociometric status. Two sources of evidence were crucial in establishing this conclusion. First, it was shown that assessment of children's social skills, made independently of the performance demands imposed by group membership, still revealed the social-skill deficits of unpopular children. The utility of the hypothetical-situations methodology for this purpose was highlighted. Second, it was shown that experimental modification of children's social skillfulness led to increases in sociometric status. The social-skill perspective, therefore, was shown to have utility for both understanding and modifying children's peer relationships.

Furthermore, we argued for and outlined a more detailed conceptualization of social skillfulness that involved both cognitive and behavioral components. This conceptualization provides a guide to the processes that may underlie the capacity to establish effective peer relations. Research directed to identifying the nature of these processes more exactly will provide the foundation for more effective intervention approaches. As our understanding of process expands, our capacity to modify the maladaptive behaviors of children with peer relationship problems will also expand.

The coaching studies that we reviewed were designed to bring about important changes in children's lives and to explicate the processes underlying change. The concern to understand process is exemplified by the inclusion of control groups that help specify the ingredients in the coaching intervention that produce change. The concern with outcomes is shown by selection of outcome variables, such as sociometric status, that have long-term predictive validity (in that they predict later social adjustment). Thus, these studies indicate the way in which an understanding of process can emerge at the same time that important problems in children's lives are addressed. In future coaching studies, explicit attention to the specific dimensions of social skillfulness holds the promise of advancing our understanding of process and further facilitating the effectiveness of intervention.

Notes

1 See Combs and Slaby (1978) for a more extensive review of this literature.
2 See Asher and Markell (1979) for a review of the research on the validity of simple rate of interaction as a way of identifying peer-relationship problems or for assessing the effectiveness of social-skill training programs.
3 A description of the coaching procedure used in our research can be found in Oden, Asher, and Hymel (1978). This description includes the script used by the coach in discussing the concepts.
4 There is also a need for a developmental perspective in designing particular training techniques. Discussion of this issue is beyond the scope of this chapter, however. For an interesting discussion of this issue see Furman (1980).

References

Allen, K. E., Hart, B., Buell, J. S., Harris, F. R., & Wolf, M. M. Effects of social reinforcement of isolate behavior of a nursery school child. *Child Development,* 1964, *35,* 511–518.

Asher, S. R., & Hymel, S. Children's social competence in peer relations: Sociometric and behavioral assessment. In J. D. Wine & M. D. Smye (Eds.), *Social competence.* New York: Guilford Press, in press.

Asher, S. R., & Markell, R. A. *Peer relations and social interaction: Assessment and intervention.* Unpublished manuscript, University of Illinois, Urbana, 1979.

Asher, S. R., Oden, S. L., & Gottman, J. M. Children's friendships in school settings. In L. G. Katz (Ed.), *Current topics in early childhood education* (Vol. 1). Norwood, N.J.: Ablex Publishing, 1977.

Asher, S. R., & Renshaw, P. D. *Social skills and social knowledge of high- and low-status kindergarten children,* in preparation.

Asher, S. R., Singleton, L. C., Tinsley, B. R., & Hymel, S. A reliable sociometric measure for preschool children. *Developmental Psychology,* 1979, *15,* 443–444.

Azrin, N. H., & Lindsley, O. R. The reinforcement of cooperation between children. *Journal of Abnormal Social Psychology,* 1956, *52,* 100–102.

Bigelow, B. J. Children's friendship expectations: A cognitive-developmental study. *Child Development,* 1977, *48,* 246–253.

Bigelow, B. J., & LaGaipa, J. J. Children's written descriptions of friendship: A multidimensional analysis. *Developmental Psychology,* 1975, *11,* 857–858.

Bonney, M. E. The relative stability of social, intellectual, and academic status in grades II to IV, and the interrelationships between these various forms of growth. *Journal of Educational Psychology,* 1943, *44,* 88–102.

Campbell, J. D., & Yarrow, M. R. Perceptual and behavioral correlates of social effectiveness. *Sociometry,* 1961, *24,* 1–20.

Chittenden, G. F. An experimental study in measuring and modifying assertive behavior in young children. *Monographs of the Society for Research in Child Development,* 1942, 7 (1, Serial No. 31).

Combs, M. L., & Slaby, D. A. Social skills training with children. In B. B. Lahey & A. E. Kazdin (Eds.), *Advances in clinical child psychology* (Vol. 1). New York: Plenum Press, 1978.

Coppotelli, H. A., & Coie, J. D. *Childhood deviance – A peer perspective.* Paper presented at the biennial meeting of the Southeastern Conference on Human Development, Atlanta, 1978.

Criswell, J. H. A sociometric study of race cleavage in the classroom. *Archives of Psychology,* 1939, No. 235, 1–82.

Damon, W. *The social world of the child.* San Francisco: Jossey-Bass, 1977.

Dunnington, M. J. Behavioral differences of sociometric status groups in a nursery school. *Child Development,* 1957, *28,* 103–111.

Evers, W. L., & Schwarz, J. C. Modifying social withdrawal in preschoolers: The effects of filmed modeling and teacher praise. *Journal of Abnormal Child Psychology,* 1973, *1,* 248–256.

Freud, A., & Dann, S. An experiment in group upbringing. *Psychoanalytic Study of the Child,* 1951, *6,* 127–168.

Furman, W. Promoting appropriate social behavior: Developmental implications for treatment. In B. B. Lahey & A. E. Kazdin (Eds.), *Advances in clinical child psychology* (Vol. 3). New York: Plenum Press, 1980.

Furman, W., Rahe, D. F., & Hartup, W. W. Rehabilitation of socially-withdrawn preschool children through mixed-age and same-age socialization. *Child Development,* 1979, *50,* 915–922.

Gottman, J. M., *Personal communication,* July, 1976.

The effects of a modeling film on social isolation in preschool children: A methodological investigation. *Journal of Abnormal Child Psychology,* 1977, *5,* 69–78.

Gottman, J., Gonso, J., & Rasmussen, B. Social interaction, social competence, and friendship in children. *Child Development,* 1975, *46,* 709–718.

Gottman, J. M., Gonso, J., & Schuler, P. Teaching social skills to isolated children. *Journal of Abnormal Child Psychology,* 1976, *4,* 179–197.

Gottman, J. M., & Parkhurst, J. T. A developmental theory of friendship and acquaintanceship processes. In W. A. Collins (Ed.), *Minnesota symposia on child psychology* (Vol. 13). Hillsdale, N.J.: Lawrence Erlbaum, 1980.

Gronlund, N. E. *Sociometry in the classroom.* New York: Harper, 1959.

Gronlund, N. E., & Anderson, L. Personality characteristics of socially accepted, socially neglected, and socially rejected junior high school pupils. *Educational Administration and Supervision,* 1957, *43,* 329–338.

Hartshorne, H., May, M. A., & Maller, J. B. *Studies in the nature of character: II. Studies in service and self-control.* New York: Macmillan, 1929.

Hartup, W. W. Peer interaction and social organization. In P. H. Mussen (Ed.), *Carmichael's manual of child psychology* (Vol. 2). New York: Wiley, 1970.

Children and their friends. In H. McGurk (Ed.), *Issues in child social development.* London: Methuen, 1978.

Hartup, W. W., Glazer, J. A., & Charlesworth, R. Peer reinforcement and sociometric status. *Child Development,* 1967, *38,* 1017–1024.

Hymel, S., & Asher, S. R. *Assessment and training of isolated children's social skills.* Paper presented at the biennial meeting of the Society for Research in Child Development, New Orleans, 1977 (ERIC Document Reproduction Service No. ED 136 930).

Ispa, J. *Familiar and unfamiliar peers as havens of security for Soviet nursery children.* Paper presented at the biennial meeting of the Society for Research in Child Development, New Orleans, 1977.

Keister, M. E. The behavior of young children in failure: An experimental attempt to discover and to modify undesirable responses of preschool children to failure. *University of Iowa Studies: Studies in Child Welfare,* 1938, *14,* 27–82.

Keller, M. F., & Carlson, P. M. The use of symbolic modeling to promote social skills in children with low levels of social responsiveness. *Child Development,* 1974, *45,* 912–919.

Kirby, F. D., & Toler, H. C. Jr. Modification of preschool isolate behavior: A case study. *Journal of Applied Behavior Analysis,* 1970, *3,* 309–314.

Koch, H. L. Popularity in preschool children: Some related factors and a technique for its measurement. *Child Development,* 1933, *4,* 164–175.

Kuhlen, R. G., & Lee, B. J. Personality characteristics and social acceptability in adolescence. *Journal of Educational Psychology,* 1943, *34*, 321–340.

Ladd, G. W. Effectiveness of a social learning method for enhancing children's social interaction and peer acceptance. *Child Development,* in press.

Ladd, G. W., & Oden S. L. The relationship between peer acceptance and children's ideas about helpfulness. *Child Development,* 1979, *50*, 402–408.

Lippitt, R. Popularity among preschool children. *Child Development,* 1941, *12*, 305–332.

McCandless, B. R., & Marshall, H. R. A picture sociometric technique for preschool children and its relation to teacher judgments of friendship. *Child Development,* 1957, *28*, 139–148.

Moore, S. G. Correlates of peer acceptance in nursery school children. In W. W. Hartup & N. L. Smothergill (Eds.), *The young child.* Washington, D.C.: National Association for the Education of Young Children, 1967.

Moore, S. G., & Updegraff, R. Sociometric status of preschool children related to age, sex, nurturance giving, and dependency. *Child Development,* 1964, *35*, 519–524.

Moreno, J. L. *Who shall survive? A new approach to the problem of human interrelations.* Washington, D.C.: Nervous and Mental Disease Publishing, 1934.

Mummery, D. An analytic study of ascendant behavior of preschool children. *Child Development,* 1947, *18*, 40–81.

O'Connor, R. D. Modification of social withdrawal through symbolic modeling. *Journal of Applied Behavior Analysis,* 1969, *2*, 15–22.

Relative efficacy of modeling, shaping, and the combined procedures for modification of social withdrawal. *Journal of Abnormal Psychology,* 1972, *79*, 327–334.

Oden, S., & Asher, S. R. Coaching children in social skills for friendship making. *Child Development,* 1977, *48*, 495–506.

Oden, S., Asher, S. R., & Hymel, S. *Procedures for coaching socially isolated children in social skills.* Unpublished manuscript, University of Illinois, Urbana, 1977.

Roff, M., Sells, S. B., & Golden, M. M. *Social adjustment and personality development in children.* Minneapolis: University of Minnesota Press, 1972.

Roistacher, R. C. A microeconomic model of sociometric choice. *Sociometry,* 1974, *37*, 219–238.

Shaw, M. E. Changes in sociometric choices following forced integration of an elementary school. *Journal of Social Issues,* 1973, *29*(4), 143–157.

Singleton, L. C., & Asher, S. R. Peer preferences and social interaction among third-grade children in an integrated school district. *Journal of Educational Psychology,* 1977, *69*, 330–336.

Racial integration and children's peer preferences: an investigation of developmental and cohort differences. *Child Development,* 1979, *50*, 936–941.

Thompson, G. G., & Powell, M. An investigation of the rating-scale approach to the measurement of social status. *Educational and Psychological Measurement,* 1951, *11*, 440–455.

Ullmann, C. A. Teachers, peers, and tests as predictors of adjustment. *Journal of Educational Psychology,* 1957, *48*, 257–267.

Walker, H. M., Greenwood, C. R., Hops, H., & Todd, N. M. Differential effects of reinforcing topographic components of social interaction: Analysis and direct replication. *Behavior Modification,* 1979, *3*, 291–321.

Zahavi, S. L., & Asher, S. R. The effect of verbal instructions on preschool children's aggressive behavior. *Journal of School Psychology,* 1978, *16*, 146–153.

11   Children's knowledge about social situations: from causes to consequences

Nancy L. Stein and Susan R. Goldman

Recent theoretical and empirical efforts in the cognitive domain of children's comprehension of stories have implications for work in the social domain of children's understanding of interpersonal interaction. Although the abilities necessary in actual social situations may differ markedly from the abilities necessary to comprehend stories about social events, some important similarities are worth exploring. In the first section of this chapter we discuss overlap at a theoretical level by describing similarities in the processes involved in understanding stories and in understanding social interactions. Our conclusion is that comprehension in each domain involves the ability to make causal inferences among events. This inferential process frequently depends on the comprehender's previously acquired knowledge of the possible reasons for a specific action and of the results of a specific action.

Next, we discuss overlap at a structural level by comparing the event structure of simple stories to that of actual social events. Event structure is shown to have important implications for empirical research on social development and the development of social skills as well as for the development of story-comprehension skills. Finally we describe some research that employs a storytelling procedure to ascertain children's prior knowledge about one type of social event, friendship. Throughout, we discuss how such cognitive research overlaps with other efforts to describe and train behavioral characteristics of successful friendship interactions.

The nature of the understanding process

Theoretical accounts of the acquisition of knowledge and the process of understanding highlight the importance of what individuals already know at the time they attempt to understand an environmental event. There is consensus regarding the general nature of this process. The following is a summary of proposals made by a diverse group of psychologists (e.g.,

297

Anderson, 1970, Bransford & McCarrell, 1974; Brown, 1975; Greeno, 1977; Newell & Simon, 1972; Piaget, 1971; Rumelhart, 1977a).

The general process of understanding involves the interaction between previously acquired knowledge systems and the information structure of the new event. The product of this interaction is an internal representation of the event. Previously acquired knowledge systems are assumed to guide the construction of meaningful internal representations of the new event. For the new event to be meaningful there must be consistency between the previously acquired knowledge systems and the additional information in the knowledge system. The understander's attempts to achieve consistency may produce changes in the organization and content of the knowledge system. Although this process has not been described in detail, an analogy has been drawn between the process of constructing a meaningful representation and scientific hypothesis testing: Initial hypotheses about meaning are successively revised, expanded, and restructured until the resulting representation seems to account for the new information (Brown, Collins, & Harris, 1978; Rumelhart, 1977a; Rumelhart & Ortony, 1977).

Research in a number of areas in psychology suggests the usefulness of this general framework in investigating the processes of knowledge acquisition and understanding (e.g., Greeno, 1977; Kintsch, 1977; Piaget & Inhelder, 1969; van Dijk, 1977). The framework points to the importance of characterizing both the information structure of the material to be understood and the knowledge systems of the understander, regardless of whether the material is a story or social event. This theoretical overlap between stories and social events can be elaborated in two ways. First we will describe the application of this framework to story-comprehension processes. Then we will illustrate that previous theoretical accounts of how we understand the behavior of others rely on assumptions that are virtually identical to those of the present framework.

Story comprehension processes

Story understanding is assumed to involve the construction of a coherent, meaningful representation of the story (Anderson, 1978; Kintsch & van Dijk, 1978; Rumelhart, 1977a). The construction of such a representation involves processes that operate on a number of different kinds of information in the story. These processes interact with one another and with previously acquired knowledge about each of these kinds of information (see Frederiksen, 1977; Kintsch & van Dijk, 1978; Perfetti & Lesgold, 1977; Rumelhart, 1977a). Successful comprehension seems to require several different kinds of knowledge, including the grammatical structure of stories and the content of the story. For stories containing problem-solving episodes, Brown, Collins, and Harris (1978) suggest that the result of the process is a "deep structure trace that is a complex hypothesis about the plans and goals of characters in the text." The source of such a hypothesis is the comprehender's ability to simulate the problem solving in which the story character is engaged. This ability depends on previously acquired problem-solving strategies.

Thus, one domain of knowledge that successful comprehension seems to require is problem solving in social situations. Furthermore, stories written for and produced by children often focus on goal-directed behavior, particularly goals that occur in social and interpersonal contexts (see Applebee, 1978; Botvin & Sutton-Smith, 1977; Stein & Glenn, 1979). Examples of common themes are friendship, obedience; and the solution of a particular personal or interpersonal problem. Such stories typically deal with the reasons for setting realistic goals and successful and unsuccessful plans for attaining such goals. Therefore, a child who attempts to understand such a story needs to rely not only on knowledge of the grammatical structure of stories but also on his or her expectations regarding social interactions and problem solving.

Comprehending the behavior of others

Social interactions involve more than one person. Therefore, in understanding social interactions one must comprehend the behavior of others as well as of oneself. There have been a number of theoretical accounts of how we understand the behavior of others (e.g., De Charms, 1968; Heider, 1958; Jones & Davis, 1965; Kelley, 1973). These accounts share an assumption that is consistent with the previously described general framework for understanding: We understand the behavior of others with respect to our understanding of our own behavior. We use our knowledge of why we would engage in a particular action to construct hypotheses about why the other person is engaging in that action. The information structure of the other person's behavior is interpreted with respect to the understander's previously acquired knowledge of his or her own behavior.

An important characteristic of intelligent human behavior is that it tends to be intentional or goal-directed (Piaget, 1968) and often involves the construction of plans. This characterisic of behavior has been assumed to play a central role in our attempts to understand the behavior of others. For example, a basic axiom of Heider's Commonsense Theory of interpersonal understanding, the axiom of personal causation, states that the observer assumes that an actor's voluntary actions "imply the existence of a plan that the actor has chosen to try to execute and also believes can be carried out" (Schmidt, 1976, p. 51). In other words, the ability to understand the behavior of another person depends on the ability of the observer to understand his or her own plans and deliberate actions. This process is similar to the comprehension process of simulating a story character's problem-solving behavior.

Therefore, theoretical accounts of comprehending stories and of comprehending the behavior of others share a common assumption: that an individual's actions are normally understood to be motivated or intentionally based. The implications of this assumption are twofold. First, it allows the prediction and explanation of certain classes of causal inferences that are made between story events. Second, it allows the prediction and explanation of an observer's attributions of intentionality, evaluations, and moral judgments of the actions of others. Acquisition and development of knowledge about interpersonal interactions and problem solving in social situations is important both for models of story comprehension and of social development. Furthermore, analytic tools that have been developed within the domain of story comprehension can be profitably applied to the analysis of the structure of actual social-interaction events. We will devote the next section to a discussion of one such analytic tool, the story grammar, and illustrate the way in which the basic structural components of a simple story are similar to the elements of an actual social interaction or observed action sequence. The discussion also points out some important differences in the information normally available in a story versus that in an observed action sequence.

Story and social event structure

The structure of simple stories

There have been a number of theoretical analyses of the structure of stories and action narratives (e.g., Kintsch, 1977; Mandler & Johnson, 1977; Rumelhart, 1975, 1977b; Stein & Glenn, 1979; van Dijk, 1977). These analyses specify a set of grammatical categories and rules for combining and ordering these categories. The categories may contain particular kinds of content. The theoretical status of the categories and the content description may be understood by analogy to sentence grammars, which state rules for combining parts of speech. For example, an adjective may precede but not follow the noun that it modifies. Each part of speech denotes a particular kind of content. A noun is a person, place, or thing. By analogy, the parts of speech of a story are its *syntactic categories*, and there are classes of content information that may occur in these categories. The following description of the grammar of a simple story is a summary of the research cited above and is typical of stories and folk tales.

A simple story has been postulated to contain two higher order syntactic categories: the SETTING and the EPISODE. The content of the SETTING typically introduces and describes the protagonist and the social, physical, and cultural context of the story. The EPISODE consists of a number of syntactic categories that are logically and causally related to one another. The information in the EPISODE generally describes a change or conflict that leads to conflict resolution. This conflict may be intrapersonal, interpersonal, or both. In the following example, the first three sentences convey SETTING information and the remainder of the story is the EPISODE.

This story is about a boy named John who lives in the city. John is nine years old. He lives in an apartment with his mother and father.
One day, John's best friend, Paul, didn't want to play with John. John felt sad and lonely and wanted Paul to play with him. John knew how much Paul liked ice cream.
So John bought an ice cream cone for Paul. Then John said, "You can have this ice-cream cone if you will play with me."
Paul said, "Okay."
John and Paul played together all afternoon and they both had a good time.

In this story, the conflict is interpersonal and is resolved by John's successful attempt to convince Paul to play with him. The EPISODE is defined by five syntactic categories that typically occur in the following order: Initiating Event, Internal Response, Attempt, Consequence, and Reaction. The Initiating Event signals a change in the story environment that was established by the SETTING. Information in this category describes an event that causes the protagonist to generate a goal. In the above example, Paul's not wanting to play with John causes John to have the goal of wanting to get Paul to play with him. Paul's behavior may be said to motivate John's goal formulation. The protagonist's goal formulation is one kind of information that may occur in the Internal Response category. In addition, the Internal Response encompasses emotional reactions to the Initiating Event, such as sadness and loneliness, degree of commitment to the goal, and thoughts about how to attain the goal. Goal formulation causes an Attempt to attain the goal, a series of overt actions carried out to achieve the goal. In the example, John buys an ice-cream cone and then offers it to Paul if Paul will play with him. The Consequence category provides outcome information about whether the attempt led to goal attainment. In the example, Paul agrees to play and then Paul and John play. Finally, the Reaction category describes the protagonist's response to the Consequence (how he feels about it or what he thinks about it) or broader consequences of goal attainment (how other story characters felt or acted in response to the protagonist's goal attainment). In the above example, "they both had a good time" is the Reaction. We might expand the Reaction, however, to include, "Paul knew he had been taken but he didn't care." A grammatically well-formed story has been postulated to include these syntactic categories in the sequential order in which they were presented.

Empirical evidence suggests that grammatical well-formedness does affect story understanding and that these proposals are reasonable models of the major syntactic categories. For example, adults' recall and summary protocols tend to contain these syntactic constituents (Kintsch, 1977; Kintsch & van Dijk, 1975; Mandler & Johnson, 1977; Rumelhart, 1977b; van Dijk, 1975). Furthermore, reading-time, summary, and recall data show that adults do expect these categories to occur in this hypothesized sequence. It takes adults longer to read and to summarize scrambled stories than stories that conform to the hypothesized sequence (Kintsch, Mandel, & Kozminsky, 1977). If presented with stories in which the ordering of categories violates the hypothesized sequence, adults tend to reorder the categories and recall a grammatically well-formed story (Stein & Nezworski, 1978).

In general, similar findings have been obtained with children, but there are some developmental differences in the importance of these categories. For younger children (ages 6 to 7), SETTINGS, Initiating Events and Consequences are more frequently recalled than Attempts; for older children (ages 9 to 10), Attempts are recalled equally well (Mandler & Johnson, 1977; Stein & Glenn, 1979). Furthermore, younger children tend to rank the Consequence as more important than the Initiating Event, whereas the reverse is true for older children (Stein & Glenn, 1979). Like adults, children demonstrate better retention of information when the hypothesized logical sequence of the categories is preserved (Stein, 1978). Deletion of major categories, especially the Initiating Event, negatively affects recall but increases the addition of nonpresented information: Children tend to add information that could occur in the missing category (Stein, 1979a, 1979b)

The syntactic-category analysis and grammatical structure of stories is relevant to work in the area of social development for at least two reasons. First, in many studies concerned with the development of knowledge about social events, the story format has been used to present the information from which a child is to make evaluative inferences. Second, social-skill training studies often use stories and films that contain the episodic structure outlined for the simple story. We will discuss both of these in order to illustrate that a better understanding of the episodic event structure of stories and films can lead to a better understanding of the acquisition of knowledge about social events and has implications for social-skill training procedures.

Using stories as the medium for presenting behavior

The results of empirical research on the acquisition of various social-cognitive abilities depend on the grammatical structure of the stories that have been used in such studies. Recent reviews of research in the area of evaluative-inferential reasoning (Shantz, 1975; Grueneich & Trabasso, in press) have pointed out that there is considerable variability in the presentation of information thought to be important in such reasoning. The presentation of motive (or intention) and outcome (or consequence) information frequently varies in both location in the story and in the explicitness of such information (Grueneich & Trabasso, in press). For example, motives are often implicit in the story and must be inferred from story statements about the character's goal, actions, and consequences of actions, and the reactions of others. This is an important factor, because empirical evidence has shown that conclusions about whether young children use motive information in their evaluative inferences depends on the explicitness of motive information (Bearison & Isaacs, 1975; Berg-Cross, 1975). In addition, Nezworski, Stein, and Trabasso (1978) have shown that if motive information (for example, giving a present to someone because it is the recipient's birthday) is explicit in the story, the importance of the location and syntactic category of the information decreases, although it does not disappear. These data suggest that if the critical information is explicit in the story and the story is grammatically well-formed, children have little trouble comprehending goal-directed behavior and then making evaluative inferences about that behavior.

However, if a story is not grammatically well formed because it is missing a major syntactic category, children tend to add to the content of the story (Stein, 1979a, 1979b). A common method of assessing one type of evaluative inference – moral judgments – is to present stories that lack a conclusion or consequence. The child's level of moral development is then inferred from the type of consequence proposed in conjunction with the child's reasoning about this story conclusion (e.g., Damon, 1977;

Selman & Byrne, 1974). These moral dilemmas require children to add to the content of the story and complete the grammatical structure. The sophistication of moral reasoning may be limited by the nature of this added content. There may also be developmental differences in the ability to anticipate alternative possibilities for the outcome of these dilemmas, and this ability may affect the nature of children's moral judgments.

Our contention, then, is that many stories that have been used in investigations of evaluative inferences require that the child not only make inferences among story events but also add to the content of the story. Developmental differences arise not only because of possible differences in the use of presented information but also because of differences in the nature of children's elaborations of the content and structure of the story. These differences are related to children's preexisting knowledge of story structure, the social situations described in the stories, and their ability to make their experiential history relevant to this new event. From both the standpoint of models of story comprehension and from that of social development it is important to describe developmental changes in the knowledge children have acquired about social situations. This knowledge is a primary determinant of the content of their inferences and their evaluations. To be able to predict the types of content inferences and evaluations that children will make we must have a better idea of what types of motives children associate with different types of goals, what actions and alternatives they view as leading to goal attainment, and what outcomes they foresee for particular actions. Goldman (1978) has attempted to examine these questions for social situations involving friendship. However, before discussing this work, we will discuss the second reason that episodic structure is relevant to social development.

Differences between stories and films: implications for social-skill training

The second reason that story research and the concept of episodic structure are relevant to social development is that social-skill training studies often use stories and films with episodic event structures similar to that of the simple story. The purpose of this section is to examine an important difference between stories and films and discuss the implications of this difference for social-skill training procedures. One aim of many social-skill training studies is to encourage children to make inferences about the motives, intentions, and feelings of the people involved in actual social events. Because stories and films differ with respect to the salience of these internal states, whether a film or story is used in the training procedure may be important to the success of the program. For example, films can greatly resemble actual social events, in that a character's thoughts must be inferred from his overt actions and from facial expressions. In contrast, the episodic structure of a well-formed story includes information about the reasons for the protagonist's actions.

The difference between films and stories has important implications for social-skill training procedures, because empirical evidence suggests that there are developmental differences in the nature of the inferences children make about characters in film (e.g., Flapan, 1968) and a developmental progression in the strategies children use for making inferences about characters who display diverse behavior (e.g., Gollin, 1958). Flapan (1968), for example, found developmental differences in the types of inferences children make when asked to explain the behavior of the characters in a film that had a problem-solving episodic structure. Twelve-year-olds explained the behavior of the characters using situational, psychological, and interpersonal reasoning; 9-year-olds used situational and psychological explanations; 6-year-olds mainly used situational reasoning. Situational reasoning refers to the concrete events and actions that were featured in the film, psychological reasoning refers to the thoughts a particular character had, and interpersonal reasoning to thoughts about others' thoughts.

Filmed episodes have also been used to examine developmental changes in strategies for evaluating characters who exhibit inconsistent behavior. Gollin (1958) analyzed children's descriptions of a protagonist who engaged in socially approved and socially disapproved actions. He proposed a developmental sequence of strategies that children use for making judgments after witnessing such diverse behavior: (1) delete divergent qualities, (2) describe actions and make inferences based on a single aspect of behavior, (3) make inferences aimed at justifying divergent actions. In Gollin's sample of 10- to 17-year-olds, the younger children tended to use the first procedure and the older children tended to employ the more inferential procedures. Stein (1979b) has found a similar developmental progression in the strategies children use when recalling stories that contain characters who behave inconsistently. First-graders tend to delete character descriptions that are incongruous with the character's actions, whereas fifth-graders tend to add information that justifies the character's incongruous behavior.

A major difference between the findings of Gollin and of Stein is the age at which a particular strategy was used rather than the developmental sequence of strategies for dealing with the inconsistencies. A possible explanation for this difference highlights an important difference between films and stories: Character evaluations may be easier to make in the story context than in the film context, because stories can state information that must be implied in films. Stories may be easier to understand than films, because the causal connections among motives for behavior, goals, subsequent actions, and outcomes can be made explicit whereas they are often implicit in films and in actual social events.

This characteristic of stories as compared to films and actual social events makes stories effective instructional tools in social-skill training. For example, a story can state a protagonist's goal explicitly and the actions he or she takes may be purposively connected to that goal, as is illustrated in the following: *John wanted to be friendly, so he went to the playground and played with some boys.* The story states the reason for John's action of going to the playground. In a film or actual social event, it is likely that we would have only John's action as the basis for our inference about his motive. Asher and Renshaw (this volume) suggest that the success of at least one social-skill intervention using a film (O'Connor, 1969, 1972) may have been the result of the verbal narration that accompanied the film. From our perspective, the verbal narration of the O'Connor film (Gottman, cited in Asher & Renshaw, this volume) makes explicit the goals, thoughts, and affective reactions of the characters in the film and the causal connections between these internal states, the character's overt actions, and the consequences of those behaviors. We would further expect that other types of social-skill training procedures will be effective to the degree that causal connections among motives, goals, actions, and outcomes are made explicit. However, the theoretical perspective outlined in the first section of the paper carries with it an important qualification: Optimal intervention procedures are those that achieve a balance between the organization of new content information and the organization of the child's preexisting conceptual knowledge (e.g., Brown, 1975; Glaser, 1976).

Thus, if one wants to teach children how to be friendly, it is important first to assess children's understanding of friendship, including the ways they know how to be friendly. Such an assessment might show that the child knows many ways to be friendly but not the context in which the action will lead to the desired outcome. Asher and Renshaw's analysis (this volume) of why social-skill training is effective includes the possibility that children do not lack social skills but rather the knowledge of when particular social skills are appropriate. Knowledge of when particular social skills are appropriate encompasses other aspects of the concept of friendship, most importantly the child's concept of the conditions under which one might want to be friendly. The use of an action or social skill that will result in friendship presupposes that the child wants to be friendly. It would be informative to know if children who differ in popularity also differ in the personal and social situations in which they formulate the goal of wanting to be friendly. Possibly, isolated children differ from popular children with respect to their reasons for wanting to be friendly. These groups of children may also differ in the goals that they formulate in response to similar motivating states. For example, a popular child who feels lonely might formulate the goal of wanting to be friendly, whereas an isolated child who feels lonely might formulate the goal of wanting to be alone. These different goals would lead to the appropriateness and utilization of different actions. Therefore, descriptive accounts of children's understanding of the reasons for wanting to be friendly, in addition to their understanding of the actions that constitute being friendly, would help us understand the dynamics of popularity and isolation. A first step toward such a descriptive account is discussed in the next section.

Children's knowledge of friendship

Goldman (1978; in press) examined children's understanding of friendship by asking them to talk about their reasons for wanting to be friendly or unfriendly, actions they could take to attain each of these goals, and the conditions that could prevent them from attaining each goal. Goldman's primary concern was to describe the information and the organization of the information that constitutes conceptual knowledge of friendship for children of different ages. Although this research does not deal with popularity differences among children, the methods used for data collection and analysis can be extended to questions regarding such individual differences.

Children's knowledge of friendship was inferred from the language they used in talking about friendship. Previous research has investigated the language children use to describe their friends (Livesley & Bromley, 1973; Peevers & Secord, 1973) and their expectations about their best friends (Bigelow, 1977). These descriptions have shown that (1) there are developmental changes in the personality attributes that are salient to children (e.g., Livesley & Bromley, 1973); and (2) for the 6- to 14-year-old age range there are developmental changes in children's descriptions of what they expect their best friends to be like but there is also agreement that a best friend should provide ego reinforcement and reciprocity of liking (Bigelow, 1977). Both of these types of studies index part of the child's concept of friendship, because both focus on properties of the other person.

They do not, however, inquire about the child's own role in the interaction. The present research uses children's verbal descriptions of their own role in solving problems involving friendship to examine the nature of children's conceptual knowledge of friendship and the developmental changes in this knowledge.

The problem solutions children were asked to construct involved two goals: wanting to be friendly and not wanting to be friendly. In order to help the children organize their comments, two tasks were included in the interviews: a storytelling task and a probe-question task. In the storytelling task children were asked to produce a story in which they were the protagonist and had a particular goal that they met. Instructions for the Want-to-be-friendly condition were the following:

I want you to make up a story today. The story is about you. Suppose one day you decided, "I want to be friendly." Tell me a story where you *want* to be friendly and *are* friendly.

Following the production of the story, a series of probe questions were asked. These questions were used (1) to help minimize the effects of developmental differences in productive language skills on conclusions about the child's knowledge of friendship; and (2) systematically to elicit further discussion from the children about reasons for wanting to be friendly, the actions they would take to be friendly, and conditions they could anticipate that might prevent them from being friendly. The same instructions and set of probe questions were repeated at another point in the interview for the Not-want-to-be-friendly goal condition.

The storytelling instructions thus gave SETTING, Goal, and Consequence information that had to be included in the story and the probe questions requested content that could occur in other categories of the episodic structure of stories and social events. Reasons for setting the goal, or Motives, are causes of goal formulation. Motives typically occur at the beginning of a story as Initiating Events or Internal Responses to Initiating Events. Actions, or Attempts, convey information about how the protagonist solves the problem that was set up in the Initiating Event. Attempts are causes of goal attainment – the means to the end. Conditions that might prevent goal attainment, or Obstacles, typically occur as the Consequence of an action and often lead to additional Attempts to meet the goal. There is, therefore, a causal relationship between information in each of these three categories and either the Goal or the Consequence of the problem solution. The selection of these specific causal relations and the rationale for the form of the interview were based on analysis of previous proposals regarding problem solving (e.g., Klahr, 1978; Simon,

1975) and on previously reported developmental changes in the form of children's verbal narrations (Glenn & Stein, 1979; Menig-Peterson & McCabe, 1978).

Ten boys and ten girls at each of three age levels (ages 6, 9, and 12) were interviewed. The rationale and additional procedural details are more fully described in Goldman (1978; in press). The interviews were tape recorded and later transcribed. A content analysis was then done on the information in the protocols. The analysis of the protocol content involved classifying the statements in each child's protocol into a number of categories that represent different aspects of problem solving in social situations. The categories should be understood as plausible classes of conceptual knowledge relating to goal attainment in realistic, everyday situations. The categories that were used to classify information about friendship are shown in Table 11-1. Three major classes of information are represented: information about the protagonist, about the role of other people, and about aspects of the external environment. Within these major classes, a number of component categories were distinguished.

As can be seen in Table 11-1, the first major class is the protagonist's states and actions. Statements from the children's protocols were classified into one of the categories in this class if the statement described the protagonist's (the child's) internal states or overt actions. The categories distinguish among types of internal states and specific overt actions. Four internal states were distinguished: physical, affective and emotional, situational, and attitudinal. Statements were classified as situational states if they described other goals and ongoing activities that were concurrent with the friendship goal. Statements were classified as attitudinal states if they described feelings and attitudes toward friendliness, toward prospective friendship objects, or toward anticipated outcomes of being either friendly or unfriendly. Examples of each of these are, respectively, "It's nice to be friendly," "She looked like a nice kid," and (I wanted to be friendly) "so people would like me." The specific action category covers statements that describe friendly or unfriendly overt actions, including both direct actions and verbal actions. This category represents specific ways to be friendly: helping, sharing, playing, telling that you like the other person; or unfriendly: hitting, not helping, teasing, calling names. All of the categories in the first major class refer to some aspect of the child's own role in the friendship situation.

The second major class of information refers to the role of other people in friendship situations. Statements from the children's protocols that referred to the ways in which other people were involved in the friendship interaction were classified into this class. In so classifying statements, no

Table 11-1. *Categories of information about problem solving in friendship situations.*

Major classes and description	Categories within each class and examples
I Protagonist's states and actions Statements that convey information about the internal states, cognitive actions, verbal actions, and direct actions of the protagonist.	A Physical state – tiredness, sleepiness, hunger, thirst. B General emotional state – anger, fear, shame, happiness. C Situational states and ongoing activities – I was watching television, I want to be alone, I have to do homework. D Feelings about friendship, the friendship object, or anticipated outcome of attaining goal – I liked him; So I'll have a friend. E Specific actions and skill states for attaining the goal – playing, helping, hitting.
II Role of other people Statements that refer to the involvement of other people in the friendship situation. Component categories specify classes of other people that children's statements referred to.	A Role of parents and family members – Mom said to play with him; Mom didn't like this kid so I couldn't play with her. B Role of nonfamily, nondyad others – My other friends teased me when I played with the new girl. C Role of friendship object – The kid I wanted to be friendly with wouldn't share his toys; He didn't like me.
III Role of environment Statements that refer to the environmental availability and accessibility of resources, including objects, activities, instruments, and locations necessary for goal attainment.	A Availability of person to be friendly with – There were no kids around. B Availability of basis for friendship interaction – We couldn't agree on what to do; We decided to play Monopoly. C Availability of common location for interaction – I went up to his house; I couldn't go to the park with the other kids.

distinction was made among statements that described the direct actions, the verbal actions, or the internal states of others. Rather, the categories within this class distinguish among the types of persons that were involved. The first category refers to the role of parents and family members. The second category refers to the role of people outside of the friendship interaction and outside of the family. Peers not directly involved in an interaction can still have an effect on the protagonist's behavior. A statement illustrative of this category is (I didn't play with her) "because my other friends would laugh at me if I did." Statements that referred to the role of the person directly involved in the dyadic friendship interaction, the friendship object, were classified into the third category: (I couldn't be friendly with him) "because he always hit me," and "He was nice to me." Note that if the child's statement referred to a group of friends with whom he or she was interacting, the statement was classified into the category of role of friendship object: "My friends wanted me to play ball with them." The second major class, then, refers to the role played by other people.

The child and these other people exist in an environment, and the characteristics of this environment also affect friendship interactions. Accordingly, the third major class referred to the role of the environment. In order for a friendship interaction to occur, the environment must be conducive to such an interaction. The categories within this class distinguish among the availability of different types of environmental resources. Statements that referred to the presence or absence of potential friendship objects were classified into the category availability of person to be friendly with. An example is, "There were lots of kids my age." The child's attempts to meet a stranger were also scored in this category: "I asked him his name," and "I said 'Hi.'" These statements are similar to previous reports of the types of actions children propose as ways to make new friends (Gottman, Gonso, & Rasmussen, 1975). Such actions may change an available stranger into a person with whom to be friendly. The second category, availability of a basis for friendship interaction, refers to statements that describe an awareness of the need to agree on a common activity or attempts to establish a common interest or activity. Examples are (I wanted to be friendly with him) "because we both like to play football," and "I asked him if he wanted to play what I was playing." The final category, availability of a common location, refers to the fact that the participants in an interaction must be in proximity to one another: "I went up to his house," and "I called my friend on the telephone."

To reiterate, these categories represent different aspects of problem solving in friendship situations. Children's knowledge of these aspects of friendship was inferred from the results of classifying the statements in their protocols. Reliability in scoring the protocol statements was 90 percent (Goldman, 1978). Once the statements were classified, two questions were of primary interest: whether there were developmental differences in the content of the knowledge base (in the set of categories of knowledge associated with friendship), and whether there were developmental differences in the organization of the knowledge base (in the types of causal relations associated with a particular category and the goal situation).

To address these questions, the results of the statement classification were scored in two ways. To answer questions associated with the content of the knowledge base, a child received credit for a particular category if it occurred during any part of the interview – the causal relation of the category to the goal was ignored in the scoring. For example, a child could give the statement "I like him" as both a Motive for being friendly and as an Obstacle to not being friendly. For purposes of the knowledge-base content analysis, the child received the same credit as a child who gave the statement only as a Motive for being friendly. However, in describing the organization of the knowledge base, the causal relation was considered. In the preceding example, the first child received credit for both Motive and Obstacle relations; the second child received only Motive relation credit.

Content of the knowledge base for friendship interactions

A knowledge base is the set of information that an individual has acquired. A particular child's knowledge base for friendship interactions was described by the set of categories of conceptual knowledge that was inferred from the classification of his or her protocol statements. Within each grade, certain categories were present in the knowledge base of at least 90 percent, or 18, of the children. These were labeled Core categories. Other categories occurred in less than 80 percent of the children's protocols and were labeled Noncore categories. One way to describe the content characteristics of the knowledge base for each age group is to consider those categories in the Core subset and those in the Noncore subset. The Core subset is a highly frequent pattern of information within an age group. By considering the co-occurrence of Noncore categories with the Core subset, we can augment the description of the set of information that constitutes the knowledge base for an age group. Developmental changes in the knowledge base can be described by comparing Core subsets and Noncore subsets across age groups.

The knowledge base for friendship interactions for each age group is shown in Table 11-2. Developmental changes in the knowledge base were elaborative and systematic. The elaborative nature of developmental changes is illustrated by the categories in the Core subset. For the oldest children, the Core subset includes all of the categories that are in the Core subsets of the 9- and 6-year olds. The Core subset of the 9-year-olds includes all the categories that are in the Core subset of the 6-year-olds. Within each age group, Core includes the protagonist's specific actions and feelings about the friendship interaction and the role of the friendship object. Within the two groups of older children, Core also includes information about the availability of a common location. Only for the oldest children does Core include information about establishing a basis for a friendship interaction, for example, "I asked him if he liked to play football." This implies an increased awareness that shared interests facilitate the establishment of friendship and that the interests of others may differ from those of the self. Younger children may know that you play with a friend but are less aware of the need to match or establish common interests. For the oldest children, Core also included protagonist's situational state – other goals the protagonist has and other activities in which the protagonist might be engaged. This implies increased awareness that friendship may conflict with an individual's independence.

Table 11-2. *Knowledge base for friendship interactions for each age group.*

Age group: 6	9	12
Categories in Core subset		
Specific actions	Specific actions	Specific actions
Protagonist's feelings about friendship	Protagonist's feelings about friendship	Protagonist's feelings about friendship
Role of friendship object	Role of friendship object	Role of friendship object
	Availability of common location	Availability of common location
		Availability of basis for friendship
		Protagonist's situational state

	Probability of co-occurrence with Core		
	6	9	12
Categories in Noncore subset			
Protagonist's states			
Physical	.11	.21	.31
General emotional	.17	.58	.75
Situational	.67	.68	Core
Role of other people			
Role of parent and family	.33	.63	.63
Role of nondyad others	.33	.26	.75
Role of environment			
Availability of person	.61	.32	.63
Availability of basis for friendship	.39	.74	Core
Availability of common location	.61	Core	Core

The Core subset represents the information that most children in an age group have acquired. What most older children know about friendship was found to be additions to what most younger children know. Acquisition of these additions seems to be systematic. This is illustrated by the likelihood that a Noncore category co-occurs with the Core subset (reported in the lower half of Table 11-2). The likelihood or probability of co-occurrence describes the frequency with which each of the categories in the Noncore subset was mentioned by children who mentioned the Core subset. The critical point is that the most frequently co-occurring Noncore categories within each of the younger groups are those categories that are part of the Core subset for the next oldest group. For example, the Core subsets of the 9- and 12-year-olds differ by two categories, availability of basis for friendship and protagonist's situational state. For the 9-year-olds, the probability that each of these categories co-occurs with the Core subset is .74 and .68 respectively, higher than the probabilities associated with any of the other Noncore categories. Similarly, the difference between the Core subsets of the 9- and 6-year-olds is availability of common location. For the 6-year-olds, the probability is .61 that this category will co-occur with the Core subset. Thus, the acquisition of knowledge about friendship interactions seems to proceed in a systematic as well as an elaborative fashion.

One final aspect of the developmental changes in knowledge-base content has implications for social-skill training research. Within an age group, individual differences among age mates decrease as age increases. This is illustrated by the changes across age in the number of categories that meet the criterion for Core information. This point is further illustrated by the presence of a smaller range in the co-occurrence probabilities associated with the Noncore categories for the older age groups. For example, over 60 percent of the 12-year-olds mention the same information, with the exception of protagonist's physical state. In contrast, there is much less agreement among the youngest children, the range is from .17 to .67. What a younger child knows about friendship seems to be less predictable than what an older child knows. A relationship between differences in conceptual knowledge about friendship and differences in popularity might be more likely in younger than in older children. Asher (1977) has suggested that certain social-skill training procedures have been effective with younger children but not with older children. A possible explanation is that the cause of isolation or low popularity in younger children is different from that in older children and related to changes in variability in the knowledge base. Older children, regardless of popularity or isolation, may share the same knowledge base for friendship, whereas for younger children differences in the knowledge base may be correlated with differences in popularity. An appropriate focus for social-skill training with older children might be on the utilization of knowledge in different group contexts (see Putallaz & Gottman, this volume). A more appropriate focus with younger children may be on the acquisition of knowledge about friendship.

However, as we noted previously, optimal intervention requires the specification of what the child knows *plus* the specification of how that information is organized. The organization of information in the knowledge base for friendship interactions describes the relevance of the various categories of knowledge to three aspects of friendship: Motives for being friendly or unfriendly, Obstacles to being friendly or unfriendly, and Attempts or ways to be friendly or unfriendly. As discussed above, descriptions of information organization may lead to better understanding of children's comprehension of actual social events and stories about social events by allowing the prediction of the types of content and evaluative inferences children will make.

Organization of the knowledge base for friendship interactions

During the comprehension of episodically structured information, children must frequently make inferences about why particular actions occur. We assume that a primary source for making such inferences is the child's previously acquired knowledge about the event, including what the child knows about the reasons for formulating goals, ways to achieve particular goals, and conditions that might prevent goal attainment. Developmental differences in inferential reasoning may arise from differences in the way the content of the knowledge base is organized as well as from differences in the content per se. One way to conceptualize the organization of the knowledge base is in terms of the causal relation associated with particular content. Goldman (1978; in press) examined the previously discussed content categories in terms of three causal roles in friendship interactions: Motives are causes of goal formulation; Attempts are causes of goal attainment; and Obstacles are causes of failure to attain the goal.

The categories of information associated with each causal relation differed. These differences are informative in that they describe children's expectations about the content of Motives, Obstacles, and Attempts involved in friendship interactions. The mean probabilities of associating each category of information with each causal relation are shown in Table 11-3. The protagonist's physical, emotional, and situational states and his or her feelings toward the friendship interaction tend to motivate goal

Table 11-3. *Mean probability of Motive, Obstacle, and Attempt relation for each type of information.*[a]

	Motive	Obstacle	Attempt
Protagonist			
Physical state	.78[b]	.47[b]	0[b]
General emotional state	.89	.28	.03
Situation state	.74	.50	.14
Feelings toward friendship and friendship object	.95	.57	.12
Specific actions	.03	0	1.00
Role of other people			
Parent and family role	.64	.50	.06
Nondyad others' role	.47	.64	0
Friendship obejct's role	.71	.68	.98
Role of environment			
Availability of person to be friendly with	.36	.26	.89
Availability of basis for friendship	.04	.18	.94
Availability of common location	0	.13	.97

[a] Maximum frequency of occurrence is 60.
[b] Frequency of occurrence less than 15.

formulation, occasionally act as obstacles to goal attainment, and are rarely associated with Attempts to attain the goal. Not surprisingly, the protagonist's specific actions are almost always associated with the Attempt. The role of other people in the friendship interactions varies with the identity of the other. Parents and family members are associated with motivating conditions, whereas nondyad others (peers not involved in the particular interactions) are associated with both Motive and Obstacle relations. The friendship object's role is associated with all three types of causal relations. Finally, the role of the environment is associated almost exclusively with Attempts to be friendly or unfriendly.

Thus, children's view of their own role in a friendship interaction is that their own thoughts and feelings can motivate them to be friendly or unfriendly and there are specific actions that they can take to accomplish their goals. Few children see themselves as causing their own failure. However, the friendship object is seen as a potential obstacle to goal attainment. In addition, the friendship object shares the motivating and attempt role that the child associates with himself or herself. People outside of the friendship interaction are seen as motivators of friendly or unfriendly interactions and as obstacles to the child's goal attainment. Finally, attempts to attain friendship interactions involve satisfying the requisite environmental conditions.

One other aspect of these data is of particular relevance to social-skill training research and attempts to train problem-solving skills. There was a great deal of consistency within the sample with respect to the types of information associated with causes of goal attainment. In contrast, there was a great deal of variability in the types of conditions that were seen as obstacles to goal attainment. One indicator of social adjustment is the number of alternatives children produce to solve a particular problem (Spivack, Platt, & Shure, 1976). However, Ladd and Oden (1979) have not found a positive relationship between the number of ways children report to be helpful and sociometric ratings of popularity. The present data indicate that there may be potentially important individual differences in the nature of anticipated obstacles that would make alternative solutions necessary in the first place. It may be that the ability to foresee potential reasons for failing to be friendly or popular is a more important predictive factor than is the ability to list a number of ways to be friendly.

In general, developmental differences in the organization of knowledge bases for friendship interactions were associated primarily with the number of different categories reported for each causal relation. These data are shown in Table 11-4. The youngest children associated fewer categories of information with each type of causal relation. These results imply more variability in the content of inferences made by older children than by younger children. Furthermore, children tend to associate a greater variety of information – a larger number of categories, with Attempts to be friendly or unfriendly than with either Motives or Obstacles to friendship interactions. This tendency appears to decrease with age and indi-

Table 11-4. *Mean number of different categories mentioned as Motives, Obstacles, or Attempts for each age group.*

	Age		
Type of causal relation	6	9	12
Motive	2.7	3.4	4.6
Obstacle	2.1	2.8	3.0
Attempts	3.4	4.3	4.6

cates that older children expect as much variability in Motives for friendship interactions as in Attempts to be friendly or unfriendly. The implication of this result is that older children may be able to understand the behavior of others in a greater range of situations than younger children.

There were few developmental differences in which categories of information were associated with each causal relation. These results show that known categories play similar causal roles for children of different ages. Developmental differences in understanding friendship interactions arise more from differences in knowledge-base content than from differences in organization of knowledge-base content. The knowledge base for younger children contains fewer information categories than the knowledge base for older children. If a category is in the knowledge base, however, its causal role is the same at all ages. Increases in children's knowledge of the information categories relevant to friendship interactions reflect a more elaborated and complex understanding of friendship. This development allows the understanding of friendship behavior across a greater variety of people and situations.

Summary and conclusions

We have attempted to show how models of story comprehension and models of problem solving in social situations are consistent with the same theoretical perspective on the nature of the understanding process. Both domains share the assumption that actions are understood to be intentionally based and that competent comprehension requires the construction of causal inferences among events. The episodic structure of events was discussed as a common link among research efforts in story comprehension, social-cognitive development, and social-skill training. Furthermore, we pointed out the importance of assessing children's conceptual knowledge of problem solving in social situations. This knowledge is the source of the child's content and evaluative inferences during comprehension of stories and actual social events. Finally, we discussed some research aimed at assessing developmental changes in children's conceptual knowledge about friendship. Changes in the content of the knowledge base were systematic and of an elaborative nature. This type of research methodology and content analysis seems to be a useful approach to describing children's knowledge. Furthermore, this type of approach can potentially lead to predictive models of comprehension that account for developmental and individual differences in the understanding of problem-solving behavior, whether that behavior occurs in stories or in everyday social interactions.

References

Anderson, R. C. Schema-directed processes in language comprehension. In A. Lesgold, J. Pellegrino, S. Fokkema, & R. Glaser (Eds.), *Cognitive psychology and instruction.* New York: Plenum Press, 1978.

Applebee, A. N. *The child's concept of story, ages two to seventeen.* Chicago, Ill.: University of Chicago Press, 1978.

Asher, S. R. *Coaching socially isolated children in social skills.* Paper presented at the annual meeting of the Association for Advancement of Behavior Therapy, Atlanta, 1977.

Bearison, D. J. & Isaacs, L. Production deficiency in children's moral judgments. *Developmental Psychology,* 1975, *11*, 732–737.

Berg-Cross, L. G. Intentionality, degree of damage, and moral judgments. *Child Development,* 1975, *46*, 970–974.

Bigelow, B. Children's friendship expectations: A cognitive-developmental study. *Child Development,* 1977, *48*, 246–253.

Botvin, G. J., & Sutton-Smith, B. The development of structural complexity in children's fantasy narratives. *Developmental Psychology,* 1977, *13*, 377–388.

Bransford, J. D., & McCarrell, N. S. A sketch of a cognitive approach to comprehension: Some thoughts about what it means to comprehend. In W. B. Weimer & D. S. Palermo (Eds.), *Cognition and the symbolic processes.* Hillsdale, N.J.: Erlbaum, 1974.

Brown, A. L. The development of memory: Knowing, knowing about knowing and knowing how to know. In H. W. Reese (Ed.), *Advances in child development and behavior* (Vol. 10). New York: Academic Press, 1975.

Brown, J. S., Collins, A., & Harris, G. Artificial intelligence and learning strategies. In H. O'Neil (Ed.), *Learning strategies.* New York: Academic Press, 1978.

Damon, W. Early conceptions of positive justice as related to the development of logical operations. *Child Development,* 1975, *46*, 301–312.

DeCharms, R. *Personal causation.* New York: Academic Press, 1968.

Flapan, D. *Children's understanding of social interaction.* New York: Teachers College Press, 1968.

Frederiksen, C. H. Structure and process in discourse production and comprehension. In M. A. Just & P. A. Carpenter (Eds.), *Cognitive processes in discourse comprehension.* Hillsdale, N.J.: Erlbaum, 1977.

Glaser, R. Components of a psychology of instruction: Toward a science of design. *Review of Educational Research,* 1976, *46*, 1–24.

Glenn, C. G., & Stein, N. L. *Syntactic structures and real world themes in children's generated stories.* Unpublished manuscript, University of Illinois, Urbana, 1979.

Goldman, S. R., *Children's semantic knowledge systems for realistic goals.* Unpublished Ph.D. dissertation, University of Pittsburgh, Pittsburgh, Pa., 1978.
Knowledge systems for realistic goals. *Discourse Processes,* in press.

Gollin, E. S. Organizational characteristics of social judgment: A developmental investigation. *Journal of Personality,* 1958, *26*, 139–154.

Gottman, J., Gonso, J., & Rasmussen, B. Social interaction, social competence and friendship in children. *Child Development,* 1975, *46*, 709–718.

Greeno, J. G. Process of understanding in problem solving. In N. J. Castellan, D. B. Pisoni, & G. R. Potts (Eds.), *Cognitive theory* (Vol. 2), Hillsdale, N.J.: Erlbaum, 1977.

Grueneich, R., & Trabasso, T. The story as a social environment: Children's comprehension and evaluation of intentions and consequences. In J. Harvey (Ed.), *Cognition, social behavior and the environment.* Hillsdale, N.J.: Erlbaum, in press.

Heider, F. *The psychology of interpersonal relations.* New York: Wiley, 1958.

Jones, E., & Davis, K. From acts to dispositions. In L. Berkowitz (Ed.), *Advances in experimental social psychology* (Vol. 2). New York: Academic Press, 1965.

Kelley, H. The processes of causal attribution. *American Psychologist,* 1973, *28,* 107–128.

Kintsch, W. *The representation of meaning in memory.* New York: Wiley, 1974.

On comprehending stories. In M. A. Just & P. A. Carpenter (Eds.), *Cognitive processes in comprehension.* Hillsdale, N.J.: Erlbaum, 1977.

Kintsch, W., Mandel, T. S., & Kozminsky, E. Summarizing scrambled stories. *Memory & Cognition,* 1977, *5,* 547–552.

Kintsch, W., & van Dijk, T. A. Recalling and summarizing stories. *Languages,* 1975, *40,* 98–116.

Toward a model of text comprehension and production. *Psychological Review,* 1978, *85,* 363–394.

Klahr, D. Goal formulation, planning and learning by preschool problem solvers. In R. Siegler (Ed.), *Children's thinking: What develops?* Hillsdale, N.J.: Erlbaum, 1978.

Ladd, G. W., & Oden, S. The relationship between peer acceptance and children's ideas about helpfulness. *Child Development,* 1979, *50,* 402–408.

Livesley, W. J., & Bromley, D. B. *Person perception in childhood and adolescence.* London: Wiley, 1973.

Mandler, J. N., & Johnson, N. S. Remembrance of things parsed: Story structure and recall. *Cognitive Psychology,* 1977, *9,* 111–151.

Menig-Peterson, C., & McCabe, A. Children's orientation of a listener to the context of their narrations. *Developmental Psychology,* 1978, *14,* 582–592.

Newell, A., & Simon, H. A. *Human problem solving.* Englewood Cliffs, N.J.: Prentice-Hall, 1972.

Nezworski, M. T., Stein, N. L., & Trabasso, T. *Story structure versus content effects on children's recall and evaluative inferences.* Paper presented at the Psychonomic Society Meetings, San Antonio, Texas, November, 1978.

O'Connor, R. D. Modification of social withdrawal through symbolic modeling. *Journal of Applied Behavior Analysis,* 1969, *2,* 15–22.

Relative efficacy of modeling, shaping, and the combined procedures for the modification of social withdrawal. *Journal of Abnormal Psychology,* 1972, *79,* 327–334.

Peevers, B. H., & Secord, P. F. Developmental changes in attribution of descriptive concepts to persons. *Journal of Personality and Social Psychology,* 1973, *27,* 120–128.

Perfetti, C. A., & Lesgold, A. M. Discourse comprehension and sources of individual differences. In M. A. Just & P. A. Carpenter (Eds.), *Cognitive processes in discourse comprehension.* Hillsdale, N.J.: Erlbaum, 1977.

Piaget, J. *Biology and knowledge: An essay on the relations between organic regulations and cognitive processes.* Beatrix Walsh (Trans.). Chicago, Ill.: University of Chicago Press, 1971.

The psychology of intelligence. Totowa, N.J.: Littlefield, Adams, 1968.

Piaget, J., & Inhelder, B. *The psychology of the child.* New York: Basic Books, 1969.

Rumelhart, D. E. Notes on a schema for stories. In D. G. Bobrow & A. Collins (Eds.), *Representation and understanding: Studies in cognitive science.* New York: Academic Press, 1975.

Toward an interactive model of reading. In S. Dornic & P. M. A. Rabbit (Eds.), *Attention and performance VI.* Hillsdale, N.J.: Erlbaum, 1977. (a)

Understanding and summarizing stories. In D. LaBerge & S. J. Samuels (Eds.), *Basic processes in reading: Perception and comprehension.* Hillsdale, N.J.: Erlbaum, 1977. (b)

Rumelhart, D. E., & Ortony, A. The representation of knowledge in memory. In R. C. Anderson, R. J. Spiro, & W. E. Montague (Eds.), *Schooling and the acquisition of knowledge.* Hillsdale, N.J.: Erlbaum, 1977.

Schmidt, C. F. Understanding human action: Recognizing the plans and motives of other persons. In J. S. Carroll & J. W. Payne (Eds.), *Cognition and social behavior*. Hillsdale, N.J.: Erlbaum, 1976.

Selman, R. L., & Byrne, D. F. A structural-developmental analysis of levels of role taking in middle childhood. *Child Development*, 1974, *45*, 803–806.

Shantz, C. U. The development of social cognition. In E. M. Hetherington (Eds.), *Review of child development research* (Vol. 5). Chicago, Ill.: University of Chicago Press, 1975.

Simon, H. A. The functional equivalence of problem-solving skills. *Cognitive Psychology*, 1975, *7*, 268–288.

Spivack, G., Platt, J. J., & Shure, M. B. *The problem-solving approach to adjustment*. San Francisco: Jossey-Bass, 1976.

Stein, N. L. The comprehension and appreciation of stories: A developmental analysis. In S. Madeja (Ed.), *The arts and cognition* (Vol. 2). St. Louis: CEMREL, 1978.

How children understand stories: A developmental analysis. In L. G. Katz (Ed.), *Current topics in early childhood education* (Vol. 2). Hillsdale, N.J.: Ablex, 1979. (a)

The concept of a story: A developmental-psycholinguistic analysis. Paper presented at the American Educational Research Association Meetings, San Francisco, March, 1979. (b)

Stein, N. L., & Glenn, C. G. An analysis of story comprehension in elementary-school children. In R. O. Freedle (Ed.), *New directions in discourse processing* (Vol. 2). Hillsdale, N.J.: Ablex, 1979.

Stein, N. L., & Nezworski, M.T. The effect of organization and instructional set on story memory. *Discourse Processes*, 1978, *1*, 177–193.

van Dijk, T. A. Semantic macro-structures and knowledge frames in discourse comprehension. In M. A. Just & P. A. Carpenter (Eds.), *Cognitive processes in comprehension*. Hillsdale, N.J.: Erlbaum, 1977.

12 Social-cognitive processes in children's friendships

Carol S. Dweck

It is clear from these chapters that rapid progress is being made in understanding children's friendships. Perhaps more important than the knowledge gleaned thus far has been the development of more sophisticated methodologies and conceptual frameworks within which research on friendships can proceed. These chapters are noteworthy in yet another respect. They represent diverse approaches to the study of the social-cognitive processes involved in peer relationships, and it is this diversity that is a discussant's delight. Thus the focus of the present discussion will be the different approaches and their implications for future work in the area.

First, with full knowledge that generalizations will not do justice to the richness of the approaches, but with the belief that they will aid in the generation of new ideas, I will characterize briefly the two main approaches exemplified in these chapters. Then I will address, again quite briefly, research suggested by joint consideration of the two approaches. Finally, I will discuss at some length several important issues that fall outside the realm of the current approaches and that require another view of the role of social-cognitive processes in children's friendships.

Social-cognitive approaches

Although all four chapters in Part II represent a social-cognitive approach to children's friendships, they represent two different traditions or research strategies within the study of social cognition. They may be distinguished by whether they place their primary emphasis on behavior or on cognitions: on the observable antecedents and consequences of social cognitions or on the social cognitions themselves.

For the purpose of this discussion, I will refer to two of the chapters as falling within the social-learning/behavioral tradition (Corsaro; Asher and Renshaw). These papers ask: What do children do, and is it appropriate to the setting in which they find themselves? Are they successful in meeting the demands of their environments? The two chapters within the cognitive-developmental tradition (Stein and Goldman; Selman) are also concerned with competence, but competence defined with regard to the cognitively mature individual. Here a child is viewed as moving through levels of understanding. The first step of the researcher in this tradition is to determine how this understanding changes with age; a later step is to see how this understanding relates to social context and social behavior.

Let us suppose that members of each tradition were to examine social cognition in a given social context. They would be likely to pinpoint quite different cognitions. For example, those within the social-learning tradition would tend to view social context as the primary determinant of social cognitions and therefore might be most interested in examining those cognitions that were clearly linked to environmental contingencies. Those within the cognitive-developmental tradition would tend more to view social cognition and changes in it as the causes of changes in social structure and social behavior. Because the latter tend to begin with cognition, they are more likely to use concepts and conceptualizations that are similar to those used in the analysis of general cognitive development.

If the representatives of these two traditions were to team up, they would inevitably generate a number of intriguing questions. For example, researchers in the social-learning tradition imply that the more skillful the child the higher will be his or her sociometric status. Yet the amalgamation of the two frameworks leads one to consider cases in which the most skilled (i.e. most mature) children might find themselves numbered among the isolates. That is, the work within the cognitive-developmental tradition suggests that perhaps a match between cognitive levels might make for the best friendships. It is apparent that a more mature child might find the concerns of a less mature child to be uninteresting, but the converse is also likely to be the case. This means that children who are in advance of their years and who seek psychological intimacy and support or mutual psychological growth from relationships not only may reject their childish peers but also may be rejected by them for their "inappropriate" behavior.

Joint consideration of the social-learning and cognitive-developmental traditions also lead one to ask in what way changing conceptions of friendship influence what social skills are important. As Asher and Renshaw suggest, the skills that make for a popular child in the early school years do not ensure popularity later on. Although concrete helping, sharing, and cooperation are desirable at any age, a more elaborate set of subtle psychological skills is required of older children. Moreover, the particular skills required for popularity among older children may become more peer-group specific. It may be the case that rather similar social-skill training is effective for diverse groups of younger children, but that for older children skill training needs to be tailored to the specific characteristics prized by the child's group. Indeed, what may win points in one subculture may be life endangering in another.

Beyond reasoning and social skills

Although each approach has already contributed a great deal and although cooperation would promise even more, there are important issues that remain outside their joint domain. These issues relate to individual differences and to group differences in social cognition. To the extent that successful friendships require fine tuning among the participants, especially as children become older, it becomes critical to consider these systematic differences. It is important to note that such differences may be entirely independent of development level and of social-skill level.

Let us examine, then, two instances in which the social problems or unsatisfactory relationships that children experience do not stem from immaturity or from skill deficits in the usual sense. One is a group difference (e.g., sex or ethnic group) that stems from often subtle differences in values, goals, and expectations. The other is an individual difference in children's ability to cope with interpersonal problems that stems from their cognitions about their social failures.

Group differences

Earlier it was suggested that a match in level of reasoning might facilitate friendships. In this section, we will consider differences within level. Specifically, individuals who belong to different groups may be matched in level of friendship reasoning but not, for example, in the specific goals, values, and social behavior patterns they bring to a relationship. That is, they may agree on the meaning and functions of friendships but may differ on the definition of the critical attributes of that level (what is meant by intimacy, independence, etc.), on values or goals within that level (for example, the degree to which they value and wish to cultivate deep understanding of unverbalized feelings), on appropriate ways of expressing their values, or on appropriate behavior for realizing their goals.

These differences may lead to an individual's inability to take the other person's perspective, even when they are eager to realize mutual goals. The term "perspective-taking" denotes seeing a situation through the eyes of others and thereby understanding how *they* are responding to it.

However, perspective-taking as it is typically understood involves the simpler process of imagining how one would respond *oneself* in that situation. This is more akin to projection than to true perspective-taking. Of course, the more similar two individuals are, the more the two processes would functionally merge. However, when there are systematic differences among individuals projection would lead to erroneous conclusions.

In many instances, the individual will not realize the failure of his or her perspective-taking, for there are many factors that conspire to create the illusion of shared perspectives. For example, a person's ability to take the perspective of others may have been validated continually within that person's group so that it might not even occur to him or her that there are plausible alternative viewpoints. Indeed such slogans as "We're all brothers under the skin" promote a denial of deep-seated differences in the structuring of experience that result from the differing socialization experiences of different groups. Moreover, individuals from different groups often use the same terms to mean quite different things, thus fostering the idea that they have communicated more precisely than they actually have. When one assumes greater similarity than is warranted, behavior that differs from one's own might be judged rather harshly. The other's behavior may be judged as though that person understood your goals and values, but deliberately chose to defy them or as though the person did not have the ability either to understand or achieve your goals.

A particularly striking example of this phenomenon is one that is usually taken for granted as "natural" – the self-segregation of the two sexes, beginning in the preschool or early grade school years and generally lasting until adolescence. This alienation between boys and girls is so predictable that researchers studying children's friendships in the grade school years often compute only same-sex sociometric measures. Although there is always much consternation surrounding the segregation of racial or ethnic groups within classrooms, few people are disturbed by the segregation of the sexes. Those who train social skills in children of this age are relatively unconcerned with promoting greater cross-sex popularity. One reason for this lack of concern may be adults' belief that the rift will inevitably disappear as cross-sex relationships develop naturally later on. However it can be argued that:

1. From a very early age, boys and girls form their own quite different and separate cultures. They appear to be developing different interests, values, and goals that relate to activities they will engage in and persons with whom they will associate.

2. With segregation, the two cultures become increasingly divergent. Girls and boys develop different ways of structuring their worlds and of

acting on it and reacting to it. Moreover, they will develop skills in different domains.

3. Despite the reunion that takes place later, these important differences remain and can create obstacles to successful relationships.

4. Early social-skill training in a new kind of perspective-taking may be a valuable way of promoting many types of cross-cultural understanding and communication.

How does this segregation begin? From evidence culled from a variety of sources (e.g., Gilligan, 1979; Lever, 1978; Luria, 1980; Maccoby & Jacklin, 1974; Whiting & Edwards, 1973), the following scenario can be constructed: In the preschool years, girls become interested in prosocial behavior – in complying with and propagating social regulations. This they do in a rather rigid, absolute manner. Because boys do not conform to the standards of obedience, cleanliness, and orderliness that girls wish to uphold, girls begin to find it unpleasant to associate with them. It can by hypothesized that girls are the initial rejectors, but as boys develop their own culture, they become the more vociferous rejectors.

In this fashion, different cultures begin. Girls engage primarily in small-group games in small spaces, games that allow them to practice and refine social rules and roles directly. Boys engage in larger-group games that are more physically active and wide ranging. These games tend to have a more extensive set of explicit rules within which the participants work (or play) toward an explicitly defined goal. The games also tend to be competitive. Girls thus learn about close personal relationships. They learn to read and respond to subtle verbal and nonverbal cues within the context of socially prescribed rules, rules that often are implicit and difficult to articulate. Boys learn to act within and upon a larger system – to articulate long-range goals and to work actively toward achieving them. They can pay less attention to giving and receiving subtle cues that relate to emotional states.

I am proposing, then, that early differences in values and interests lead to differing experiences and eventually to different world views and areas of competence. These differences have profound consequences for all phases of children's lives: their achievement orientations, their interpersonal relationships, their self-concepts. Thus two children who are at the same level of reasoning, who are both highly skilled socially and adept at perspective-taking within their groups, may not be able to take each other's perspectives and to relate to each other successfully.

Similar problems may occur across racial or ethnic groups. Children may judge other children within their own framework and find that they fail to meet their standards. Here too, perspective-taking that involves projecting oneself into another's situation may yield misleading judgments. What must be learned, then, is first, that another's perspective may differ from what yours (or that of others like you) would be in that situation; and second, that other perspectives may be valid given different frameworks. Thus the strategy that is implied for promoting intergroup relationships is one that stresses the multiplicity of interpretations for any event and that interests children in understanding behavior that differs from what theirs would be. This is not to suggest that children *must* be friends with those who have different views, values, or interests, but that an informed choice is preferable to an uninformed one.

Individual differences: learned helplessness

Like the group differences discussed above, there are individual differences in cognitive style that are independent of skills and reasoning. These stylistic variables may inhibit a display of skills by prompting avoidance or withdrawal or by impairing performance in social situations. A particularly important stylistic variable may be the means children employ to cope with setbacks in interpersonal situations. In this section, I will describe our findings on learned helplessness and mastery orientation in achievement situations and then discuss the applicability of this analysis to children's social relationships.

We have identified two distinct patterns of reaction to challenges in intellectual problem-solving situations (Diener & Dweck, 1978, 1980; Dweck, 1975; Dweck & Reppucci, 1973). When failure, confusion, or difficulties occur, some children (learned helpless) rather quickly give up. Their effort wanes and their problem-solving strategies deteriorate. In contrast, other children (mastery-oriented) become increasingly engaged with the task. Their efforts are intensified as they attempt new strategies for achieving success. Yet these children are not smarter or more adept at our tasks than the helpless ones. We have found that each of these two responses is accompanied by a highly predictable set of cognitions and affective reactions. First, children who show deterioration of performance in the face of failure interpret their failure differently than do mastery-oriented children. They tend to attribute failure to factors beyond their control, such as a lack of ability. The implications of such an attribution for future success and for the child's sense of competence are discouraging. Specifically, it implies for the child that future efforts are unlikely to be fruitful and that, in fact, the more effort that is applied, the more negatively does failure reflect on this competence. The term "learned helplessness" refers to this belief that one's failures are insurmountable.

Children who maintain or improve their performance under failure tend to place different interpretations on these failures. First, they are far less likely to see themselves as having failed at all. They instead view difficulties as temporary obstacles or minor setbacks or even welcome them as opportunities to demonstrate or develop their abilities. Second, when they are asked to interpret the causes of the failures or difficulties they experience, they attribute them to changeable factors such as lack of effort or bad luck. These attributions imply that persistence or the attempt to find new strategies for problem solving are likely to be fruitful. Thus, changes in performance under failure are related to attributions for failure. Moreover, we have found that if we alter a helpless child's attributions for failure (from lack of ability to lack of effort), we can make the child's response to failure more mastery oriented. In fact, following such "attribution retraining" the formerly helpless children generally showed *improved* performance after failure (Dweck, 1975).

The difference between the helpless and mastery-oriented responses to failure is perhaps best conveyed by describing the different processes that are triggered by failure. In several studies, we asked children to verbalize their thoughts while performing a task on which they initially succeeded and then experienced difficulty (e.g., Diener & Dweck, 1978). The children were told that all statements, task-relevant or task-irrelevant, were welcome. The verbalizations of the helpless and mastery-oriented children did not differ prior to failure, but as soon as the children confronted the more difficult problems dramatic differences emerged. Helpless children seemed to focus on themselves and to ruminate about their plight. Specifically, they soon began attributing failure to unchangeable personal characteristics such as lack of ability. They began to express negative affect toward the task, which they had enjoyed a great deal only shortly before, and to express a desire to withdraw from the situation. This, of course, was accompanied by a serious deterioration in the sophistication of their strategy use. The mastery-oriented children, in marked contrast, tended not to make attributions at all. When we directly asked for attributions, mastery-oriented children attributed their failures to lack of effort, but when we tapped only spontaneous verbalizations, they did not orient toward causes of failure. Instead, they mobilized their resources to plan strategies for attaining success. They engaged in a good deal of constructive self-instruction and self-monitoring and expressed continual optimism that they would shortly be successful. What is more, a number of mastery-oriented children expressed greater interest in and enjoyment of the task now that it posed a greater challenge. In line with this, master-oriented children tended to maintain or even increase the sophistication of their problem-solving strategies over the failure trials. It should be reemphasized that the difference between the helpless and mastery-oriented children is not that of possessing or not possessing the requisite skills but of displaying those skills when they are called into question.

It is inevitable that children will meet with rejection in social situations and that they will encounter obstacles in attempting to form friendships. It appears reasonable to assume that the cognitions and affect that precede, accompany, and follow such events will be critical in determining how the child copes with these setbacks, just like in achievement situations. In line with what we have found in achievement situations, there may well be a syndrome of helplessness and mastery orientation that occurs in social situations. Helpless children are quicker to perceive rejection and to attribute it to factors beyond their control, and to withdraw from the situation or exhibit deterioration of social performance if required to remain in the situation. In addition, helpless children are characterized by a focus on their own distress and by ruminations about their competence as well as by a negative prognosis of their eventual acceptance. In contrast, mastery-oriented children are less apt to interpret the behavior of others as signifying rejection, but if they do, and choose to pursue the relationship, they seek constructive means of rectifying the situation. Even if the situation did not yield to their efforts, they would still be less likely to see the failure as a condemnation of their likeability or as signifying the inevitability of future rejections.

The potential utility of this analysis is highlighted when it is viewed in the context of past work on children's interpersonal coping and peer relationships. Most previous investigations have neglected the role of perceptions of control and have concentrated instead on cognitive and social skills, with the assumption that problems in coping must primarily result from deficits in these skills (Allen, Hart, Buell, Harris, & Wolf, 1964; Baer & Wolf, 1970; Keller & Carlson, 1974; O'Connor, 1969, 1972). Yet programs that have focused on skill or overt behavior alone have not reliably promoted or maintained effective peer relationships. The most effective programs have been the ones that appear to be teaching the contingency between the child's actions and the social outcomes he or she experiences (see Gottman, Gonso, & Schuler, 1976; Oden & Asher, 1977).

Focusing on perception of control over aversive outcomes brings to the fore a number of important possibilities not addressed by earlier researchers, who considered only rejected and isolated children and implicitly assumed that popular ones were free of potentially serious problems in interpersonal coping. However, just as learned helplessness in achievement situations appears to be unrelated to competence, responses to negative social outcomes may be less closely related to social skills than one might expect: Popular as well as unpopular individuals may have coping problems. For instance, some popular children may interpret their few experiences with social rebuff as indications of permanent rejection not open to change by their actions, paralleling the student who attributes a single low grade to lack of ability, despite all previous evidence to the contrary. Moreover, it may be that some children are isolated not because they lack knowledge about appropriate behavior but because they fear or have experienced social rejection and view it as insurmountable.

As a first step in evaluating the applicability of this helplessness analysis to social situations, Goetz and Dweck (1980) examined children's attributions for social rejection and their ability to cope constructively with social rebuffs. In other words, we sought to determine whether attributions would predict coping patterns in social situations as they do in academic and intellectual ones. In order to tap causal attributions for social rejection, a questionnaire was developed that depicted a series of hypothetical social situations in which children are either rejected or accepted by same-sex peers. Responses on this measure were then related to responses in a situation in which each child dealt with potential social rejection by a peer of the same sex. In this way, we could determine whether causal attributions that imply difficulty in surmounting rejection are in fact associated with deterioration of social behavior in the face of rejection.

In the questionnaire, children were presented with instances of rejection and were asked to evaluate a list of reasons the rejection may have occurred. Both the situations and their causes were selected as the most representative of those generated by children in the course of extensive interviews. (For example: "Suppose you move into a new neighborhood. A girl you meet does not like you very much. Why would this happen to you?") The reasons include such factors as personal ineptitude, a characteristic of the rejector, chance, misunderstandings, and a mutual mismatch of temperaments or preferences.

Just as failure attributions to some factors, such as effort, imply surmountability, so would rejection attributions to misunderstanding. Similarly, attributing rejection to one's lack of ability implies a relatively enduring outcome, as would an ability attribution for an academic failure.

Given the parallel implications of interpersonal and intellectual attributions, one would also expect parallel reactions.

The results from the questionnaire indicate marked individual differences in the causes to which children attribute social rejection. To test the hypothesized relationship between attributions and responses to rejection, a method of sampling each child's interpersonal strategies both before and after social rejection was devised. Children tried out for a pen-pal club. They formulated a sample getting-to-know-you letter (a first letter to a pen pal), which was the basis for the acceptance decision. The child was told that the letter should convey "the kind of person you are" and that when she or he was ready the letter would be recorded for transmission to a peer evaluator, who was said to represent the pen-pal committee. Shortly after the child recorded the letter the experimenter appeared to receive a message (via her headphones) from the evaluator and relayed the evaluator's initial decision to the child – in this case, not to admit the child into the club. To assess the effect of the evaluation on subsequent responses, the child was told that he or she had a chance to try again to send another message to the same evaluator. A short while after the second communication, enthusiastic acceptance was relayed to the child, and his or her home address was recorded to place on file for the club. (Pen pals were actually obtained for all children in the study.)

These prerejection and postrejection communications were then rated by trained, independent judges along a number of dimensions designed to reflect the child's strategy for attaining acceptance and to reveal alterations in strategy. As with the attribution measure, the results show that there are striking differences in strategies for coping with interpersonal rejection. Responses ranged from mastery-oriented patterns, with more and different strategies used after rejection, to complete withdrawal: About 10 percent of the children could not formulate a second message to the rejecting evaluator, even after gentle prodding and prompting. Only after the experimenter explicitly attributed the rejection to an idiosyncrasy of the committee member would these children produce a message for a different evaluator, which enabled us to provide acceptance feedback.

Furthermore, the results supported our analysis: The coping strategies were indeed related to attributions for rejection. Most striking was the finding that those children who showed disruption in their attempts to gain social approval (giving up entirely or failing to alter their message appreciably on the second round) were the ones who emphasized on the questionnaire personal incompetence as the cause of rejection, regardless of their level of popularity. (It should be noted that children who scored low on measures of popularity were somewhat more likely than those who scored high to emphasize attributions to personal incompetence, but, as reported, across popularity levels these attributions were linked with little constructive change in strategy.) Moreover, this disruption occurred even though their original messages were equivalent in length and quality to those of the children who coped more effectively.

The fact that the relationship between incompetence attributions and maladaptive response to rejection was found regardless of the popularity level of the rejected individual suggests that popularity alone is not a sufficient index of a child's social adjustment. Any adequate definition of social adjustment or social skills must include the ability to cope with and surmount adversity and to resolve conflicts. Retreat from such situations or incapacitation in their presence will have a number of undesirable consequences and may well limit the range of an individual's social, academic, and professional success.

Conclusion

The advent of social cognition in the study of children's friendships has had many exciting repercussions. Yet few researchers have addressed what appears to be a major question: What is unique about *social* skills and *social* cognitions? Of course, one need not answer this question to justify the study of social skills and cognition. Certainly the centrality of the social domain in children's lives justifies its study on purely pragmatic grounds. And yet this centrality suggests that social skills and social cognitions may differ in important and interesting ways from skills and cognitions that are not social. For example, compared to more purely intellectual skills, they may differ in their primary mode of transmission, in the kind and amount of practice involved, in the explicitness with which rules are articulated, and in how context-specific such rules tend to be. It is likely that social cognition does deserve a privileged status, but it is from answers to questions like these that this status will be earned.

Nonetheless, the study of social cognition has provided a bridge between research traditions that were formerly rather distinct, to the great advantage of each. For example, those in the cognitive-developmental tradition are now more likely to ask how their measures of reasoning relate to indexes of social skills or popularity; those in the social-learning tradition are now more likely to search for the cognitive underpinnings of the behaviors they study and train. Moreover, systematic individual and group differences may be explored within each framework and may provide further grounds for the integration of the two. The future of this field clearly promises many intriguing and important findings.

Social-cognitive processes in children's friendships
Social-cognitive processes in children's friendships 333

References

Allen, K. E., Hart, B., Buell, J. S., Harris, F. R., & Wolf, M. M. Effects of social reinforcement of isolate behavior of a nursery-school child. *Child Development*, 1964, *35*, 511–518.
Baer, D. M., & Wolf, M. M. Recent examples of behavior modification in preschool settings. In C. Neuringer & J. L. Michael (Eds.), *Behavior modification in clinical psychology*. New York: Appleton-Century-Crofts, 1970.
Diener, C. I., & Dweck, C. S. An analysis of learned helplessness: Continuous changes in performance, strategy, and achievement cognitions following failure. *Journal of Personality and Social Psychology*, 1978, *36*, 451–462.
An analysis of learned helplessness (II): The processing of success. *Journal of Personality and Social Psychology*, 1980, *39*, 940–952.
Dweck, C. S. The role of expectations and attributions in the alleviation of learned helplessness. *Journal of Personality and Social Psychology*, 1975, *31*, 674–685.
Dweck, C. S., & Repucci, N. D. Learned helplessness and reinforcement responsibility in children. *Journal of Personality and Social Psychology*, 1973, *25*, 109–116.
Gilligan, C. Woman's place in man's life cycle. *Harvard Educational Review*, 1979, *41*, 431–446.
Goetz, T. E., & Dweck, C. S. Learned helplessness in social situations. *Journal of Personality and Social Psychology*, 1980, *39*, 246–255.
Gottman, J., Gonso, J., & Schuler, P. Teaching social skills to isolated children. *Journal of Abnormal Child Psychology*, 1976, *4*, 179–197.
Keller, M. F., & Carlson, P. M. The use of symbols modeling to promote social skills in preschool children with low levels of social responsiveness. *Child Development*, 1974, *45*, 912–919.
Lever, J. Sex differences in the complexity of children's play and games. *American Sociological Review*, 1978, *43*, 471–483.
Luria, Z. *Personal communication*, 1980.
Maccoby, E. E., & Jacklin, C. N. *The psychology of sex differences*. Stanford, Cal.: Stanford University Press, 1974.
O'Connor, R. D. Modification of social withdrawal through symbolic modeling. *Journal of Applied Behavior Analysis*, 1969, *2*, 15–22.
Relative efficacy of modeling, shaping, and the combined procedures for modification of social withdrawal. *Journal of Abnormal Psychology*, 1972, *79*, 327–334.
Oden, S., & Asher, S. R. Coaching children in social skills for friendship making. *Child Development*, 1977, *48*, 495–506.
Whiting, B., & Edwards, C. P. A cross-cultural analysis of sex differences in the behavior of children aged three through eleven. *Journal of Social Psychology*, 1973, *91*, 171–188.

Author index

Subject index

academic ability
and cross-race interaction, 78–80, 94
and cross-sex interaction, 95
and interventions, 200
and mentally retarded children, 158, 160–1, 164
and peer interaction, 78–80, 94, 95, 158, 160–1, 164, 190–1
and racial stereotypes, 74–5
and sociometric status, 92, 106, 117
race differences in, 74–5, 78–80
access to peer groups, *see* entry strategies
aggressive behavior, 5, 8, 13, 18, 64–5, 68, 75–6, 119, 158, 279
and sociometric status, 119, 158, 279
race differences, 75–6
altercasting, 36, 41
altruistic behavior, 1, 4, 7
assertive behavior, 16–18
assimilation into a peer group, 126–8
attributions
in academic situations, 327–9
in social situations, 329–32

balance theory, 93, 98
behavioral observations
as outcome measures, 20–1, 280–3
see also observational methods

child welfare institutes, 2, 8, 19
chumship, 33
classroom structure
and peer acceptance of mainstreamed children, 155–6
and social isolation, 107–8
and sociometric status, 95–7, 111
class size
and peer interaction, 97
and sociometric status, 97, 111, 117
cliques, 14, 99, 110, 111

cognitive consistency, 98
cognitive development
and social development, 1, 3, 18, 19, 243
theory of, 6, 9, 18, 30, 32, 208, 243, 248
see also structural-developmental approach to social development
communication skills, 32, 161, 208, 210–11, 277
companionship choices, 6, 8–9, 10, 41, 156
competence versus performance, *see* social knowledge versus performance
conceptions of friendship, 219–25, 230–4, 234–6, 243–9, 250–1, 258–61, 264–9, 307–8, 323–4
and cognitive-developmental theory, 248
and conflict resolution, 258–61
and exclusion, 219–24
and interpersonal problem solving, 266–9
and social behavior, 266–9
and social perspective taking, 246–7, 249
developmental stages, 250–1, 264–6, 307–8, 323–4
functional applications, 249, 252–3
conflict in peer interaction, 8, 11, 12, 40, 253, 256, 258–61
see also conflict resolution
conflict resolution, 258–63
contact hypothesis, 56–7, 154–7, 159–63, 177, 189
and cross-race interaction, 56–7, 160
and group membership, 189
and mainstreaming, 154–7, 159–63, 177
and school staffing, 57
cooperative behavior, 4–5, 7, 17–18, 56, 277

342